Practical Web 2.0 Applications with PHP

Quentin Zervaas

Apress®

Practical Web 2.0 Applications with PHP

Copyright © 2008 by Quentin Zervaas

ISBN-13 (pbk): 978-1-59059-906-8

ISBN-10 (pbk): 1-59059-906-3

ISBN-13 (electronic): 978-1-4302-0474-9

ISBN-10 (electronic): 1-4302-0474-5

Printed and bound in the United States of America 9 8 7 6 5 4 3 2 1

Lead Editor: Ben Renow-Clarke
Technical Reviewer: Jeff Sambells
Editorial Board: Steve Anglin, Ewan Buckingham, Tony Campbell, Gary Cornell, Jonathan Gennick, Jason Gilmore, Kevin Goff, Jonathan Hassell, Matthew Moodie, Joseph Ottinger, Jeffrey Pepper, Ben Renow-Clarke, Dominic Shakeshaft, Matt Wade, Tom Welsh
Project Manager: Richard Dal Porto
Copy Editors: Andy Carroll, Kim Wimpsett
Assistant Production Director: Kari Brooks-Copony
Production Editor: Liz Berry
Compositor: Diana Van Winkle
Proofreader: Lisa Hamilton
Indexer: Broccoli Information Management
Artist: Diana Van Winkle
Cover Designer: Kurt Krames
Manufacturing Director: Tom Debolski

Distributed to the book trade worldwide by Springer-Verlag New York, Inc., 233 Spring Street, 6th Floor, New York, NY 10013. Phone 1-800-SPRINGER, fax 201-348-4505, e-mail orders-ny@springer-sbm.com, or visit http://www.springeronline.com.

For information on translations, please contact Apress directly at 2855 Telegraph Avenue, Suite 600, Berkeley, CA 94705. Phone 510-549-5930, fax 510-549-5939, e-mail info@apress.com, or visit http://www.apress.com.

The source code for this book is available to readers at http://www.apress.com.

Contents at a Glance

Contents

■CHAPTER 4   User Registration, Login, and Logout 73

■CHAPTER 5   Introduction to Prototype and Scriptaculous 123

About the Author

QUENTIN ZERVAAS is a web developer based in Adelaide, South Australia, where he has been self-employed since 2003. After receiving his bachelor's degree in computer science from the University of Adelaide in 2001, Quentin worked for several web development firms before branching out on his own, developing a wide range of custom web applications for customers all around the world.

Quentin has recently started a new company called Recite Media (`http://www.recite.com.au`) with two partners. Recite Media develops web applications primarily for other development or design companies to resell. Its flagship product, Recite CMS, is being used by some of Australia's largest companies.

Quentin also runs and writes for his PHP development resource site, PhpRiot (`www.phpriot.com`), which provides a number of useful articles on a wide variety of PHP-related topics.

After completing his role as the technical reviewer for *Beginning Ajax with PHP: From Novice to Professional* (Apress, 2006), he decided to undertake writing this book.

About the Technical Reviewer

JEFFREY SAMBELLS is a graphic designer and self-taught web application developer best known for his unique ability to merge the visual world of graphics with the mental realm of code. After obtaining his bachelor's of technology degree in graphic communications management with a minor in multimedia, Jeffrey originally enjoyed the paper-and-ink printing industry, but he soon realized the world of pixels and code was where his ideas would prosper.

Jeffrey has previously published articles related to print design and has contributed to award-winning graphical and Internet software designs. His latest book, *AdvancED DOM Scripting: Dynamic Web Design Techniques* (friends of ED, 2007), was an instant success. In late 2005, Jeffrey also became a PHP 4 Zend Certified Engineer; he updated the certification to PHP 5 in September 2006 to become one of the first PHP 5 Zend Certified Engineers. Jeffrey also maintains a blog at `http://jeffreysambells.com` where he discusses his thoughts about everything from web development to photography.

He currently lives and plays in Ontario, Canada, with his wife, Stephanie; his daughter, Addison; and their little dog, Milo.

Introduction

Many of today's web development books and articles cover single aspects of the development life cycle, delving only into specific features rather than looking at the whole picture.

In this book, we will develop a complete web application. Although we will be using various third-party libraries and tools to aid in development, we will be developing the application from start to finish.

The focus of this book is on Web 2.0, a catchphrase that has been in use for a few years now and is typically used to refer to web sites or web applications that have particular characteristics. Some of these characteristics include the following:

- Correctly using HTML/XHTML, CSS, and other standards

- Using Ajax (Asynchronous JavaScript and XML) to provide a responsive application without requiring a full refresh of pages

- Allowing syndication of web site content using RSS

- Adding wikis, blogs, or tags

Although not everybody is an advocate of the "Web 2.0" phrase, the term does signify forward progress in web development. And although not everybody has the need to provide a wiki or a blog on their web site, the other characteristics listed (such as correct standards usage) provide a good basis for a web site and should be used by all developers, regardless of how they want their web site or application categorized.

I wrote this book because I want to share with other users how I build web sites. Having been a web developer for ten years now (full-time for the past seven), I have a solid understanding of a wide range of web-related topics and have much to offer newer developers or developers looking to expand their own knowledge.

Who This Book Is For

This book has been written primarily for intermediate to expert PHP programmers. Although programmers of all levels will benefit from this book, we do jump in to the deep end very quickly, so some prior knowledge of PHP is assumed.

Having said that, if you're relatively new to PHP, you will definitely benefit from this book because it will formalize some of the techniques you have already learned and will show you some different ways of approaching various problems.

In this book, I have made the assumption that you are familiar with HTML and CSS, although since most of the code developed in this book is PHP and JavaScript, an advanced knowledge of HTML and CSS is not critical. All JavaScript code is explained thoroughly, which, in combination with the Prototype JavaScript library we will be using, makes the listings relatively straightforward.

How This Book Is Structured

We will start the book by determining which features to implement in our web application and then implement each one as we progress through the book. Each chapter will add a new set of features to the application, until reaching the final chapter where we look at strategies for deploying the application.

The specific type of application we develop in this book (a multiuser blogging system) is not particularly important; rather, it is used simply as a tool to show you the process of developing a web application. Each chapter is specifically designed to demonstrate particular aspects of development that may arise regardless of the type of application:

- **Chapter 1, Application Planning and Design.** We begin the book by looking at what defines Web 2.0, as well as looking briefly at the features that will be implemented in the application. Additionally, this chapter covers various aspects of the web development life cycle that should be considered when planning and implementing web applications.

- **Chapter 2, Setting Up the Application Framework.** In this chapter, we begin to implement the web application. This process begins by correctly setting up the environment (that is, installing the correct web server software) and then by creating the initial file structure of the site. In addition to connecting to the database with PHP, we will handle user requests with the Zend Framework and manage HTML code using the Smarty Template Engine.

- **Chapter 3, User Authentication, Authorization, and Management.** This chapter gives the first look at using a database. We look at how to easily manage database data when we implement the user system. Additionally, we look at how a role-based permissions system works and then implement it into the application.

- **Chapter 4, User Registration, Login, and Logout.** Continuing from Chapter 3, this chapter shows how to implement a user registration system. Since this is the first time the book deals with user-submitted data, this chapter looks at how to correctly deal with such data when we create the registration and login forms.

- **Chapter 5, Introduction to Prototype and Scriptaculous.** Since we make heavy use of JavaScript and Ajax in later chapters, we move away from the main application in this chapter while we explore two of the most useful JavaScript libraries available. Prototype helps programmers develop easily maintainable cross-platform JavaScript code, while Scriptaculous simplifies the process of adding appealing visual effects to web pages.

- **Chapter 6, Styling the Web Application.** In this chapter, we step back slightly from the web application in that we focus more on the user experience rather than on the main application features. We first look at implementing various navigational items (which also gives us a first taste of developing custom Smarty plug-ins), and we then complete the chapter by implementing a simple and clean web design into the application.

- **Chapter 7, Building the Blogging System.** This chapter moves on to beginning the implementation of the blogging system. In this chapter, we give users the ability to add, edit, and delete their blog posts. One of the key concepts covered is how to correctly allow user-submitted HTML while keeping the site safe and secure for visitors.

- **Chapter 8, Extending the Blog Manager.** This chapter largely builds on what was implemented in Chapter 7. A comprehensive Ajax example is included in this chapter that we will use to help users manage their blogs. We also integrate an open source What You See Is What You Get (WYSIWYG) editor into a blog post creation form.

- **Chapter 9, Personalized User Areas.** At this point in the book, users can create a new account as well as manage their very own blogs. In this chapter, we make their blogs public in the application. We give each user a public home page within our application web site in which all of their blog posts are shown. This chapter shows how to implement more advanced URL schemes, as well as shows you how to enable users to customize their own experience by managing their own profiles and settings.

- **Chapter 10, Implementing Web 2.0 Features.** Although several of the features we define as Web 2.0 (such as standards compliancy and Ajax) apply throughout web applications, a few concrete features are often defined as being part of the Web 2.0 movement. In this chapter, we will look at some of these, including microformats, web feeds (RSS and Atom), and tagging.

- **Chapter 11, A Dynamic Image Gallery.** In this chapter, we expand the capabilities of the blogging system by allowing users to upload photos for each of their blog posts. This allows us to see how to correctly handle not only file uploads but also image-specific issues, such as dynamically generating thumbnails.

- **Chapter 12, Implementing Site Search.** This chapter is essentially split into two parts: creating search indexes based on user blog posts and then allowing site visitors to search for posts. Indexing data can be a complicated topic, but by using the tools provided by the Zend Framework, the task is made simpler. After implementing the basic search functionality, we extend it to use an intuitive Ajax-based autocompleter, similar to that of Google Suggest.

- **Chapter 13, Integrating Google Maps.** You as a developer can use many freely available web services on the Internet to improve your own web site. In this chapter, we extend the blog capabilities further to allow users to add locations to their blog posts using Google Maps. We create an advanced sample implementation of Google Maps that combines the Google Maps API with our database using Ajax, as well as learn how to manage map data in real-time.

- **Chapter 14, Deployment and Maintenance.** In this, the final chapter, we cover a number of miscellaneous topics related to developing a polished application. This is partly an extension of some functionality implemented in Chapter 2 but also introduces several new ideas (such as application deployment).

Prerequisites

A number of third-party applications and libraries are used in this book. We discuss downloading and installing each of these as required, but for your reference, the following are used:

- PHP 5.2.3

- Apache 2.2 on Linux (and its variants) or Windows (earlier versions of Apache may also work)

- MySQL 5 or PostgreSQL 8

- Prototype 1.5.1.1

- Scriptaculous 1.7.1 beta 3

- Zend Framework 1.0.2 or newer

- Smarty Template Engine 2.6.18

- FCKeditor 2.4.3 (an open source JavaScript WYSIWYG editor)

In addition to these applications and libraries, in this book I use several custom PHP classes that I have implemented. Each of these is available in the application source, which can be downloaded as per the following instructions.

Downloading the Code

All code listings in this book are available from the book's web site at http://www.myphpbook.com. The source code for this book is also available to readers at http://www.apress.com on this book's page on the Apress web site. You can download the full web application as it stands at the end of any of the chapters.

Additionally, I've included a number of bonus add-ons in the source code, including an administration area and a blog post commenting system.

Contacting the Author

If you have any questions about the code in this book, your first stop should be the book's web site at http://www.myphpbook.com. This web site contains answers to frequently asked questions as well as various other web development resources.

Alternatively, you can contact me directly at quentin.zervaas@apress.com. Please ensure your questions relate directly to the content of the book. It is likely I will publish your questions and the answers on the FAQ section of the book's web site.

CHAPTER 1

■ ■ ■

Application Planning and Design

In this book we will be creating a blogging web application that will allow us to cover not only all of the different PHP and database considerations involved, but also a number of different Web 2.0 principles (such as Ajax and tagging). The blogging application will allow users to create and manage their own blog. Each user will have their own public page on which their blog posts are published.

Figure 1-1 shows how the application will be structured. As you can see, we will use a database to store application data, and we will create separate logical areas in the application to manage each feature as required. Additionally, one of the core aspects of Web 2.0 applications is using standards-compliant XHTML and CSS. We will focus on developing clean markup and well-structured JavaScript classes to ensure maximum compatibility and accessibility.

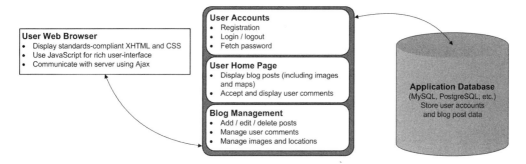

Figure 1-1. *The basic structure of our web application*

There are a number of different aspects of the application that we must cover, including database connectivity, template management, user authentication and permissions, and consumption of third-party web services.

In this chapter we will look at all features of the web application from a "black box" point of view. Each specific feature will be broken down in its respective chapter; here we will look at the application as a whole and discuss various options that need to be considered.

In essence, this chapter can be viewed as an informal design document, including an analysis of all required features and a look at design from a high-level. In developing the web application, we will be using both custom-written code as well as various third-party libraries (such as Prototype for JavaScript development, Smarty for template management in PHP, and the Zend Framework for several other features).

What Is Web 2.0?

So exactly what defines a web site as being "Web 2.0"? There are many different opinions on this, making it difficult to pinpoint an exact definition; however, some of the features typically associated with Web 2.0 sites are as follows:

- **Using standards-compliant HTML and CSS.** This allows sites to work across many platforms and helps with accessibility. This includes the use of microformats to generate friendly HTML that can be used across a variety of platforms (as we will see in Chapter 10).

- **Using Ajax to provide a rich user interface.** By performing trivial operations in the background using XMLHttpRequest, web pages can be more functional and intuitive.

Note XMLHttpRequest is a JavaScript API that allows a background HTTP request to occur while a user is viewing a web page. This means that the current page can be updated based on a response from the server without the user navigating to another page on the web site. The phrase "making an Ajax request" (or similar) typically refers to performing an HTTP request in the background using XMLHttpRequest.

- **Sharing data using web feeds and web services.** Users like to aggregate many feeds to easily receive content updates from their favorite sites using web feeds (such as RSS or Atom). Additionally, web services can enable one site to use data from other sites (for instance, we will display maps on our site using Google Maps).

- **Incorporating social networking tools.** Blogs and forums can enable users to communicate with each other.

While none of these features or aspects of development are new, we use the Web 2.0 term to describe the current generation of web sites that make good use of HTML and CSS while perhaps improving their interface with Ajax and social-networking tools. These are sites that "do things right." However, that's not to say that a site that uses any of these features is necessarily a good site.

Database Connectivity

In this application, we will need to save a number of different types of data, including

- User accounts

- User settings

- User-submitted data (such as blog posts, images, tags)

We will make use of a database abstraction layer to insert, update, and delete data from the database. This allows us to develop PHP code that will work regardless of the type of underlying database server. Within this book we will make use of MySQL, but if you want to use PostgreSQL instead, it would simply be a matter of changing the application's database connection settings.

We will be using the Zend Framework's Zend_DB class to handle the database abstraction. This is essentially an interface to the PDO extension for PHP 5. We will cover the installation of all required software in Chapter 2.

■Note In this book, all "database code" (i.e., PHP code that interacts with the database) will be self-contained within its relevant class or function. This means that if you want to use a different database abstraction layer (such as PEAR DB, ADOdb, or your own custom layer), it will be fairly straightforward to implement in place of Zend_Db.

Web Site Templates

One of the reasons PHP has become so popular is that you can easily include PHP code directly within the HTML code you want to output. This makes developing simple and small web applications very easy; however, this typically doesn't scale well. When an application grows large, it becomes difficult either to add new functionality within a bunch of HTML markup or to change the site design by sifting through the PHP code.

To deal with this, we aim to separate our *application logic* from our *display logic*. Essentially, this means the code that does the hard work (such as processing forms, reading data from the database, or checking user permissions) is performed in one place, while the HTML that will be output to the end user is stored in its own template file.

In Chapter 2 we will look at Model-View-Controller (MVC), which is a design pattern specifically describing this separation of application and display logic. We will be using the Smarty Template Engine to manage the display of templates, as this is a very popular and powerful template engine (Smarty will essentially make up the "view" portion of MVC, as we will see in Chapter 2).

Web Site Features

So far we have only looked at peripheral aspects of web application development, so let's take a look at some specifics. Let's look at what the end users of the web application would see.

Main Home Page and User Home Page

The home page of our web application will display blog posts from all users in a single journal. Registered users will be able to decide whether or not their posts are public and therefore are displayed on the home page.

In addition to the main home page, each user will have a public home page. This will display all of their blog posts in a single listing.

User Registration

We will need to create an account registration tool so new users can sign up and create a blog with our web application.

Essentially, this tool will need to do the following:

- Validate their details (we will use Ajax to help us with this).

- Use CAPTCHA to prevent automated registrations.

■Note A CAPTCHA is typically an image made up of a series of random characters that must be entered by the user when submitting a form. This technique is used to differentiate between humans and computers. It is discussed further in Chapter 4.

- Create their account in the database.

- E-mail them to confirm their account details.

Account Login and Management

Once a user has created and confirmed their account, they will be able to log in to their account. This part of the application will allow them to do several things:

- Manage their blog (see the next section).

- Update their account details (such as their e-mail address).

- Log out from their account.

User Blogs

The blog functionality is the core feature of the application, and we will use it to demonstrate a wide variety of web development and Ajax programming concepts. There are many features we must implement to make a useful blogging system. Users must be able to do the following:

- Add, edit, and delete blog posts.

- Tag posts.

- Upload images to blog posts, and display an image gallery for the user's account.

- Tie geographical data (maps) to the blogs.

Web Site Search

A keyword search tool is vital in any content-based web site. As such, we need to provide users with a way of searching for any content that appears on the site.

It needs to be easy to use and efficient, and it must provide meaningful results. To make it easier to use, we will develop an auto-completing search box (similar to that of Google Suggest—see `http://www.google.com/webhp?complete=1`).

Application Management

Administration of a web site or application is very important, and it is often overlooked or underdeveloped. An administration area is used to perform day-to-day management of the web application, such as viewing web site statistics or posting news to the site.

It often doesn't receive the attention it deserves because it requires spending development time (which means money) on an area of the site that the target demographic never sees.

In Chapter 14 we will look at various strategies for application deployment, management, and maintenance. Because this area is not for "public consumption," advanced features and a rich interface aren't as important as they are on the main area of the site, and we won't be focusing on the development of this area. However, we will look at the features you should consider when developing an administration area for the blogging application.

Other Aspects of Development

In addition to the specific features of our web application, there are some other aspects we must consider in the development process. No chapters are specifically devoted to any of these topics, but they do form the basis for content that is covered throughout the book.

Search-Engine Optimization

While we are not looking to achieve high search-engine rankings with this particular web application (after all, it's not a real-world web site we are developing), we will still aim to develop our code in a way that is optimal for search engines. This means that if you choose to extend the application developed in this book, a strong basis for search-engine ranking will have been formed.

Specifically, this means the following:

- Using friendly URLs. A friendly URL is basically a URL that doesn't contain a lot of extraneous characters. For example, if you had a document called "About Us," a URL such as `http://www.example.com/about-us` would be user friendly, while a URL such as `http://www.example.com/documents.php?id=1234` would not be so friendly.

- Correctly using HTML markup (such as headings, paragraphs, and tables).

- Correctly using HTTP status codes and content types (where relevant).

PHPDoc-Style Commenting

All classes we develop will be commented using PHPDoc-style comments, allowing us to easily build API documentation for all our classes. PHPDoc is based on Sun's Javadoc system, which is a simple method of commenting all functions, arguments, variables, and packages so developers can easily reuse them.

While this is not essential for the development of our web application, it is a good habit to get into when developing. Additionally, you may find it useful when following code examples in this book to have a PHPDoc comment block before each function.

Note The code displayed in this book typically won't include any PHPDoc comments since listings will be described in the text; however, they will be included in the downloadable code for this web application where possible.

PHPDoc works by placing a block of comments before each function, class, or variable definition. It is not mandatory in all situations—only where you feel it is necessary.

Each comment block begins with a description, and then is followed by a series of one or more optional parameters. For example, when adding PHPDoc comments to a function, you specify the input parameters and return value data. Obviously, the PHPDoc comments you would write for a variable definition would contain different information.

The following code shows an example of a PHPDoc comment for a simple user-defined function:

```php
<?php
    /**
     * mySimpleFunction
     *
     * A simple function to return a friendly message
     * to the user based on their name and age
     *
     * @param   string  $name   The name of the user
     * @param   int     $age    The age of the user
     * @return  string          The generated welcome message
     */
    function mySimpleFunction($name, $age)
    {
        $str = sprintf('Hello %s, your age is %d', $name, $age);
        return $str;
    }
?>
```

The first thing to note is how the block of comments begins. The /** token indicates to the PHPDoc parser that a PHPDoc comment block is beginning.

The first line of the block is a short description. My own personal preference here is to simply use the name of the function, class, or variable.

The next section in the comment block is a longer description. Here I try to describe what the function, class, or variable does from a black-box perspective. That is, what it does, not how it works. Any specific functionality considerations or funky logic that takes place is dealt with in standard comments within the code.

■**Note** Although it is not required, the usual convention is to include an asterisk at the beginning of each line of the /** … */ block. This is primarily to improve readability and to easily identify entire PHPDoc blocks.

The final section of the comment block contains the various PHPDoc parameters used by the parser to link the API documentation together better and to provide you with useful documentation. Each parameter begins with @, directly followed by the name of the parameter. Following that is the information required for that particular parameter.

In this example, you can see the @param and @return parameters. @param is used to specify aspects of the function arguments: first, the type of argument (in this case, our first argument is a string); next, its name (which in this case is $name); and finally, a brief description of what the input data should contain. The @return parameter is used to give information about the data returned from the function: the type of data is specified, followed by a brief description of what the return data contains.

For more information about phpDocumentor, read the "phpDocumentor Guide to Creating Fantastic Documentation" at http://www.phpdoc.org/tutorial.php.

Security

We will be looking closely at the security of our web site, as this very important aspect of web development is often overlooked or implemented incorrectly.

For instance, we will focus on making sure attacks such as SQL injection, cross-site scripting (XSS), and cross-site request forgeries (CSRF) do not occur. This is especially important in sites that not only make use of JavaScript and Ajax, but also make heavy use of user-submitted data. We achieve this by correctly filtering submitted data while correctly "escaping" user-submitted data when it is returned to users' browsers.

Application Logging

An aspect of development that ties in closely to both the security and performance considerations is that of logging. We will maintain a log file within our application to record significant events. For example, we will record a log entry whenever somebody tries to log in but provides incorrect information.

Maintainability and Extensibility

In addition to using some well-known third-party classes and libraries, we will also be developing our own custom classes in such a way that they can easily be expanded upon in the future.

In the next section, we will consider the use of unit testing. Note that unit testing aids greatly in developing applications that can easily be extended (as well as aiding in extending the application); however, this exceeds the scope of the book. You should keep unit testing in mind for your own future application development if you don't already use it.

Some of the ways we will make our code easily maintainable and extensible include

- Using a template engine to separate application logic from display logic.

- Using database abstraction to handle database server interaction.

- Making heavy use of the object oriented programming (OOP) features in PHP 5 to organize code.

Version Control and Unit Testing

There are two other reasonably important aspects of the web development process that we won't be covering in this book, but that you should at least be aware of: version control and unit testing. While they are important, they don't directly concern the concepts and libraries we will be looking at in this book.

Almost all web development projects I undertake use some form of version control (typically Subversion). This allows me to track any and all changes made to the files, and it also aids with code deployment. If you're not familiar with Subversion, I encourage you to use it for your own development projects. You can download it from `http://subversion.tigris.org`, and you can download the free O'Reilly book on Subversion from `http://svnbook.red-bean.com`.

Unit testing is another important tool that should be used when developing your own web sites (or when developing libraries you can use in multiple applications). A unit test is a script designed to test the functionality of a class (or of an entire package, or just individual methods inside a class).

You can perform automated testing using multiple unit tests, which will assist in finding regression bugs if they occur (that is, bugs that occur incidentally as a result of changing code that previously worked).

All of the code provided in this book has been tested, so including unit tests with all of the code would be somewhat redundant. For your own unit testing, you can use a package such as Simple Test (`http://www.lastcraft.com/simple_test.php`).

Summary

In this chapter, we have looked at the required features of our Web 2.0 application, and briefly at how they will be implemented. From here on in, we will work on the actual application development, starting with the initial setup in Chapter 2.

■■■

Setting Up the Application Framework

In the last chapter, we covered the features that we will be implementing in our web application. Before we can get started on these features, however, we must set up our development environment. In this chapter, we will be completing a number of tasks, beginning with setting up the required server software.

Following that, we will create a filesystem structure that will serve as the basis for our web application. There are a number of different types of files in our web application, and we will keep them as organized as possible. For example, we need one directory for the web server to use as the base directory from which to serve files, we need another directory to hold custom and third-party PHP libraries, and we need another to hold web site templates.

Next, we will set up the database. The actual creation of database schema and various queries will be covered in later chapters, but here we will write the PHP code required to connect to the database.

Then we will write code to handle client requests to our web site. We will use the Model-View-Controller design pattern to handle requests, and we will look more closely at this model in this chapter.

Finally, we will install the Smarty Template Engine into our application and set up some basic templates. We will expand on these templates as we continue through this book, but the material provided here should explain the basics of Smarty.

Also in this chapter, we will create a configuration file for our web application. This file allows you to deploy the web applications to different servers easily. For example, we will be storing database connection settings in this file, meaning that you can switch databases or the database password simply by modifying this file.

Web Server Setup

Setting up a web server correctly can be a complex task, and I cannot cover all scenarios in this book. However, I will cover the setup used for all code in this book.

I have used a somewhat typical LAMP setup (Linux/Apache/MySQL/PHP), broken down as follows:

- Operating system: Linux
- Web server: Apache 2.2
- Database server: MySQL 5
- Server-side scripting language: PHP 5.2.3

Operating System

The code in this book has been developed and tested on Linux, FreeBSD, and Microsoft Windows XP. There are no differences in code required for any of these platforms. Note also that references to Linux can typically also include similar platforms such as FreeBSD and Mac OS X.

For Windows there are slight differences in the configuration of the web server, as well as in the application configuration file we will develop later in this chapter. Each of these differences is noted in the relevant places.

Installing the Apache HTTP Server

Apache HTTP Server 2.2 is the web server of choice for this book—it is the latest stable release of Apache at the time of writing. This web server is available for Linux and Windows. Since I can't guarantee all PHP code in this book will work correctly on IIS, you should use Apache if you are using Windows. Alternatively, you may choose to use an older version of Apache (such as 1.3 or 2.0). There should be no problems with doing so, but this cannot be guaranteed.

You can download Apache 2.2 from `http://httpd.apache.org`. We will use a typical configuration, enabling all modules (including `mod_rewrite`, which we require in order to use `Zend_Controller`). You may also wish to include extra options that aren't included by default (such as SSL).

To install Apache on Windows, you can download the installer from the Apache web site, which will take you through the installation step by step.

The easiest way to install Apache (as well as PHP and MySQL) on Linux is to use the packaging system that comes with your operating system (such as Ports on FreeBSD). However, if you do not use a packaging system, you can install Apache 2.2.4 on Linux by downloading the `httpd-2.2.4.tar.gz` file (or a newer version if one is available) and using the following commands:

```
# tar -zxf httpd-2.2.4.tar.gz
# cd httpd-2.2.4
# ./configure --enable-modules=all
# make
# make install
```

Note that by default this will install Apache into the `/usr/local/apache2` directory.

Assuming each of these steps were successful, the Apache files should now be installed. You can configure the web server by editing the `/usr/local/apache2/conf/httpd.conf` file. Once that has been done, you can start the web server by issuing the following command:

```
# /usr/local/apache2/bin/apachectl start
```

If there is an error in the configuration, you will be notified. Alternatively, you can issue the `configtest` command instead of `start` with `apachectl` to ensure that the configuration is correct.

We will look at the Apache configuration required for our web application in the "Configuring the Web Server" section later in this chapter.

Installing MySQL 5

Next you must install MySQL 5. You can download it from `http://dev.mysql.com/downloads`.

Just like Apache, the Windows version of MySQL 5 is very straightforward to install as it uses an installer. If you are installing on Linux, it is recommended that you download the binary distribution, as MySQL can be a slow program to compile from source. I recommend installing MySQL to the `/usr/local` directory, although you may prefer a different setup.

Assuming you have downloaded the 5.0.41 version, the commands to install MySQL on Linux are as follows:

```
# cd /usr/local
# tar -zxf /path/to/mysql-5.0.41-linux-i686.tar.gz
# ln -s mysql-5.0.41-linux-i686 mysql
# cd mysql
# ./configure
```

Setting up the server using a symbolic link to `/usr/local/mysql` allows you to upgrade the server version in the future much more easily.

Once you have run the configure script, you can start the MySQL server with the following command:

```
# ./bin/mysqld_safe &
```

Note that this assumes you are already in the `/usr/local/mysql` directory.

It is now recommended that you add `/usr/local/mysql/bin` to your system path so you can easily load MySQL programs when required (such as `mysql`, `mysqladmin`, and `mysqldump`).

Installing PHP 5.2.3

The code developed in this book is designed to run on PHP 5.2.3 (or later). We will be using many PHP 5-specific features, so you will not be able to run the code in this book on PHP 4. Strictly speaking, you can use a version of PHP 5 earlier than 5.2.3, but it is best to use the latest available version. Note that the Zend Framework requires a minimum PHP version of 5.1.4.

Download PHP 5.2.3 (or later) from the PHP web site (`http://www.php.net/downloads.php`), and use the following commands to compile a fresh version of PHP. Note that these commands only include the minimum options required for compatibility with the code in this book.

```
# tar -zxf php-5.2.3.tar.gz
# cd php-5.2.3
# ./configure --with-apxs2 \
    --with-gd --with-curl \
    --with-mysql --with-pdo-mysql \
    --with-jpeg-dir --with-png-dir \
    --with-freetype-dir --with-zlib
# make
# make install
```

Once these commands have successfully executed, PHP should be compiled and installed, including the PEAR library in `/usr/local/lib/php`.

Note Please ensure that your version of PHP is built with the GD library enabled, as we will use it in this book for generating CAPTCHA images (Chapter 4) and for resizing uploaded images (Chapter 11).

When you run the make install command, the Apache httpd.conf file will be modified to load the PHP library; however, you may still need to add the following lines to ensure that Apache recognizes files with the extension .php as PHP files:

```
AddType application/x-httpd-php .php
AddType application/x-httpd-php-source .phps
```

This second line is optional, but it is included with the PHP documentation, so I have included it here.

You should also modify the DirectoryIndex directive in httpd.conf so index.php files are treated as index files. You can simply add index.php to this command so it looks something like the following:

```
DirectoryIndex index.php index.html
```

Application Filesystem Structure

Let's now take a look at the filesystem structure we will be using for the web application. The precise naming and organization of the directories in the web application is not in itself critical—it is simply important that everything is easy to find and manage.

In this book, we will develop the entire application within a directory called /var/www/phpweb20 (with "phpweb20" referring to the title of this book). You can, of course, use whichever directory on your own server that you choose, although we will refer back to this directory name on several occasions.

Web Root Directory

We need to define a root directory for the web server to access. This is the directory specified in the Apache configuration, and it is where Apache looks for files when a user requests a page in the web site. I will call this directory htdocs (the full path is /var/www/phpweb20/htdocs).

Most of the files in our application will exist outside of this directory (such as PHP classes and web site templates), which prevents users from directly accessing these files.

Data Storage Directory

Next, we need a directory for storing application data (that is, data in addition to that in the database). Here we will store log files (both from Apache, and those we create ourselves), files uploaded by users, as well as any other temporary data.

I will call this directory data, and it will contain a number of subdirectories for each of the different types of data stored. These subdirectories are logs, uploaded-files, and tmp.

PHP Classes Directory

We next need a directory called `include`, which will be used to store all PHP functions and libraries. Any third-party scripts we use (such as Smarty) will also be stored in this directory in addition to our own code. Application controllers (scripts that define the different actions users can perform on the web site) will be stored in a directory called `Controllers` in the `include` directory.

When we create the Apache virtual host for our application (in the "Configuring the Web Server" section of this chapter), we will include the `include` directory in the PHP `include_path` directive, so our application will know where to find this code.

Templates Directory

Finally, we need a directory to hold all the web site templates. We could put these directly inside either the `htdocs` directory or the `include` directory; however, they are not PHP code (although they do contain display logic), and they shouldn't be directly accessible (although they do contain HTML markup). We will put them in a directory called `templates`.

Full Directory Structure

Putting this all together, the directory structure of our web application will look like this:

```
/
|- /data
|    |- /logs
|    |- /uploaded-files
|    |- /tmp
|- /htdocs
|- /include
|    |- /Controllers
|- /templates
```

To create this structure in Linux, you would issue the following commands:

```
# mkdir /var/www/phpweb20
# cd /var/www/phpweb20
# mkdir data
# mkdir data/logs
# mkdir data/uploaded-files
# mkdir data/tmp
# mkdir htdocs
# mkdir include
# mkdir include/Controllers
# mkdir templates
```

When you view the directory listing, you should see the following:

```
# ls
data/ htdocs/ include/ templates/
```

■**Note** You will need sufficient permissions to create this directory structure. You may instead prefer to keep the code for this book in your home directory. I chose to use /var/www since it is a commonly used area on web servers to hold web sites, and it is short and easy to refer back to when required. (On a typical Windows setup, you won't need any special permissions to create the required directories.)

Installing the Zend Framework

The Zend Framework is an open-source library of PHP 5 components that can be used to solve tasks that commonly arise in everyday web development. It is actively contributed to by a large number of developers, and it is backed by Zend (the company that writes the Zend Engine, which has powered PHP since PHP 4). We will be using this framework in our application, as it allows us to focus on developing a Web 2.0 application, rather than getting bogged down in the details of building an entire application infrastructure.

These are some of the components we will be using:

- Zend_Auth and Zend_Acl: Used to authenticate users when they try to log in and to check their permissions (see Chapter 3)

- Zend_Controller: Used to handle client requests and direct the requests to the appropriate classes (see later this chapter)

- Zend_Db: Used to interact with the application MySQL database

- Zend_Mail: Used to send e-mails to users

- Zend_Validate and Zend_Filter: Used to check and sanitize user-submitted data in forms

- Zend_Search: Used for full-text searching

We will use more components, but, as you can see, we will be making heavy use of the framework.

Download the Zend Framework from http://framework.zend.com. In this book, I used version 1.0.2, but you should use the most up-to-date version available. Use these commands to extract the library to the include directory:

```
# cd /var/www/phpweb20
# wget http://framework.zend.com/releases/ZendFramework-1.0.2/
ZendFramework-1.0.2.tar.gz
# tar -zxf ZendFramework-1.0.2.tar.gz
# mv ZendFramework-1.0.2/library/Zend include
```

The last command moves the actual library files from the extracted archive into the application directory. The additional files in the archive include documentation and unit testing and are not really required. You may wish to remove the downloaded files once you have installed the framework, as they are no longer needed.

Configuring the Web Server

A typical development setup is to use your normal computer (such as your Windows or Mac OS machine) to write your code, while running the web server on another server. In such a case, you need to access the web server over a network. For example, I use a Windows machine for my day-to-day work, while my web server is a FreeBSD machine elsewhere in the office.

Tip I aim to keep my development web server configured identically to my production server, as this helps to eliminate any unforeseeable issues that may arise when deploying my code (such as different versions of linked libraries).

For the purposes of this book, I assume the web application is accessible using the web address http://phpweb20. In order to access my web server using this hostname, I make a fake DNS entry in my Windows host file so my browser will resolve the phpweb20 hostname to 192.168.0.80. This is the entry I add in my Windows hostname file (c:\windows\system32\drivers\etc\hosts in Windows XP):

```
192.168.0.80 phpweb20
```

Note Setting up a host as described here is not related to the development of the web application, but rather allows you to access it in your web browser. Creating fake hostnames is a simple trick for development purposes, eliminating the need for a DNS server or a real domain. Once you deploy your application live, you will need to use a real hostname so other people can access your web site.

If you have control over a real DNS server, you may instead prefer to create your own hostname. (Just keep in mind that I continually refer to phpweb20 throughout this book.)

Note You could use IP-based hosting, which would allow you to simply access http://192.168.0.80. Since name-based hosting in Apache is arguably the most common setup, I've chosen instead to use the method described previously (that is, setting up a fake hostname). Obviously, using a real hostname is better, but I've tried to simplify matters by not requiring it for this book.

Creating a Virtual Host in Linux

To configure the web server, we must first create the <VirtualHost> entry for Apache. I like to store this configuration data in its own file within my application directory, and then use the Include directive from the main Apache httpd.conf file. This means changes can be made to the local configuration, and the main configuration will pick up the changes automatically when the server is restarted. Listing 2-1 shows the contents of the /var/www/phpweb20/httpd.conf file.

Listing 2-1. *Virtual Host Configuration for Apache on Linux (httpd.conf)*

```
<VirtualHost 192.168.0.80>
    ServerName phpweb20
    DocumentRoot /var/www/phpweb20/htdocs

    <Directory /var/www/phpweb20/htdocs>
        AllowOverride All
        Options All
    </Directory>

    php_value include_path .:/var/www/phpweb20/include:/usr/local/lib/pear
    php_value magic_quotes_gpc off
    php_value register_globals off
</VirtualHost>
```

In your main httpd.conf file (commonly found in /usr/local/apache2/conf/httpd.conf for a default Linux install), you would add the following line:

```
Include /var/www/phpweb20/httpd.conf
```

■**Note** For this VirtualHost directive to work, you must have previously included the NameVirtualHost 192.168.0.80 in your main web server configuration before loading this virtual host.

There may be other directives you wish to add to your configuration, but this is a pretty standard configuration. It allows you to override configuration per directory as required with a .htaccess file (because of the AllowOverride directive), and it tells the PHP module where to look for included files. In this example, it will first look in the current directory, then in the /var/www/phpweb20/include directory, then finally in the PEAR library. Note that the specific location of PEAR may change depending on your Linux distribution or operating system.

■**Note** As a general rule, the PHP register_globals setting should be set to off. If this setting is on, the form, URL, session, and cookie variables will be made into global variables, which is generally a bad thing. The problem is that for many years the default was to have this setting enabled, so some web servers will have it enabled while others won't. All code in this book will work with register_globals turned off, just as all code you develop should (unless there's a particular reason to do otherwise). The same applies to the magic_quotes_gpc setting, which is used to automatically escape submitted data. While it is not necessarily a bad thing in general, all the code we develop will escape data as required; this setting should not be relied upon and is therefore disabled.

Creating a Virtual Host in Windows

Creating a virtual host in Windows is similar to the process in the previous section, except that the paths must be adjusted. Note also that the PHP `include_path` directive uses a semicolon as the separator rather than a colon, since a colon is used to indicate a drive label.

Listing 2-2 shows the Windows equivalent of Listing 2-1. Once again, you will need to include it in the main web server configuration file, typically found in `C:\Program Files\Apache Software Foundation\Apache2.2\conf\httpd.conf` on Windows.

Listing 2-2. *Web Server Configuration for Apache on Windows (httpd.conf)*

```
<VirtualHost *:80>
    ServerName phpweb20
    DocumentRoot "c:/www/phpweb20/htdocs"

    <Directory "c:/www/phpweb20/htdocs">
        AllowOverride None
        Options All
    </Directory>

    php_value include_path ".;c:/www/phpweb20/include;c:/program files/php/pear"
    php_value magic_quotes_gpc off
    php_value register_globals off
</VirtualHost>
```

Restarting Your Web Server

After making changes to your web server configuration, you must restart your web server. In Linux, the typical way to do this is with the following command:

```
# apachectl restart
```

In Windows, you can restart Apache by going to Control Panel ➤ Administrative Tools ➤ Services and selecting restart on the Apache2 service.

Once your server has been restarted, you should be able to access `http://phpweb20` directly in your browser (or by entering the server IP address directly, although if you're using a name-based virtual host system as described previously, this will not show files from the application directory).

Setting Up the Database

The next thing we need to do is create the MySQL database that we will be using in the web application. We will call this database `phpweb20`, and we will create a user called `phpweb20` to access this database.

To create the database, load the MySQL client program (`mysql`) and issue the `CREATE DATABASE` command as shown here:

```
# mysql -u root

Welcome to the MySQL monitor.  Commands end with ; or \g.
Your MySQL connection id is 1 to server version: 5.0.27-standard

mysql> CREATE DATABASE phpweb20;
Query OK, 1 row affected (0.00 sec)

mysql> use phpweb20
Database changed
```

Next, we must create the `phpweb20` user and assign a password to the account:

```
mysql> grant all on phpweb20.* to phpweb20@localhost identified by 'myPassword';
Query OK, 0 rows affected (0.01 sec)
```

■**Warning** I use the password `myPassword` for this book, but if you plan on deploying this application and using it as a real-world site, it is essential that you use a different password than the one created here, as anybody who has read this book will be able to access your database if you don't.

To ensure that the database and user have been correctly created, try exiting from the MySQL client and connecting using the new details. To do so, type the following command and then enter your password when prompted:

```
# mysql -u phpweb20 -p phpweb20
```

We will next take a quick look at handling client requests, and then we will return to our MySQL database and look at the PHP code for accessing the database.

Using the Model-View-Controller Pattern

The Model-View-Controller (MVC) design pattern is a commonly used method of designing web applications. In simple terms, it separates the presentation of the application from the underlying application logic.

The three parts of the pattern work as follows:

- **Model:** This represents the application logic. It performs the "hard work" of the application, such as interacting with the database, processing credit card transactions, or sending e-mails to users.

- **View:** The *view* represents the user interface. In the case of our application, this will typically be HTML code. We will be using the Smarty Template Engine to manage the view aspect of our application.

- **Controller:** The *controller* joins the *view* to the *model*. That is, it responds to events (such as when a user submits a web form), potentially updating the state of the application by interacting with the *model*.

Figure 2-1 shows how the three parts of MVC fit together in a typical web application.

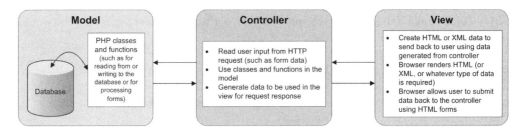

Figure 2-1. *How the Model-View-Controller design pattern fits together in our application*

We will be using the `Zend_Controller` class to handle the controller aspect of MVC. All user requests will be handled by this class, which will then result either in a new web page being displayed to the user (using Smarty), or in some update to the application (such as a new blog post being written to the database).

Separating Application Logic from Presentation Logic

To better demonstrate how MVC works, let's use the example of a simple news-article publishing system both using MVC and not using it.

The most basic way to retrieve a series of news articles from a database and display them would be to create a PHP script that connects to a database, queries the database, then loops over the results and outputs some HTML for each article. The following code shows what such a script might look like.

```php
<?php
    mysql_connect(...);
    $result = mysql_query('select * from news order by article_date desc');
?>
<html>
    <body>
        <h1>News Articles</h1>

        <?php while ($row = mysql_fetch_object($result)) { ?>
            <h2><?php echo $row->headline ?></h2>

            <p>
                <?php echo $row->body ?>
            </p>
        <?php } ?>
    </body>
</html>
```

In the preceding script, the application logic is the code that connects to the database server and retrieves the rows from the news table. The presentation logic is the HTML code that outputs the articles.

The problem with a script like this is that it can be hard to maintain, especially if you change the way the news system works (for instance, if you wanted to rename the table to news_articles). While it appears that you only need to change the code in place, consider what would happen if you wanted to display your news articles on other pages also. You would need to duplicate this code and then maintain it accordingly.

Now consider using the MVC pattern to implement this code. There are essentially two key changes that would be made. The first would be to move the code that retrieves articles from the database into a reusable component (either a PHP class or function). We would then call this new function to retrieve the articles so they could be output using HTML. In MVC terms, this new class or function is the *model*.

The second change would be to separate the call to retrieve the articles from the actual HTML. While this change isn't quite as important as the first change, it is still important as it allows you to change your HTML code without having to worry about how the data used in the HTML is generated. In MVC terms, this is separating the *controller* from the *view*.

Figure 2-2 shows how the previous code would be structured to use MVC.

Figure 2-2. *The news article example represented in MVC*

In the MVC version, you would effectively have three files. The model:

```php
<?php
    function get_articles()
    {
        mysql_connect(...);
        $result = mysql_query('select * from news order by article_date desc');

        $articles = array();
        while ($row = mysql_fetch_objects($result)) {
            $articles[] = $row;
        }

        return $articles;
    }
?>
```

The controller:

```php
<?php
    $articles = get_articles();

    display_template('articles.tpl');
?>
```

▦**Note** `display_template()` is a fictional function that represents some mechanism used to render templates.

And the view:

```html
<html>
    <body>
        <h1>News Articles</h1>

        <?php foreach ($articles as $row) { ?>
            <h2><?php echo $row->headline ?></h2>

            <p>
                <?php echo $row->body ?>
            </p>
        <?php } ?>
    </body>
</html>
```

While this example is fairly trivial, considering how the news articles are maintained (that is, inserted, edited, or deleted) will highlight the advantages of MVC. It is a nightmare to maintain code that mixes SQL insert statements directly within the HTML output for the corresponding page.

Directing All Requests to index.php

To implement our application using MVC, we will use the `Zend_Controller` class. First, though, we must alter our web server configuration to direct all page requests to `Zend_Controller`, even if the requested location is not a real file on the filesystem. All requests to files that do exist on the filesystem (such as our images and CSS files) will be handled normally by Apache; however, all other requests will be handled by the application bootstrap file (which will be located in /var/www/phpweb20/htdocs/index.php).

The directives in Listing 2-3 should be placed in a file called .htaccess inside ./htdocs. Note that these could be placed in the httpd.conf file we created earlier, but doing it here allows us to make changes without restarting the web server. The `RewriteRule` directive in Listing 2-3 routes any request that doesn't correspond to an actual file or directory through index.php.

Note The `AllowOverride` directive in the Apache configuration we created earlier allows us to change the configuration within a `.htaccess` file.

Listing 2-3. *Routing All Web Site Requests Through the index.php File (.htaccess)*

```
RewriteEngine on
RewriteCond %{SCRIPT_FILENAME} !-f
RewriteCond %{SCRIPT_FILENAME} !-d
RewriteRule ^(.*)$ index.php/$1
```

The first line in Listing 2-3 enables `mod_rewrite` for the directory in which `.htaccess` is located (including subdirectories).

The second and third lines set up conditions for rewriting the request to `index.php`. The second line says "if the requested file doesn't correspond to a file relative to the web root then use the rewrite rule," while the third line says the same thing but for nonexistent directories.

The final line is then executed if either of the conditions is satisfied. The requested filename is made available to `index.php` by adding it to the request string.

Introduction to the Zend_Controller Class

Let's now begin with the `Zend_Controller` class. Since we have already installed the Zend Framework, we can access this class easily. You will learn how to use this class in this section.

First, we will create the `index.php` file in the `./htdocs` directory (to which requests are routed using `mod_rewrite`). This file will drive our entire web site. Every single user request will be handled by this file (aside from requests for files such as images or CSS). This file is the *bootstrap* file.

Note From here onwards in the book, when I use the filesystem path `./` I am referring to `/var/www/phpweb20`. For example, the path `/var/www/phpweb20/htdocs/index.php` will now be referred to as `./htdocs/index.php`.

All this bootstrap file needs to do is load and initialize the `Zend_Controller_Front` class, then call the `dispatch()` method, which will call the necessary code to handle the request. Note that `Zend_Controller_Front` is a singleton class, meaning that only one instance of the class may exist. This is why the `getInstance()` method is used to instantiate it. Listing 2-4 shows the contents of the `index.php` file.

Listing 2-4. *Handling Client Requests Using Zend_Controller (index.php)*

```php
<?php
    require_once('Zend/Loader.php');
    Zend_Loader::registerAutoload();

    $controller = Zend_Controller_Front::getInstance();
    $controller->setControllerDirectory('../include/Controllers');
    $controller->dispatch();
?>
```

We will use the registerAutoload() method from Zend_Loader to automatically load Zend Framework classes. Doing this means you don't have to use require_once for any of the Zend Framework classes you use (apart from Zend_Loader).

■**Note** If you decide to use Zend Framework in any other apps that already use PHP's class autoloading, you will either have to modify your autoloader or manually include the Zend Framework library files. The filenames correspond to classes simply by replacing underscores in the class name with a slash and appending .php. For instance, Zend_Controller_Front can be included using require_once('Zend/Controller/Front.php').

How Requests Work with Zend_Controller

If you were to run the code in Listing 2-4 (by visiting http://phpweb20), nothing useful would happen—an error would be shown. At this point, we need to look at how requests work with Zend_Controller.

■**Note** Depending on your PHP configuration, errors may in fact be logged to the filesystem rather than displayed on screen, so be sure to look for a log file if you encounter unexpected behavior but no error messages. We will deal with error handling (such as "404 File Not Found") in Chapter 14.

In Listing 2-4 we called the setControllerDirectory() method. This is used to specify the directory that holds our web application's *controllers*—that is, classes that are used to handle requests to the application.

For example, you might have a controller called news, used for displaying both a summary of all news articles on your site, and for displaying individual articles. To create this controller, you would create a class called NewsController and save it in the Controllers directory (./include/Controllers/NewsController.php).

When Zend_Controller routes a user request, it automatically looks in the controller directory for a file called *Name*Controller.php, where *Name* corresponds to the controller name specified. The name is automatically capitalized, meaning a controller named news corresponds to a file called NewsController.php.

■**Note** The typical naming convention in PHP (including in the Zend Framework) is to capitalize each word in a class name (regardless of whether each word is separated by an underscore). Conversely, class methods use camel caps, meaning all words in the method name begin with an uppercase letter except for the first word. As an extra caveat, I prefer to capitalize all words for static class methods. This lets me know instantly that the method is static without needing to understand the function.

Other conventions include using two underscores for PHP's magic method (these names are built into PHP, such as __get(), __set(), __unset(), and __isset()), while method names beginning with one underscore indicate private or protected methods (which can only be called with the class or package respectively).

To then access this controller in your application, you would visit http://phpweb20/news. To view a specific news article, you might create an action called display, which would be accessed at http://phpweb20/news/display. To create this action, you would define a method called displayAction() inside of NewsController. Figure 2-3 shows how the URL is broken down to correspond to a controller class name and an action handler function within that class.

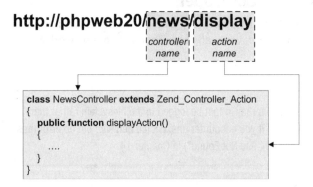

Figure 2-3. *Breaking down a URL into the controller and action*

The following code demonstrates this. We won't be using this particular class in our application, but we will be creating similar classes.

```php
<?php
    class NewsController extends Zend_Controller_Action
    {
        public function indexAction()
        {
            echo 'News article index';
        }
```

```
        public function displayAction()
        {
            echo 'News article details';
        }
    }
?>
```

■**Note** In addition to displaying the string echoed in the preceding function, an error message would also be displayed due to the way Zend_Controller automatically displays templates. We will look at this more closely later in the "Automatic View Rendering with Zend_Controller" section of this chapter.

If we were to include this controller in our application (by saving it to ./include/ Controllers/NewsController.php), we would visit http://phpweb20/news/display to display the "New article details" text. In this URL, news is the controller, and display is the action.

The default controller and action are both index. Here are some examples:

- http://phpweb20 is equivalent to http://phpweb20/index, as is http://phpweb20/index/index

- http://phpweb20/news is equivalent to http://phpweb20/news/index

Creating the IndexController

At this point in our application development, we must create a controller for the root of the site. That is, a controller called index that defines an action called index. Listing 2-5 shows the contents of IndexController.php, which we will save to the ./include/Controllers directory.

■**Note** As mentioned previously, Zend_Controller looks for the controller file by capitalizing the first letter of the controller name and appending Controller.php to it. So in this case, the index controller code belongs inside a file called IndexController.php.

Listing 2-5. *The Index Controller, Which Is Used for the Web Application Home Page (IndexController.php)*

```
<?php
    class IndexController extends Zend_Controller_Action
    {
        public function indexAction()
        {
            echo 'Web site home';
        }
    }
?>
```

While this particular controller doesn't yet do anything useful, we will be adding to it, as well as creating new controllers as we move on in this book. In fact, not only will we extend this controller, but we will add functionality that will extend to all controllers. To allow for this, we will extend the Zend_Controller_Action class in a new class called CustomControllerAction. Listing 2-6 shows the contents of CustomControllerAction.php, which should be stored in the ./include directory.

Listing 2-6. *The Controller Action That All of Our Application Controllers Will Extend from (CustomControllerAction.php)*

```php
<?php
    class CustomControllerAction extends Zend_Controller_Action
    {
        public $db;

        public function init()
        {
            $this->db = Zend_Registry::get('db');
        }
    }
?>
```

At this stage, we have only defined the init() function, which is automatically called by Zend_Controller_Front when a controller is loaded. Currently it simply fetches the database handle from the application registry and stores it in the db property. This allows us to refer to $this->db from any of our controllers. If we want an init() function in any of the child classes, we must also call parent::init() from that class so that the init() function in Listing 2-6 is also called.

■**Note** Listing 2-6 relies on the application database connection being in the variable registry that we will use Zend_Registry to manage. We create the database connection and look at the Zend_Registry component in the "Connecting to the Database" section.

We now need to modify our IndexController class to extend CustomControllerAction instead of Zend_Controller_Action. Listing 2-7 shows the updated code for IndexController.php.

Listing 2-7. *Modifying the Index Controller to Use the New Controller Action (IndexController.php)*

```php
<?php
    class IndexController extends CustomControllerAction
    {
        public function indexAction()
        {
```

```
            echo 'Web site home';
        }
    }
?>
```

Defining Application Settings

Before we go any further in developing our application code, we're going to define some application settings. We will store these settings in a file called settings.ini, and we will use the Zend_Config_Ini class to access them.

Note Zend_Config also allows storage of settings in an XML file instead of an Ini file. The Zend_Config_XML class would be used instead of Zend_Config_Ini. If you prefer, you can use the XML solution instead, since it makes no real difference to the functionality of the application.

The initial settings we will be storing are the database connection details and application path settings. We will not be implementing any mechanism to update these settings—if you want to change application settings, you will need to edit the values in this file. We will add further settings to this file as required.

Listing 2-8 shows the initial application settings we will be using (/var/www/phpweb20/ settings.ini). Update any of these values as you require.

Listing 2-8. *The Initial Application Settings (settings.ini)*

```
[development]

database.type     = pdo_mysql
database.hostname = localhost
database.username = phpweb20
database.password = myPassword
database.database = phpweb20

paths.base      = /var/www/phpweb20
paths.data      = /var/www/phpweb20/data
paths.templates = /var/www/phpweb20/templates

logging.file = /var/www/phpweb20/data/logs/debug.log
```

The first line of this file defines a section in the file. It is possible to have multiple configurations in the same file, and I have specified a section called development. You might also define sections called staging and production in the same file, allowing you to use different database details or a different path without having to edit the file when you deploy the application.

Initially the logging file will not exist, but assuming the write permissions are correctly set on the logs directory, debug.log will automatically be created when required.

Note You must define at least one section in a configuration file when using Zend_Config, as the section to load must be specified when the file is loaded.

Once settings.ini is set up, we need to load it in the index.php file using the Zend_Config_Ini class. Listing 2-9 shows an updated version of index.php, now including both the request handling code, as well as the code to load the configuration.

Listing 2-9. *Using the Zend_Config_Ini Class to Load the Application Settings (index.php)*

```php
<?php
    require_once('Zend/Loader.php');
    Zend_Loader::registerAutoload();

    $config = new Zend_Config_Ini('../settings.ini', 'development');
    Zend_Registry::set('config', $config);

    $controller = Zend_Controller_Front::getInstance();
    $controller->setControllerDirectory($config->paths->base .
                                '/include/Controllers');
    $controller->dispatch();
?>
```

Tip In Chapter 14 we will implement error handling in this code to deal with fatal errors (such as being unable to connect to the database server). In the meantime, Zend_Controller will suppress these errors, making potential debugging difficult. You may wish to add $controller->throwExceptions(true) to index.php after $controller has been created (and before the request is dispatched) to make identifying any potential errors easier.

As you can see, the Zend_Config_Ini class is instantiated, passing the settings filename as the first argument and the settings section as the second argument.

Following this, we use the Zend_Registry class. This allows us to store the $config object in a global registry so we can easily access this object again throughout the script's execution without needing to reinstantiate Zend_Config_Ini. This is a technique we will also use with the database connection.

Now, to access any of our configuration variables, we can simply use $config->*key*. For instance, to access the database.password setting, we would use $config->database->password in our code. Note that we have also updated the setControllerDirectory() call to use the path we set in the config to find the controller classes for Zend_Controller.

Connecting to the Database

Now that we have all of our database settings stored in the $config variable, we can easily create our database connection. For this, we use the Zend_Db class. We must first build an array with the database connection settings, and then call Zend_Db::factory() to find the appropriate database handler.

What does this mean, exactly? In our configuration, we specified the database type as pdo_mysql, and the factory() method will find the appropriate handler for this database type. If you wanted to use PostgreSQL instead, you could simply update the database.type value in settings.ini to pdo_pgsql, and if you had this driver installed with your PHP installation, it would use that one instead.

The following example code will connect to a database using the pdo_mysql driver:

```php
<?php
    require_once('Zend/Loader.php');
    Zend_Loader::registerAutoload();

    $params = array('host'     => 'localhost',
                    'username' => 'phpweb20',
                    'password' => 'myPassword',
                    'dbname'   => 'phpweb20');

    $db = Zend_Db::factory('pdo_mysql', $params);
?>
```

Note that I have hard-coded the connection settings in this example; the code in our application will call the appropriate settings we defined previously.

■Note Zend_Db doesn't initiate a connection to the database until a query is actually executed, so, technically speaking, in this example no connection is actually made.

Our next step is to include the database connection code in our index.php file—there are two key additions we must make. The first is to fetch the connection values from $config instead of hard-coding them. The second is to write the $db object to the Zend_Registry so we can use it throughout our application.

Listing 2-10 shows the updated index.php file, this time connecting to the database and writing the $db object to the registry.

Listing 2-10. *The index.php File, Now Connecting to the Application Database (index.php)*

```php
<?php
    require_once('Zend/Loader.php');
    Zend_Loader::registerAutoload();
```

```
// load the application configuration
$config = new Zend_Config_Ini('../settings.ini', 'development');
Zend_Registry::set('config', $config);


// connect to the database
$params = array('host'     => $config->database->hostname,
                'username' => $config->database->username,
                'password' => $config->database->password,
                'dbname'   => $config->database->database);

$db = Zend_Db::factory($config->database->type, $params);
Zend_Registry::set('db', $db);


// handle the user request
$controller = Zend_Controller_Front::getInstance();
$controller->setControllerDirectory($config->paths->base .
                                    '/include/Controllers');
$controller->dispatch();
?>
```

Testing the Database Connection

Now that we have written the database connection code, it is best to ensure that the connection actually works. As mentioned previously, a connection is not actually made to the database server until a query is executed, so to test the connection we need to execute a basic SQL query. Add an extra line of code after creating the $db object in index.php as follows:

```
$db->query('select 1');
```

If you visit http://phpweb20 now, an error will be shown if the connection to the database could not be made (such as Zend_Db_Adapter_Exception: SQLSTATE…). Remember to remove this test query from your code afterwards.

■**Note** In Chapter 14 we will add code to handle application errors such as invalid database connections.

The Smarty Template Engine

Smarty is a template engine written for PHP that allows you to easily separate your application output and presentation logic from your application logic. We looked at what this means earlier in this chapter when covering the Model-View-Controller design pattern, but what does it actually mean in terms of using Smarty?

Basically, anything we want to show to the user (that is, the HTML output) will be stored in a template file (which we will denote with a file extension of .tpl). After a user request has been processed, whether that means processing a form or fetching a list of news articles to display, we will use Smarty to output that template file.

A template file contains a series of placeholders used to dynamically output content. So in the case of displaying a list of news articles, the template file would loop over the articles and provide HTML code for each one. In addition, prior to displaying the template, we must tell the template about any data we want to be able to show in it. So in the case of news articles, we must *assign* the articles to the template prior to displaying the template.

To demonstrate this, I will return to the NewsController example we looked at above in the "How Requests Work with Zend_Controller" section. The following example shows the basic algorithm used to assign data to a template and then display that template. For this code to work, we must set template_dir and compile_dir accordingly. These settings indicate the filesystem paths where templates are stored and where compiled templates should be written, respectively. This is covered in more detail in the "Downloading and Installing Smarty" section later in the chapter.

```php
<?php
    class NewsController extends Zend_Controller_Action
    {
        public function indexAction()
        {
            require_once('Smarty/Smarty.class.php');

            $articles  = array('News Article 1',
                               'Another News Article',
                               'Even More News');

            $smarty = new Smarty();
            $smarty->template_dir = '/var/www/phpweb20/templates';
            $smarty->compile_dir = '/var/www/phpweb20/data/tmp/templates_c';
            $smarty->assign('news', $articles);
            $smarty->display('news/index.tpl');
        }
    }
?>
```

The first thing to do is define some data to assign to the template. In this case, I've created a simple array called $articles, which contains some fake news headlines. After instantiating and configuring the $smarty object, I assign the $articles array to $smarty, and finally output the news/index.tpl file. Based on the specified template_dir, the full path of this template would be ./templates/news/index.tpl.

Now let's see what the news/index.tpl template might look like. There's a lot going on in this template.

```
<h1>News</h1>

{if $news|@count == 0}
    <p>
        No news found!
    </p>
```

```
{else}
    <ul>
        {foreach from=$news item=article}
            <li>{$article|escape}</li>
        {/foreach}
    </ul>
{/if}
```

The first thing to note is that I haven't included all of the normal HTML tags (such as the document type and <html> and <body> tags). Typically we would include these tags, but I have tried to keep the clutter out of this template.

Next is an if/else statement. Note that it is wrapped in curly braces. These are the default delimiters for Smarty template code. Note also that if expressions in Smarty are not wrapped in parentheses as they would be in PHP.

Note also that in this template, I use $news to refer to the article data. In the previous news example, I assigned the $articles variables to the template using the name news.

When processing the data, I first check whether the $news array is empty by using the PHP count() function. In fact, what I am doing is using a Smarty *modifier*. Modifiers are applied using a vertical pipe. Essentially, the variable is passed to the modifier as its first argument. Smarty comes with several built-in modifiers, but you can also use any PHP function as a modifier. Because PHP's count() accepts an array as an argument, I put the @ character before count. If I didn't, Smarty would loop over the array and pass each array element to count(), rather than the array as a whole.

It is also possible to pass arguments to modifiers. For instance, if you wanted to retrieve the first three characters of a string using substr(), you could do so using $myStr|substr:0:3, which is equivalent to calling substr($myStr, 0, 3) in PHP. To output a variable, simply wrap the variable in curly braces. So to output the first three characters of a string in the template, you would use {$myStr|substr:0:3} in the template.

■**Note** You can also chain several modifiers together. In the preceding example, you could change the output to display the first three characters of a string in uppercase by also applying strtoupper() as a modifier. To do this, you would use {$myStr|substr:0:3|strtoupper}. Modifiers are applied in order from left to right.

In the template, I next use the {foreach} tag to loop over the $news array. This behaves almost identically to foreach() in PHP. The array is passed in using the from argument, and the current element of the array is assigned to variable specified in the item argument. So in the preceding example, the PHP equivalent of {foreach from=$news item=article} is foreach ($news as $article). If I also wanted the array key, I would specify the key argument: {foreach from=$news item=article key=k} would be equivalent to foreach ($news as $k => $article) in PHP.

Now I output each element of the array inside of the foreach loop. I could simply use {$article}, but I have improved this slightly by using the escape modifier (this is a Smarty modifier, not a PHP function). This modifier should be frequently used when outputting data inside of HTML documents, as it will escape HTML entities to make the document valid. In other words, it will turn > into >, < into <, and & into &, among others.

Finally, I close the foreach loop using {/foreach}. Note how this is similar to how HTML tags work. Similarly, the {if} clause is closed using {/if}.

Why Not Use a Different Template Engine?

Smarty is certainly not the only choice as far as template engines go. Most PHP developers will have a different opinion as to which template engine to use. The concerns with Smarty generally consist of the following:

- The Smarty code is large (approximately 150KB of code for Smarty.class.php and Smarty_Compiler.class.php combined) and expensive (in terms of processing power) to use for every request on your web site.

- Why use a metalanguage to output content when PHP is designed to do exactly this?

Certainly, these are both valid concerns. We'll take a quick look at each of these and practical ways to deal with them.

Improving Smarty Performance

First, let me say that in real terms, unless you have a high-traffic web site, and/or a slow web server, the overhead caused by using Smarty will typically not be noticeable. Regardless, it is always good to look at ways of improving the performance of your web applications.

Smarty compiles templates into native PHP code whenever they are changed. When a web site is in production, templates will generally not be modified and therefore not be recompiled. This means that the Smarty_Compiler.class.php class is not loaded, effectively reducing the amount of code to be parsed by about 90KB.

Next, you can always use code accelerators (such APC or PHP Accelerator) to decrease the overhead of loading the Smarty library. Additionally, you can cache the output from any or all of your web pages (using Smarty's caching functionality, or using something like Zend_Cache).

■**Note** The Alternative PHP Cache (APC) is free to download and can easily be installed using the PECL installer. It is used for caching and optimizing PHP code on the web server, thereby improving server performance. If you're using Linux, you can simply type pecl install apc from the command line, add extension="apc.so" to your php.ini, and then restart your web server. Check the output from phpinfo() to confirm that it is correctly installed.

Using a Metalanguage for Templates

While using PHP code directly for templates is a perfectly viable solution, it can be very useful to use a metalanguage for templates instead. Here are some of the advantages of using Smarty templates over native PHP code:

- The code is shorter and more easily readable. For example, using {$foo} to output the $foo variable provides less clutter than <?php echo $foo ?> or <?= $foo ?>.

- Smarty provides built-in security features, which when activated will control what can be done in a template. That is, it heavily restricts access to normal PHP functions. Technically speaking, using native PHP for templates could result in unrelated operations taking place in a template (such as writing to a file or sending an e-mail). Take, for example, a content management system (CMS). In addition to being able to update web site content, a CMS will typically allow users to modify the web site templates. Enforcing control over what can and can't be contained in a template has huge benefits in this type of situation, where user-submitted data is used.

- It can be less daunting for non-programmers to create templates. For example, if you employ somebody to convert a web design into HTML and CSS, it will be simpler for them to use Smarty than PHP.

- Smarty can be extended in so many ways that some really powerful effects can be achieved. The most obvious example is in the use of modifiers. Another powerful (but often overlooked) feature is creating custom *blocks*. For example, you could make a custom Smarty block called `roundedbox`, which you could use to output content inside a box with rounded corners. Although Firefox can provide this in CSS (using the `-moz-border-radius` selector), it is not available in Internet Explorer (`border-radius` is included in CSS3, not yet implemented in major browsers). You could then use template code as follows in your template: `{roundedbox} some content {/roundedbox}`. Since drawing rounded boxes without a native CSS solution requires the use of HTML tables or nested divs, you can hide the implementation details away in the `roundedbox` block handler.

Of course, it would be unfair to ignore the disadvantages of using a metalanguage for templates. Here are some of the disadvantages of using Smarty templates over native PHP code:

- There is extra overhead in parsing and compiling the templates in PHP code. Note, however, that this is only ever done when a template is changed, and therefore the overhead is almost zero in the long term.

- Users must learn an extra language, and while Smarty is really good at some things, there are some drawbacks. For example, if you want to output an array into a three-column table, you will generally end up with a clutter of `{assign}`, `{math}`, and `{section}` tags. However, you can also extend to create built-in functions or include a separate template to hide this clutter.

The Zend Framework does, in fact, provide a templating solution that uses native PHP files. While we looked at the `Zend_Controller` component earlier in this chapter (the *controller* part of MVC), there is also the `Zend_View` component (the *view* part of MVC). This component works similarly to Smarty, except that the templates it uses are written in native PHP code. If you prefer to use this instead of Smarty, you will need to adapt the templates we create accordingly.

Downloading and Installing Smarty

You can download the Smarty code from the Smarty web site (`http://smarty.php.net`). The latest version at the time of writing is 2.6.18, but you should use the most current version. The following commands can be used in Linux to download Smarty and move it to the application include directory (./include).

```
# cd /var/www/phpweb20
# wget http://smarty.php.net/do_download.php?download_file=Smarty-2.6.18.tar.gz
# tar -zxf Smarty-2.6.18.tar.gz
# cd Smarty-2.6.18
# mv libs ../include/Smarty
# cd ../include/Smarty
```

The contents of the directory should look like this:

```
# ls
Config_File.class.php   Smarty_Compiler.class.php   internals/
Smarty.class.php        debug.tpl                   plugins/
```

■Note You may wish to remove the downloaded and extracted files that are left over after installing Smarty, as they are no longer required.

In order to use Smarty, we need to configure the template_dir and compile_dir properties of each instantiated Smarty object.

- template_dir is the location where all of our application templates are stored. We earlier specified this when creating our directory structure and settings file to be /var/www/phpweb20/templates.

- compile_dir is a directory where Smarty saves compiled templates. Since Smarty templates use their own metalanguage, Smarty compiles each template to native PHP code in order to speed subsequent execution. Whenever a template file is modified, Smarty automatically recompiles that template and saves it to the compile directory.

The compile_dir directory needs to be writable by the web server. We will be using the /var/www/phpweb/data/tmp/templates_c directory for this (it is convention to use templates_c as the directory name for compiled Smarty templates). We earlier created the ./data/tmp directory, but we must now create the templates_c directory and give write permissions to it. The following commands can be issued to do so:

```
# cd /var/www/phpweb20/data/tmp/
# mkdir templates_c
# chmod 777 templates_c/
```

In order to render a template with Smarty, we would now use code similar to the following. Note that the foo.tpl template doesn't really exist (but if it did its full path would be /var/www/phpweb20/templates/foo.tpl).

```
<?php
    require_once('Smarty/Smarty.class.php');
```

```php
    $smarty = new Smarty();
    $smarty->template_dir = '/var/www/phpweb20/templates';
    $smarty->compile_dir = '/var/www/phpweb20/data/tmp/templates_c';
    $smarty->display('foo.tpl');
?>
```

We shouldn't be hard-coding these paths—we have them stored in our configuration file, so we should use them. Let's look at the same code using the paths from settings.ini. (Note that I am assuming that the $settings variable has already been created and set up as in our index.php bootstrap file.)

```php
<?php
    // assume that $config is already defined
    require_once('Smarty/Smarty.class.php');

    $smarty = new Smarty();
    $smarty->template_dir = $config->paths->templates;
    $smarty->compile_dir = $config->paths->data . '/tmp/templates_c';
    $smarty->display('foo.tpl');
?>
```

Automatic View Rendering with Zend_Controller

When using Zend_Controller, a plug-in called ViewRenderer is automatically loaded, and it displays a view script (that is, a template) based on the names of the requested controller and action. This means that when we use Smarty we don't have to instantiate the Smarty class or call the display() method to output templates; ViewRenderer will do all of this for us.

In order for this to work, we must extend the Zend_View_Abstract class to interact with the Smarty class. We will create a class called Templater, and we must then tell Zend_Controller about this class in the index.php bootstrap file.

We will store this class in the application ./include directory in a file called Templater.php. Additionally, we will create the ./include/Templater/plugins directory, in which we will store any custom Smarty plug-ins that we write throughout this book. By storing all of our own extensions in a separate directory, we can easily upgrade to the latest version of Smarty without having to track which of our files need moving.

To create the required directories, use the following commands:

```
# cd /var/www/phpweb20/include/
# mkdir -p Templater/plugins
```

Tip The -p argument to mkdir results in intermediate directories being created as required. That is, if the Templater directory doesn't exist, it will be created before creating the plugins directory.

We can now create the Templater class, in which we specify template_dir and compile_dir. Additionally, we must tell Smarty to look in the Templater/plugins/ directory for plug-ins (in addition to Smarty's own plugins directory).

To implement this class, we must implement several key methods so that ViewRenderer can interact with Smarty. The most important of these methods are as follows:

- getEngine(): This must return an instance of Smarty. Since this may be called multiple times, we should cache the Smarty instance so it is only created once. We do this by creating the Smarty object in the constructor.

- __set(): This assigns a variable to the template. Essentially this means we can replace $smarty->assign('foo', 'bar') with $this->view->foo = 'bar' in any controller action.

- __get(): This returns a variable that has previously been assigned to a template.

- render(): This method renders a template. This is effectively the same as calling $smarty->display(), except that this method should return the output (not display it directly), so we must use fetch() instead of display() on the Smarty object.

Listing 2-11 shows the code for Templater.php, which in keeping with Zend Framework's class naming structure means we must store this class in the ./include directory.

Listing 2-11. *Extending Smarty for Use with Our Web Application (Templater.php)*

```php
<?php
    class Templater extends Zend_View_Abstract
    {
        protected $_path;
        protected $_engine;

        public function __construct()
        {
            $config = Zend_Registry::get('config');

            require_once('Smarty/Smarty.class.php');

            $this->_engine = new Smarty();
            $this->_engine->template_dir = $config->paths->templates;
            $this->_engine->compile_dir = sprintf('%s/tmp/templates_c',
                                        $config->paths->data);

            $this->_engine->plugins_dir  = array($config->paths->base .
                                            '/include/Templater/plugins',
                                        'plugins');
        }

        public function getEngine()
        {
            return $this->_engine;
        }
```

```php
    public function __set($key, $val)
    {
        $this->_engine->assign($key, $val);
    }

    public function __get($key)
    {
        return $this->_engine->get_template_vars($key);
    }

    public function __isset($key)
    {
        return $this->_engine->get_template_vars($key) !== null;
    }

    public function __unset($key)
    {
        $this->_engine->clear_assign($key);
    }

    public function assign($spec, $value = null)
    {
        if (is_array($spec)) {
            $this->_engine->assign($spec);
            return;
        }

        $this->_engine->assign($spec, $value);
    }

    public function clearVars()
    {
        $this->_engine->clear_all_assign();
    }

    public function render($name)
    {
        return $this->_engine->fetch(strtolower($name));
    }

    public function _run()
    { }
}
?>
```

Integrating Smarty with the Web Site Controllers

Finally, we need to make Zend_Controller use the Templater class instead of its default Zend_View class. To do this, we must use the following code, which we will shortly add to the application bootstrap file:

```
$vr = new Zend_Controller_Action_Helper_ViewRenderer();
$vr->setView(new Templater());
$vr->setViewSuffix('tpl');
Zend_Controller_Action_HelperBroker::addHelper($vr);
```

Note that we must call setViewSuffix() to indicate that templates finish with a file extension of .tpl. By default, Zend_View will use the extension .phtml. Listing 2-12 shows how the controller part of index.php looks once this code has been added.

Listing 2-12. *Telling Zend_Controller to Use Smarty Instead of its Default View Renderer (index.php)*

```
<?php
    // ... other code

    // handle the user request
    $controller = Zend_Controller_Front::getInstance();
    $controller->setControllerDirectory($config->paths->base .
                                        '/include/Controllers');

    // setup the view renderer
    $vr = new Zend_Controller_Action_Helper_ViewRenderer();
    $vr->setView(new Templater());
    $vr->setViewSuffix('tpl');
    Zend_Controller_Action_HelperBroker::addHelper($vr);

    $controller->dispatch();
?>
```

■**Note** Viewing the web site now will still display the "Web site home" message. However, a Smarty error will occur, since we haven't yet created the corresponding template file for the index action of the index controller.

Now, whenever a controller action is executed, Zend_Controller will automatically look for a template based on the controller and action name. Let's use the index action of the index controller as an example, as shown in Listing 2-13.

Listing 2-13. *Our New Index Controller, Now Outputting the index.tpl File (IndexController.php)*

```php
<?php
    class IndexController extends CustomControllerAction
    {
        public function indexAction()
        {
        }
    }
?>
```

When you open `http://phpweb20` in your browser, the action in Listing 2-13 will now be executed, and the `Templater` class we just created will automatically render the template in `./templates/index/index.tpl`.

Since the `index.tpl` template doesn't yet exist, however, we must now create it. Again, we will simply output the "Web site home" message, but we will also create header (`header.tpl`) and footer (`footer.tpl`) templates that will be included in all web site templates. This allows us to make modifications to the web site in one place and have them carry over to all pages in the site.

To include the `header.tpl` and `footer.tpl` templates in `index.tpl`, we use Smarty's `{include}` tag. Listing 2-14 shows the contents of `index.tpl`, which can be found in `./templates/index/index.tpl`.

Listing 2-14. *The Template for the Index Action of the Index Controller (index.tpl)*

```
{include file='header.tpl'}

Web site home

{include file='footer.tpl'}
```

If you try to view this page in your browser without creating the `header.tpl` and `footer.tpl` files, an error will occur, so let's now create these templates. Listing 2-15 shows the contents of `header.tpl`, while Listing 2-16 shows `footer.tpl`. These files are both stored in the `./templates` directory (not within a subdirectory, as they don't belong to a specific controller).

Listing 2-15. *The HTML Header File, Which Indicates a Document Type of XHTML 1.0 Strict (header.tpl)*

```html
<!DOCTYPE html
    PUBLIC "-//W3C//DTD XHTML 1.0 Strict//EN"
    "http://www.w3.org/TR/xhtml1/DTD/xhtml1-strict.dtd">
<html xmlns="http://www.w3.org/1999/xhtml" lang="en" xml:lang="en">
  <head>
    <title>Title</title>
    <meta http-equiv="Content-Type" content="text/html; charset=iso-8859-1" />
  </head>
  <body>
    <div>
```

Listing 2-16. *The HTML Footer File, Which Simply Closes Off Tags Opened in the Header (footer.tpl)*

```
    </div>
  </body>
</html>
```

As you can see, the header and footer are straightforward at this stage. We will develop them further as we move along, such as by adding style sheets, JavaScript code, and relevant page titles. The Content-Type <meta> tag was included here because the document will not validate correctly without it (using the W3C validator at http://validator.w3.org). You may need to specify a different character set than iso-8859-1, depending on your locale.

Note that I have specified a document type of XHTML 1.0 Strict. All HTML developed in this book will conform to that standard. We can achieve this by correct use of cascading style sheets, inclusion of JavaScript, and correctly escaping user-submitted data in the HTML (an example of this is the Smarty escape modifier we looked at earlier in this chapter).

If you now load the http://phpweb20 address in your web browser, you will see the simple "Web site home" message. If you view the source of this document, you will see that message nested between the <div> open tag from header.tpl, and the </div> close tag from footer.tpl. Note that the <div> is included as it violates the standard to have text directly inside the <body> tag.

Adding Logging Capabilities

The final thing we will look at in this chapter is adding logging capabilities to our application. To do this, we will use the Zend_Log component of the Zend Framework, which we will use in various places in our application. For example, we will record an entry in the log every time a failed login occurs in the members section.

Although it is possible to do some pretty fancy things with logging (such as writing entries to a database, or sending e-mails to a site administrator), all we will do now is create a single log file to hold log entries. This file can then be used to debug any possible problems that arise not only during development of the web application, but also in its day-to-day operation.

We will store the log file in the /var/www/phpweb20/data/logs directory that we created earlier. This directory must be writable by the web server:

```
# cd /var/www/phpweb20/data/
# chmod 777 logs
```

The procedure for using Zend_Log is to firstly instantiate the Zend_Log class, and then add a *writer* to it. A writer is a class that does something with the log messages, such as writing them to a database or sending them straight to the browser. We will be using the Zend_Log_Writer_Stream writer to write log messages to the file specified in our settings.ini file (the logging.file value).

The following code shows this procedure. First, a filesystem writer is created, which is then passed as the only argument to the constructor of the Zend_Log class:

```php
<?php
    $writer = new Zend_Log_Writer_Stream('/path/to/log');
    $logger = new Zend_Log($writer);
?>
```

We can now add this code to our `index.php` bootstrap file. We want to create the `Zend_Log` object as soon as possible in the application, so we can record any problems that occur in the application. Since we rely on the `logging.file` value from `settings.ini`, we can create our logger as soon as this configuration file has been loaded.

■**Note** It is possible to have multiple writers for a single logger. For example, you might use `Zend_Log_Writer_Stream` to write all log messages to the filesystem and use a custom e-mail writer to send log messages of a critical nature to the system administrator. In Chapter 14 we will implement this specific functionality.

Listing 2-17 shows the new version of `index.php`, which now creates `$logger`, an instance of `Zend_Log`. The path of the log file is found in the `$config->logging->file` variable. Additionally, it is written to the registry so it can be accessed elsewhere in the application.

Listing 2-17. *The Updated Version of the Application Bootstrap File, Now with Logging (index.php)*

```php
<?php
    require_once('Zend/Loader.php');
    Zend_Loader::registerAutoload();


    // load the application configuration
    $config = new Zend_Config_Ini('../settings.ini', 'development');
    Zend_Registry::set('config', $config);


    // create the application logger
    $logger = new Zend_Log(new Zend_Log_Writer_Stream($config->logging->file));
    Zend_Registry::set('logger', $logger);


    // connect to the database
    $params = array('host'     => $config->database->hostname,
                    'username' => $config->database->username,
                    'password' => $config->database->password,
                    'dbname'   => $config->database->database);

    $db = Zend_Db::factory($config->database->type, $params);
    Zend_Registry::set('db', $db);


    // handle the user request
    $controller = Zend_Controller_Front::getInstance();
```

```
    $controller->setControllerDirectory($config->paths->base .
                                        '/include/Controllers');

    // setup the view renderer
    $vr = new Zend_Controller_Action_Helper_ViewRenderer();
    $vr->setView(new Templater());
    $vr->setViewSuffix('tpl');
    Zend_Controller_Action_HelperBroker::addHelper($vr);

    $controller->dispatch();
?>
```

Writing to the Log File

To write to the log file, we call the `log()` method on the `$logger` object. The first argument is the message we want to log, and the second argument is the priority level of the message.

The following is a list of the built-in log priorities (from the Zend Framework manual):

- Zend_Log::EMERG (Emergency: system is unusable)

- Zend_Log::ALERT (Alert: action must be taken immediately)

- Zend_Log::CRIT (Critical: critical conditions)

- Zend_Log::ERR (Error: error conditions)

- Zend_Log::WARN (Warning: warning conditions)

- Zend_Log::NOTICE (Notice: normal but significant condition)

- Zend_Log::INFO (Informational: informational messages)

- Zend_Log::DEBUG (Debug: debug messages)

■**Note** It is also possible to create your own logging priorities, but for development in this book we will only use these built-in priorities.

So, if you wanted to write a debug message, you might use $logger->log('Test', Zend_Log::DEBUG). Alternatively, you could use the priority name as the method on $logger, which is essentially just a simple shortcut. Using this method, you could use $logger->debug('Test') instead.

As a test, you can add that line to your index.php file after you instantiate Zend_Log, as follows:

```
<?php
    // ... other bootstrap code

    // create the application logger
```

```
$logger = new Zend_Log(new Zend_Log_Writer_Stream($config->logging->file));
Zend_Registry::set('logger', $logger);
$logger->debug('Test');

// ... other bootstrap code
?>
```

Now, load `http://phpweb20` in your browser and then check the contents of `debug.log`. You will see something like this:

```
# cat debug.log
2007-04-23T01:19:27+09:00 DEBUG (7): Test
```

As you can see, the message has been written to the file, showing the timestamp of when it occurred, as well as the priority (DEBUG, which internally has a code of 7). Remember to remove the line of code from `index.php` after trying this!

Note It is possible to change the formatting of the log messages using a `Zend_Log` *formatter*. By default, the `Zend_Log_Formatter_Simple` formatter is used. Zend Framework also comes with a formatter that will output log messages in XML. Not all writers can have their formatting changed (such as if you write log messages to a database—each event item is written to a separate column).

At this stage, we won't be doing anything further with our application logger. However, as mentioned, we will use it to record various events as we continue with development, such as recording failed logins.

Summary

In this chapter we've begun to build our web application. After setting up the development environment, we set up the application framework, which includes structuring the files in our web application, configuring application settings, connecting to the database, handling client requests, outputting web pages with Smarty, and writing diagnostic information to a log file.

In the next chapter, we will begin to implement the user management and administration aspects of our web application. We will be making heavy use of the `Zend_Auth` and `Zend_Acl` components of the Zend Framework.

CHAPTER 3

■■■

User Authentication, Authorization, and Management

In Chapter 2 we looked at the Model-View-Controller design pattern, which allowed us to easily separate our application logic from the display logic, and we implemented it using Zend_Controller_Front. We will now extend our application controller to deal with user authentication, user authorization, and user management.

At this stage, you may be wondering what the difference between *authentication* and *authorization* is.

- **Authentication:** Determines whether a user is in fact who they claim to be. This is typically performed using a unique username (their *identity*) and a password (their *credentials*).

- **Authorization:** Determines whether a user is allowed to access a particular *resource*, given that we now know who they are from the authentication process. Authorization also determines what an unauthenticated user is allowed to do. In our application, a resource is essentially a particular action or page, such as the action of submitting a new blog post.

In this chapter, we will set up user authentication in our application using the Zend_Auth component of the Zend Framework. This includes setting up database tables to store user details. We will then use the Zend_Acl component to manage which resources in the application each user has access to. Additionally, we must tie in our permissions system to work with Zend_Controller_Front.

Creating the User Database Table

Since our application will hold user accounts for multiple users, we need to track each of these user accounts. To do so, we will create a database table called users. This table will contain one record for each user, and it will hold their username and password, as well as other important details.

There will be three classes of users that access our web application: *guests*, *members*, and *administrators*. A user visiting the application will be automatically classed as a guest until they log in as a member. In order to distinguish members from administrators, the users table will include a column that denotes the *role* of each user. We will use this column when implementing the access control lists with Zend_Acl.

Note In a more complex system, you might assign multiple roles to users; however, for the sake of simplicity we will allow only one role per user. Any user classed as an administrator will also be able to perform all functions that a member can. Additionally, you could also use another table to store user types, but once again, for the sake of simplicity we will forego this and keep a static list of user types in our code.

The core data we will store for each user in the users table will be as follows:

- user_id: An internal integer used to represent the user.

- username: A unique string used to log in. In effect, this will be a public identifier for the user. We will display the username on blog posts and other publicly available content, rather than their real name, which many users prefer to keep anonymous.

- password: A string used to authenticate the user. We will store passwords as a hash using the md5() function. Note that this means passwords cannot be retrieved; instead they must be reset. We will implement all code required to do this.

- user_type: A string used to classify the user (either admin or member, although you will easily be able to add extra user types in the future based on what you learn in this book).

- ts_created: A timestamp indicating when the user account was created.

- ts_last_login: A timestamp indicating when the user last logged in. We will allow this field to have a null value, since the user won't have yet logged in when the record is created.

Listing 3-1 shows the SQL commands required to create the users table in MySQL. All SQL schema definitions are stored in the schema-mysql.sql file in the main application directory. If you're using PostgreSQL, you can find the corresponding schema in schema-pgsql.sql instead.

Note How you choose to store the database schema for your own web applications is entirely up to you. I've simply structured it this way so you can easily refer to it as required (and so you have easy access to it when downloading the code for this book).

Listing 3-1. *SQL Used to Create the Users Table in MySQL (schema-mysql.sql)*

```
create table users (
    user_id        serial         not null,
    username       varchar(255)   not null,
    password       varchar(32)    not null,

    user_type      varchar(20)    not null,

    ts_created     datetime       not null,
```

```
    ts_last_login    datetime,

    primary key (user_id),
    unique (username)
) type = InnoDB;
```

The user_id column is defined as type serial, which is the same as using bigint unsigned not null auto_increment. I personally prefer using serial, as it is shorter and simpler to type, and it also works in PostgreSQL.

The username column can be up to 255 characters in length, although we will put a restriction on this length in the code. The password will be stored as an MD5 encrypted string, so this column only needs to be 32 characters long.

Next is the user_type column. The length of this column isn't too important, although any new user types you add will be limited to 20 characters (this is only an internal name, so it doesn't need to be overly descriptive). This string is used when performing ACL checks.

Finally, there are the two timestamp columns. MySQL does in fact have a data type called timestamp, but I chose to use the datetime type instead, as MySQL will automatically update columns that use the timestamp type. In PostgreSQL, you need to use the timestamptz data type instead (see the schema-pgsql.sql file for the table definition). The following "Timestamps" section provides more details about how timestamps work in PHP.

■**Tip** Listing 3-1 instructs MySQL to use the InnoDB table type when creating a table, thereby providing us with SQL transaction capability and enforcing foreign key constraints. The default table type used otherwise is MyISAM.

You must now create this table in your database. There are two ways to do this. First, you can pipe the entire schema-mysql.sql file into your database using the following command:

```
# mysql -u phpweb20 -p phpweb20 < schema-mysql.sql
```

When you type this command you will be prompted to enter your password. This will create the entire database from scratch.

Alternatively, you can connect directly to the database, and copy and paste the table schema using the following command:

```
# mysql -u phpweb20 -p phpweb20
```

Since we will be building on the database as we go, I recommend the second method for simply adding each new table as required.

Timestamps

The way dates and times are handled in PHP, MySQL, and PostgreSQL is often misunderstood. Before we go any further, I will quickly cover some important points to be aware of when using dates and times in MySQL.

MySQL does not store time zone information with its date and time data. This means that your MySQL server must be set to use the same time zone as PHP; otherwise you may notice odd behavior with timestamps. For example, if you want to use the PHP date() function to format a timestamp from a MySQL table, be cautious—if you use the MySQL unix_timestamp() function when retrieving that timestamp, the incorrect date will be retrieved if the time zones do not match up.

There are three major drawbacks to using the date field types in MySQL:

- If you need to move your database to another server (let's say you change web hosts), the moved data will be incorrect if the server uses a different time zone. The server configuration would need to be modified, which most web hosts will not do for you.

- Various issues can arise concerning when daylight savings starts and finishes (assuming your location uses daylight savings).

- It is difficult to store timestamps from different time zones. You must convert all timestamps to the server time zone before inserting them.

If you think these aren't problems that will occur often, you are probably right, although here's a practical example. A web application I wrote stored the complete schedule for a sports league (among other things). Week to week, all games took place in different cities, and therefore in different time zones. For accurate scheduling data to be output on the web application (for instance, "3 hours until game time"), the time zone data needed to be accurate.

PostgreSQL does not have the datetime data type. Instead, I prefer to use the timestamptz column, which stores a date, time, and time zone. If you don't specify the time zone when inserting a value into this column, it uses the server's time zone (for instance, both 2007-04-18 23:32:00 and 2007-04-18 23:32:00+09:30 are valid; the former will use the server's time zone and the latter will use +09:30).

In the sports schedule example, I used PostgreSQL, which allowed me to easily store the time zone of the game. PostgreSQL's equivalent of unix_timestamp(ts_column) is extract(epoch from ts_column). Using timestamptz, this returns an accurate value that can be used in PHP's date() function. It also seamlessly deals with daylight savings.

User Profiles

You may have noticed that the users table (Listing 3-1) didn't store any useful information about the user, such as their name or e-mail address. To store this data, we will create an extra table called users_profile.

By using an extra table to store this information, we can easily store an arbitrary amount of information about the user without modifying the users table at all. For instance, we can store their name, e-mail address, phone number, location, favorite food, or anything else. Additionally, we can use this table to store preferences for each user.

Each record in the users_profile table corresponds to a single user profile value. That is, one record will correspond to a user's e-mail address, while another record will hold their name. There is slightly more overhead in retrieving this data at runtime, but the added flexibility makes it well worth it. All that is required in this table is three columns:

- user_id: This column links the profile value to a record in users.

- profile_key: This is the name of the profile value. For instance, we would use the value email here if the record holds an e-mail address.

- profile_value: This is the actual profile value. If the profile_key value is email, this column would hold the actual e-mail address.

■**Tip** We use the text field type for profile_value because this allows us to store a large amount of data if required. There is no difference in performance between the varchar and text types in MySQL and PostgreSQL. In fact, MySQL internally creates a varchar field as the smallest possible text field based on the specified precision.

Listing 3-2 shows the MySQL table definition for users_profile. We will implement code to manage user profiles later in this chapter.

Listing 3-2. *SQL Used to Create the users_profile Table in MySQL (schema-mysql.sql)*

```
create table users_profile (
    user_id         bigint unsigned not null,
    profile_key     varchar(255)    not null,
    profile_value   text            not null,

    primary key (user_id, profile_key),
    foreign key (user_id) references users (user_id)
) type = InnoDB;
```

As mentioned previously, the serial column type (used for the user_id column in Listing 3-1) is an alias for an auto-incrementing unsigned bigint column. Since the user_id column in this table refers back to the users table, we manually use the bigint unsigned type because we don't want this column to auto-increment.

We use the user_id and profile_key columns as the primary key for the users_profile table, as no profile values can be repeated for each user. However, a user can have several different profile values.

■**Note** If you're using PostgreSQL, the int data type is used for user_id, as this is what the PostgreSQL serial type uses. Once again, the PostgreSQL version of the table can be found in schema-pgsql.sql.

Introduction to Zend_Auth

Now that we've created the users table, we have something to authenticate against using Zend_Auth. Before we get to that, though, we must understand exactly how Zend_Auth works.

First, we must understand the terminology Zend_Auth uses. The unique information that identifies a user is referred to as their *identity*. After a user successfully authenticates, we store their identity in a PHP session so we can identify them in subsequent page requests.

> **▓Note** It is possible to write custom storage methods, but the most common storage method will arguably be in a PHP session. `Zend_Auth` provides the `Zend_Auth_Storage_Session` class for this. This class, in turn, uses the `Zend_Session` component, which is essentially a wrapper to PHP's `$_SESSION` variable (although it does provide greater functionality). To create some other storage method, you simply implement the `Zend_Auth_Storage_Interface` interface. For example, if you wanted to "remember a user" in between sessions, you could create a storage class that writes identity data to a cookie. You would then create an adapter (discussed shortly) to authenticate against cookie data. Be careful with this though, as it could potentially be dangerous if done incorrectly, since cookie data can be forged. One safeguard against this could be to give them a restricted role until they provide their credentials again, as Amazon.com does: it will remember your identity but not allow you to make any changes to your account unless you re-enter your password. Another example of using custom session storage is in a load-balanced environment (where multiple web servers are used for a single site). Disk-based sessions will not typically be available across all servers, so a subsequent user request may be handled on a different server than the previous request. Storing session data in the database alleviates this problem.

In order to authenticate a user, they must provide *credentials*. In the case of the application we are writing, we will use the `password` column from the `users` table as the user's credentials.

We use an *adapter* to check the given identity and credentials against our database. Adapters in `Zend_Auth` implement the `Zend_Auth_Adapter_Interface` interface. Thankfully, the Zend Framework comes with an adapter that we can use to check our MySQL database. If we wanted to authenticate users against a different storage method (such as LDAP or a password file generated by Apache's `htpasswd`), we would need to write a new adapter.

We will be using the `Zend_Auth_Adapter_DbTable` adapter, which is designed to work with the `Zend_Db` component. If you choose instead to write your own adapter, the only method you need to implement is the `authenticate()` method, which returns a `Zend_Auth_Result` object. This object contains information about whether authentication was successful, as well as diagnostic messages (such as whether the provided credentials were incorrect, or authentication failed because the identity wasn't found or for some other reason).

By default, `Zend_Auth_Adapter_DbTable` returns only the submitted username in the `Zend_Auth_Result` object. However, we need to store additional information about the user (such as their name and, more importantly, their user type). When we look at processing user logins with `Zend_Auth`, we will deal with this.

Instantiating Zend_Auth

`Zend_Auth` is a singleton class, which means only one instance of it can exist (like the `Zend_Controller_Front` class we used in Chapter 2). As such, we can use the static `getInstance()` method to retrieve that instance. We must then set the storage class (remember, we are using sessions) using the `setStorage()` method. If you use multiple storage methods, you will need to call this every time you want to access identity data in each storage location. Typically though, you will only need to call this once: at the start of each request.

The following code is used to set up the `Zend_Auth` instance. As you can see, it is fairly straightforward in its initial usage:

```
<?php
    $auth = Zend_Auth::getInstance();
    $auth->setStorage(new Zend_Auth_Storage_Session());
?>
```

We will be using the $auth object in several places in our web application. First, it will be used when we check user permissions with Zend_Acl (in the "Introduction to Zend_Acl" section later in this chapter). It will also be used in application login and logout methods, as we need to store and then clear the identity data for each of these methods.

As we did with our application configuration and database connection, we will store the $auth object in the application registry using Zend_Registry. Listing 3-3 shows the index.php bootstrap file as it stands with Zend_Auth.

Listing 3-3. *The Application Bootstrap File, Now Using Zend_Auth (index.php)*

```
<?php
    require_once('Zend/Loader.php');
    Zend_Loader::registerAutoload();


    // load the application configuration
    $config = new Zend_Config_Ini('../settings.ini', 'development');
    Zend_Registry::set('config', $config);


    // create the application logger
    $logger = new Zend_Log(new Zend_Log_Writer_Stream($config->logging->file));
    Zend_Registry::set('logger', $logger);


    // connect to the database
    $params = array('host'     => $config->database->hostname,
                    'username' => $config->database->username,
                    'password' => $config->database->password,
                    'dbname'   => $config->database->database);

    $db = Zend_Db::factory($config->database->type, $params);
    Zend_Registry::set('db', $db);


    // setup application authentication
    $auth = Zend_Auth::getInstance();
    $auth->setStorage(new Zend_Auth_Storage_Session());


    // handle the user request
    $controller = Zend_Controller_Front::getInstance();
    $controller->setControllerDirectory($config->paths->base .
                                   '/include/Controllers');
    $controller->registerPlugin(new CustomControllerAclManager($auth));
```

```
    // setup the view renderer
    $vr = new Zend_Controller_Action_Helper_ViewRenderer();
    $vr->setView(new Templater());
    $vr->setViewSuffix('tpl');
    Zend_Controller_Action_HelperBroker::addHelper($vr);

    $controller->dispatch();
?>
```

Authenticating with Zend_Auth

In Chapter 4 we will be implementing the login and logout forms for our web application, but before we get to that we will take a look at how the login and logout process actually work. As mentioned previously, we will be using the Zend_Auth_Adapter_DbTable authentication adapter. Prior to using this adapter, you must already have a valid Zend_Db object.

Because Zend_Auth_Adapter_DbTable is flexible and is designed to work with any database configuration, you must tell it how your storage is set up. Thus, you must include the following when instantiating it:

- The name of the database table being used (our table is called users).

- The column that holds the user identity (we are using the username column in the users table).

- The column that holds the user credentials (we are using the password column).

- And finally, the *treatment* used on the credentials. This is essentially a function that (if specified) wraps around the credentials. Remember that we are storing an MD5 hash of the password in the password column. Therefore, we pass md5(?) as this final argument. The question mark tells Zend_Db where to substitute in the password value.

Once Zend_Auth_Adapter_DbTable is instantiated (we will use the variable name $adapter), we can set the identity (username) and credentials (password). To do this, we use setIdentity() and setCredential().

Next, we will call the authenticate() method on the $auth object (the instance of Zend_Auth). The single argument passed to authenticate() is the adapter ($adapter). An instance of Zend_Auth_Result is then returned. We can call isValid() on this object to see whether the user successfully authenticated. If they didn't, we can either call getMessages() on the result to determine why, or we can generate our own error message based on the result from getCode().

■**Note** Although Zend_Auth_Result allows us to easily distinguish between an invalid username and an invalid password, this typically isn't information you should present to the user. Doing so can implicitly let them know when a username exists or not, which can aid malicious users in gaining unauthorized access to your application. The example in Listing 3-4 differentiates between these errors purely to demonstrate how you can detect them. The code we add to our application will not inform users whether it was their user-name or their password that was incorrect.

Listing 3-4 shows the code used to instantiate Zend_Auth_Adapter_DbTable and to authenticate against the users table. At this stage, we are simply providing a fake username and
password, as we haven't yet populated the users table. As you can see, we also handle
authentication errors and output a message indicating the reason for failure.

Listing 3-4. *Authenticating Against a Database Table Using Zend_Auth and Zend_Db*
(listing-3-4.php)

```php
<?php
    require_once('Zend/Loader.php');
    Zend_Loader::registerAutoload();


    // connect to the database
    $params = array('host'     => 'localhost',
                    'username' => 'phpweb20',
                    'password' => 'myPassword',
                    'dbname'   => 'phpweb20');


    $db = Zend_Db::factory('pdo_mysql', $params);


    // setup application authentication
    $auth = Zend_Auth::getInstance();
    $auth->setStorage(new Zend_Auth_Storage_Session());

    $adapter = new Zend_Auth_Adapter_DbTable($db,
                                             'users',
                                             'username',
                                             'password',
                                             'md5(?)');


    // try and login the "fakeUsername" user
    $adapter->setIdentity('fakeUsername');
    $adapter->setCredential('fakePassword');
    $result = $auth->authenticate($adapter);

    if ($result->isValid()) {
        // user successfully authenticated
    }
    else {
        // user not authenticated

        switch ($result->getCode()) {
            case Zend_Auth_Result::FAILURE_IDENTITY_NOT_FOUND:
                echo 'Identity not found';
                break;
            case Zend_Auth_Result::FAILURE_IDENTITY_AMBIGUOUS:
                echo 'Multiple users found with this identity!';
```

```
                    break;
            case Zend_Auth_Result::FAILURE_CREDENTIAL_INVALID:
                echo 'Invalid password';
                break;
            default:
                var_dump($result->getMessages());
        }
    }
?>
```

You can also check whether or not a user is authenticated using the $auth object. The hasIdentity() method indicates whether or not a user is authenticated. Then, to determine which user that is, you can use the getIdentity() method.

Similarly, you can use the clearIdentity() method to log a user out. If you are using sessions as the storage method, this effectively unsets the identity from the session.

As mentioned previously, when $auth->authenticate() succeeds using Zend_Auth_Adapter_DbTable, only the username is stored for the identity data. In Chapter 4, when we implement the user login form, we will alter the identity data to include other user details, such as the user type.

Introduction to Zend_Acl

Zend_Acl is a component of the Zend Framework that provides access control list (ACL) functionality. While it doesn't fundamentally require the use of Zend_Auth, we will combine these two components to control what users can and cannot do in our web application.

Essentially what Zend_Acl does is determine whether a *role* has sufficient privileges to access a *resource*.

- **Resource:** Some object (not an object in the OOP sense, just some "thing") in a web application to which access can be controlled. An example of a resource is an action in a web application, such as approving the content of an article before it is published, or deleting a user from the system. Additionally, you can provide finer-grained control over privileges to resources. So, in the example of approving an article, the resource would be the article-management system (or a particular article, depending on how you look at it), while the privilege would be the approve action.

- **Role:** Some object that requests access to resources. In our web application, a role refers to a user of certain privileges.

Although this language might be somewhat confusing, each user in our application (that is, each record in the users table) has a particular user type. We refer to this as a user's role.

Note It is possible to make a role or a resource inherit from another role or resource, respectively. For example, let's say you assign certain privileges to Role A. If you make Role B inherit from Role A, it will get all of the privileges that Role A has, in addition to any extra privileges you add to Role B. This can make your permissions system confusing (especially when inheriting from more than one other role or resource), so we will try to keep it as simple as possible in our application.

We will control access to particular resources (such as publishing a blog post or resetting a password) based on a user's role. As mentioned when creating the `users` table, the three types of users (the three user roles) will be `guest`, `member`, and `administrator`.

The typical flow for using `Zend_Acl` in a web application is as follows:

1. Instantiate the `Zend_Acl` class (let's call this object $acl).

2. Add one or more roles to $acl using the `addRole()` method.

3. Add resources to $acl using the `add()` method.

4. Add the full list of privileges for each role (that is, use `allow()` or `deny()` to indicate which resources roles have access to).

5. Use the `isAllowed()` method on $acl to determine whether a particular role has access to a particular resource/privilege combination.

6. Repeat step 5 as often as necessary while the script executes.

A Zend_Acl Example

Let's take a look at actually using the `Zend_Acl` class. In this example, I will use the role names we will be using in our application. The privileges I set up here should give you an idea of exactly what we will be doing when we integrate `Zend_Acl` into our application.

The first thing I need to do to manage and check permissions is to instantiate the `Zend_Acl` class. The constructor takes no arguments:

```
$acl = new Zend_Acl();
```

Next, I create each of the roles that I'm checking permissions for. As mentioned previously, we will be using three different roles: `guest`, `member`, and `administrator`.

```
$acl->addRole(new Zend_Acl_Role('guest'));
$acl->addRole(new Zend_Acl_Role('member'));
$acl->addRole(new Zend_Acl_Role('administrator'));
```

After creating the roles, I can create the resources. In fact, I could swap the order; the key thing is that both roles and resources must be added before defining or checking permissions.

For this example, I will only add account and admin as the resources that will be granted permissions. There will be other resources in our application, but only items that will be granted permissions need to be added here, because when checking permissions, we check for the existence of the requested resource. It's up to you as the developer how you handle a permissions check for a nonexistent resource. In this case, I will simply allow access to a requested resource if it hasn't been added to $acl.

```
$acl->add(new Zend_Acl_Resource('account'));
$acl->add(new Zend_Acl_Resource('admin'));
```

The next step is to define the different permissions required in the application. This is achieved by making a series of calls to `allow()` and `deny()` on the `Zend_Acl` instance. The first argument to this function is the role, and the second is the resource. You can add finer-grained control by specifying the third parameter (the permission name).

In the permissions system for our application, the name of the controller (in the context of `Zend_Controller`) is the resource, while the controller action is the permission name. As in the following example, we can allow or deny access to an entire controller (as we will do for guest in the `admin` controller), or we can open up one or two specific actions within a controller (as we will do for the `login` and `fetchpassword` actions for guest).

```
$acl->allow('guest');            // allow guests everywhere ...
$acl->deny('guest', 'admin');    // ... except in the admin section ...
$acl->deny('guest', 'account');  // ... and the account management section
$acl->allow('guest', 'account',  // ... although let them log in
          array('login', 'fetchpassword'));
```

In addition to defining what guests can do, I also want to define what members are allowed to do. Members are privileged users, so I allow them more access than guests:

```
$acl->allow('member');           // members can go everywhere ...
$acl->deny('member', 'admin');   // ... except for the site admin section
```

Next I define the permissions for administrators, who are even more privileged than members:

```
$acl->allow('administrator');    // administrators can go everywhere!
```

Once all the permissions have been defined, they can be queried to determine what can and can't be accessed. Here are some examples:

```
// check permissions
$acl->isAllowed('guest', 'account');            // returns false
$acl->isAllowed('guest', 'account', 'login');   // true

$acl->isAllowed('member', 'account');           // true
$acl->isAllowed('member', 'account', 'login');  // true
$acl->isAllowed('member', 'admin');             // false

$acl->isAllowed('administrator', 'admin');      // true
```

Note that in our application the role names will be dynamically determined based on the user that is logged in, and the resource and permission names will be determined by the requested controller and action.

Realistically, the call to `isAllowed()` will be in an `if` statement, such as this:

```php
<?php
    if ($acl->isAllowed('member', 'account')) {
        // display member account area
    }
?>
```

■Tip If you try to check the permissions of an undefined resource, an exception will be thrown. It is up to you how you want to handle this. For example, you may choose to automatically deny the request, or you may choose to automatically allow it. Another option could be to fall back to a different resource if the given resource is not found; the `has()` function is used to check the existence of a resource. The same principle applies to roles. In our application, a user will fall back to guest if their role is not found (this would result from a bogus value in the `user_type` column of the `users` table).

Our actual permissions system will be almost identical to this example, in that members can access the account resource, while guests cannot, and administrators can access all areas.

■Note The code uses both the term `admin` and `administrator`. The user type (that is, the role) is called `administrator`, while the controller (that is, the resource) is called `admin`. In other words, only users of type `administrator` will be able to access the `http://phpweb20/admin` URL.

Combining Zend_Auth, Zend_Acl, and Zend_Controller_Front

The next step in developing our web application is to integrate the Zend_Auth and Zend_Acl components. In this section, we will change the behavior of the application controller (that is, the instance of Zend_Controller_Front), to check permissions using Zend_Acl prior to dispatching a user's request. When checking permissions, we will use the identity stored with Zend_Auth to determine the role of the current user.

To control permissions, we will treat each controller as a resource, and treat the action handlers in these controllers as the permissions associated with the resource. For instance, later in this chapter we will create the AccountController.php file, which is used to control everything relating to user accounts (such as logging in, logging out, fetching passwords, and updating user details). The AccountController controller will be the resource for Zend_Acl, while the privileges associated with this resource are the actions just mentioned (login, logout, fetch password, update details).

■Note There are many ways to structure a permissions system. In this application, we will simply control access to action handlers in controller files. This is relatively straightforward, as we can automate all ACL checks dynamically based on the action and controller name in a user request.

The way we achieve this setup of using controller and action names to dictate permissions is to write a plug-in for Zend_Controller (by extending the Zend_Controller_Plugin_ Abstract class). This plug-in defines the preDispatch() method, which receives a user request before the front controller dispatches the request to the respective action. Effectively, we are intercepting the request and checking whether the current user has sufficient privileges to execute that action.

To register a plug-in with Zend_Controller, we call the registerPlugin() method on our Zend_Controller_Front instance. Before we do that, let's create the plug-in, which we will call CustomControllerAclManager. We will create all roles and resources for Zend_Acl in this class, as well as checking permissions.

Listing 3-5 shows the contents of the CustomControllerAclManager.php file, which we will store in the /var/www/phpweb20/include directory.

Listing 3-5. *The CustomControllerAclManager Plug-in, Which Checks Permissions Prior to Dispatching User Requests (CustomControllerAclManager.php)*

```php
<?php
    class CustomControllerAclManager extends Zend_Controller_Plugin_Abstract
    {
        // default user role if not logged or (or invalid role found)
        private $_defaultRole = 'guest';

        // the action to dispatch if a user doesn't have sufficient privileges
        private $_authController = array('controller' => 'account',
                                         'action'     => 'login');

        public function __construct(Zend_Auth $auth)
        {
            $this->auth = $auth;
            $this->acl = new Zend_Acl();

            // add the different user roles
            $this->acl->addRole(new Zend_Acl_Role($this->_defaultRole));
            $this->acl->addRole(new Zend_Acl_Role('member'));
            $this->acl->addRole(new Zend_Acl_Role('administrator'), 'member');

            // add the resources we want to have control over
            $this->acl->add(new Zend_Acl_Resource('account'));
            $this->acl->add(new Zend_Acl_Resource('admin'));

            // allow access to everything for all users by default
            // except for the account management and administration areas
            $this->acl->allow();
            $this->acl->deny(null, 'account');
            $this->acl->deny(null, 'admin');

            // add an exception so guests can log in or register
            // in order to gain privilege
```

```
        $this->acl->allow('guest', 'account', array('login',
                                                    'fetchpassword',
                                                    'register',
                                                    'registercomplete'));

    // allow members access to the account management area
    $this->acl->allow('member', 'account');

    // allows administrators access to the admin area
    $this->acl->allow('administrator', 'admin');
}

/**
 * preDispatch
 *
 * Before an action is dispatched, check if the current user
 * has sufficient privileges. If not, dispatch the default
 * action instead
 *
 * @param   Zend_Controller_Request_Abstract    $request
 */
public function preDispatch(Zend_Controller_Request_Abstract $request)
{
    // check if a user is logged in and has a valid role,
    // otherwise, assign them the default role (guest)
    if ($this->auth->hasIdentity())
        $role = $this->auth->getIdentity()->user_type;
    else
        $role = $this->_defaultRole;

    if (!$this->acl->hasRole($role))
        $role = $this->_defaultRole;

    // the ACL resource is the requested controller name
    $resource = $request->controller;

    // the ACL privilege is the requested action name
    $privilege = $request->action;

    // if we haven't explicitly added the resource, check
    // the default global permissions
    if (!$this->acl->has($resource))
        $resource = null;

    // access denied - reroute the request to the default action handler
    if (!$this->acl->isAllowed($role, $resource, $privilege)) {
        $request->setControllerName($this->_authController['controller']);
```

```
                    $request->setActionName($this->_authController['action']);
                }
            }
        }
?>
```

The class constructor is where we define roles, resources, and permissions. In Listing 3-5 we first make the administrator role inherit from the member role. This means that any permission given to members is also given to administrators. Additionally, we can then give the administrator role privileges on its own to access the admin area.

Next, we set up the default permissions (that is, permissions that apply to all roles). These allow access to everything except for the account and admin resources. Obviously, a guest needs the chance to authenticate themselves and become a privileged user, so we must open up access to the login and fetchpassword privileges. Additionally, if they are not yet registered, we need to grant them access to register and registercomplete (a helper action used to confirm registration to a user).

Once a guest becomes authenticated (thereby becoming either a member or an administrator), they need to be able to access the account resource. Since the administrator role inherits from the member role, permitting members access to the account resource also gives access to administrators.

Finally, we open up the admin areas to administrators only. In other words, guests and members cannot access this area.

Now, let's take a look at the preDispatch() method, which takes the user request as an argument. First, we set up the role and resource so the ACL check will work correctly. If the resource is not found, we set the $resource variable to null, which means the default permission will be used for the given role. Based on the way we have set this up (that is, allowing access to everything), this effectively means the ACL check will return true. If the role is not found, we use the guest role instead.

■Note We are accessing the user_type property of the identity stored with Zend_Auth. We haven't yet looked at storing this property with the identity when performing a login, but we will cover this in Chapter 4, when we implement the login action to our account controller.

Finally, we call isAllowed() to determine whether the $role role has access to the $privilege privilege of resource $resource. If this returns true, we do nothing and let the front controller dispatch loop continue. If this returns false, we reroute the dispatcher to execute the login action of the account controller. In other words, when an unprivileged user tries to do something they are not allowed to do, they will be redirected to a login screen.

■Note One side effect of this behavior is that if a member tries to access the admin area, they will be shown a login screen, even though they are already logged in. You could modify the code to show the login screen if no identity is found in $auth, but show a different screen if the user is logged in but has insufficient privileges.

Managing User Records with DatabaseObject

DatabaseObject is a class I developed several years ago that I make heavy use of in nearly all of my PHP development tasks. It acts as an extra layer on top of a database connection, which makes reading, writing, and deleting rows from a database very simple. You can find the full DatabaseObject.php file in the ./include directory of the downloadable source code.

Essentially, I extend the abstract DatabaseObject class for each major table in an application. So to manage records in the users table of our web application, we will create a class called DatabaseObject_User. Once we instantiate this class, we can then call the load() method to fetch a record from the database, use the save() method to either insert or update data in the database (depending on whether or not a record has already been loaded), and call delete() to delete a loaded record.

■Note When I first wrote DatabaseObject, neither PHP 5 nor the Zend Framework were out yet, but I have since updated this class to use PHP 5 and to work with the Zend_Db component. If you are not using Zend_Db, you will have to make appropriate changes.

Instead of looking at the implementation details, we will take a look at the available functions and exactly how DatabaseObject can be used:

- load(): Loads a record by performing a select query. Returns true if the record is loaded.

- isSaved(): Returns true if a record has previously been loaded with load().

- save(): Saves the current data to the database. If the record wasn't previously loaded, an insert statement is used; otherwise the loaded record is updated with an SQL update.

- delete(): If a record has been loaded, this function performs an SQL delete query.

- getId(): Retrieves the database ID of a saved record.

There are also a number of callbacks you can define, which are automatically called as required. The callbacks that can be defined are as follows:

- postLoad(): Called after a record is successfully loaded. It could be used to load data from other tables as required.

- preInsert(): Called prior to inserting a new record (note that in this case save() distinguishes inserts from updates). It could be used to set values dynamically (such as a timestamp recording the date of insert).

- postInsert(): Called after a new record is saved. In the case of our users table, we will use this to send an e-mail to the new user.

- preUpdate(): Called prior to an existing record being updated. It could be used to set values dynamically (such as a timestamp recording the date of update).

- postUpdate(): Called after an existing record is updated.

- `preDelete()`: Called prior to an existing record being deleted. If other tables depend on this data, you would delete the data from those tables here, before the data is deleted from this table.

- `postDelete()`: Called after a record has been deleted. It could be used to delete a file on the filesystem that relates to this record.

All callbacks (except for `postLoad()`) must return either `true` or `false`. If `false` is returned, the entire transaction is rolled back. For example, if you return `false` from `postDelete()`, the record is not deleted, and any queries you perform in `preDelete()` are also rolled back. It is important to remember to define the return value if you implement any of these functions.

Note Because of the way `DatabaseObject` works, all tables that use it must follow a similar structure. That is, the table must have a single primary key field, with an auto-incrementing sequence. The `users` table we created earlier in this chapter follows this structure by defining the `user_id` field as a serial. This wasn't the case for `users_profile`, and we will be managing data in this table slightly differently.

The DatabaseObject_User Class

Now that we've looked at how `DatabaseObject` works, we will create a child class to manage records in the `users` table. Once we have created this class, we will look at how to actually use it.

To create this class, all we really need to do is define the name of the database table and the name of its primary key field, and then define the list of columns in the table. If required, you can also set the types of the columns, which makes `DatabaseObject` treat the data accordingly. At this stage, all we will be using is the `DatabaseObject::TYPE_TIMESTAMP` type.

Listing 3-6 shows the contents of `User.php`, which should be stored in the `DatabaseObject` directory (so the full path is `/var/www/phpweb20/include/DatabaseObject`). Note that naming it in this manner means the Zend Framework autoloader will automatically include this code when required.

Listing 3-6. *The Initial Version of the DatabaseObject_User Class (User.php)*

```php
<?php
    class DatabaseObject_User extends DatabaseObject
    {
        public function __construct($db)
        {
            parent::__construct($db, 'users', 'user_id');

            $this->add('username');
            $this->add('password');
            $this->add('user_type', 'member');
            $this->add('ts_created', time(), self::TYPE_TIMESTAMP);
            $this->add('ts_last_login', null, self::TYPE_TIMESTAMP);
        }
    }
?>
```

In Listing 3-6, we first call the parent constructor. This method accepts the database connection as the first argument (an instance of Zend_Db_Adapter), the database table name as the second argument, and the column name of the primary key as the third argument.

Next, we add the list of fields using add(). The first argument is the name of the field, the second argument if specified is its default value, and the third argument is the type. If no type is specified, the value is simply treated as is.

In the listing, you can see that the ts_created and ts_last_login fields are both timestamps. We set the ts_created field to be the current time, and we set ts_last_login to null, as the user has not yet logged in.

■**Note** We could alternatively set the default value of ts_created to null, and then dynamically set the value in the preInsert() callback instead. There's no real difference, unless there is a huge time difference between instantiating the object and calling its save() method.

The other thing we have done is set the default value of the user_type field to member. Earlier in this chapter we covered the three types of users: guests, members, and administrators. By definition, a guest is somebody who doesn't have a user account (and therefore has no row in the users table), so we set the default value to member.

Now is a good time to define the user types in this code. Our code should allow us to add more user types in the future and to only ever have to change this one list (disregarding the fact that we would likely need to change the ACL permissions). We could alternatively store the list of user types in a database table, but for the sake of simplicity we will store them in a static array in the DatabaseObject_User class.

Additionally, we can extend the __set() method to intercept the value being set so we can ensure that the value is valid.

■**Note** PHP 5 allows the use of a magic __set() method, which is automatically called (if defined) when code tries to modify a nonexistent property in an object. DatabaseObject uses this method to set values to be saved in the database table. We can also define this in the DatabaseObject_User child class in order to alter a value before calling __set() in the parent class. PHP 5 also allows a similar __get() method, which is automatically called if a nonexistent property is read. DatabaseObject also uses this method.

Before we look at the code that does this, there is one further value we must intercept and alter before it is written to the database: the password. We mentioned earlier that we are saving passwords as MD5 hashes of their original value. As such, we must call md5() on the password value prior to saving it to the database.

■**Note** You can use either the PHP version of md5() or you can call it in the SQL query. For the sake of simplicity and cross-database compatibility, we will use the PHP function.

Listing 3-7 shows the new version of User.php, which now defines the list of user types, as well as ensuring that a valid user type is set. It also changes the password value, when it is set, to be an MD5 hash.

Listing 3-7. *The New Version of DatabaseObject_User, Now Setting the Password and User Type Correctly (User.php)*

```php
<?php
    class DatabaseObject_User extends DatabaseObject
    {
        static $userTypes = array('member'        => 'Member',
                                  'administrator' => 'Administrator');

        public function __construct($db)
        {
            parent::__construct($db, 'users', 'user_id');

            $this->add('username');
            $this->add('password');
            $this->add('user_type', 'member');
            $this->add('ts_created', time(), self::TYPE_TIMESTAMP);
            $this->add('ts_last_login', null, self::TYPE_TIMESTAMP);
        }

        public function __set($name, $value)
        {
            switch ($name) {
                case 'password':
                    $value = md5($value);
                    break;

                case 'user_type':
                    if (!array_key_exists($value, self::$userTypes))
                        $value = 'member';
                    break;
            }

            return parent::__set($name, $value);
        }
    }
?>
```

Using DatabaseObject_User

Now that we have created the DatabaseObject_User class, let's look at how to use it. Listing 3-8 shows the typical usage of a DatabaseObject child class: we first set some properties and then call the save() method (which will perform an SQL insert). Next we modify some properties on the same object and then call save() again (this time an SQL update will be performed). Finally, we try to load an existing record and then delete it from the database table.

Listing 3-8. *Sample Usage of the DatabaseObject_User Class (listing-3-8.php)*

```php
<?php
    require_once('Zend/Loader.php');
    Zend_Loader::registerAutoload();

    // connect to the database
    $params = array('host'     => 'localhost',
                    'username' => 'phpweb20',
                    'password' => 'myPassword',
                    'dbname'   => 'phpweb20');

    $db = Zend_Db::factory('pdo_mysql', $params);

    // Create a new user
    $user = new DatabaseObject_User($db);
    $user->username = 'someUser';
    $user->password = 'myPassword';
    $user->save();

    // Now update that user and save new details
    $user->user_type = 'admin';
    $user->ts_last_login = time();
    $user->save();

    // Find a user with user_id of 5 and delete them
    $user2 = new DatabaseObject_User($db);
    if ($user2->load(5)) {
        $user2->delete();
    }
?>
```

If we were to look at the users table after running this script, it might look something like this:

```
mysql> select user_id, username, password from users;
+---------+----------+----------------------------------+
| user_id | username | password                         |
+---------+----------+----------------------------------+
|       7 | someUser | deb1536f480475f7d593219aa1afd74c |
+---------+----------+----------------------------------+
```

Managing User Profiles

When we created the users table earlier in this chapter, we also created a table called users_profile, which we use to hold user profile data. The way this table is structured, we can add any number of values to correspond with each user account. This may include personal details, such as the user's name or e-mail address, or it may include other settings, such as whether or not the user wants to receive a monthly newsletter.

Because I use a system like this for most web applications I work on, I have developed a generic class called Profile to manage data of this nature. Profile is an abstract class that must be extended for each table you want to write to. We will create a class called Profile_User to extend Profile.

The profile is typically used as follows:

1. Create a new instance of Profile_User. One instance is responsible for the profile data of one user.

2. Set the user ID and load the existing profile data for that user.

3. Set new values, update existing values, or delete existing values as required.

4. Save the profile data.

In order to autoload the classes with Zend_Loader, we can store the Profile.php file in the ./include directory, while we store User.php (which holds the Profile_User class) in ./include/Profile.

No methods need to be implemented in the Profile_User class—all we need to do is specify the database table used to store profile data. Additionally, we need to add a single utility method to set the user ID.

Since we are storing profile data for all users in a single table, we need to add a *filter* to the parent Profile class so it correctly reads and writes the profile data.

Listing 3-9 shows the contents of User.php, which defines the Profile_User child class.

Listing 3-9. *The Profile_User Child Class, Used to Initialize Profile Management for Users (User.php)*

```php
<?php
    class Profile_User extends Profile
    {
        public function __construct($db, $user_id = null)
        {
            parent::__construct($db, 'users_profile');

            if ($user_id > 0)
                $this->setUserId($user_id);
        }

        public function setUserId($user_id)
        {
            $filters = array('user_id' => (int) $user_id);
            $this->_filters = $filters;
```

```
        }
    }
?>
```

To instantiate `Profile_User`, the database connection is passed, as well as an optional user ID. If you don't specify a user ID, you can call the `setUserId()` method. Once the user ID has been set, you can call the `load()` method to load existing profile data from the database.

■**Note** You must make a call to `setUserId()` before calling `load()` or `save()`; otherwise the data may be saved incorrectly or an error will occur.

Using Profile_User

Now that we have looked at the code for `Profile_User`, let's take a look at an example of how to use the class. For this example, let's assume a user has already been created in the `users` table with an ID of `1234` (remember from our schema that the `user_id` field in `users_profile` is a foreign key to `users`, so the corresponding record must exist).

The first thing we must do is instantiate the class and load the data:

```php
<?php
    $profile = new Profile_User($db, 1234);
    $profile->load();
?>
```

Alternatively, we can call `setUserId()` instead of passing the ID in the constructor. We will be using this method when we integrate `Profile_User` with `DatabaseObject_User`.

```
$profile = new Profile_User($db);
$profile->setUserId(1234);
$profile->load();
```

Now we can set a new profile value (or update an existing one) just by accessing the object property, like so:

```
$profile->email = 'user@example.com';
```

We can delete a profile value by calling `unset()`:

```
unset($profile->email);
```

And we can check whether a profile value exists by calling `isset()`:

```
if (isset($profile->email)) {
    // do something
}
```

Finally, we must save any changes that we make to the database by calling the `save()` method:

```
$profile->save();
```

Listing 3-10 shows a more complete example of using `Profile_User`, this time including the database creation code.

Listing 3-10. *A Complete Example of Setting Profile Data and Displaying a Simple Message (listing-3-10.php)*

```php
<?php
    require_once('Zend/Loader.php');
    Zend_Loader::registerAutoload();


    // connect to the database
    $params = array('host'     => 'localhost',
                    'username' => 'phpweb20',
                    'password' => 'myPassword',
                    'dbname'   => 'phpweb20');


    $db = Zend_Db::factory('pdo_mysql', $params);


    $profile = new Profile_User($db);
    $profile->setUserId(1234);
    $profile->load();

    $profile->email = 'user@example.com';
    $profile->country = 'Australia';
    $profile->save();

    if (isset($profile->country))
        echo sprintf('Your country is %s', $profile->country);
?>
```

If you were to check the data in the `users_profile` table after running this example, it would look something like the following:

```
mysql> select * from users_profile where user_id = 1234;
+---------+-------------+------------------+
| user_id | profile_key | profile_value    |
+---------+-------------+------------------+
|    1234 | country     | Australia        |
|    1234 | email       | user@example.com |
+---------+-------------+------------------+
2 rows in set (0.00 sec)
```

Integrating Profile_User with DatabaseObject_User

Now that we have a way of managing user profiles, we must integrate this into our DatabaseObject_User class so that all user data can easily be managed in a single place. Essentially what we must do is as follows:

- Instantiate the Profile_User class within DatabaseObject_User.

- Load the profile data automatically when a user is loaded.

- Save the profile data automatically when the user record is saved.

- Delete the profile data automatically when the user record is deleted.

Additionally, we must deal with the fact that the user ID is not known when creating a new user record with DatabaseObject_User. As such, we must correctly use the callbacks that DatabaseObject makes available. We will use them as follows:

- In the load callback (postLoad()), we will set the user ID and load the profile data.

- Before an insert occurs (preInsert()), we will generate a password for the user. For now, we will use the PHP uniqid() function to generate a password, but we will improve on this in Chapter 4 when we need to send an e-mail out to new users.

- After an insert occurs (postInsert()), we will set the user ID and save the profile data.

- After an update occurs (postUpdate()), we will save the profile data (the user ID is known at this point).

- Before a delete occurs (preDelete()), we will delete all profile data. Note that this must occur before the user is deleted (as opposed to being done in postDelete()), because a foreign key constraint violation will occur if we do it the other way around (that is, users_profile depends on users, so data can't be removed from users that is referenced in users_profile).

Listing 3-11 shows the new version of DatabaseObject_User, which defines each of these callbacks. Importantly, the postInsert() and postUpdate() callbacks also return true, which is required for the database transaction to complete.

Listing 3-11. *DatabaseObject_User with Profile Management Functionality Built in (User.php)*

```php
<?php
    class DatabaseObject_User extends DatabaseObject
    {
        static $userTypes = array('member'        => 'Member',
                                  'administrator' => 'Administrator');

        public $profile = null;

        public function __construct($db)
        {
            parent::__construct($db, 'users', 'user_id');
```

```php
        $this->add('username');
        $this->add('password');
        $this->add('user_type', 'member');
        $this->add('ts_created', time(), self::TYPE_TIMESTAMP);
        $this->add('ts_last_login', null, self::TYPE_TIMESTAMP);

        $this->profile = new Profile_User($db);
    }

    protected function preInsert()
    {
        $this->password = uniqid();
        return true;
    }

    protected function postLoad()
    {
        $this->profile->setUserId($this->getId());
        $this->profile->load();
    }

    protected function postInsert()
    {
        $this->profile->setUserId($this->getId());
        $this->profile->save(false);
        return true;
    }

    protected function postUpdate()
    {
        $this->profile->save(false);
        return true;
    }

    protected function preDelete()
    {
        $this->profile->delete();
        return true;
    }

    public function __set($name, $value)
    {
        switch ($name) {
            case 'password':
                $value = md5($value);
                break;
```

```
            case 'user_type':
                if (!array_key_exists($value, self::$userTypes))
                    $value = 'member';
                break;
        }

        return parent::__set($name, $value);
    }
}
?>
```

In addition to the callbacks defined in this code, Profile_User is instantiated in the constructor. Note that because we have used the PHP 5 __set() and __get() overloaders in DatabaseObject, we must also define the $profile property in the class definition.

■Important When calling the save() method on the profile, we pass false as an argument, which prevents Profile from using a database transaction to save the data. We want to prevent this because DatabaseObject has already initiated a transaction, so the saving of profile data falls within this transaction. In other words, if we were to return false from postUpdate(), the transaction would be rolled back, meaning the changes to the user table wouldn't be saved, and the profile data would remain unchanged in the database.

With these new features added to DatabaseObject_User, we can now easily manipulate all user data as required. Listing 3-12 shows an example of creating a new user and setting the profile data all in one step.

Listing 3-12. *Creating a New User and Setting the Profile Data All in One Step (listing-3-12.php)*

```php
<?php
    require_once('Zend/Loader.php');
    Zend_Loader::registerAutoload();

    // connect to the database
    $params = array('host'     => 'localhost',
                    'username' => 'phpweb20',
                    'password' => 'myPassword',
                    'dbname'   => 'phpweb20');

    $db = Zend_Db::factory('pdo_mysql', $params);

    // Create a new user
    $user = new DatabaseObject_User($db);
    $user->username = 'someUser';
    $user->password = 'myPassword';
```

```
// Set their profile data
$user->profile->email = 'user@example.com';
$user->profile->country = 'Australia';

// Save the user and their profile
$user->save();

// Load some other user and delete them
$user2 = new DatabaseObject_User($db);
if ($user2->load(1234))
    $user2->delete();
?>
```

Summary

In this chapter we created the infrastructure for managing users in our web application. First, we looked at the Zend_Auth and Zend_Acl components from the Zend Framework. We discovered the differences between authentication and authorization, and how they apply to our application.

Next, we integrated both of these components with Zend_Controller_Front, restricting access to our application based on the requested controller and action. We then looked at how database data can easily be managed using the DatabaseObject and Profile classes, which we extended in order to manage user data.

In the next chapter, we will continue the process of building the application's user system by allowing users to create new accounts, log in, and update their profiles using the code we have developed in this chapter.

CHAPTER 4

■ ■ ■

User Registration, Login, and Logout

In Chapter 3 we looked closely at the user authentication and authorization aspects of the web application. We learned that authentication is when a user proves they are who they say they are, while authorization determines what that user is and isn't allowed to do. We created the necessary database tables to hold user details as well as the code to manage the database records. We then used the `Zend_Auth` and `Zend_Acl` components of the Zend Framework to control which areas of the web site users can access.

In this chapter we will build on the code from Chapter 3 by implementing a user registration system. Once registered, users will be able to log in and update their details. This chapter covers everything related to creating user accounts and authenticating (that is, logging in). This includes the use of CAPTCHA images as well as allowing users to reset their forgotten passwords.

Adding User Registration to the Application

Implementing a user registration system is a fairly involved process, not only because there's a lot to do in setting up a user account, but also because it's the first real interaction between the web application and the end-user that we've looked at in this book.

The process of accepting user registrations will involve the following:

- Adding navigation so the user can find the registration form

- Displaying the registration form to the user, including a CAPTCHA image

- Accepting and validating the submitted details, including checking availability of usernames

- Displaying errors back to the user if something goes wrong

- Saving the database record, e-mailing the user, and displaying a confirmation page if all went well

We won't do all of this in exactly this order, but we will build up the registration system until it incorporates all of these features.

The fields users will be filling in for registration are as follows:

- **A username.** This value must be unique and contain only alphanumeric characters (letters and numbers).

- **Their name.** We will split this up into first name and last name.

- **Their e-mail address.** We require this so we have a valid point of contact for the user. To ensure that we have a real e-mail address, the account password is automatically generated and sent to this address. This is a simple but effective way of preventing false e-mail addresses from being entered.

Creating the Form Processor for User Registration

In order to keep the code that is responsible for processing the user registration form separate from other parts of the application (such as the account controller that displays the registration form), we will create a class called FormProcessor_UserRegistration. This class will extend from FormProcessor, another utility class (available in the book's code base in ./include/FormProcessor.php) that I wrote to aid in my own web application development. The FormProcessor class is fairly simple and doesn't do anything aside from hold the form values you tell it to, and hold form error messages that you can display.

The Initial FormProcessor_UserRegistration Class

To extend FormProcessor, all we need to do is implement the *abstract* function process(), which accepts a Zend_Controller_Request_Abstract object as an argument and returns true if the form was successfully processed or false if an error occurred. The instance of Zend_Controller_Request_Abstract is an object generated by Zend_Controller_Front, which holds all data relating to the current request, such as get and post data.

■**Note** In actual fact, the instance of Zend_Controller_Request_Abstract is an instance of Zend_Controller_Request_Http that we will eventually pass to process(). The Zend_Controller_Request_Http class extends from Zend_Controller_Request_Abstract.

As mentioned above, FormProcessor also provides methods for storing error messages:

- addError($name, $message): Sets a new error message with the given name. If the error message already exists, that error name is assigned an array with multiple messages.

- hasError($name): Checks whether an error message with the specified name has been set. By omitting the $name parameter, this method can also be used to check whether any errors have been set at all.

- getError($name): Retrieves the error message for the given name. If no corresponding error message has been set, null is returned.

Additionally, there is a function called `sanitize()` that is used to strip HTML tags from the string and trim whitespace from the start and end of the string. This is achieved primarily using `Zend_Filter`, a Zend Framework component that can manipulate strings with filters (we will look briefly at `Zend_Filter` in Chapter 7).

■**Note** The `FormProcessor.php` file is available from the downloadable source code for this book. It belongs in the `./include` directory so it can be automatically loaded as required.

Let's now take a look at the `FormProcessor_UserRegistration` class. Listing 4-1 shows the beginnings of this class—we will add to it throughout this section. This file is located in `./include/FormProcessor/UserRegistration.php`.

Listing 4-1. *The Beginnings of the User Registration Form Processor (UserRegistration.php)*

```php
<?php
    class FormProcessor_UserRegistration extends FormProcessor
    {
        protected $db = null;
        public $user = null;

        public function __construct($db)
        {
            parent::__construct();

            $this->db = $db;
            $this->user = new DatabaseObject_User($db);
            $this->user->type = 'member';
        }

        public function process(Zend_Controller_Request_Abstract $request)
        {
            // validate the username

            // validate first and last name

            // validate the e-mail address

            // validate CAPTCHA phrase

            // save database record if no errors

            // return true if no errors have occurred
            return !$this->hasError();
        }
    }
?>
```

The first thing this code does is define the constructor, in which the database connection is accepted and an instance of DatabaseObject_User is created. This object will remain unsaved until the form is successfully processed and $this->user->save() is called.

Next the abstract method process() is implemented. This method returns true if the form was processed correctly and false if an error occurred. As such, we can use the hasError() method to determine the return value.

To implement the process() method, we must fetch the submitted values from the $request object and process them accordingly. First, we must check the username by doing the following:

1. Check that a username was entered. If one wasn't, we need to notify the user that the username is a required field.

2. If a username was entered, check that it is in a valid format. Our usernames will consist of only alphanumeric characters (that is, only letters and numbers). If an invalid username was entered, we should create an appropriate error message.

3. If the username is valid, check whether or not somebody else has already registered with this username.

In order to check these conditions, we will implement two new functions in DatabaseObject_User: usernameExists() and IsValidUsername(), as shown in Listing 4-2.

Listing 4-2. *New Functions Added to DatabaseObject_User (User.php)*

```php
<?php
    class DatabaseObject_User extends DatabaseObject
    {
        // ... other code

        public function usernameExists($username)
        {
            $query = sprintf('select count(*) as num from %s where username = ?',
                            $this->_table);

            $result = $this->_db->fetchOne($query, $username);

            return $result['num'] > 0;
        }

        static public function IsValidUsername($username)
        {
            $validator = new Zend_Validate_Alnum();
            return $validator->isValid($username);
        }
    }
?>
```

Let's take a look at each of these changes before returning to the FormProcessor_UserRegistration class.

The usernameExists() Method

We call this method to determine whether or not the passed-in username already exists. If the username is in use, then true is returned; otherwise false is returned.

The IsValidUsername() Method

This method simply checks whether or not a username is valid, returning true if it is and false if not. To check the validity of the username, we use the Zend_Validate component of the Zend Framework. We are only checking for alphanumeric characters, so we can use the Zend_Validate_Alnum class.

Obviously, we could write a simple regular expression (such as /^[a-z0-9]+$/i) to check this, but Zend_Validate allows us to easily chain different validators together, meaning that in the future you could easily change the method for validating a username. Additionally, using Zend_Validate is a good practice to get into, as we will be using it throughout this book when validating form data (we will see it again shortly when we check users' e-mail addresses).

This method is static, as it does not rely on an instance of DatabaseObject_User.

Adding Username Validation to FormProcessor_UserRegistration

Since we have the new username-related methods available in DatabaseObject_User, we can now proceed to validate and set a username according to the rules outlined previously. Listing 4-3 shows the new version of process(), which now takes the submitted username from the request post data (using the getPost() method on $request) and validates it.

Listing 4-3. *Validating the Submitted Username (UserRegistration.php)*

```php
<?php
    class FormProcessor_UserRegistration extends FormProcessor
    {
        // ... other code

        public function process(Zend_Controller_Request_Abstract $request)
        {
            // validate the username
            $this->username = trim($request->getPost('username'));

            if (strlen($this->username) == 0)
                $this->addError('username', 'Please enter a username');
            else if (!DatabaseObject_User::IsValidUsername($this->username))
                $this->addError('username', 'Please enter a valid username');
            else if ($this->user->usernameExists($this->username))
                $this->addError('username', 'The selected username already exists');
            else
                $this->user->username = $this->username;

            // return true if no errors have occurred
            return !$this->hasError();
        }
    }
?>
```

As you can see in this code, we first check that the username isn't an empty string, then we check that it's a valid username, and then we make sure that it doesn't already exist. If we determine the username is valid, we accept the value and update the DatabaseObject_User instance.

Note The IsValidUsername() method will return false if the string is empty, thereby making the first check somewhat redundant. However, checking for an empty string separately allows us to generate a different error message.

Validating the User's Name

As mentioned earlier, we will require users to enter both a first name and last name (in separate fields) when registering. To keep things simple, we won't do any validation on this data other than making sure they're not empty strings. You may want to add further validation to this data yourself. We will also call the sanitize() method to ensure any HTML tags are stripped out.

Listing 4-4 shows a stripped-down version of FormProcessor_UserRegistration, which retrieves, validates, and sets the first and last name of the user.

Listing 4-4. *Validating the User's First and Last Name (UserRegistration.php)*

```php
<?php
    class FormProcessor_UserRegistration extends FormProcessor
    {
        // ... other code

        public function process(Zend_Controller_Request_Abstract $request)
        {
            // validate first and last name

            $this->first_name = $this->sanitize($request->getPost('first_name'));
            if (strlen($this->first_name) == 0)
                $this->addError('first_name', 'Please enter your first name');
            else
                $this->user->profile->first_name = $this->first_name;

            $this->last_name = $this->sanitize($request->getPost('last_name'));
            if (strlen($this->last_name) == 0)
                $this->addError('last_name', 'Please enter your last name');
            else
                $this->user->profile->last_name = $this->last_name;

            // return true if no errors have occurred
            return !$this->hasError();
        }
    }
?>
```

Validating the User's E-mail Address

The final submitted item we must validate is the user's e-mail address. We do this by first checking that an e-mail address was submitted, and then by checking that it is in the correct format for an e-mail address.

To check this second condition, we will use the Zend_Validate_EmailAddress class. This class is a part of the Zend_Validate component and will tell us whether or not an e-mail address is valid.

■**Note** Zend_Validate_EmailAddress can even go one step further than checking for a valid e-mail format: it can also check that the given hostname in the e-mail address has valid DNS MX records. We won't be using this feature, though, as it's the user's problem if they want to fool the system—they simply won't receive their password if they enter a false address.

Listing 4-5 shows the code for FormProcessor_UserRegistration, which validates the e-mail address using Zend_Validate_EmailAddress. Note once again that we first check for an empty string so we can generate a different error message.

Listing 4-5. *Using Zend_Validate_EmailAddress to Check the Validity of a Submitted E-mail Address (UserRegistration.php)*

```php
<?php
    class FormProcessor_UserRegistration extends FormProcessor
    {
        // ... other code

        public function process(Zend_Controller_Request_Abstract $request)
        {
            // validate the e-mail address

            $this->email = $this->sanitize($request->getPost('email'));
            $validator = new Zend_Validate_EmailAddress();

            if (strlen($this->email) == 0)
                $this->addError('email', 'Please enter your e-mail address');
            else if (!$validator->isValid($this->email))
                $this->addError('email', 'Please enter a valid e-mail address');
            else
                $this->user->profile->email = $this->email;

            // return true if no errors have occurred
            return !$this->hasError();
        }
    }
?>
```

The Complete FormProcessor_UserRegistration Class

We have now covered all of the validation tasks required for our `FormProcessor_UserRegistration` class. The final section of code we must insert is a call to `$this->user->save()` to save the record into the `users` table. We will first check whether or not an error has occurred before saving the record. If there is an error, no record will be saved and the user will be shown the error messages (that is, once we have created the registration form template).

Listing 4-6 shows the entire `FormProcessor_UserRegistration` class. In the next section we will write the code responsible for using this class.

Listing 4-6. *The Complete FormProcessor_UserRegistration Class (UserRegistration.php)*

```php
<?php
    class FormProcessor_UserRegistration extends FormProcessor
    {
        protected $db = null;
        public $user = null;

        public function __construct($db)
        {
            parent::__construct();

            $this->db = $db;
            $this->user = new DatabaseObject_User($db);
            $this->user->type = 'member';
        }

        public function process(Zend_Controller_Request_Abstract $request)
        {
            // validate the username
            $this->username = trim($request->getPost('username'));

            if (strlen($this->username) == 0)
                $this->addError('username', 'Please enter a username');
            else if (!DatabaseObject_User::IsValidUsername($this->username))
                $this->addError('username', 'Please enter a valid username');
            else if ($this->user->usernameExists($this->username))
                $this->addError('username', 'The selected username already exists');
            else
                $this->user->username = $this->username;

            // validate the user's name

            $this->first_name = $this->sanitize($request->getPost('first_name'));
            if (strlen($this->first_name) == 0)
                $this->addError('first_name', 'Please enter your first name');
            else
                $this->user->profile->first_name = $this->first_name;
```

```
        $this->last_name = $this->sanitize($request->getPost('last_name'));
        if (strlen($this->last_name) == 0)
            $this->addError('last_name', 'Please enter your last name');
        else
            $this->user->profile->last_name = $this->last_name;

        // validate the e-mail address
        $this->email = $this->sanitize($request->getPost('email'));
        $validator = new Zend_Validate_EmailAddress();

        if (strlen($this->email) == 0)
            $this->addError('email', 'Please enter your e-mail address');
        else if (!$validator->isValid($this->email))
            $this->addError('email', 'Please enter a valid e-mail address');
        else
            $this->user->profile->email = $this->email;

        // if no errors have occurred, save the user
        if (!$this->hasError()) {
            $this->user->save();
        }

        // return true if no errors have occurred
        return !$this->hasError();
    }
}
?>
```

Displaying the Registration Form and Processing Registrations

The next step in creating the registration form is to create the account controller as well as the register action inside of it. In Chapter 3 we set up the access control lists so that only registered members could access the account section. That permission refers specifically to this controller (in other words, if a user tries to access http://phpweb20/account, they can only access the actions in the specified controller if they have the necessary permissions).

The other permissions we defined were exemptions so that unregistered users (guests) would be able to access the register, registercomplete, login, and fetchpassword actions. There's nothing special we need to put in the controller to deal with these permissions—it has already been done in the CustomControllerAclManager class.

The Initial AccountController Class

Listing 4-7 shows the beginnings of the AccountController class, which extends CustomControllerAction. At this stage we will only define the registerAction() method—as we continue with development, we will add more actions to this controller (such as the index action, which will be executed when users successfully authenticate). The AccountController class is stored in the AccountController.php file, which belongs in the ./include/Controllers directory.

Listing 4-7. *Creating the Account Controller and Defining the Register Action (AccountController.php)*

```php
<?php
    class AccountController extends CustomControllerAction
    {
        public function registerAction()
        {
            $fp = new FormProcessor_UserRegistration($this->db);
            $this->view->fp = $fp;
        }
    }
?>
```

■**Note** Since we haven't yet created the `register.tpl` template, loading `http://phpweb20/account/register` in your browser will result in a Smarty error.

In the `registerAction()` method, we first instantiate the `FormProcessor_UserRegistration` class. We then assign it to the displayed template. This template (`register.tpl`) will show the HTML form to the user trying to register.

The reason we assign the form processor to this template is so that any errors can be displayed to the user. The template can then read the errors in the form processor using the `hasError()` and `getError()` methods.

Additionally, when displaying errors in a form, you should prepopulate the fields the user has already entered. The form processor provides access to these values easily via the magic `__get()` method. For instance, to retrieve the username value, you would use `$fp->username` in the template.

Developing the Templates

Before we go any further, let's quickly add some navigation to the `header.tpl` template we created in Chapter 2, so we can navigate to the registration page. Listing 4-8 shows the contents of `./templates/header.tpl` with some basic navigation. We will improve on this later in the book, but for now this will suffice.

Listing 4-8. *Including Basic Navigation on the Header Template (header.tpl)*

```html
<!DOCTYPE html
    PUBLIC "-//W3C//DTD XHTML 1.0 Strict//EN"
    "http://www.w3.org/TR/xhtml1/DTD/xhtml1-strict.dtd">
<html xmlns="http://www.w3.org/1999/xhtml" lang="en" xml:lang="en">
    <head>
        <title>Title</title>
        <meta http-equiv="Content-Type" content="text/html; charset=iso-8859-1" />
    </head>
    <body>
        <div>
```

```
<a href="/">Home</a>
| <a href="/account/register">Register</a>

<hr />
```

We can now start building the `register.tpl` template. There are some fundamental things we need to include in a form template:

- A clearly labeled form so the user knows what the form is for.

- A label for each field in the form.

- The HTML form element with any submitted values prepopulating the field. Additionally, since this contains user-submitted data, we must escape the HTML entities accordingly (as we saw in Chapter 2).

- Any errors that have occurred.

- A clearly labeled submit button.

The easiest way to lay out a form is to use HTML tables; however, these are not necessarily the best thing to use for accessibility and for good CSS practice. Instead, we are going to use the `fieldset`, `legend`, and `label` HTML tags to aid with layout. Additionally, each form element is wrapped in a `div` so it can be positioned properly.

Figure 4-1 shows what this form looks like after the user has submitted it yet omitted some fields. At this stage, the page looks somewhat bland, but we will not concern ourselves with the CSS until Chapter 6 (eventually, errors will be highlighted and the form fields will be spaced so they can be more easily understood).

Figure 4-1. *The registration form displaying some data-entry errors*

Listing 4-9 shows the contents of `register.tpl`, which is stored in the `./templates/account` directory (you will need to create this directory if you have not already done so).

Listing 4-9. *The HTML Template for User Registration (register.tpl)*

```
{include file='header.tpl'}

<form method="post" action="/account/register">

<fieldset>
    <legend>Create an Account</legend>

    <div class="error"{if !$fp->hasError()} style="display: none"{/if}>
        An error has occurred in the form below. Please check
        the highlighted fields and resubmit the form.
    </div>

    <div class="row" id="form_username_container">
        <label for="form_username">Username:</label>
        <input type="text" id="form_username"
                name="username" value="{$fp->username|escape}" />
        {include file='lib/error.tpl' error=$fp->getError('username')}
    </div>

    <div class="row" id="form_email_container">
        <label for="form_email">E-mail Address:</label>
        <input type="text" id="form_email"
                name="email" value="{$fp->email|escape}" />
        {include file='lib/error.tpl' error=$fp->getError('email')}
    </div>

    <div class="row" id="form_first_name_container">
        <label for="form_first_name">First Name:</label>
        <input type="text" id="form_first_name"
                name="first_name" value="{$fp->first_name|escape}" />
        {include file='lib/error.tpl' error=$fp->getError('first_name')}
    </div>

    <div class="row" id="form_last_name_container">
        <label for="form_last_name">Last Name:</label>
        <input type="text" id="form_last_name"
                name="last_name" value="{$fp->last_name|escape}" />
        {include file='lib/error.tpl' error=$fp->getError('last_name')}
    </div>

    <div class="submit">
        <input type="submit" value="Register" />
    </div>
```

```
</fieldset>

</form>

{include file='footer.tpl'}
```

■Note You will still need to create the `error.tpl` template in Listing 4-10 before `register.tpl` can be viewed without any PHP or Smarty errors.

In Listing 4-9, the entire form is wrapped in a `<fieldset>` tag, which is useful for splitting a form into separate parts. This form only contains a small number of fields though, so it only uses one part.

For each element in the form, we essentially use the same markup: a named `<div>` containing a label for the element, as well as the form element. Finally the `error.tpl` template is included, which we use to output any errors for the respective element. We also include a global form error message at the top of the form. This is especially useful for long forms, where an individual error may go unnoticed.

Listing 4-10 shows the contents of `error.tpl`, which we will store in `./templates/lib`. There is no great significance to the name of this directory (`lib`), but as a general habit I like to store reusable templates that don't directly correspond to a specific controller action inside a separate directory.

■Note If you were to create a controller called `lib`, you would need to use a different directory for these helper templates.

Listing 4-10. *A Basic Template Used to Display Form Errors (error.tpl)*

```
{if $error|@is_array || $error|strlen > 0}
    {assign var=hasError value=true}
{else}
    {assign var=hasError value=false}
{/if}
<div class="error"{if !$hasError} style="display:none"{/if}>
    {if $error|@is_array}
        <ul>
            {foreach from=$error item=str}
                <li>{$str|escape}</li>
            {/foreach}
        </ul>
    {else}
        {$error|escape}
    {/if}
</div>
```

The way we determine whether an error has occurred is to check the `$error` variable passed to this template (when called in `register.tpl`). If it is an empty string, there are no errors. Otherwise `FormProcessor::getError()` will return a single error as a nonempty string, and multiple error messages with the same name will be returned as an array.

The other significant thing to notice in this template is that we still generate the HTML `div` even if there is no error. We do this to create a placeholder for error messages we might generate on the client side using JavaScript. Later in this book we will add some client-side validation to this form (such as checking the availability of a username in real time), so we will write error messages to this error container.

Handling the Form Submission

At this stage in the development of the registration form, if you were to click the submit button, nothing would happen other than the empty form being redisplayed. When the page reloads, the register action handler should process the request by either using the `FormProcessor_UserRegistration` class to check the form and save the user data, or to simply display the form.

Note If an error occurs while processing the form (such as the user entering a username already in use), the code is designed to fall through to displaying the form again. On this subsequent rendering of the form, the submitted values will be available to redisplay in the template, along with any generated error messages.

We'll accomplish this by first checking for a post request (using `$request->isPost()`), and then calling `process()` accordingly. Once the form has been successfully processed, the browser is redirected to the `registercomplete` action. This redirection to a new action prevents the user from refreshing the page (and therefore resubmitting their registration data, which would fail at this point since the username now exists).

In order to show the user a custom thank-you message (that is, one that includes some part of their registration details), we need to first write the ID (this is the `user_id` column of the `users` table, which has a data type of `serial`) of the new user to the session before redirecting them to `registercompleteAction()`. Inside the `registercomplete` action, we look for a stored user ID, and if one exists we display a message. If a valid user ID is not found in the session, we simply forward their request back to the register page.

Listing 4-11 shows the account controller with the call to `process()`, as well as the redirection to the `registercomplete` action once a valid registration occurs. We use the `_redirect()` method provided by `Zend_Controller_Front`, as this performs an HTTP redirect (as opposed to `_forward()`, which forwards the request internally). The lines you need to add to your existing version of `registerAction()` are displayed in bold.

Listing 4-11. *Completing the Processing of a User's Registration (AccountController.php)*

```php
<?php
    class AccountController extends CustomControllerAction
    {
        public function registerAction()
        {
```

```
        $request = $this->getRequest();

        $fp = new FormProcessor_UserRegistration($this->db);

        if ($request->isPost()) {
            if ($fp->process($request)) {
                $session = new Zend_Session_Namespace('registration');
                $session->user_id = $fp->user->getId();
                $this->_redirect('/account/registercomplete');
            }
        }

        $this->view->fp = $fp;
    }

    public function registercompleteAction()
    {
        // retrieve the same session namespace used in register
        $session = new Zend_Session_Namespace('registration');

        // load the user record based on the stored user ID
        $user = new DatabaseObject_User($this->db);
        if (!$user->load($session->user_id)) {
            $this->_forward('register');
            return;
        }

        $this->view->user = $user;
    }
}
?>
```

In the registerAction() method, we call $this->getRequest() to retrieve the request object from Zend_Controller_Front, which contains all the data related to the user's request, such as get and post data. This is the object we pass to FormProcessor_UserRegistration when calling process().

Note that since process() will return false if an error occurs, the code will simply fall right through to displaying the register.tpl template again, which means the errors that occurred will be displayed. On the other hand, if the call to process() returns true, we can assume a new user was created in the database. As such, we can write the user's ID to the session and redirect the browser to /account/registercomplete.

■**Note** We could write directly to the $_SESSION superglobal; however, Zend_Session provides a better way of managing session data. It allows fairly straightforward management of session namespaces, meaning the session is organized in a way that won't cause data conflicts. Additionally, we are already using Zend_Session to store user authentication data (that is, their identity).

In the `registercompleteAction()` method, we check for a stored user ID and then try to load a new `DatabaseObject_User` object accordingly. If the record isn't found, we forward the request back to the `registerAction()`. This would happen if a user requested the /account/ registercomplete URL directly without completing the registration.

■**Note** After calling the `_forward()` method in this case, we return from the `registercompleteAction()` method. If we didn't, the remainder of `registercompleteAction()` would be executed, since the new action would only be dispatched after the current one was complete. The first argument to `_forward()` is the action, and the second is the controller. If the second argument is omitted (as in this case), the current controller is used.

Finally, we must create the `registercomplete.tpl` template (which also belongs in the `./templates/account` directory). We will use this template to show a basic "thank you for registering" message. Listing 4-12 shows this template, which makes mention of a password being sent to the user. We will add this e-mail functionality in the "Adding E-mail Functionality" section of this chapter.

Listing 4-12. *The Message Displayed to Users Upon Successful Registration (registercomplete.tpl)*

```
{include file='header.tpl'}

<p>
    Thank you {$user->profile->first_name|escape},
    your registration is now complete.
</p>
<p>
    Your password has been e-mailed to you at {$user->profile->email|escape}.
</p>

{include file='footer.tpl'}
```

Adding CAPTCHA to the User Registration Form

Now that we have the core functionality of the user registration system working, we can improve it slightly by adding a simple yet effective security measure to ensure that registrations come only from real people and not computer programs. This security measure is called CAPTCHA, which stands for Completely Automated Public Turing test to tell Computers and Humans Apart. There are many different types of CAPTCHA tests available, but we will be using what is probably the most common one. This is where a series of characters are shown as an image, and the user is required to identify these characters by typing them in as part of the form they are submitting.

We will be using the `Text_CAPTCHA` component from PEAR (the PHP Extension and Application Repository) to generate our CAPTCHA images. Note that we will be using a CAPTCHA test for several forms in our web application, not just the registration form.

An example of a CAPTCHA image that Text_CAPTCHA generates is shown in Figure 4-2. The random lines and shapes help to fool optical character recognition (OCR) software that may try to automatically decipher the CAPTCHA.

Figure 4-2. *A sample CAPTCHA image generated by PEAR's Text_CAPTCHA*

Circumventing CAPTCHA

Although the point of the CAPTCHA test is to tell computers and humans apart, it is technically possible to write a program that can solve a CAPTCHA automatically. In the case of the text CAPTCHA we will be using, OCR software could be used to determine the characters in the image.

Because of this, we try to distort the images to a point where using OCR software is not possible, but not too far so that humans cannot determine which characters are being displayed. This means avoiding characters such as zero and the letter O completely, which can easily be confused.

CAPTCHA and Accessibility

Another important consideration when implementing a CAPTCHA test in your web applications is accessibility. If somebody is unable to pass the test, they will be unable to complete the form protected by the CAPTCHA test. As such, it is important to have alternative methods available.

One possible solution is to implement an audio CAPTCHA in addition to the text CAPTCHA. This would involve generating an audio file that reads back letters, numbers, or words, which the user must then type in.

Another alternative is to have a manual registration system, where the user can e-mail their details to the site administrator who can then save their details on their behalf. In Chapter 14 we will discuss the implementation of an administration area in our web application. Part of this administration area will be a user management section where an administrator could manually create new users.

PEAR's Text_CAPTCHA

To generate CAPTCHA images, we will be using the Text_CAPTCHA component from PEAR. Text_CAPTCHA will generate the series of characters to appear in the image and then create an image with those characters appearing at a random angles in random locations. It will also add some random noise to prevent OCR software from reading the letters. This noise is a series of lines and shapes that will be placed randomly on the image.

Before you can use Text_CAPTCHA, you must install it. It is available for download from http://pear.php.net/package/Text_CAPTCHA, or you can use the PEAR installer to simplify installation.

Text_CAPTCHA also relies on the Text_Password and Image_Text components, so you must also install them. To install these packages using the PEAR installer, use the following commands:

```
# pear install -f Text_CAPTCHA
# pear install -f Image_Text
```

Because neither of these packages have a stable release at time of writing, I used the –f argument, which forces installation of a non-stable version. The first command should automatically install Text_Password, but if it doesn't, use the following command:

```
# pear install Text_Password
```

Text_CAPTCHA also needs a TrueType font available in order to write letters to the CAPTCHA image. Any font will do for this, as long as its characters are easy to read. The font file I use in this book is the bold version of Vera (VeraBD.ttf), available from the Gnome web site (http://www.gnome.org/fonts/). I chose this font because its license terms allow it to be freely distributed. The font should be stored in the application data directory (/var/www/phpweb20/data/VeraBD.ttf).

Generating a CAPTCHA Image

In order to add CAPTCHA capabilities to our application, we need to create a new controller action that will be responsible for outputting the image. The CAPTCHA is not specific to user registration, so we will call this controller utility, as there may be other utility actions we want to add later.

Listing 4-13 shows the contents of UtilityController.php, which we will store in ./include/Controllers. Presently there is just one action, which is responsible for generating and outputting the image.

Listing 4-13. *Generating a CAPTCHA Image Using Text_CAPTCHA (UtilityController.php)*

```php
<?php
    class UtilityController extends CustomControllerAction
    {
        public function captchaAction()
        {
            $captcha = Text_CAPTCHA::factory('Image');

            $opts = array('font_size' => 20,
                          'font_path' => Zend_Registry::get('config')->paths->data,
                          'font_file' => 'VeraBd.ttf');

            $captcha->init(120, 60, null, $opts);

            // disable auto-rendering since we're outputting an image
            $this->_helper->viewRenderer->setNoRender();

            header('Content-type: image/png');
            echo $captcha->getCAPTCHAAsPng();
        }
    }
?>
```

■**Important** In Listing 4-13, we must disable the autorendering of templates that Zend_Controller_ Front will do. If we don't include the call to setNoRender(), captchaAction() will try to render a template belonging in ./templates/utility/captcha.tpl. Since the captchaAction() method outputs the generated CAPTCHA image, there is no such template.

In order to use Text_CAPTCHA, we first call the factory() method to use the Image driver. We then create an array of options to specify properties of the font that will be used. As mentioned previously, the TrueType font is stored in the application data directory, so we use the application config to tell Text_CAPTCHA about this directory.

Next we call the init() method, which specifies the height, width, and CAPTCHA phrase, as well as the font options. In this code we pass null as the third parameter, which means the phrase will be randomly generated by Text_Password.

■**Tip** You may prefer to store some of the "magic values" in Listing 4-13 (such as font name and size) in the application settings (./settings.ini).

Finally, we send the image to the browser using the getCAPTCHAAsPng() method. We must also send the correct Content-type header to the browser, so it knows to interpret the data as an image.

As it stands, we cannot yet use this code in our registration form because FormProcessor_UserRegistration needs to know the CAPTCHA phrase in order to determine whether or not the user entered it correctly. We must modify captchaAction() so that it generates a new phrase and writes it to the session. On subsequent requests to captchaAction(), we then check for the existence of the phrase in the session. If the value exists, we use that for the image rather than generating a new one.

■**Note** The way we are implementing CAPTCHA images is so that if a user enters the phrase incorrectly, they are shown the same CAPTCHA image again. An alternative is to generate a new phrase every time they get it wrong. The important thing to remember in this implementation is to clear the phrase once it has been successfully entered. We will cover this shortly.

Listing 4-14 shows a modified version of captchaAction(), which now checks for an existing phrase, and then writes the phrase that was used in the image back to the session.

Listing 4-14. *Storing CAPTCHA Phrases in the Session for Reuse (UtilityController.php)*

```php
<?php
    class UtilityController extends CustomControllerAction
    {
        public function captchaAction()
        {
            $session = new Zend_Session_Namespace('captcha');

            // check for existing phrase in session
            $phrase = null;
            if (isset($session->phrase) && strlen($session->phrase) > 0)
                $phrase = $session->phrase;

            // generate CAPTCHA
            $captcha = Text_CAPTCHA::factory('Image');

            $opts = array('font_size' => 20,
                          'font_path' => Zend_Registry::get('config')->paths->data,
                          'font_file' => 'VeraBd.ttf');
```

```
            $captcha->init(120, 60, $phrase, $opts);

            // write the phrase to session
            $session->phrase = $captcha->getPhrase();

            // disable auto-rendering since we're outputting an image
            $this->_helper->viewRenderer->setNoRender();

            header('Content-type: image/png');
            echo $captcha->getCAPTCHAAsPng();
        }
    }
?>
```

You can now view the generated CAPTCHA image directly in your browser by visiting
http://phpweb20/utility/captcha. (This is how I generated Figure 4-2.) Unlike all of the previous controller actions we have implemented so far, which returned HTML code, this action
returns image data (along with the corresponding headers so browsers knows how to display
the data).

Adding the CAPTCHA Image to the Registration Form

The next step in integrating the CAPTCHA test is to display the image on the registration form.
To do this, we simply use an HTML <img> tag to show the image, and we add a text input so the
user can enter the phrase.

Listing 4-15 shows the relevant HTML code we need to add to the register.tpl form created earlier in this chapter (located in ./templates/account). The convention with CAPTCHA
images is to add them at the end of the form, above the submit button.

Listing 4-15. *Displaying the CAPTCHA Image on the Registration Form (register.tpl)*

```
{include file='header.tpl'}

<form method="post" action="/account/register">

<fieldset>
    <legend>Create an Account</legend>

    <!--
        // other form fields
      -->

    <div class="captcha">
        <img src="/utility/captcha" alt="CAPTCHA image" />
    </div>

    <div class="row" id="form_captcha_container">
        <label for="form_captcha">Enter Above Phrase:</label>
```

```
            <input type="text" id="form_captcha"
                name="captcha" value="{$fp->captcha|escape}" />
            {include file='lib/error.tpl' error=$fp->getError('captcha')}
        </div>

        <div class="submit">
            <input type="submit" value="Register" />
        </div>
    </fieldset>

    </form>

{include file='footer.tpl'}
```

One thing to notice in this code is that we still prepopulate the captcha field in this form. This is so the user only has to enter it successfully once. For example, if they enter an invalid e-mail address but a valid CAPTCHA phrase, they shouldn't have to enter the CAPTCHA phrase again after fixing their e-mail address. Figure 4-3 shows the registration form with the CAPTCHA image and the corresponding text input field.

Figure 4-3. *The registration form with a CAPTCHA image and text input field to receive the phrase from the user*

Validating the CAPTCHA Phrase

Finally, we must check that the submitted CAPTCHA phrase matches the one stored in the session data. To do this, we need to add a new check to the process() method in FormProcessor_ UserRegistration. We also need to clear the saved phrase once the form is completed. This is so a new phrase is generated the next time the user tries to do anything that requires CAPTCHA authentication.

Listing 4-16 shows the additions to FormProcessor_UserRegistration that check for a valid phrase and clear out the phrase upon completion.

Listing 4-16. *Validating the Submitted CAPTCHA Phrase (UserRegistration.php)*

```php
<?php
    class FormProcessor_UserRegistration extends FormProcessor
    {

        // ... other code

        public function process(Zend_Controller_Request_Abstract $request)
        {
            // validate CAPTCHA phrase

            $session = new Zend_Session_Namespace('captcha');
            $this->captcha = $this->sanitize($request->getPost('captcha'));

            if ($this->captcha != $session->phrase)
                $this->addError('captcha', 'Please enter the correct phrase');

            // if no errors have occurred, save the user
            if (!$this->hasError()) {
                $this->user->save();
                unset($session->phrase);
            }

            // return true if no errors have occurred
            return !$this->hasError();
        }
    }
?>
```

Adding E-mail Functionality

The final function we must add to the user registration system is one that sends the newly registered user a confirmation of their account, as well as their randomly generated password so they can log in. Sending them their password by e-mail is an easy way to validate their e-mail address.

To send e-mail from our application, we will use the Zend_Mail component of the Zend Framework. We could instead use the PHP mail() function, but by using a class such as this (or even PEAR's Mail_Mime), we can do a whole lot more, such as attaching files (including images) and sending HTML e-mail. We won't be doing either in this book, but if you ever wanted to add such functionality, the key code would already be in place.

Listing 4-17 shows a basic example of using Zend_Mail. This script sends a single e-mail to the address specified with the call to addTo(). You can use this script to ensure that your e-mail server is correctly sending e-mail (remember to update the recipient address to your own).

Listing 4-17. *Example Usage of Zend_Mail to Send an E-mail (listing-4-17.php)*

```php
<?php
    require_once('Zend/Loader.php');
    Zend_Loader::registerAutoload();

    $mail = new Zend_Mail();
    $mail->setBodyText('E-mail body');
    $mail->setFrom('from@example.com');
    $mail->addTo('to@example.com');
    $mail->setSubject('E-mail Subject');
    $mail->send();
?>
```

Before we can make our user registration system send out an e-mail, we must first add functionality to DatabaseObject_User for sending e-mail to users—this will allow us to easily send other e-mail messages to users as well (such as instructions for resetting a forgotten password).

We will use Smarty for e-mail templates, just as we do for outputting the web site HTML. Our e-mail templates will be structured so the first line of the template is the e-mail subject, while the rest of the file constitutes the e-mail body.

Listing 4-18 shows the sendEmail() function, which we will add to the DatabaseObject_User class. It takes the filename of a template as the argument, and feeds it through Smarty before using Zend_Mail to send the resulting e-mail body to the user.

Listing 4-18. *A Helper Function Used to Send E-mail to Users (User.php)*

```php
<?php
    class DatabaseObject_User extends DatabaseObject
    {
        // ... other code

        public function sendEmail($tpl)
        {
            $templater = new Templater();
            $templater->user = $this;

            // fetch the e-mail body
            $body = $templater->render('email/' . $tpl);
```

```
        // extract the subject from the first line
        list($subject, $body) = preg_split('/\r|\n/', $body, 2);

        // now set up and send the e-mail
        $mail = new Zend_Mail();

        // set the to address and the user's full name in the 'to' line
        $mail->addTo($this->profile->email,
                    trim($this->profile->first_name . ' ' .
                        $this->profile->last_name));

        // get the admin 'from' details from the config
        $mail->setFrom(Zend_Registry::get('config')->email->from->email,
                    Zend_Registry::get('config')->email->from->name);

        // set the subject and body and send the mail
        $mail->setSubject(trim($subject));
        $mail->setBodyText(trim($body));
        $mail->send();
    }

    // ... other code
    }
?>
```

In this code, we first instantiate the Templater class and assign to it $this, so we can access all user details (including the profile) from within the e-mail template passed in via the $tpl argument.

Next, we use the render() method to retrieve the template output. In this function, we want the string returned, so we can extract the subject and then send it via e-mail. Additionally, this code forces all e-mail templates to be within the e-mail directory inside the template directory (./templates/email).

The call to preg_split() is what we use to extract the subject. The regular expression used simply finds a newline (\n) or a carriage return (\r) to split on. The third argument (the number 2) splits the string into a maximum of two items.

The other important thing to notice in this code is how we set the from e-mail address and name: we add two new values in the application settings file (settings.ini). Listing 4-19 shows the updated version of settings.ini. The values here are somewhat generic; you can set them to reflect your own needs.

Listing 4-19. *The Updated Application Settings with System Administrator Contact Details (settings.ini)*

```
[development]

database.type       = pdo_mysql
database.hostname   = localhost
```

```
database.username   = phpweb20
database.password   = myPassword
database.database   = phpweb20

paths.base      = /var/www/phpweb20
paths.data      = /var/www/phpweb20/data
paths.templates = /var/www/phpweb20/templates

logging.file = /var/www/phpweb20/data/logs/debug.log

email.from.name  = "System Administrator"
email.from.email = "noreply@localhost"
```

Now we can update the postInsert() method in DatabaseObject_User to send the user a welcome e-mail. As you may recall from Chapter 3, this callback method is executed after a new record has successfully been inserted into the database using DatabaseObject's save() method. Listing 4-20 shows the updated version of postInsert(), which will send an e-mail using user-register.tpl once the user's profile has been saved.

Listing 4-20. *Adding an Automated Call to sendEmail() when a New User is Added (User.php)*

```php
<?php
    class DatabaseObject_User extends DatabaseObject
    {
        // ... other code

        protected function postInsert()
        {
            $this->profile->setUserId($this->getId());
            $this->profile->save(false);

            $this->sendEmail('user-register.tpl');
            return true;
        }

        // ... other code
    }
?>
```

All that remains now is to create the e-mail template and make the new password available from within that template. When we initially created DatabaseObject_User, we used the uniqid() function generate a random password. We will now update this to use the PEAR Text_Password class we installed for our CAPTCHA implementation to generate a better password. Additionally, since passwords are stored in the database using MD5, we must record the password before it is encrypted so we can include it in the e-mail template.

We will do this by storing the generated password as a property in the current DatabaseObject_User object so it is available from the template. We will also need to initialize this property at the top of the class. Listing 4-21 shows the changes to the preInsert() callback of DatabaseObject_User, and the new initialization of the $_newPassword property. This property must be public so the template can access its value.

Listing 4-21. *Creating a Pronounceable Password with Text_Password (User.php)*

```php
<?php
    class DatabaseObject_User extends DatabaseObject
    {
        // ... other code

        public $_newPassword = null;

        // ... other code

        protected function preInsert()
        {
            $this->_newPassword = Text_Password::create(8);
            $this->password = $this->_newPassword;
            return true;
        }

        // ... other code
    }
?>
```

Finally, we can create the user-register.tpl template. As mentioned previously, the first line of this file will be used as the e-mail subject. This is useful, as it allows us to include template logic in the e-mail subject as well as in the body. We will include the user's first name in the e-mail subject.

Listing 4-22 shows the contents of user-register.tpl, which is stored in ./templates/ email. You may want to customize this template to suit your own requirements.

Listing 4-22. *The E-mail Template Used when New Users Register (user-register.tpl)*

```
{$user->profile->first_name}, Thank You For Your Registration
Dear {$user->profile->first_name},

Thank you for your registration. Your login details are as follows:

    Login URL: http://phpweb20/account/login
    Username: {$user->username}
    Password: {$user->_newPassword}

Sincerely,

Web Site Administrator
```

Figure 4-4 shows how the e-mail will look when received by the user. Hopefully the user's e-mail client will make the login URL clickable. You could choose to use an HTML e-mail instead, but if the e-mail client can't automatically highlight links in a text e-mail, it probably can't render HTML e-mails either.

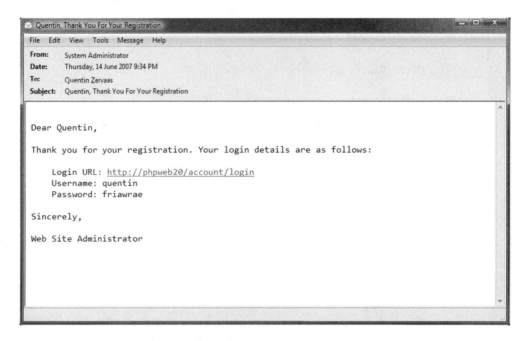

Figure 4-4. *An example of the e-mail sent to a user when they register*

Implementing Account Login and Logout

Now that users have a way of registering on the system, we must allow them to log in to their account. We do that by adding a new action to the account controller, which we will call login. In Chapter 3 we looked at how to authenticate using Zend_Auth (see Listing 3-5). We will now implement this functionality.

The basic algorithm for the login action is as follows:

1. Display the login form.

2. If the user submits the form, try to authenticate them with Zend_Auth.

3. If they successfully authenticate, write their identity to the session and redirect them to their account home page (or to the protected page they originally requested).

4. If their authentication attempt was unsuccessful, display the login form again, indicating that an error occurred.

In addition to this, we also want to make use of our logging capabilities. We will make a log entry for both successful and unsuccessful login attempts.

Creating the Login Template

Before we implement the `login` action in our account controller, we'll quickly take a look at the login form. Listing 4-23 shows the `login.tpl` template, which we will store in `./templates/account`.

Listing 4-23. *The Account Login Form (login.tpl)*

```
{include file='header.tpl'}

<form method="post" action="/account/login">

<fieldset>
    <input type="hidden" name="redirect" value="{$redirect|escape}" />

    <legend>Log In to Your Account</legend>

    <div class="row" id="form_username_container">
        <label for="form_username">Username:</label>
        <input type="text" id="form_username"
                name="username" value="{$username|escape}" />
        {include file='lib/error.tpl' error=$errors.username}
    </div>

    <div class="row" id="form_password_container">
        <label for="form_password">Password:</label>
        <input type="password" id="form_password"
                name="password" value="" />
        {include file='lib/error.tpl' error=$errors.password}
    </div>

    <div class="submit">
        <input type="submit" value="Login" />
    </div>
</fieldset>

</form>

{include file='footer.tpl'}
```

This form is very similar in structure to the registration form, except it only contains input fields for username and password. Additionally, we use the `password` type for the `password` field, instead of the `text` type. This template also relies on the presence of an array called `$errors`, which is generated by the login action.

This form also includes a hidden form variable called `redirect`. The value of this field indicates the relative page URL where the user will end up once they successfully log in. This is necessary because sometimes a user will go directly to a page that requires authentication, but they will not yet be authenticated. If users were automatically redirected to their account home, they would then have to navigate back to the page they originally wanted, which they would find annoying. We will set the value for $redirect in the login action.

Figure 4-5 shows the login form. Again, it is bland, but we will improve on it in Chapter 6.

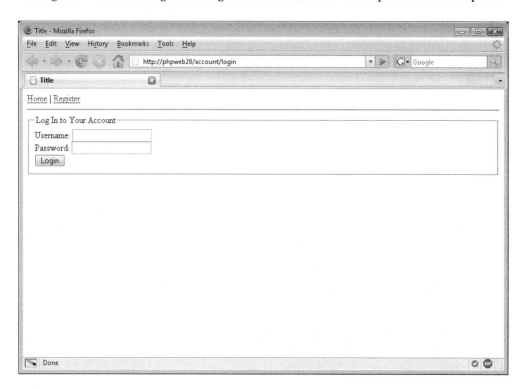

Figure 4-5. *The user login form*

Adding the Account Controller Login Action

Now we need to add the loginAction() method to the account controller. This is the most complex action handler we've created so far, although all it does is perform the four points listed at the start of the "Implementing Account Login and Logout" section.

Listing 4-24 shows the code for loginAction(), which belongs in the AccountController.php file.

Listing 4-24. *Processing User Login Attempts (AccountController.php)*

```php
<?php
    class AccountController extends CustomControllerAction
    {
        // ... other code

        public function loginAction()
        {
            // if a user's already logged in, send them to their account home page
            $auth = Zend_Auth::getInstance();
```

```
if ($auth->hasIdentity())
    $this->_redirect('/account');

$request = $this->getRequest();

// determine the page the user was originally trying to request
$redirect = $request->getPost('redirect');
if (strlen($redirect) == 0)
    $redirect = $request->getServer('REQUEST_URI');
if (strlen($redirect) == 0)
    $redirect = '/account';

// initialize errors
$errors = array();

// process login if request method is post
if ($request->isPost()) {

    // fetch login details from form and validate them
    $username = $request->getPost('username');
    $password = $request->getPost('password');

    if (strlen($username) == 0)
        $errors['username'] = 'Required field must not be blank';
    if (strlen($password) == 0)
        $errors['password'] = 'Required field must not be blank';

    if (count($errors) == 0) {

        // setup the authentication adapter
        $adapter = new Zend_Auth_Adapter_DbTable($this->db,
                                                 'users',
                                                 'username',
                                                 'password',
                                                 'md5(?)');

        $adapter->setIdentity($username);
        $adapter->setCredential($password);

        // try and authenticate the user
        $result = $auth->authenticate($adapter);

        if ($result->isValid()) {

            $user = new DatabaseObject_User($this->db);
            $user->load($adapter->getResultRowObject()->user_id);
```

```
                    // record login attempt
                    $user->loginSuccess();

                    // create identity data and write it to session
                    $identity = $user->createAuthIdentity();
                    $auth->getStorage()->write($identity);

                    // send user to page they originally request
                    $this->_redirect($redirect);
                }

                // record failed login attempt
                DatabaseObject_User::LoginFailure($username,
                                                  $result->getCode());
                $errors['username'] = 'Your login details were invalid';
            }
        }

        $this->view->errors = $errors;
        $this->view->redirect = $redirect;
    }
}
?>
```

The first thing this function does is check whether or not the user has already been authenticated. If they have, they are redirected back to their account home page.

Next we try to determine the page they were originally trying to access. If they have submitted the login form, this value will be in the redirect form value. If not, we simply use the $_SERVER['REQUEST_URI'] value to determine where they came from. If we still can't determine where they came from, we just use their account home page as the default destination. We haven't yet created the action to display their account home page; we will do that in the "Implementing Account Management" section later in this chapter.

■Note Because the ACL manager forwarded the request to the login handler (as opposed to using an HTTP redirect), the server variable REQUEST_URI will contain the location originally requested. If a redirect was used to display the login form, you could use the HTTP_REFERER value instead.

We then define an empty array to hold error messages. This is done here so it can be assigned to the template whether a login attempt has occurred or not.

Next we check whether or not the login form has been submitted by checking the $request object's isPost() method (we also did this earlier when processing user registrations). If it has been submitted, we retrieve the submitted username and password values from the request data. If either of these is empty, we set corresponding error messages and proceed to display the login template again.

Once we have determined that both a username and password have been submitted, we try to authenticate the user. This code is very similar to that of Listing 3-4.

If we determine that the login attempt was successful, we perform three actions:

1. **Record the successful login attempt.** When a user successfully logs in, we want to make a note of this in the application log file. To do so, we will add a utility function to DatabaseObject_User called loginSuccess(). This function will also update the ts_last_login field in the user table to record the timestamp of the user's most recent login. We will look at the loginSuccess() function shortly. This function must be called after a user record has been loaded in DatabaseObject_User.

2. **Update the identity data stored in session to include all of the values in the corresponding database row for this user.** By default, only the supplied username will be stored as the identity; however, since we want to display other user details (such as their name or e-mail address) we need to update the stored identity to include those other details:

    - We can retrieve the data we want to save as the identity by using the createAuthIdentity() method in DatabaseObject_User. This function returns a generic PHP object holding the user's details.

    - The storage object returned from Zend_Auth's getStorage() method has a method called write(), which we can use to overwrite the existing identity with the data returned from createAuthIdentity().

3. **Redirect the user to their previously requested page.** This is achieved simply by calling the _redirect() method with the $redirect variable as its only argument.

Alternatively, if the login attempt failed, the code will continue on. At this point, we call the LoginFailure() method from the DatabaseObject_User class to write this failed attempt to the log file. We will look at this method shortly.

We then write a message to the $errors array and continue on to display the template. As mentioned in Chapter 3, we can determine the exact reason why the login attempt failed, and we will record this reason in the log file. However, this isn't information that should be provided to the user.

■**Note** Until you add the functions in the next section, a PHP error will occur if you try to log in.

Logging Successful and Failed Login Attempts

To log both successful and unsuccessful login attempts, we will implement two utility functions in DatabaseObject_User: loginSuccess() and LoginFailure().

Listing 4-25 shows these functions as they appear within the DatabaseObject_User class (User.php). Note that LoginFailure() is a static method, while loginSuccess() must be called after a user record has been loaded. I've also included the createAuthIdentity() method as described in the previous section.

Listing 4-25. *Auditing Login Attempts by Writing Them to the Application Log (User.php)*

```php
<?php
    class DatabaseObject_User extends DatabaseObject
    {
        // ... other code

        public function createAuthIdentity()
        {
            $identity = new stdClass;
            $identity->user_id    = $this->getId();
            $identity->username   = $this->username;
            $identity->user_type  = $this->user_type;
            $identity->first_name = $this->profile->first_name;
            $identity->last_name  = $this->profile->last_name;
            $identity->email      = $this->profile->email;

            return $identity;
        }

        public function loginSuccess()
        {
            $this->ts_last_login = time();
            $this->save();

            $message = sprintf('Successful login attempt from %s user %s',
                               $_SERVER['REMOTE_ADDR'],
                               $this->username);

            $logger = Zend_Registry::get('logger');
            $logger->notice($message);
        }

        static public function LoginFailure($username, $code = '')
        {
            switch ($code) {
                case Zend_Auth_Result::FAILURE_IDENTITY_NOT_FOUND:
                    $reason = 'Unknown username';
                    break;
                case Zend_Auth_Result::FAILURE_IDENTITY_AMBIGUOUS:
                    $reason = 'Multiple users found with this username';
                    break;
                case Zend_Auth_Result::FAILURE_CREDENTIAL_INVALID:
                    $reason = 'Invalid password';
                    break;
                default:
                    $reason = '';
            }
```

```
            $message = sprintf('Failed login attempt from %s user %s',
                                $_SERVER['REMOTE_ADDR'],
                                $username);

        if (strlen($reason) > 0)
            $message .= sprintf(' (%s)', $reason);

        $logger = Zend_Registry::get('logger');
        $logger->warn($message);
    }

    // ... other code
    }
?>
```

The first thing we do in LoginSuccess() is update the users table to set the ts_last_login field to the current date and time for the user that has just logged in. It is for this reason (updating the database) that we pass in the database connection as the first argument.

We then fetch the $logger object from the application registry so we can write a message indicating that the given user just logged in. We also include the IP address of the user.

LoginFailure() is essentially the same as loginSuccess(), except we do not make any database updates. Also, the function accepts the error code generated during the login attempt (retrieved with the getCode() method on the authentication result object in Listing 4-24), which we use to generate extra information to write to the log. We log this message as a warning, since it's of greater importance than a successful login.

Please be aware that if you try to log in now you will be redirected to the account home page (http://phpweb20/account) which we will be creating shortly.

Tip The reason you want to track failed logins separately from successful logins (using different priority levels) is that a successful login typically indicates "normal operation," while a failed login may indicate that somebody is trying to gain unauthorized access to an account. Being able to filter the log easily by the message type helps you easily identify potential problems that have occurred or are occurring. In Chapter 14 we will look at how to make use of this log file.

Logging Users Out of Their Accounts

It is important to give users the option of logging out of their accounts, as they may want to ensure that nobody can use their account (maliciously or otherwise) after they are finished with their session.

It is very straightforward to log a user out when using Zend_Auth. Because the presence of an identity in the session is what determines whether or not a user is logged in, all we need to do is clear that identity to log them out.

To do this, we simply use the clearIdentity() method of the instance of Zend_Auth. We can then redirect the user somewhere else, so they can continue to use the site if they please. I simply chose to redirect them back to the login page.

Listing 4-26 shows the logoutAction() method which is used to clear user identity data. Users can log out by visiting http://phpweb20/account/logout.

Listing 4-26. *Logging Out a User and Redirecting Them Back to the Login Page (AccountController.php)*

```php
<?php
    class AccountController extends CustomControllerAction
    {
        // ... other code

        public function logoutAction()
        {
            Zend_Auth::getInstance()->clearIdentity();
            $this->_redirect('/account/login');
        }
    }
?>
```

■**Note** You could use _forward('login') in Listing 4-26 instead of _redirect('/account/login') if you wanted to. However, if you forwarded the request to the login page, the $redirect variable in loginAction() would be set to load the logout page (/account/logout) as soon as a user logged in—they would never be able to log in to their account unless they manually typed in a different URL first!

Dealing with Forgotten Passwords

Now that we have added login functionality, we must also allow users who have forgotten their passwords to access their accounts. Because we store the user password as an MD5 hash of the actual password, we cannot send them the old password. Instead, when they complete the fetch-password form, we will generate a new password and send that to them.

We can't automatically assume that the person who filled out the fetch-password form is the account holder, so we won't update the actual account password until their identity has been verified. We do this by providing a link in the sent e-mail that will confirm the password change. This has the added advantage of allowing them to remember their old password after filling out the form and before clicking the confirmation link.

The basic algorithm for implementing fetch-password functionality is as follows:

1. Display a form to the user asking for their username.

2. If the supplied username is found, generate a new password and write it to their profile, and then send an e-mail to the address associated with the account informing them of their new password.

3. If the supplied username is not found, display an error message to the user.

So that we don't have to mess around with application permissions, we will handle three different actions in the new fetch-password controller action:

1. Display and process the user form.

2. Display the confirmation message.

3. Update the user account when the password-update confirmation link is clicked and indicate to the user that this has occurred.

Resetting a User's Password

Before we implement the required application logic for fetch password, let's create the web page template we will use. Listing 4-27 shows the contents of fetchpassword.tpl, which we will store in the account template directory. This template handles each of the three cases outlined previously.

Listing 4-27. *The Template Used for the Fetch-Password Tool (fetchpassword.tpl)*

```
{include file='header.tpl'}

{if $action == 'confirm'}
    {if $errors|@count == 0}
        <p>
            Your new password has now been activated.
        </p>
        <ul>
            <li><a href="/account/login">Log in to your account</a></li>
        </ul>
    {else}
        <p>
            Your new password was not confirmed. Please double-check the link
            sent to you by e-mail, or try using the
            <a href="/account/fetchpassword">Fetch Password</a> tool again.
        </p>
    {/if}
{elseif $action == 'complete'}
    <p>
        A password has been sent to your account e-mail address containing
        your new password. You must click the link in this e-mail to activate
        the new password.
    </p>
{else}
    <form method="post" action="/account/fetchpassword">

        <fieldset>
            <legend>Fetch Your Password</legend>

            <div class="row" id="form_username_container">
```

```
        <label for="form_username">Username:</label>
        <input type="text" id="form_username" name="username" />
        {include file='lib/error.tpl' error=$errors.username}
    </div>

    <div class="submit">
        <input type="submit" value="Fetch Password" />
    </div>

</fieldset>

</form>
{/if}

{include file='footer.tpl'}
```

This template is divided into three parts. The first is used when a user tries to confirm their new password. Within this section is a section for successful confirmation, and another to display a message if the confirmation URL is invalid.

The next section (for the complete action) is used after the user submits the fetch-password form with a valid username. The final section is the default part of the template, which is shown when the user initially visits the fetch-password tool, or if they enter an invalid username.

Now let's take a look at the new controller action. I called this action handler fetchpasswordAction(), as you can see in Listing 4-28. This code is to be added to the AccountController.php file in ./include/Controllers.

Listing 4-28. *Handling the Fetch-Password Request (AccountController.php)*

```php
<?php
    class AccountController extends CustomControllerAction
    {
        // ... other code

        public function fetchpasswordAction()
        {
            // if a user's already logged in, send them to their account home page
            if (Zend_Auth::getInstance()->hasIdentity())
                $this->_redirect('/account');

            $errors = array();

            $action = $this->getRequest()->getQuery('action');

            if ($this->getRequest()->isPost())
                $action = 'submit';

            switch ($action) {
```

```
            case 'submit':
                $username = trim($this->getRequest()->getPost('username'));
                if (strlen($username) == 0) {
                    $errors['username'] = 'Required field must not be blank';
                }
                else {
                    $user = new DatabaseObject_User($this->db);
                    if ($user->load($username, 'username')) {
                        $user->fetchPassword();

                        $url = '/account/fetchpassword?action=complete';
                        $this->_redirect($url);
                    }
                    else
                        $errors['username'] = 'Specified user not found';
                }
                break;

            case 'complete':
                // nothing to do
                break;

            case 'confirm':
                $id = $this->getRequest()->getQuery('id');
                $key = $this->getRequest()->getQuery('key');

                $user = new DatabaseObject_User($this->db);
                if (!$user->load($id))
                    $errors['confirm'] = 'Error confirming new password';
                else if (!$user->confirmNewPassword($key))
                    $errors['confirm'] = 'Error confirming new password';

                break;
        }

        $this->view->errors = $errors;
        $this->view->action = $action;
    }
}
?>
```

In this code, we first redirect the user back to the account home page if they are authenticated. Next we try to determine the action the user is trying to perform. When a user initially visits the fetch-password page (http://phpweb20/account/fetchpassword), no action will be set. As such, the entire switch statement will be skipped.

If the request method for the current request is POST, we assume the user submitted the fetch-password form, so we update the $action variable accordingly. If the form has been filled out correctly and a valid username has been specified, the DatabaseObject_User::

fetchPassword() method is called. This is a utility function we will define shortly (along with confirmNewPassword()). Once this has been called, we redirect back to the fetch-password page, indicating that the action has completed by putting action=complete in the URL. As you can see in the switch statement, there is nothing to actually do for this action; it is just included there for completeness.

The other action is the confirm action. This code is executed when the user clicks on the link we send them in the fetch-password e-mail (which we will look at shortly). We then try to confirm their new password using the submitted key value.

Functions for Resetting Passwords

There are two functions we need to add to DatabaseObject_User to implement the password resetting. The first is called fetchPassword(), which does the following:

1. Generates a new password using Text_Password.

2. Writes the new password to the user profile.

3. Writes the current date and time to the user profile, so we can ensure the new password can only be confirmed within one day.

4. Generates a key that must be supplied by the user to confirm their new password. We also write this to the user profile.

5. Saves the profile.

6. Sends an e-mail to the user using the fetch-password.tpl e-mail template (separate from the fetchpassword.tpl page template created previously).

The second function we will add is called confirmNewPassword(), which confirms the user's new password after they click the link in the e-mail sent to them. This function works as follows:

1. Checks that the new password, timestamp, and confirmation key exist in the profile.

2. Checks that the confirmation is taking place within a day of the stored timestamp.

3. Checks that the supplied key matches the key stored in the user profile.

4. Updates the user record to use the new password.

5. Removes the values from the profile.

6. Saves the user (which will also save the profile).

Listing 4-29 shows these two new functions, which belong in the DatabaseObject_User class (User.php).

Listing 4-29. *Utility Functions Used for Resetting a User's Password (User.php)*

```php
<?php
    class DatabaseObject_User extends DatabaseObject
    {
        // ... other code
```

```
public function fetchPassword()
{
    if (!$this->isSaved())
        return false;

    // generate new password properties
    $this->_newPassword = Text_Password::create(8);
    $this->profile->new_password     = md5($this->_newPassword);
    $this->profile->new_password_ts  = time();
    $this->profile->new_password_key = md5(uniqid() .
                                         $this->getId() .
                                         $this->_newPassword);

    // save new password to profile and send e-mail
    $this->profile->save();
    $this->sendEmail('user-fetch-password.tpl');

    return true;
}

public function confirmNewPassword($key)
{
    // check that valid password reset data is set
    if (!isset($this->profile->new_password)
        || !isset($this->profile->new_password_ts)
        || !isset($this->profile->new_password_key)) {

        return false;
    }

    // check if the password is being confirm within a day
    if (time() - $this->profile->new_password_ts > 86400)
        return false;

    // check that the key is correct
    if ($this->profile->new_password_key != $key)
        return false;

    // everything is valid, now update the account to use the new password

    // bypass the local setter as new_password is already an md5
    parent::__set('password', $this->profile->new_password);

    unset($this->profile->new_password);
    unset($this->profile->new_password_ts);
    unset($this->profile->new_password_key);

    // finally, save the updated user record and the updated profile
```

```
            return $this->save();
        }

        // ... other code
    }
?>
```

Now we just need to create the e-mail template. In this e-mail, we will generate the URL that the user needs to click on in order to reset their password. If you refer back to the fetchpasswordAction() function in AccountController.php (Listing 4-28), you will see that the arguments required are the action parameter (set to confirm), the id parameter (which corresponds to the user_id column in the users table), and the key parameter (which is the new_password_key value we generated in DatabaseObject::fetchPassword()).

Listing 4-30 shows the e-mail template, which we will store in user-fetch-password.tpl in the ./templates/email directory. Remember that the first line is the e-mail subject.

Listing 4-30. *The E-mail Template Used to Send a User Their New Password (user-fetch-password.tpl)*

```
{$user->profile->first_name}, Your Account Password
Dear {$user->profile->first_name},

You recently requested a password reset as you had forgotten your password.

Your new password is listed below. To activate this password, click this link:

    Activate Password: http://phpweb20/account/fetchpassword? ➥
action=confirm&id={$user->getId()}&key={$user->profile->new_password_key}
    Username: {$user->username}
    New Password: {$user->_newPassword}

If you didn't request a password reset, please ignore this message and your password
will remain unchanged.

Sincerely,

Web Site Administrator
```

Figure 4-6 shows a sample of the e-mail that is sent when a new password is requested. Take special note of the URL that is generated, and the different parts in the URL that we use in fetchpasswordAction().

■**Note** One small potential problem is the length of the URL in the e-mail. Some e-mail clients may wrap this URL across two lines, resulting in it not being highlighted properly (or if the user manually copies and pastes the URL, they may miss part of it). You may prefer to generate a shorter key or action name to reduce its length.

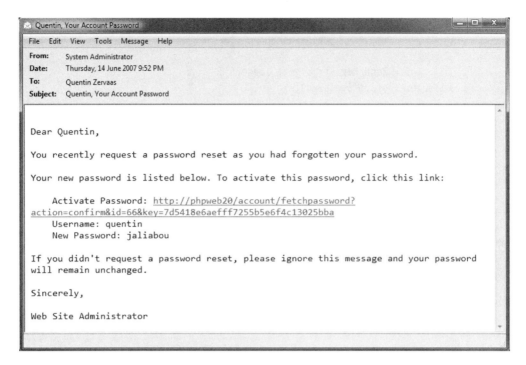

Figure 4-6. *The fetch password e-mail sent to a user*

There's one more small issue we must now address: if a user requests a new password, and then logs in with their old password without using the new password, we want to remove the new password details from their profile. To do this, we update the loginSuccess() method in DatabaseObject_User to clear this data. Listing 4-31 shows the updated version of this method as it appears in the User.php file. We place the three calls to unset() before calling the save() method, so the user record only needs saving once.

Listing 4-31. *Clearing the Password Reset Fields if They Are Set (User.php)*

```php
<?php
    class DatabaseObject_User extends DatabaseObject
    {
        // ... other code

        public function loginSuccess()
        {
            $this->ts_last_login = time();
            unset($this->profile->new_password);
            unset($this->profile->new_password_ts);
            unset($this->profile->new_password_key);
            $this->save();

            $message = sprintf('Successful login attempt from %s user %s',
```

```
                              $_SERVER['REMOTE_ADDR'],
                              $this->username);

            $logger = Zend_Registry::get('logger');
            $logger->notice($message);
        }

        // ... other code
    }
?>
```

Finally, as shown in Listing 4-32, we must add a link to the original login form (login.tpl in ./templates/account) so the user can access the fetch-password tool if required.

Listing 4-32. *Linking to the Fetch-Password Tool from the Account Login Page (login.tpl)*

```html
<!-- // ... other code -->

<fieldset>
    <legend>Log In to Your Account</legend>

    <!-- // ... other code -->

    <div>
        <a href="/account/fetchpassword">Forgotten your password?</a>
    </div>
</fieldset>

<!-- // ... other code -->
```

Implementing Account Management

Earlier in this chapter we implemented the login and logout system for user accounts. When a user successfully logged in, the code would redirect them to the page they initially requested. In many cases, this will be their account home page (which has the URL http://phpweb20/account). So far, however, we haven't actually implemented this action in the AccountController class.

In this section, we will first create this action (indexAction()), although there isn't terribly much that this will do right now. Next, we will update the site header template so it has more useful navigation (even if it is still unstyled). This will include additional menu options for logged-in users only. Finally, we will allow users to update their account details.

Creating the Account Home Page

After a user logs in, they are allowed to access their account home page by using the index action in the account controller. Listing 4-33 shows the code for indexAction() in AccountController.php, which at this stage doesn't do anything of great interest, other than display the index.tpl template in ./templates/account.

Listing 4-33. *The Account Home Page Action Controller (AccountController.php)*

```php
<?php
    class AccountController extends CustomControllerAction
    {
        public function indexAction()
        {
            // nothing to do here, index.tpl will be displayed
        }

        // ... other code
    }
?>
```

Before we look at index.tpl, we will make a small but important change to the
CustomControllerAction.php file. We are going to change it so the logged-in user's identity
data is automatically assigned to the template, thereby making it available within all site templates. This is the data we generated in the createAuthIdentity() method in Listing 4-25.

Additionally, we will assign a variable called $authenticated, which is true if identity data
exists. We could use {if isset($identity)} in our templates instead of this variable, but we
would then be making an assumption that the presence of the $identity means the user is
logged in (and vice versa).

To make this change, we need to implement the preDispatch() method, as shown in
Listing 4-34. This method is automatically called by Zend_Controller_Front at the start of dispatching any action. We can make this change to CustomControllerAction, since all controllers
in our application extend from this class.

Listing 4-34. *Assigning Identity Data Automatically to Templates (CustomControllerAction.php)*

```php
<?php
    class CustomControllerAction extends Zend_Controller_Action
    {
        function init()
        {
            $this->db = Zend_Registry::get('db');
        }

        public function preDispatch()
        {
            $auth = Zend_Auth::getInstance();
            if ($auth->hasIdentity()) {
                $this->view->authenticated = true;
                $this->view->identity = $auth->getIdentity();
            }
            else
                $this->view->authenticated = false;
        }
    }
?>
```

Now let's look at the index.tpl file, which currently displays a simple welcome message. We can use the first_name property from the identity to personalize the message. Listing 4-35 shows this template, which is stored in ./templates/account.

Listing 4-35. *Displaying a Welcome Message After a User Logs In to Their Account Home Page (index.tpl)*

```
{include file='header.tpl'}

Welcome {$identity->first_name}.

{include file='footer.tpl'}
```

At this point, you can try to log in by visiting http://phpweb20/account and entering your account details (remember that thanks to the permissions, trying to access this URL will display the page at http://phpweb20/account/login).

Updating the Web Site Navigation

When we last looked at the navigation in header.tpl, all we had was a home link and a register link. We are now going to improve this navigation to include a few new items:

- Log in to account link

- Information about the currently logged in user (if any)

- A member's-only submenu, including a logout link

To implement the second and third points, we need to check the $authenticated variable we are now assigning to the template. Additionally, once a user has logged in, the login and register links are no longer relevant, so we can hide them.

Listing 4-36 shows the updated version of header.tpl, which now includes some basic template logic for the HTML header. For now we are just using vertical pipes to separate menu items, but we will use CSS to improve this in Chapter 6.

Listing 4-36. *Making the Site Navigation Member-Aware (header.tpl)*

```
<!DOCTYPE html
    PUBLIC "-//W3C//DTD XHTML 1.0 Strict//EN"
    "http://www.w3.org/TR/xhtml1/DTD/xhtml1-strict.dtd">
<html xmlns="http://www.w3.org/1999/xhtml" lang="en" xml:lang="en">
    <head>
        <title>Title</title>
        <meta http-equiv="Content-Type" content="text/html; charset=iso-8859-1" />
    </head>
    <body>
        <div>
            <a href="/">Home</a>
```

```
{if $authenticated}
    | <a href="/account">Your Account</a>
    | <a href="/account/details">Update Your Details</a>
    | <a href="/account/logout">Logout</a>
{else}
    | <a href="/account/register">Register</a>
    | <a href="/account">Log In</a>
{/if}

{if $authenticated}
    <hr />
    <div>
        Logged in as
        {$identity->first_name|escape} {$identity->last_name|escape}
        (<a href="/account/logout">logout</a>)
    </div>
{/if}

<hr />
```

Figure 4-7 shows the account home page that users are directed to after logging in. Note the new navigation elements, as well as the information about the currently logged-in user.

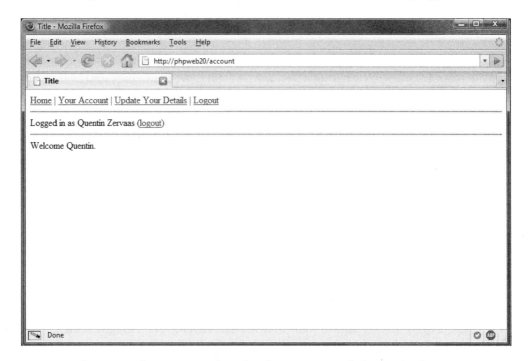

Figure 4-7. *The account home page with updated navigation and identity display*

Allowing Users to Update Their Details

The final thing we need to add to the user account section for now is the ability for users to update their details. In the new header.tpl shown in Figure 4-7, there is a link labeled Update Your Details, which will allow users to do this.

Because this code is largely similar to the user registration system, I have not included all of the repetitive details. The key differences between user registration and updating details are as follows:

- We are updating an existing user record rather than creating a new one.

- We do not allow the user to update their username.

- We allow the user to set a new password.

- We do not need the CAPTCHA test.

- Because the user is already logged in, we must update their Zend_Auth identity accordingly.

■**Note** While there isn't anything inherently bad about allowing users to change their own usernames, it is my own preference to generally not allow users to do so (an exception might be if their e-mail address is used as their login username). One reason why it is bad to allow the changing of usernames is that other users get to know a user by their username; in the case of this application, we will be using the username to generate a unique user home page URL. Changing their username would result in a new URL for their home page.

When allowing users to change their password, we will show them a password field and a password confirmation field, requiring them to enter the new password twice in order to change it. Additionally, we will include a note telling them to leave the password field blank if they do not want to change their password. This is because we cannot prepopulate the password field with their existing password, since we only store an MD5 hash of it.

To implement the update details function, we must do the following:

- **Create a new form processor class called FormProcessor_UserDetails, which is similar to FormProcessor_UserRegistration.** This class will read the submitted form values and process them to ensure they are valid. If no errors occur when validating the data, the existing user record is updated.

- **Create a new action called detailsAction() in AccountController that instantiates FormProcessor_UserDetails, and passes to it the ID of the logged-in user.** This function also updates the Zend_Auth identity by calling the createAuthIdentity() function in DatabaseObject_User that we created earlier.

- **Create a confirmation page to confirm to the user that their details have been updated.** To do this, we will create a new action handler called detailscompleteAction(), which simply tells the user that their details have been saved.

Figure 4-8 shows what the form looks like when initially displayed to users. Note the pre-populated fields, as well as the lack of a username field and the addition of a password field.

You may want to display the username as a read-only field, but that is a personal preference. If the user tries to remove a value and then submit the form, a corresponding error message will be shown, just as in the registration form.

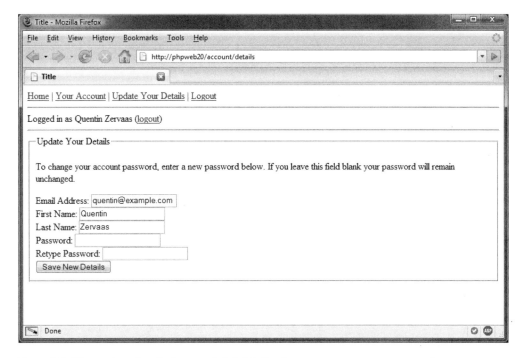

Figure 4-8. *The update details form as it is initially shown to users*

All the code for this section is included with the downloadable application source code.

Summary

In this chapter we implemented a user registration system, which allows users to create a new account by filling out a web form. This form requires users to enter a CAPTCHA phrase to prove that they are people (and not computer programs). Once the user's registration is complete, their details are saved to the database using DatabaseObject_User and Profile_User, and the users are then sent an e-mail containing their account details.

We then added code to the application to allow users to log in to their accounts. We saved their identity to the current session using Zend_Auth so it would be accessible on all pages they visit.

Additionally, we added logging capabilities to the login system, so both successful and unsuccessful login attempts would be recorded.

Finally, we created a basic account home page, to which users will be redirected after logging in. We also added code to let them update their account details.

In the next chapter we will move slightly away from the development of the web application while we take a look at two JavaScript libraries: Prototype and Scriptaculous. We will be using these libraries to help give our application a funky interface and make it "Web 2.0."

CHAPTER 5

■■■

Introduction to Prototype and Scriptaculous

In this chapter we will be looking at two JavaScript libraries that are designed to help with Web 2.0 and Ajax application development.

First, we will look at Prototype, a JavaScript framework developed by Sam Stephenson. Prototype simplifies JavaScript development by providing the means to easily write for different platforms (browsers). For example, implementing an Ajax subrequest using XMLHttpRequest can be achieved with the same code in Internet Explorer, Firefox, and Safari.

Next, we will look at Scriptaculous, a JavaScript library used to add special effects and improve a web site's user interface. Scriptaculous is built upon Prototype, so knowing how to use Scriptaculous requires knowledge of how Prototype works. Scriptaculous was created by Thomas Fuchs.

We will cover the basic functions of Prototype and look at how it can be used in your web applications. Then we will look at some of the effects that can be achieved with Scriptaculous. Finally, we will look at an example that makes use of Prototype, Scriptaculous, Ajax, and PHP.

The code covered in this chapter will not form part of our final web application, but in forthcoming chapters we will use the techniques from this chapter to add various effects and to help with coding clean and maintainable JavaScript.

Downloading and Installing Prototype

The Prototype JavaScript framework can be downloaded from http://prototypejs.org.

At time of writing, the latest release version of Prototype is 1.5.1.1, and it is a single JavaScript file that you include in your HTML files. For example, if you store your JavaScript code in the /js directory on your web site, you would use the following HTML code to include Prototype:

```
<html>
    <head>
        <title>Loading the Prototype library</title>
        <script type="text/javascript" src="/js/prototype.js"></script>
    </head>
    <body>

    </body>
</html>
```

■**Note** At time of writing, Prototype 1.5.1.1 is the latest stable release; however, version 1.6 is close to being released. This new version will introduce several key features and improvements in the event handling model of Prototype (as well as many other enhancements).

Prototype Documentation

You can find comprehensive documentation for all the functionality provided by Prototype at `http://prototypejs.org/api`. I highly recommend you look through this site, as it will provide details about Prototype beyond what I can cover in this chapter.

Additionally, you may find value in perusing the Prototype source code. Doing so may give you a feel not only for how certain functions work but also to see a good example of how to use various aspects of Prototype.

Selecting Objects in the Document Object Model

There are several functions available in Prototype for selecting elements in the Document Object Model (DOM). I recommend that you use the Prototype functions wherever possible instead of methods you may be more used to using (such as `document.getElementById()`), since they are simpler, they work across different browsers, and they provide you with extra functionality (as you will shortly see).

The $() Function

The $() function is used to select an element from the Document Object Model (DOM)—in other words, it selects an element on your HTML page. This function is extremely useful and may be one of the most commonly used functions in your JavaScript development.

Essentially, $() is a replacement for using `document.getElementById()`, except that it will also do the following:

- Return an array of elements if you pass in multiple arguments (each returned element corresponds to the argument position; that is, the 0 element corresponds to the first argument).

- Extend the returned element(s) with extra Prototype functionality (which we will cover in this chapter).

Because of this second point, you should always use $() (or one of the other Prototype element selectors we will look at shortly) to select elements in your JavaScript code when you are using Prototype. This will give you the full range of functionality that Prototype provides.

Listing 5-1 shows several examples of selecting elements with the $() function. Note that you can pass in an element's ID or you can pass in the element directly (which effectively will just add the extra Prototype functionality to the element).

Listing 5-1. *Example Usage of the $() Element Selector (listing-5-1.html)*

```html
<html>
    <head>
        <title>Listing 5-1: Example usage of the $() function</title>
        <script type="text/javascript" src="/js/prototype.js"></script>
    </head>
    <body>
        <div id="my-example-div">
            <form method="post" action="nowhere.html" name="f">
                <input type="text" name="title" value="Example" id="form-title" />
            </form>
        </div>

        <script type="text/javascript">
            // select the div and change its color to red
            var exampleDiv = $('my-example-div');
            exampleDiv.style.backgroundColor = '#f00';

            // select the text input and show its value
            var exampleInput = $('form-title');
            alert(exampleInput.value);

            // now select it again using its DOM path and show its value
            var exampleInput = $(document.f.elements.title);
            alert(exampleInput.value);
        </script>
    </body>
</html>
```

The getElementsByClassName() Function

If you have multiple elements on a page, all with the same class, you can use the
getElementsByClassName() function to select all of them. An array will be returned, with
each element corresponding to one element with the given class name.

This can be an expensive function to call, as internally every element is analyzed to see if
it is of the specified class. Because of this, you should also specify a parent element when calling this function. Doing so means only elements within the parent element are checked.

You would typically use this function when you want a make the same update to all elements of a particular class. For example, suppose you had an HTML page with several boxes
on it, each having the class name .box, contained within a div called #box-container. If you
wanted to add a Hide All or Show All button on your HTML page, you could select all elements using document.getElementsByClassName('box', 'box-container'), and then loop over
each element and hide or show it accordingly. Listing 5-2 demonstrates this.

Listing 5-2. *Sample Usage of getElementsByClassName (listing-5-2.html)*

```html
<html>
  <head>
    <title>
        Listing 5-2: Hiding or showing boxes using
        document.getElementsByClassName()
    </title>

    <script type="text/javascript" src="/js/prototype.js"></script>

    <style type="text/css">
      .box {
        width : 300px; text-align : center;
        background : #f60; color : #fff;
        margin : 10px; font-weight : bold;
      }
      .box h1 { margin : 0; }
    </style>
  </head>
  <body>

    <div>
      <input type="button" value="Hide All" onclick="hideAll()" />
      <input type="button" value="Show All" onclick="showAll()" />
    </div>

    <div id="box-container">
      <div class="box">
        <h1>Box 1</h1>
      </div>

      <div class="box">
        <h1>Box 2</h1>
      </div>
    </div>

    <script type="text/javascript">
      function hideAll()
      {
        // find all 'box' elements
        var elts = document.getElementsByClassName('box', 'box-container');

        // now loop over them and hide them
        for (i = 0; i < elts.length; i++)
          elts[i].hide();
      }
```

```
    function showAll()
    {
      // find all 'box' elements
      var elts = document.getElementsByClassName('box', 'box-container');

      // now loop over them and hide them
      for (i = 0; i < elts.length; i++)
        elts[i].show();
    }
  </script>
  </body>
</html>
```

In the preceding code, you will see a call to a method called hide() and a call to a method called show(). These are both functions provided by Prototype, which simply hide or show the respective element. These are examples of the extra functionality provided when using the Prototype element selectors. We will cover more of these later in this chapter.

After the code fetches all of the box elements, it loops over them in both the showAll() and hideAll() functions to show or hide the element.

There is another way you can shorten this code and easily apply the same code to all returned elements: you can use either the each() method or the invoke() method. These are two functions Prototype adds to all arrays. Listing 5-3 shows the methods in Listing 5-2 rewritten to use each().

Listing 5-3. *Using each() to Iterate Over the Returned Elements (listing-5-3.html)*

```
<script type="text/javascript">
  function hideAll()
  {
    // find all 'box' elements and hide them
    document.getElementsByClassName('box', 'box-container').each(
        function(s) {
            s.hide();
        }
    );
  }

  function showAll()
  {
    // find all 'box' elements and show them
    document.getElementsByClassName('box', 'box-container').each(
        function(s) {
            s.show();
        }
    );
  }
</script>
```

This code passes a function as the argument to each(). This function is executed once for each item in the array each() is called on. The argument passed to this function is the element in question, thereby allowing us to call hide() or show() directly on it.

■**Note** Although I didn't use it in this case, the second argument passed to the function inside each() contains the loop number. For example, function(s, idx) { … } would pass 0 in the idx parameter for the first element, 1 for the second, and so on.

Alternatively, you can use invoke() instead of each(). This allows you to call a single method on each element, with an arbitrary number of arguments. This would work perfectly in this hide/show example, as we are just calling these methods for each box. However, if you needed to execute multiple lines of code, you would need to go back to using each().

Listing 5-4 shows the hideAll() and showAll() functions with a call to invoke(). Note that the method you want to invoke on each array element is passed as a string.

Listing 5-4. *Using invoke() to Call a Single Method on Each Array Element (listing-5-4.html)*

```
<script type="text/javascript">
  function hideAll()
  {
    // find all 'box' elements and hide them
    document.getElementsByClassName('box', 'box-container').invoke('hide');
  }

  function showAll()
  {
    // find all 'box' elements and show them
    document.getElementsByClassName('box', 'box-container').invoke('show');
  }
</script>
```

■**Tip** You can also call getElementsByClassName() directly on an element (rather than passing it as the first argument). For instance, you could select all .box-container elements as in the previous example by using $('box').getElementsByClassName('box-container').

The $$() Function

The $$() function (not to be confused with the $() function discussed previously) is a very powerful function that allows you to select elements using CSS rules. All returned elements are extended with extra Prototype functionality, just as $() does. Note, however, that an array is returned, even if only a single element is found. The ordering of elements in the array is the order of the elements in the document.

A CSS rule is a string used to specify elements in Cascading Style Sheets (CSS) documents, using a combination of element names (such as div), class names (such as .box), and element ID names (such as #box-content). For example, in Listing 5-2 we could have used var elts = $$('#box-container .box') instead of using the call to document.getElementsByClassName(). Here are some more examples:

- $$('form'): Selects all forms on a page

- $$('div.box'): Selects all div elements that have the class name box

- $$('div#logo img'): Selects the img element within the div called #logo

- $$('input[type=radio]'): Selects all inputs that are radio buttons

So why not just use $$() solely, and forget about $() and getElementsByClassName()? Yes, $$() can do exactly what the other two functions can do, but it is more expensive to call. That is, it is less efficient.

If you want to select an element whose ID you know, you should use $('element-id') instead of $$('#element-id'), since the former is more efficient (also, using $$() returns an array, and $() doesn't in this case). If you want to select all elements with a certain class (such as class .box inside a div with ID #box-container), you should use $('box-container'). getElementsByClassName('box') instead of $$('#box-container .box').

One recommendation from the Prototype documentation (found on http://proto-typejs.org/api), is that if you do use $$(), try to narrow the search down by specifying a parent element's ID at the start of the CSS rule. In other words, $$('#box-container .box') would be more efficient than $$('.box'), as the former would only search within the #box-container element for elements with class .box, while the latter would search the entire DOM.

If you are familiar with CSS, using $$() will be far easier to read and write, but from a per-formance point of view you should try to avoid it if there is a more efficient solution. For simplicity, I will continue to use $$() in the examples.

The getElementsBySelector() Function

It is possible to use the same syntax as in $$() but to only look within a particular element rather than the whole document. This can be achieved by calling the getElementsBySelector() func-tion directly on an element.

For example, you can use $('box-container').getElementsBySelector('.box') to find all elements that have class .box inside the #box-container element.

Prototype's Hash Object

Prototype provides an object type called Hash, which is essentially a normal JavaScript object that has been extended. I am covering it here simply because I will be referring to the Hash object in the future. It could also be referred to as an associative array, but I will call it a hash.

If you are unfamiliar with JavaScript objects, they can be created and used as follows:

```
<script type="text/javascript">
    var person = {
                name : 'John Smith',
```

```
              age  : 30
          };
    alert('The age of ' + person.name + ' is ' + person.age);
</script>
```

To extend this object with extra Prototype functionality, the $H() function is used. This essentially converts the created object into a hash. So the preceding code would be modified as follows:

```
<script type="text/javascript">
    var person = $H({
                    name : 'John Smith',
                    age  : 30
                });
    alert('The age of ' + person.name + ' is ' + person.age);
</script>
```

Doing this not only allows you to understand what a hash is, but it also provides the following extra functionality:

- each(): Allows you to loop over each key/value pair, similar to how you would with arrays in Prototype.

- remove(): Removes a value from the hash based on the specified key (for example, person.remove('age') will remove the age element from the hash in the previous example).

- toQueryString(): Serializes the keys and values into a usable query string (so the preceding person hash would become name=John+Smith&age=30).

■**Note** Sometimes you will need to create a hash but you will not require the extended functionality (such as when defining options to be passed to Ajax.Request). In this case, you can forego calling $H(), but I will still refer to it as a hash even though strictly speaking it is a generic JavaScript object.

Other Element Extensions

In the previous section I stated that when using a function such as $() or $$() in Prototype, the returned elements are extended. That is, they are given extra functionality that is not normally available when programming in JavaScript. We looked at a couple of these added functions (namely show() and hide()), but there are many more functions provided. We will take a brief look at the some of the more useful of these and at how you can use them in your everyday JavaScript development.

Note that which extensions are added depends on the type of element. That is, some new functions will be only available for arrays, and others only for strings. Some new functions are available to all elements.

Showing and Hiding Elements

As we saw before, the show() method makes a hidden element visible (or does nothing if the element is already visible), while the hide() method hides a visible element hidden (or does nothing if the element is already hidden).

In addition, there is a toggle() method. This will hide a visible element or show a hidden element. You can check whether an element is hidden or not by using the visible() method, which returns true if the element is visible and false if not.

Additionally, you can remove an element from the DOM completely by calling its remove() method.

Retrieving Dimensions of Elements

Prototype provides a method called getDimensions(), which returns the width and height of an element (in the width and height properties). You can retrieve an element's width by just using getWidth(), or its height by using getHeight(), but if you need both of these values you should use a single call to getDimensions(). This is because both getWidth() and getHeight() will internally make a call to getDimensions(), thereby resulting in an extra unnecessary function call.

The following example shows a simple function that accepts the ID of an element and then determines and displays its dimensions in an alert box:

```
<script type="text/javascript">
    function displayDimensions(id)
    {
        var dims = $(id).getDimensions();
        alert('This size of this box is ' + dims.width + 'x' + dims.height);
    }
</script>
```

Managing Classes of Elements

You can easily manipulate an element's classes with Prototype, which may be of great use for achieving mouseover effects or to allow the user to mark an item as selected.

The following functions are available to elements:

- addClassName(): Applies a class to an element. This might be useful if you have a highlight class for a selected element.

- removeClassName(): Removes a class from an element. This would typically be used at some point after calling addClassName().

- toggleClassName(): Adds or removes a class name (if the element doesn't have the class, it is added; it is removed if the element already has it).

- hasClassName(): Checks whether an element has a particular class.

Let's now look at a practical example of using these methods. Listing 5-5 is slightly more complex than previous examples; it highlights a box when your mouse pointer moves over it, and removes the highlight when the pointer is moved away.

Listing 5-5. *Demonstrating addClassName() and removeClassName() (listing-5-5.html)*

```html
<html>
    <head>
        <title>
            Listing 5-5: Manipulating element class name with Prototype
        </title>

        <script type="text/javascript" src="/js/prototype.js"></script>

        <style type="text/css">
            .box {
                width : 300px; text-align : center;
                background : #f60; color : #fff;
                margin : 10px; font-weight : bold;
            }
            .box h1 { margin : 0; }
            .box.highlight { background : #f00; }
        </style>
    </head>
    <body>
        <div id="box-container">
            <div class="box">
                <h1>Box 1</h1>
            </div>

            <div class="box">
                <h1>Box 2</h1>
            </div>
        </div>

        <script type="text/javascript">
            // find all the box elements, then loop over each one and
            // add the onmouseover and onmouseout events to it
            $$('#box-container .box').each(
                function(s)
                {
                    s.onmouseover = function() {
                        this.addClassName('highlight');
                    };
                    s.onmouseout = function() {
                        this.removeClassName('highlight');
                    };
                }
            );
        </script>
    </body>
</html>
```

In this example, there are a series of boxes (with class `.box`) inside of `#box-container`, and various styles are defined for this box. I have also defined a `.highlight` style, which will make the box turn red when the mouse is over it.

■**Note** The JavaScript code in this example would be unnecessary if the `:hover` selector worked across all browsers. In Firefox, you could simply use CSS like `div.box:hover { background : #f00; }`, but this will not work in Internet Explorer (except on links) so the JavaScript solution is required.

Essentially, what I want this code to do is as follows:

1. Retrieve all `.box` elements.

2. Add an `onmouseover` event to each element, which adds the `.highlight` class.

3. Add an `onmouseout` event to each element, which removes the `.highlight` class.

I first use `$$('#box-container .box')` to select all the boxes, and then use `each()` on the array of returned elements, as I want to execute several lines of code for each element. (See Listing 5-3 for more information about using `each()`.)

Next I set the `onmouseover` and `onmouseout` events for each element with a call to `addClassName()` and `removeClassName()` respectively. Note that in the event handler, `this` refers to the element on which the event occurred.

■**Caution** In order to keep the example somewhat simple, I used a non-preferred way of observing events in JavaScript. The problem with how I added these events is that if either of the `onmouseover` or `onmouseout` events had previously been defined on the `.box` elements, I would have overwritten that handler. Conversely, if another script executes after this code, my event handlers may be overwritten. Prototype provides an event handling class that deals with these issues and allows events to be observed correctly between all platforms. We will cover this `Event` class in the "Event Handling in Prototype" section later in this chapter.

Manipulating Strings with Prototype

All string elements are extended with several methods, including the following:

- `truncate()`: Shortens a string to a specified length, and optionally appends a string at the end (such as …). For example, you could turn "My short string" into "My short…".

- `strip()`: Removes whitespace from the beginning and end of a string.

- `stripTags()`: Removes any HTML tags from a string.

- `stripScripts()`: Removes any scripts (such as JavaScript) from a string.

- escapeHTML(): Turns HTML elements into their respective entities (for example, replacing < with <)

- unescapeHTML(): Performs the opposite of escapeHTML() (for example, turning < into <).

There are several more functions available, but these are among the most useful.

Note Even if you are using functions such as stripTags() and stripScripts() on user-submitted data, you should still be performing these same operations at the server if the data is submitted, since you cannot guarantee the data has passed through the JavaScript code when it reaches the server.

Ajax Operations in Prototype

One of the key reasons for choosing to use Prototype in this book was not only the extended functionality applied to all elements—which in itself is extremely useful—but also for its Ajax support. Cross-browser Ajax solutions can easily be created by using the Prototype Ajax class.

Typical usage of this class involves first defining a hash of options (such as form data that should be submitted in the request), and then instantiating one of Ajax.Request, Ajax.Updater, or Ajax.PeriodicalUpdater:

- Ajax.Request: Generally used for a one-time request. This is the core Ajax method available, and it is the function you will call directly to initiate most Ajax operations.

- Ajax.Updater: Behaves in the same way as Ajax.Request, except its specific purpose is to populate an element on your HTML page with the response data from a request. This can also be achieved by using Ajax.Request, but Ajax.Updater simplifies the process for this specific operation.

- Ajax.PeriodicalUpdater: Behaves the same way as Ajax.Updater in that it populates an element with the Ajax response data; however, it will continue to execute with a specified frequency. For instance, if you need to retrieve fresh data every N seconds, you can use this method. Another way to look at it is that Ajax.PeriodicalUpdater performs a request with Ajax.Updater every N seconds.

Ajax Request Options

When initiating an Ajax request with Prototype, the one key thing you need is the URL you are requesting. In addition to this, you can define a set of options that dictate the behavior of the request. These options are not required to perform the request (default options are defined internally); however, it is rare that you wouldn't need to set various options or callbacks.

The options you will typically need to set are as follows:

- method: The HTTP method used for the request. This is typically get or post (with post being the default). Note that there are other types of HTTP requests possible, but they are typically not used and are beyond the scope of this book.

- parameters: The form data that is included in the request, regardless of whether it is a get or post request. Prototype can accept a wide variety of data formats here (such as a string you have already encoded, or simply a hash). It will convert the data into the required format to complete the request.

The following is an example of an options hash that can be used for a Prototype Ajax request:

```
<script type="text/javascript">
    var options = {
        method      : 'post',
        parameters : 'action=save&id=1234'
    };
</script>
```

And here is an example of getting the value of a text input field from the existing page and including it in the options hash:

```
<input type="text" id="my-input" />
<script type="text/javascript">
    function createOptions()
    {
        var options = {
            method      : 'post',
            parameters : 'action=save&id=1234',
            postBody   : 'someValue=' + $('my-input').getValue()
        };
    }
</script>
```

In this example, the getValue() function retrieves a form element's value. This is a function added to form elements by Prototype so their values can be retrieved regardless of their type (whether textarea, checkbox, radio, or other type).

Ajax Callback Functions

For all Ajax requests you make with Prototype, there are a number of callback functions that can be defined. Each specified callback function will be called automatically at appropriate stages of the Ajax request lifecycle.

■Note You can perform Ajax requests without specifying any event callbacks; however, it will not be possible to use the returned result if you don't define any callbacks. Sometimes you may not care about the response data, but most of the time you will.

Typically, you will define the callback prior to initiating the Ajax request, and then pass in the function name with the request options (as discussed in the previous section). Each callback receives the XMLHttpRequest object as its first parameter, thereby allowing you to easily read the response data (including HTTP status code) if it is available.

The following are the main callback functions you will typically need to define when handling an Ajax request:

- onSuccess: This callback is called upon successful completion of a request. A request is successful if no error occurs and if the HTTP status code is in the 2xx family.

- onFailure: If a request completes successfully but returns an HTTP status code not in the 2xx family, this callback is invoked.

- onComplete: After a request has completed and all other callbacks have been called, the onComplete callback is triggered. In reality, you will probably not need this callback in your requests unless you have some kind of cleanup code that needs to be executed whether a request succeeds or not.

Note Many Ajax programmers (both in the past and even now) simply check for an exact status code of 200 when trying to determine success. Not all successful HTTP requests will necessarily return this status code, however, so the onSuccess callback should be used instead. Prototype will automatically deal with each of these status codes.

Here's an example of defining the onComplete and onFailure callbacks, combined with the other options you may need in an Ajax request:

```
<script type="text/javascript">
    var options = {
        method     : 'post',
        parameters : 'action=save&id=1234',
        onSuccess  : function(transport)
        {
            alert('Ajax request succeeded!');
        },
        onFailure  : function(transport)
        {
            alert('Oh no - something went wrong!');
        }
    };
</script>
```

The callback functions I have defined are somewhat useless, but hopefully they demonstrate how the Ajax request is set up.

In reality, I much prefer to define the actual function as its own separate block, and then pass in the function name as the argument in the options hash. An example of this is shown next. Note that technically speaking it is a function pointer that is used as the value in the options hash—it's not simply a string with the function name.

```
<script type="text/javascript">
    function handleSuccess(transport)
    {
        alert('Ajax request succeeded!');
    }

    function handleFailure(transport)
    {
        alert('Oh no - something went wrong!');
    }

    var options = {
        method     : 'post',
        parameters : 'action=save&id=1234',
        onSuccess  : handleSuccess,
        onFailure  : handleFailure
    };
</script>
```

In addition to the onSuccess and onFailure callbacks (which encompass a large number of HTTP status codes), Prototype also allows you to easily handle each status code independently. To do this, you define an onXYZ callback, where XYZ corresponds to the HTTP status code you want to handle.

For example, if you wanted a specific function to be called when a 404: File Not Found error occurred, you would pass the on404 callback to the Ajax request options. The following example demonstrates this by creating several callbacks, each to handle various error codes:

```
<script type="text/javascript">
    function handleUnauthorized(transport)
    {
        alert('401 Error - You are not authorized');
    }

    function handleForbidden(transport)
    {
        alert('403 Error - You are forbidden');
    }

    function handleFileNotFound(transport)
    {
        alert('404 Error - File was not found');
    }

    var options = {
        on401 : handleUnauthorized,
        on403 : handleForbidden,
```

```
        on404 : handleFileNotFound
    };
</script>
```

The XMLHttpRequest Callback Argument

In all of the preceding examples, I have included an argument called transport in the callback functions. As I mentioned previously, this argument is the XMLHttpRequest object created as a result of the call to Ajax.Request.

■**Note** The primary reason for naming this argument transport (and not xhr or something similar) is simply convention. You can call it what you like, but to be consistent you should just call it transport.

You can use transport in your callback functions to read the response data. The following properties are available inside the transport variable:

- responseText: The response from the request as a string.

- responseXML: The response from the request as an XMLDocument object. This allows you to manipulate the response in the same way you would with the normal DOM. I will demonstrate this shortly, in the "An Ajax.Request Example" section.

- status: The HTTP status code resulting from the request (such as 200 for a successful request, or 404 for a file-not-found error).

- statusText: A textual description for the HTTP status code (such as OK for a status response of 200).

So you could modify the handleSuccess() callback from the previous example to show the response data in an alert box using the following code:

```
<script type="text/javascript">
    function handleSuccess(transport)
    {
        alert(transport.responseText);
    }
</script>
```

JavaScript Object Notation (JSON)

JavaScript Object Notation, or JSON, is a data-exchange format that is very useful in Ajax-enabled web applications. In essence, JSON is JavaScript code. It is typically used to serialize JavaScript arrays or objects (what I referred to as hashes earlier) into a simple format that can be exchanged between client and server.

■**Note** My own personal preference is to use JSON data as the response to Ajax requests, since it's much easier to manipulate the data. However, since we're covering Ajax, it's good to know how the X in Ajax works. As such, I will use XML for the main example in this chapter, but in following chapters, when we add Ajax functionality to our application, we will use JSON and not XML.

JSON is used as an alternative to XML for data exchange in Ajax requests because it results in a much smaller payload (since there are no opening/closing tags), and it is typically simpler to access within JavaScript code. For example, the JavaScript code you might use to represent data for a book may look like this:

```
var book = {
    title  : 'Practical PHP Web 2.0 Applications',
    author : 'Quentin Zervaas'
};
```

Now consider the code you would use in PHP to represent this same data:

```
<?php
    $book = array(
        'title'  => 'Practical PHP Web 2.0 Applications',
        'author' => 'Quentin Zervaas'
    );
?>
```

If I wanted to represent this PHP snippet in JavaScript, I would need to somehow create JavaScript code like the preceding, which means creating a string of JSON data. PHP provides a function called json_encode() to do exactly this. The Zend Framework also provides the Zend_Json class, which is what we'll be using. Earlier versions of PHP do not have the json_encode() function, and by using Zend_Json we don't have to worry about that.

Now, if I wanted to represent the preceding PHP code as JavaScript code, I could call Zend_Json::encode() to do so:

```
<script type="text/javascript">
    var book = <?php echo Zend_Json::encode($book) ?>
</script>
```

This function will generate a string that looks like this:

```
{ title  : 'Practical PHP Web 2.0 Applications', author : 'Quentin Zervaas' };
```

While this example serves no great purpose, it demonstrates what is possible with JSON. When a request is made with XMLHttpRequest, the server can return a JSON-encoded string so that the JavaScript code can interpret the results.

To interpret the returned data, you can use the JavaScript eval() function, which will evaluate as JavaScript code whatever is passed as its first argument. Thankfully, Prototype simplifies this for us by providing the evalJSON() method. For example, to decode JSON data returned from an Ajax request, you could use code similar to the following:

```
<script type="text/javascript">
    function handleSuccess(transport)
    {
        var json = transport.responseText.evalJSON(true);
    }
</script>
```

In this example, the evalJSON() is an extended method Prototype provides to all strings. The first argument to this method tells Prototype to check for data that isn't well formed. If the string is not well-formed JavaScript code, eval() is not called internally as a safety precaution.

Note When Prototype 1.6.0 is released, the responseJSON property will also be available in the response from Ajax requests, saving us the trouble of manually decoding the JSON data as in the preceding example.

I will continue using XML in this chapter, just to give you a full taste of how Ajax solutions can be implemented. Our first real taste of JSON will be in Chapter 6, when we add client-side form validation to the user registration form we created in Chapter 4.

An Ajax.Request Example

Now that we have looked at defining options and callbacks for a request, we can take a look at Ajax.Request, the primary Prototype function used for Ajax. In this example, the code will request an XML file that resides on a web server. It will then loop over the data in the XML file and output it to the browser. At this stage, we won't be doing anything fancy with the data—we will save the fanciness for when we cover Scriptaculous.

Listing 5-6 shows the XML data. This is just made-up data that has no real meaning other than demonstrating the use of Ajax.Request. This data is stored in a file called listing-5-6.xml.

Listing 5-6. *Sample XML Data to Be Processed in the Ajax.Request Example (listing-5-6.xml)*

```
<people>
    <person name="John" age="30" />
    <person name="Mary" age="25" />
</people>
```

The basic code outline we will use to perform the Ajax request is as follows. We will flesh it out a bit more shortly.

```
<script type="text/javascript">
    function handleSuccess(transport)
    {
        // todo
    }

    function handleFailure(transport)
    {
```

```
        // todo
    }

    function loadXml()
    {
        var url = 'listing-5-6.xml';
        var options = {
            method    : 'get',
            onSuccess : handleSuccess,
            onFailure : handleFailure
        };

        new Ajax.Request(url, options);
    }
</script>
```

Note Since Ajax.Request is in fact a class (as opposed to simply being a function), it must be invoked using the new keyword. If new is omitted, the call to Ajax.Request will not work.

As you can see, the first argument to Ajax.Request is the URL being requested. In this example, we are simply getting an XML file, but in real-world applications this is likely to be a server-side script (such as a PHP script). The second argument is the list of request options.

Here you can also see that we've defined callbacks for both success and failure, although they do not yet do anything.

Handling XML Data from an Ajax Request

As mentioned previously, we can access the responseXML property of the XMLHttpRequest object passed in to the callback. This property is an XMLDocument object, which allows us to manipulate it just as we would the DOM.

Referring back to our listing-5-6.xml file in Listing 5-6, we could call getElementsByTagName('person') to find all of the individual people records in the returned XML. Note that the documentElement property is the root node of the XML document, so you can't actually call getElementsByTagName() directly on the responseXML property. In reality, it would look more like this:

```
<script type="text/javascript">
  var people = transport.responseXML.documentElement.getElementsByTagName('person');
</script>
```

This will return an array called people containing all of the person records in the XML document. Strictly speaking, this is actually an HTMLCollection (not an array), but by using the Prototype $A() function, we can turn it into an array and gain the extra array functionality Prototype provides (such as each() and invoke()).

So, we can modify the handleSuccess() callback to loop over each person, outputting their name in an alert box. This functionality is still somewhat crude, but we will improve it further shortly. We can use the DOM getAttribute() method to fetch a person's name from the returned person data, as follows:

```
<script type="text/javascript">
    function handleSuccess(transport)
    {
        var xml = transport.responseXML;
        var people = $A(xml.documentElement.getElementsByTagName('person'));

        people.each(function(s) {
            alert(s.getAttribute('name'));
        });
    }
</script>
```

If we want to output a more meaningful message for each returned person, we need to build up a string using the data associated with each user. To do this, we will use Prototype's Template class. This class probably isn't something you will often use with Prototype, but it is worth knowing about (particularly since we will use it in later code listings).

The Template class allows you to define a template string with placeholders for change-able data. You can then call the evaluate() method on the created template, passing in the data you want to include. The following code shows an updated version of handleSuccess(), which now uses the Template class in combination with Prototype's each() enumerator:

```
<script type="text/javascript">
    function handleSuccess(transport)
    {
        var xml = transport.responseXML;
        var people = $A(xml.documentElement.getElementsByTagName('person'));

        var tpl = new Template('The age of #{name} is #{age}');

        people.each(function(s, idx) {
            var data = {
                name : s.getAttribute('name'),
                age  : s.getAttribute('age')
            };

            alert(tpl.evaluate(data));
        });
    }
</script>
```

Handling XML That Isn't Well Formed

In all of the preceding examples of handleSuccess(), we have assumed that the XML data is well formed. That is, we assume it is valid and that no errors are contained in the document. This is not always going to be the case, especially for dynamically generated XML. Just because an Ajax request is successful doesn't mean the returned data is correct. Additionally, if the document is well formed but is missing properties that we require (for instance, if the age property is missing from one or more records), this is not an error per se.

Prototype does not provide XML-handling functionality, so detecting XML errors across different platforms is not a straightforward task. We will treat an XML parsing error in our code the same way we treat no records being returned.

For the sake of completeness, here is code you can use to detect XML parsing errors:

```
<script type="text/javascript">
    // detect a parse error in Internet Explorer
    if (xml.parseError) {
        if (xml.parseError.errorCode != 0) {
            str = xml.parseError.reason
                + ' on line ' + xml.parseError.line
                + ' position ' + xml.parseError.linepos);
            alert(str);
        }
    }

    // detect a parse error in Mozilla
    else if (xml.documentElement.nodeName == 'parsererror') {
        alert(xml.documentElement.firstChild.data);
    }
</script>
```

Completing the onFailure Error Handler

The final part of this example is the handleError() callback. In this particular example, we are doing nothing more than showing an alert box for each person record found. To accompany this, we will simply display an alert box containing the error if one has occurred.

```
<script type="text/javascript">
    function handleFailure(transport)
    {
        alert('Error: ' + transport.statusText);
    }
</script>
```

The Complete Ajax.Request Example

Listing 5-7 contains the complete code for the Ajax.Request example.

Listing 5-7. *The Complete Ajax.Request Example (listing-5-7.html)*

```
<html>
    <head>
        <title>
            Listing 5-7: The complete Ajax.Request example
```

```
        </title>
        <script type="text/javascript" src="/js/prototype.js"></script>
    </head>
    <body>
        <div>
            <input type="button" value="Load XML" id="load-xml" />
        </div>

        <script type="text/javascript">
            function handleSuccess(transport)
            {
                var xml = transport.responseXML;
                var people = $A(xml.documentElement.getElementsByTagName('person'));

                var tpl = new Template('The age of #{name} is #{age}');

                people.each(function(s, idx) {
                    var data = {
                        name : s.getAttribute('name'),
                        age  : s.getAttribute('age')
                    };
                    alert(tpl.evaluate(data));
                });
            }

            function handleFailure(transport)
            {
                alert('Error: ' + transport.statusText);
            }

            function loadXml()
            {
                var url = 'listing-5-6.xml';
                var options = {
                    method    : 'get',
                    onSuccess : handleSuccess,
                    onFailure : handleFailure
                };

                new Ajax.Request(url, options);
            }

            Event.observe('load-xml', 'click', loadXml);
        </script>
    </body>
</html>
```

When you load `listing-5-7.html` in your browser, all you will see is a form button that says `Load XML`. At the end of the code, the `click` event handler is added to this button using `Event.observe()`, which simply calls the `loadXml()` function when the event is triggered.

Note that we could have created the button with a line like this:

```
<input type="button" value="Load XML" id="load-xml" onclick="loadXml()" />
```

However, as noted earlier in this chapter, using the Prototype event-handling code is the preferred way to observe events.

■**Note** If you don't quite follow how the event-observing code works, don't worry; we'll cover it in the next section.

Event Handling in Prototype

One key benefit Prototype offers developers is enhanced DOM event handling. Writing code to handle events across different browsers can be difficult, but with Prototype these issues can be avoided.

One difficulty when not using Prototype is that event handlers can easily be overwritten. For example, if you have HTML code that includes `<body onload="doSomething()">` and also loads an external JavaScript file containing `window.onload = doSomethingElse`, which function is called? Certainly not both of them!

Prototype solves this problem by allowing us to add to existing event observers. This means that if you observe the same event on the same element twice, both event handlers will be triggered when the event occurs.

Observing an Event

To observe an event with Prototype, use the `Event.observe()` method. This method takes three arguments:

- The element on which the event is being observed.

- The event to observe; this is a string containing the event name. The event names are the same ones you might already be used to in JavaScript, except they don't begin with `on`. For instance, to observe the `onmouseover` event, you would specify `mouseover` as the second argument.

- The function to execute when the event is triggered.

Going back to the "body onload" example, rather than using `<body onload="doSomething()">`, you would use the following to correctly observe this event:

```
Event.observe(window, 'load', something);
```

This code would appear either in an external JavaScript file or within `<script>` tags in your HTML document.

■**Note** This example might be slightly confusing, since you observe the `window` element in
`Event.observe()`, whereas the inline version was in the `body` tag. Technically speaking, when using
`<body onload="">`, this event is being attached to the `window` DOM element. Also, the reference to the
`something` function is a function pointer, so you don't include the brackets; if you did, it would mean
the result of the `something()` function would be used as the third argument.

Note that you can also call the `observe()` function directly on an element. In this case, you
omit the first argument. For instance, you might add an image to your web page with the following HTML code:

```
<img src="image.jpg" id="my-image" />
```

You can observe the `onclick` event on this image by using `Event.observe()` as you saw
already:

```
Event.observe('my-image', 'click', something);
```

Or you can first retrieve the element and then call `observe()` on it:

```
$('my-image').observe('click', something);
```

Finding Out Which Element an Event Occurred On

When a function is triggered by an event occurring, the event object is passed in as the first
argument to the callback. This lets you find out certain things about the event, such as the element on which the event occurred (so if the `onclick` event was observed on several elements,
you could find out exactly which element was clicked on).

To find the element, you call the `Event.element()` function. I'll use the example of clicking
on an image:

```
<img src="image.jpg" id="my-image" />

<script type="text/javascript">
    $('my-image').observe('click', something);
</script>
```

Next I can write the `something()` function, which is called when the image is clicked. I
assume the first argument will be the event (which I like to simply call e). I can then pass e to
`Event.element()` to return the image element.

```
<script type="text/javascript">
    function something(e)
    {
        var img = Event.element(e);
    }
</script>
```

Canceling an Event

A common technique we will use in this book when writing Ajax code is to trigger an Ajax request when a form submit button is clicked. The problem with this is that the web browser will perform a normal postback when the button is clicked, meaning a new page will be loaded in the browser. To prevent this from occurring, the `Event.stop()` method must be called. This is a very useful method, since it is difficult to write code to achieve this across all browsers.

As an example, let's say I have the following form code:

```
<form method="post" action="/someUrl" id="my-form">
    <input type="submit" value="Submit Form" />
</form>
```

Rather than submitting the form data back to the server, I want to run a function called `handleFormSubmission()` when the `Submit Form` button is clicked. First, I must observe the `onsubmit` event, and then call `Event.stop()` when handling the event:

```
<script type="text/javascript">
    $('my-form').observe('submit', handleFormSubmission);

    function handleFormSubmission(e)
    {
        Event.stop(e);

        // now do something here such as an Ajax request
    }
</script>
```

The best part about using code such as this is that it allows you to prevent normal postback when the user is running a browser capable of running JavaScript, yet it still submits the form as normal when a non-JavaScript browser is used. This helps you provide a rich user experience when the browser is capable of it, but it is also an accessible non-JavaScript solution.

Creating JavaScript Classes in Prototype

Yet another great thing about Prototype is its ability to easily create JavaScript classes. While this has always been possible with JavaScript, Prototype makes the process much simpler and helps you generate cleaner and more manageable code.

Creating a Class

The typical process for creating a class with Prototype is as follows:

1. Create the new class by calling `Class.create()`. Internally, this causes the class's constructor function to be automatically run when the class is instantiated.

2. Define the class's `prototype` object (not to be confused with the name of the library you are using). This defines the properties and methods of the class.

3. When defining the class's `prototype` object, implement the class constructor. The name of the constructor is `initialize()`, which can take any number of arguments (just as when writing any other JavaScript function).

For example, to create a simple class called `Book`, which takes a title as its first argument, the following code could be used:

```
Book = Class.create();

Book.prototype = {
    initialize : function(title)
    {
        this.title = title;
    }
};
```

You can implement your own functions as required. For example, you could make a function that returns the book title as follows:

```
Book = Class.create();

Book.prototype = {
    initialize : function(title)
    {
        this.title = title;
    },

    getTitle : function()
    {
        return this.title;
    }
};

var book = new Book('Practical PHP Web 2.0 Applications');
alert(book.getTitle());
```

■**Tip** Since each function is an element of the class's `prototype` object, they must be separated by commas. Forgetting the comma is a very common cause of syntax errors when developing classes in JavaScript.

Binding Function Calls to Objects

A very important aspect of developing classes with Prototype is the use of the `bind()` and `bindAsEventListener()` functions. Please ensure you understand how these functions work, as they are used frequently in the JavaScript code in this book.

These functions bind an object's context to a class method so that when you call `this` in the method, it refers to the correct object. Because this is a difficult concept to grasp, I'll use examples to explain it further. Once I have shown you how binding works, I'll show you the difference between `bind()` and `bindAsEventListener()`, since there is only a subtle difference between the two.

To demonstrate how binding works, I'll create a class that observes the `onclick` event on an image. When the image is clicked, I will display an alert to the user notifying them that the image was clicked.

First, I'll create the class. The `initialize` method accepts the image element as its only argument, and then observes the `onclick` event. Also, I'll define the `notifyUser()` method, which will be called by the event handler when the image is clicked.

```
ImageHandler = Class.create();

ImageHandler.prototype = {
    initialize : function(img)
    {
        $(img).observe('click', handleClick);
    },


    notifyUser : function()
    {
        alert('The image was clicked');
    }
};
```

So far so good. The image element is set as the first argument to the constructor, and the onclick event is observed on it. But wait, I haven't implemented the `handleClick()` method, which is called by the event observer. I'll add it to the class:

```
ImageHandler = Class.create();

ImageHandler.prototype = {
    initialize : function(img)
    {
        $(img).observe('click', handleClick);
    },

    notifyUser : function()
    {
        alert('The image was clicked');
    },

    handleClick : function(e)
    {
        this.notifyUser();
    }
};
```

The event handler function is now there. But will it be called when the image is clicked? No—the observer will call the global handleClick() function, not the handleClick() method inside the ImageHandler class. I need to add this in front of the handleClick() call:

```
initialize : function(img)
{
    $(img).observe('click', this.handleClick);
},
```

There's one small problem with this. The correct function will now be called when the image is clicked, but it will be called from the event-handling part of the system. In the handleClick() function, I refer to this.notifyUser(). Unfortunately, calling this here will not refer to the current instance of ImageHandler.

This is where bind() comes in. I must bind the event-handler function to the current object. Rather than using this.handleClick as the event handler, I actually need to use this.handleClick.bind(this), as follows:

```
ImageHandler = Class.create();

ImageHandler.prototype = {
    initialize : function(img)
    {
        $(img).observe('click', this.handleClick.bind(this));
    },

    notifyUser : function()
    {
        alert('The image was clicked');
    },

    handleClick : function(e)
    {
        this.notifyUser();
    }
};
```

By calling bind() on the function, I'm effectively saying, "when I refer to this in the ImageHandler's handleClick() function, it should refer to the object I'm passing to bind(), which is an instance of ImageHandler."

The difference between bind() and bindAsEventListener() is that when you use bindAsEventListener() the event object will be passed in as the first argument to the bound function. Typically, you will always use bindAsEventListener() when observing events, not bind(). So, in actual fact, the preceding code to observe the image click needs to be as follows:

```
$(img).observe('click', this.handleClick.bindAsEventListener(this));
```

When implementing callbacks for an Ajax response, you only use bind(), as the response isn't triggered by an event. For example, the following code initiates an Ajax request when the object is initialized. The Ajax request will call handleSuccess() if the request is successfully performed. I will tell Prototype to bind the instance of `AjaxBindExample` to the `handleSuccess()` function:

```
AjaxBindExample = Class.create();

AjaxBindExample.prototype = {
    initialize : function(img)
    {
        var options = {
            onSuccess : this.handleSuccess.bind(this)
        };

        new Ajax.Request('/someUrl', options);
    },

    handleSuccess : function(transport)
    {
        this.doSomething();
    },

    doSomething : function()
    { }
};
```

From Prototype to Scriptaculous

Prototype is a very useful JavaScript framework, and we just covered a large amount of the functionality it provides. We didn't cover everything available in Prototype, however, as it is simply not all relevant to most of the code you will write in your Web 2.0 applications.

We now move on to Scriptaculous, a JavaScript library used to add special effects to web sites. Scriptaculous is built upon Prototype, as it makes extensive use of nearly all classes provided by Prototype—even ones we haven't yet looked at, such as `Position` (used for element positioning and other issues related to the complex task of cross-browser layout). We will briefly cover exactly what Scriptaculous can do, then go over the installation of the library on your web pages, and finally look at an extensive example, which will make use of Scriptaculous effects and controls, Prototype classes, Ajax, and PHP.

Before we go any further, though, let's look at what Scriptaculous can do for us. We won't go into all features in detail, but we will cover the more important ones, and anything else that will be required in this book.

Prebuilt Controls

Scriptaculous provides a number of prebuilt controls that can easily be included on your page. A control is a complex element for user interaction, typically used within or in place of forms.

The controls available in Scriptaculous are as follows:

- `Autocompleter`: A text field that automatically provides suggestions based on user-input (somewhat similar to Google Suggest—http://www.google.com/webhp?complete=1&hl=en).

■**Note** In Chapter 12 we will implement a JavaScript class that behaves similarly to Google Suggest rather than using the one provided by Scriptaculous. This allows us to look at some of the nitty-gritty code involved in developing such a class.

- `InPlaceEditor`: A class that allows a user to edit content on a web page directly. For example, if you had a list of files, you could use `InPlaceEditor` to allow users to rename a file by clicking on it. The filename would be replaced by a text input field, allowing the new filename to be entered inline.

- `Slider`: A slider that a user can click and drag to change a value. Sliders are very customizable, including their styles, available values, and orientation (horizontal or vertical).

Drag and Drop

With Scriptaculous, it is easy to define *draggable* areas (using the `Draggables` class) and *droppable* areas (using the `Droppables` class) on your HTML pages. This allows you to achieve effects such as the following very easily:

- Sort a list of items using the `Sortables` class, meaning that list items can be clicked on and dragged to their new location (and the new order can be saved in real time transparently using Ajax).

- Drag an item from one list to another. For example, if you were managing product images for an online store, you might have a gallery of all the unused images. You could drag an image from this list onto a list of product images. Once again, you could save this state change transparently using Ajax.

Visual Effects

There are five core effects in Scriptaculous:

- `Effect.Opacity`: Changes the opacity (transparency) of an element. This is done gradually over a specified period of time. For instance, you could fade something from 100 percent opacity to 50 percent opacity over a period of 2 seconds.

- `Effect.Scale`: Changes the size of an element to the specified dimensions. This allows you to easily grow or shrink an element.

- `Effect.MoveBy`: Moves an element by a specified number of pixels (in both the X and Y directions).

- `Effect.Highlight`: Highlights an element with a given color. Both a starting color and finishing color are specified, and the element changes color from the starting color to the finish color. This effect would typically be used to draw attention to a particular area of the page, such as to notify the user that an Ajax request has completed.

- `Effect.Parallel`: Combines one or more effects into a single effect.

In addition to these core effects, there are a large number of combination effects, built using the core effects. They include the following:

- `Effect.Appear`: Makes a hidden element appear, going from complete transparency to 100 percent opacity.

- `Effect.Fade`: Makes an element completely transparent (the opposite of `Effect.Appear`). At the completion of the effect, it will also hide the element from the document (that is, it will set the element's CSS `display` property to `none`).

- `Effect.Grow`: Grows an element from a size of 0x0 to its normal size. At the start of the effect, the element is shrunk to 0x0 and then grown gradually to normal size. Typically the element will be hidden prior to calling this effect.

- `Effect.Shrink`: Scales an element gradually down to a size of 0x0 (the opposite of `Effect.Grow`).

There are many more effects available, and you can write your own. The Scriptaculous web site (`http://script.aculo.us`) has more examples of the effects you can use.

DOM Element Builder

Scriptaculous provides a class called `Builder`, which is used to dynamically create new elements in the DOM. It is effectively a replacement for the `document.createElement()` available in modern browsers.

■**Tip** The upcoming release of Prototype (version 1.6.0) will include a built-in DOM element builder. This means you can use Prototype to create new DOM elements rather than using Scriptaculous. Throughout this book, however, we will be using the Scriptaculous `Builder` class when we need to dynamically create new DOM elements. You can still create DOM elements using the browser's built-in functions, but the solution provided by Scriptaculous is much cleaner and simpler.

JavaScript Unit Testing

The final class provided by Scriptaculous is called `Test`, which provides unit testing capabilities for JavaScript. The idea is to write a series of test cases alongside your code as you are developing it. This allows you to assert that your code still works correctly in the future even after making changes. It is useful for discovering bugs early on that you might not have discovered until later.

To use this class, you must manually include the unittest.js file in your HTML document. We will not be using this class in this book.

Downloading and Installing Scriptaculous

You can download Scriptaculous from http://script.aculo.us. The version used in this book is 1.7.1b3, and it requires Prototype 1.5.1.1 (typically when a new version of Prototype is released, a corresponding version of Scriptaculous is also released).

After extracting the downloaded archive, all you need are the files in the src directory; I like to put these files in a directory called scriptaculous. Note that Prototype is also included in the archive (inside the lib directory), but you may already have the file installed. If not, this is the same file that you would download from http://www.prototypejs.org.

Assuming you created the scriptaculous directory within a directory called /js (just as you did for Prototype), you would load Scriptaculous in your HTML pages using code similar to the following:

```html
<html>
    <head>
        <title>Loading the Scriptaculous library</title>
        <script type="text/javascript" src="/js/prototype.js"></script>
        <script type="text/javascript"
                src="/js/scriptaculous/scriptaculous.js"></script>
    </head>
    <body>

    </body>
</html>
```

As you can see, Prototype is loaded prior to Scriptaculous. If you do not do this, an exception will be thrown by Scriptaculous.

Tip If you do not need to use Scriptaculous on a particular page, you should avoid loading it to improve download speeds of the page and slightly reduce system overhead when loading the page. In addition to the main scriptaculous.js file, there are six JavaScript files that are automatically loaded. This totals seven HTTP requests and about 150KB just for Scriptaculous (the unit testing library, unittest.js, isn't automatically loaded). In addition to this, Prototype is another 94KB.

Combining Prototype, Scriptaculous, Ajax, and PHP in a Useful Example

In order to demonstrate how to actually use Scriptaculous, we are going to write a script that utilizes it and makes use of the Prototype features we have covered so far in this chapter.

We will create a script that allows a user to sort a list of items using drag and drop. The script will do the following:

1. Once the user loads the page, use Ajax to fetch the list of items to be sorted and display them to the user

2. Allow the user to click and drag items to new locations to change the list order

3. Save the new order of the list after the user releases an item in a new location

4. Notify the user when the new order has been saved

We will look at everything that is involved, including these functions:

- Fetching the list of items using Ajax and using the DOM to create an unordered list (`<ul></ul>`) in which to display the items.

- Making the list of items into a drag-and-drop list using the Scriptaculous `Sortable` class.

- Styling the list of items in a manner that makes it easy for the user to drag items.

- Handling Ajax events, including errors that may occur.

- Using PHP in the background to save the list order. The list will be saved in a MySQL database.

The code will be structured as follows:

- `index.php`: A simple HTML page containing placeholders in which to show the sortable list and to show status messages.

- `styles.css`: An external CSS file used to style the HTML page.

- `items.php`: A PHP utility script used to manage the list of items, including connecting to the database, retrieving the list of items, and updating the order of the items.

- `processor.php`: A PHP script to respond to the two different Ajax requests.

- `scripts.js`: An external JavaScript file (in addition to Prototype and Scriptaculous) to handle the client-side application logic. This will be responsible for making the two Ajax requests required (fetching the list of items, and saving its new order).

■**Note** These files should be kept separate from the main web application we began in earlier chapters, since these files will not form part of the final application. This code will work just fine from a subdirectory.

Figure 5-1 shows how the page will look once the example is complete. This is an action shot of the "Door" item being dragged to the bottom of the list.

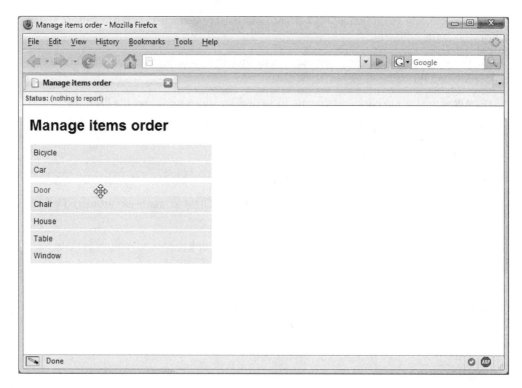

Figure 5-1. *Dragging an item in the list to a new location*

Creating the Main HTML Page: index.php

First we need to create the main index HTML page, as shown in Listing 5-8. This is the page users will load in the browser.

Listing 5-8. *The HTML Code Used to Display the List to the User (index.php)*

```
<html>
    <head>
        <title>Manage items order</title>
        <script type="text/javascript" src="/js/prototype.js"></script>
        <script type="text/javascript"
                src="/js/scriptaculous/scriptaculous.js"></script>
        <script type="text/javascript" src="scripts.js"></script>
        <link type="text/css" rel="stylesheet" href="styles.css" />
    </head>
    <body>
        <div id="status-container">
            Status:
            <span id="status">(nothing to report)</span>
        </div>
```

```
    <div id="content">
        <h1>Manage items order</h1>

        <div id="container">
            (items not yet loaded)
        </div>
    </div>
</body>
</html>
```

In this code we first load the Prototype and Scriptaculous libraries, followed by our own JavaScript file (`scripts.js`). The files must be loaded in this order, as Scriptaculous relies on Prototype, and our script relies on both. Then the external CSS file is loaded.

Next, we include a container called #status-container to show a status message. When a new status message is set, it will be displayed inside of #status. The text inside of #status is the default text, meaning that after a new status message is shown, #status will revert back to this text.

We then define a div called #content. This is only used because of how we will style #status-container. Inside of this is a div called #container—this is where the sortable list will appear. Note that we could define the <ul></ul> tag here, and then add elements to it later, but instead of doing that I've included a message saying the items aren't yet loaded. This message will be replaced by the list after it is loaded.

That is all that is required in this file. If you're wondering how the script is initiated, we will actually define the onload event inside of `scripts.js`; after everything is loaded, the list will be fetched using Ajax.

■Note This file could just as easily be called `index.html` as it doesn't contain any PHP code; however, I like to keep all files consistently named, rather than have a mix of `.php` and `.html` files.

Styling the Application: styles.css

Now let's look at the CSS file for our application, `styles.css`. Listing 5-9 shows the code for this file. It should be stored in the same directory as the `index.php` file.

Listing 5-9. *The CSS Code Used to Style the Example Application (styles.css)*

```css
body {
    margin : 0;
    font-family : sans-serif;
    font-size : 12px;
}

ul.sortable {
    list-style-type : none; width : 300px; margin : 0; padding : 0;
}
```

```
ul.sortable li {
    margin : 2px; padding : 5px; background : #eee; cursor : move;
}

#status-container {
    color : #333; background : #f7f7f7; font-weight : bold; font-size : 11px;
    border-bottom : 1px solid #666; padding : 3px;
}

#status {
    font-weight : normal;
}

#content {
    margin : 10px;
}
```

The main things to be aware of in this file are the `ul.sortable` and `ul.sortable li` selectors. These give the list items the look and feel of items that can be moved. We also change the mouse pointer to `move` to indicate that the elements can be dragged when the cursor is above them.

Creating and Populating the Database: schema.sql

As mentioned previously, we will be using a MySQL database in this example to store the list items. The database is called `ch05_example`. Assuming you already have permissions set up correctly in your MySQL server, use the following query to create your database:

```
mysql> create database ch05_example;
```

You may need to grant the correct permissions so that the database can be accessed. To use the same username and password as we used in Chapter 2, you can use the following command:

```
mysql> grant all on ch05_example.* to phpweb20@localhost identified by 'myPassword';
```

You can then populate this database using the SQL queries inside `schema.sql`, as shown in Listing 5-10.

Listing 5-10. *The SQL Queries Used to Populate the Database (schema.sql)*

```
create table items (
    item_id     serial       not null,
    title       varchar(255)  not null,
    ranking     int,

    primary key (item_id)
);

insert into items (title) values ('Bicycle');
```

```
insert into items (title) values ('Car');
insert into items (title) values ('Chair');
insert into items (title) values ('Door');
insert into items (title) values ('House');
insert into items (title) values ('Table');
insert into items (title) values ('Window');
```

■**Note** The SQL code in `schema.sql` will also work just fine in PostgreSQL (although the commands to create the database and user will be different).

You can either paste these commands directly into the MySQL console, or you could run the following command (from the Linux or Windows command prompt):

```
$ mysql -u phpweb20 -p ch05_example < schema.sql
```

In the preceding table schema, the `ranking` column is used to store the order of the list items. This is the value that is manipulated by clicking and dragging items using the Scriptaculous `Sortable` class.

■**Note** At this stage we aren't storing any value for the `ranking` column. This will only be saved when the list order is updated. In the PHP code, you will see that if two or more rows have the same `ranking` value, they will then be sorted alphabetically.

Managing the List Items on the Server Side: items.php

We must now write the server-side code required to manage the list items. Essentially, we need a function to load the list of items, and another to save the order of the list. (We will look at how these functions are utilized shortly.)

In addition to these two functions, we also need to include a basic wrapper function to connect to the database. In larger applications you would typically use some kind of database abstraction (such as the `Zend_Db` class we integrated in Chapter 2).

All of the code in this section belongs in the `items.php` file.

Connecting to the Database

Listing 5-11 shows the code used to connect to the MySQL database.

Listing 5-11. *The dbConnect() Function, Which Connects to a MySQL Database Called ch05_example (items.php)*

```
<?php
    function dbConnect()
    {
```

```php
$link = mysql_connect('localhost', 'phpweb20', 'myPassword');
if (!$link)
    return false;

if (!mysql_select_db('ch05_example')) {
    mysql_close($link);
    return false;
}

return true;
}
```

If the connection cannot be made (either to the server, or to the database after connecting to the server) then `false` is returned; otherwise `true` is returned. Since selecting the database in MySQL is a separate step from connecting to the server, we include a call to close the connection if the database cannot be selected.

Retrieving the List Items

The `getItems()` function returns an array of all the items in the list. Items are returned in an associative array, with the item ID as the key and the item title as the array value. Listing 5-12 shows the code for `getItems()`.

Listing 5-12. *The getItems() Function, Which Returns an Associative Array of the Rows from the Table Items (items.php)*

```php
function getItems()
{
    $query = 'select item_id, title from items order by ranking, lower(title)';
    $result = mysql_query($query);

    $items = array();
    while ($row = mysql_fetch_object($result)) {
        $items[$row->item_id] = $row->title;
    }

    return $items;
}
```

In this function, we sort the list by each item's `ranking` value. This is the value that is updated when the list order is changed. Initially, there is no `ranking` value for items, so we use the `title` column as the secondary ordering field.

Processing and Saving the List Order

Finally, we must save the new list order to the database after a user drags a list item to a new location. In the `processItemsOrder()` function, we retrieve the new order from the post data (using PHP's `$_POST` superglobal), and then update the database. If this action fails, `false` is returned; this will occur if the new ordering data isn't found in `$_POST`. If the new list order is saved, `true` is returned.

Listing 5-13 shows the processItemsOrder() function.

Listing 5-13. *The processItemsOrder() Function, Which Takes the New List Order from the Post Data and Saves It to the Database (items.php)*

```php
function processItemsOrder($key)
{
    if (!isset($_POST[$key]) || !is_array($_POST[$key]))
        return false;

    $items = getItems();

    $ranking = 1;
    foreach ($_POST[$key] as $id) {
        if (!array_key_exists($id, $items))
            continue;

        $query = sprintf('update items set ranking = %d where item_id = %d',
                        $ranking,
                        $id);

        mysql_query($query);
        $ranking++;
    }

    return true;
}
?>
```

Processing Ajax Requests on the Server Side: processor.php

In the previous section, we covered the code used to manage the list of items. We will now look at processor.php, the script responsible for handling Ajax requests and interfacing with the functions in items.php.

As mentioned earlier, there are two different Ajax requests to handle. The first is the load action, which returns the list of items as XML. This action is handled by calling the getItems() function, and then looping over the returned items and generating XML based on the data.

The second action is save, which is triggered after the user changes the order of the sortable list. This action results in a call to the processItemsOrder() function we just looked at.

Listing 5-14 shows the contents of the processor.php file.

Listing 5-14. *Loading and Saving Ajax Requests (processor.php)*

```php
<?php
    require_once('items.php');

    if (!dbConnect())
        exit;
```

```php
        $action = isset($_POST['action']) ? $_POST['action'] : '';

    switch ($action) {
        case 'load':
            $items = getItems();
            $xmlItems = array();
            foreach ($items as $id => $title)
                $xmlItems[] = sprintf('<item id="%d" title="%s" />',
                                        $id,
                                        htmlSpecialChars($title));

            $xml = sprintf('<items>%s</items>',
                            join("\n", $xmlItems));

            header('Content-type: text/xml');
            echo $xml;
            exit;

        case 'save':
            echo (int) processItemsOrder('items');
            exit;
    }
?>
```

The first thing we do in this code is include the `items.php` file and call `dbConnect()`. If this function call fails, there's no way the Ajax requests can succeed, so we exit right away. The JavaScript code we will look at in the next section will handle this situation.

We then use a `switch` statement to determine which action to perform, based on the value of the `action` element in the `$_POST` array. This allows for easy expansion if another Ajax request type needs to be added. If the action isn't recognized in the `switch`, nothing happens and the script execution simply ends.

Handling the Load Action

To handle the `load` action, we first retrieve the array of items. We then loop over them and generate XML for the list. We use `htmlSpecialChars()` to escape the data so that valid XML is produced. Technically speaking, this wouldn't be sufficient in all cases, but for this example it will suffice.

The resulting XML will look like the following:

```xml
<items>
    <item id="1" title="Bicycle" />
    <item id="2" title="Car" />
    <item id="3" title="Chair" />
    <item id="4" title="Door" />
    <item id="5" title="House" />
    <item id="6" title="Table" />
    <item id="7" title="Window" />
</items>
```

Finally, we send this XML data. To tell the requester what kind of data is being returned, the `content-type` header is sent with `text/xml` as its value.

Handling the Save Action

All processing for the `save` action is taken care of by the `processItemsOrder()` function, so it is relatively simple to handle this request. The `items` value is passed as the first argument, as this corresponds to the value in the post data holding the item order.

The `processItemsOrder()` function returns `true` if the list order was successfully updated. To indicate this to the JavaScript, we return `1` for success. Any other value will be treated as failure. As such, we can simply cast the return value of `processItemsOrder()` using `(int)` to return a `1` on success.

Creating the Client-Side Application Logic: scripts.js

We will now look at the JavaScript code used to make and handle all Ajax requests, including loading the items list initially, making it sortable with Scriptaculous, and handling any changes in the order of the list. All the code listed in this section is from the `scripts.js` file in this chapter's source code.

Application Settings

We first define a few settings that are used in multiple areas. Using a hash to store options at the start of the script makes altering code behavior very simple. Listing 5-15 shows the hash used to store settings.

Listing 5-15. *The JavaScript Hash That Stores Application Settings (scripts.js)*

```
var settings = {
    containerId         : 'container',
    statusId            : 'status',
    processUrl          : 'processor.php',
    statusSuccessColor  : '#99ff99',
    statusErrorColor    : '#ff9999'
};
```

The `containerId` value specifies the ID of the element that holds the list items (that is, where the `<ul></ul>` of list items will go). The `statusId` value specifies the element where status messages will appear.

The value for `processUrl` is the URL where Ajax requests are sent. `statusSuccessColor` is the color used to highlight the status box when an Ajax request is successful, while `statusErrorColor` is used when an Ajax request fails.

Initializing the Application with init()

To begin this simple Ajax application, we call the `init()` function. Listing 5-16 shows the code for `init()`.

Listing 5-16. *The init() Function, Which Begins this Example Ajax Application (scripts.js)*

```
function init()
{
    $(settings.statusId).defaultContent = $(settings.statusId).innerHTML;
    loadItems();
}
```

You might find the first line of this function to be slightly confusing. Essentially, what it does is save the initial content from the status container in a new property called defaultContent (remember that in index.php we had the string (nothing to report) in the status container). This allows us to change the contents of the status container back to this value after showing a new status message.

Next, we call the loadItems() function, which fetches the list of items from the server and displays them to the user. We will look at this function shortly.

In order to call this function, we use the onload event. Using Prototype's Event.observe() method, we set the init() function to run once the page has finished loading. This is shown in Listing 5-17.

Listing 5-17. *Setting init() to Run once the Page Finishes Loading—Triggered by the window.onload Event (scripts.js)*

```
Event.observe(window, 'load', init);
```

■Note As we saw earlier in this chapter, using Event.observe() to handle the page onload event is preferred over using <body onload= "init()">.

Updating the Status Container with setStatus()

Before we go over the main function calls in this example, we will look at the setStatus() utility function. This function is used to update the status message, and it uses Scriptaculous to highlight the status box (with green for success, or red for error).

Listing 5-18 shows the code for setStatus(). The first argument to this function specifies the text to appear in the status box. Note that there is also an optional second argument that indicates whether or not an error occurred. If setStatus() is called with this second argument (with a value of true), the message is treated as though it occurred as a result of an error. Essentially, this means the status box will be highlighted with red.

Listing 5-18. *The setStatus() Function, Which Displays a Status Message to the User (scripts.js)*

```
function setStatus(msg)
{
    var isError = typeof arguments[1] == 'boolean' && arguments[1];
    var status = $(settings.statusId);

    var options = {
```

```
            startcolor  : isError ?
                                settings.statusErrorColor :
                                settings.statusSuccessColor,
            afterFinish : function() {
                                this.update(this.defaultContent);
                            }.bind(status)
    };

    status.update(msg);
    new Effect.Highlight(status, options);
}
```

The options hash holds the options for the Scriptaculous effect we will be using
(Effect.Highlight). First, we specify the starting color based on whether or not an error
occurred, and then we specify code to run after the effect has completed.

In the init() function, we stored the initial content of the status container in the
defaultContent property. Here we change the status content back to this value after the effect
completes.

Notice that we are making use of bind(), which was explained earlier in this chapter. Even
though we haven't created this code in a class, we can bind a function to an arbitrary element,
allowing us to use this within that function to refer to that element.

Next, we call the Prototype update() method to set the status message. We then create a
new instance of the Effect.Highlight class to begin the highlight effect on the status box.
Once again, because this is a class, it must be instantiated using the new keyword.

Loading the List of Items with loadItems()

The loadItems() function initiates the load Ajax request. This function is somewhat straightforward—it is the onSuccess callback loadItemsSuccess that is more complicated.

Listing 5-19 shows the code for loadItems(), including a call to the setStatus() function
we just covered.

Listing 5-19. *The loadItems() Function, Which Initiates the Load Ajax Request (scripts.js)*

```
function loadItems()
{
    var options = {
        method     : 'post',
        parameters : 'action=load',
        onSuccess  : loadItemsSuccess,
        onFailure  : loadItemsFailure
    };

    setStatus('Loading items');
    new Ajax.Request(settings.processUrl, options);
}
```

In this code, we specify the action=load string as the parameters value. This action value
is used in processor.php to determine which Ajax request to handle.

Handling the Response from the Ajax Request in loadItems()

We will now look at the onSuccess and onFailure callbacks for the Ajax request in the previous section. The onFailure callback is handled by the loadItemsFailure() function shown in Listing 5-20, while the onSuccess callback is handled by the loadItemsSuccess() function shown in Listing 5-21.

Listing 5-20. *The onFailure Callback Handler (scripts.js)*

```
function loadItemsFailure(transport)
{
    setStatus('Error loading items', true);
}
```

In this function, we simply set an error status message by passing true as the second parameter to setStatus().

Listing 5-21. *The onSuccess Callback Handler (scripts.js)*

```
function loadItemsSuccess(transport)
{
    // Find all <item></item> tags in the return XML, then cast it into
    // a Prototype Array
    var xml   = transport.responseXML;
    var items = $A(xml.documentElement.getElementsByTagName('item'));

    // If no items were found there's nothing to do
    if (items.size() == 0) {
        setStatus('No items found', true);
        return;
    }

    // Create an array to hold items in. These will become the <li></li> tags.
    // By storing them in an array, we can pass this array to Builder when
    // creating the surrounding <ul></ul>. This will automatically take care
    // of adding the items to the list
    var listItems = $A();

    // Use Builder to create an <li> element for each item in the list, then
    // add it to the listItems array
    items.each(function(s) {
        var elt = Builder.node('li',
                            { id : 'item_' + s.getAttribute('id') },
                            s.getAttribute('title'));

        listItems.push(elt);
    });

    // Finally, create the surrounding <ul> element, giving it the className
```

```
            // property (for styling purposes), and the 'items' values as an Id (for
            // form processing - Scriptaculous uses this as the form item name).
            // The final parameter is the <li> element we just created
            var list = Builder.node('ul',
                                    { className : 'sortable', id : 'items' },
                                    listItems);

            // Get the item container and clear its content
            var container = $(settings.containerId);
            container.update();

            // Add the <ul> to the empty container
            container.appendChild(list);

            // Finally, make the list into a Sortable list. All we need to pass here
            // is the callback function to use after an item has been dropped in a
            // new position.
            Sortable.create(list, { onUpdate : saveItemOrder.bind(list) });
}
```

The preceding code has been documented inline to show you how it works. The only new things in this code we haven't yet covered are the calls to the Scriptaculous functions `Builder.node()` and `Sortable.create()`.

The following code shows the HTML equivalent of the elements created using the `Builder.node()` function:

```
<ul id="items" class="sortable">
    <li id="item_1">Bicycle</li>
    <li id="item_2">Car</li>
    <li id="item_3">Chair</li>
    <li id="item_4">Door</li>
    <li id="item_5">House</li>
    <li id="item_6">Table</li>
    <li id="item_7">Window</li>
</ul>
```

This list is then made into a sortable list by passing it as the first parameter to `Sortable.create()`. Additionally, the `saveItemOrder()` function is specified as the function to be called after the user moves a list item to a new location. Once again, we use `bind()`, allowing us to use `this` inside of `saveItemOrder()` to refer to the #items list.

Handling a Change to the List Order with saveItemOrder()

A call to the `saveItemOrder()` function will initiate the second Ajax request, save. This function shouldn't be called directly, but only as the callback function on the sortable list, to be triggered after the list order is changed. Listing 5-22 shows the code for `saveItemOrder()`.

Listing 5-22. *The saveItemOrder Callback, Triggered After the Sortable List Order is Changed (scripts.js)*

```
function saveItemOrder()
{
    var options = {
        method     : 'post',
        parameters : 'action=save&' + Sortable.serialize(this),
        onSuccess  : saveItemOrderSuccess,
        onFailure  : saveItemOrderFailure
    };

    new Ajax.Request(settings.processUrl, options);
}
```

In this code, we once again create an options hash to pass to Ajax.Request(). This time, we set the action value inside of parameters to save. Additionally, we use Sortable.serialize() to create appropriate form data for the order of the list. This is the data that is processed in the PHP function processItemsOrder() from items.php.

The value of parameters will look something like the following:

```
action=save&items[]=1&items[]=2&items[]=3&items[]=4&items[]=5&items[]=6&items[]=7
```

Each value for items[] corresponds to a value in the items database table (with the item_ part automatically removed).

Handling the Response from the Ajax Request in saveItemOrder()

Finally, we must handle the onSuccess and onFailure events for the save Ajax request. Listing 5-23 shows the code for the onFailure callback saveItemOrderFailure(), while Listing 5-24 shows the code for the onSuccess callback saveItemOrderSuccess().

Listing 5-23. *The saveItemOrderFailure() Callback, Used for the onFailure Event (scripts.js)*

```
function saveItemOrderFailure(transport)
{
    setStatus('Error saving order', true);
}
```

If saving the order of the list fails, we simply call setStatus() to indicate this, marking the status message as an error by passing true as the second parameter.

Handling the onSuccess event is also fairly straightforward. To determine whether the request was successful, we simply check to see if the response contains 1. If so, the request was successful. Once again we call setStatus() to notify the user. If the request wasn't successful, we call saveItemOrderFailure() to handle the error.

Listing 5-24. *The saveItemOrderSuccess() Callback, Used for the onSuccess Event (scripts.js)*

```
function saveItemOrderSuccess(transport)
{
```

```
    if (transport.responseText != '1')
        return saveItemOrderFailure(transport);

    setStatus('Order saved');
}
```

If you now load the index.php file created in Listing 5-8 in your web browser you will be shown a list of items that you can now drag and drop. When you drop an item to a new location an Ajax request will be performed, updating the order saved in the database.

Summary

As you have seen in this chapter, the Prototype JavaScript library is a very powerful library that provides a lot of useful functionality, as well as making cross-browser scripting simpler. We also looked at the Scriptaculous library and created a simple Ajax application that made use of its highlight effect and sortable control.

In the next chapter, we will build on the HTML code we created in Chapter 2 by using some powerful CSS techniques to style our web application. Once we have the HTML and CSS in place, we can add new functionality that makes use of the JavaScript techniques we have learned in this chapter.

CHAPTER 6

■ ■ ■

Styling the Web Application

At this stage in the development of our Web 2.0 application, we have created some basic templates and a few different forms (for user registration and login), but we haven't applied any customized styling to these forms. In this chapter we are going to start sprucing up our site. In addition to making the forms we have already created look much better, we are also going to put styles and layout in place to help with development in following chapters.

We will be covering a number of topics in this chapter, including the following:

- Adding navigation and search engine optimization elements, such as the document title, page headings, and breadcrumb trails

- Creating a set of generic global styles that can easily be applied throughout all templates (such as forms and headings) using Cascading Style Sheets (CSS)

- Allowing for viewing on devices other than a desktop computer (such as creating a print-only style sheet for "printer-friendly" pages)

- Integrating the HTML and CSS into the existing Smarty templates, and using Smarty templates to easily generate maintainable HTML

- Creating an Ajax-based form validator for the user registration form created in Chapter 4

Adding Page Titles and Breadcrumbs

Visually indicating to users where they are in the structure of a web site is very important for the site's usability, and many web sites overlook this. A user should easily be able to identify where they are and how they got there without having to retrace their steps.

To do this, we must assign a title to every page in our application. Once we have the titles, we can set up a *breadcrumb* system. A breadcrumb trail is a navigational tool that shows users the hierarchy of pages from the home page to where they currently are. Note that this differs from how the web browser's history works—the breadcrumb system essentially shows all of the parent sections the current page is in, not the trail of specific pages the user visited to get to the current page.

A breadcrumb system might look like this:

```
Home > Products > XYZ Widget
```

In this example, the current page would be XYZ Widget, while Home would be hyperlinked to the web site's home page, and Products would link to the appropriate page.

To name the pages, we need to define a title in each action handler of each controller (for example, to add a title to the account login page we will add it to the loginAction() method of the AccountController PHP class). Some titles will be dynamically generated based on the purpose of the action (such as using the headline of a news article as the page title when displaying that article), while others will be static. You could argue about whether the title of a page should be determined by the application logic (that is, in the controller file) or by the display logic (determined by the template). In some special cases titles will need to be determined in the template, but it is important to always define a page title in the controller actions to build up a correct breadcrumb trail. If the page titles were defined within templates, it would be very difficult to construct the breadcrumb trail.

Note In larger web applications, where the target audience includes people not only from your country but also other countries, you need to consider internationalization and localization (also known as i18n and L10n, with the numbers indicating the number of letters between the starting and finishing letters). Internationalization and localization take into account a number of international differences, including languages and formatting of numbers, currencies, and dates. In the case of page titles, you would fetch the appropriate page title for the given language based on the user's settings, rather than hard-coding the title in the PHP code. The Zend_Translate component of the Zend Framework can help with implementation of i18n and L10n.

To implement the title and breadcrumb system, we need to make two changes to the way we create application controllers:

1. We must implement the Breadcrumbs class, which is used to hold each of the breadcrumb steps. The Breadcrumbs object will be assigned to the template, so we can easily output the trail in the header.tpl file.

2. We must build a trail in each controller action with the steps that lead up to the action. The steps (and number of steps) will be different for each action, depending on its specific purpose.

The Breadcrumbs Class

This is a class that simply holds an array of the steps leading up to the current page. Each element of the array has a title and a link associated with it. Listing 6-1 shows the code for Breadcrumbs, which we will store in Breadcrumbs.php in the /var/www/phpweb20/include directory.

Listing 6-1. *Tracking the Trail to the Current Page with the Breadcrumbs Class (Breadcrumbs.php)*

```php
<?php
    class Breadcrumbs
    {
        private $_trail = array();
```

```php
    public function addStep($title, $link = '')
    {
        $this->_trail[] = array('title' => $title,
                                'link'  => $link);
    }

    public function getTrail()
    {
        return $this->_trail;
    }

    public function getTitle()
    {
        if (count($this->_trail) == 0)
            return null;

        return $this->_trail[count($this->_trail) - 1]['title'];
    }
    }
?>
```

This class is very short and straightforward, consisting of just three methods: one to add a step to the breadcrumbs trail (addStep()), one to retrieve the trail (getTrail()), and one to determine the page title using the final step of the trail (getTitle()).

To use Breadcrumbs, we instantiate it in the init() method of the CustomControllerAction class. This makes it available to all classes that extend from this class. Additionally, we will add a link to the web site home page by calling addStep('Home', '/') after we instantiate Breadcrumbs.

■Note This object is freshly created for every action that is dispatched. This means that even if you forward from one action to another in the same request, the breadcrumbs trail is recreated (since the controller object is reinstantiated).

Next, we need to add the postDispatch() function to CustomControllerAction. This function will be executed once a controller action has completed. We will use this function to assign the breadcrumbs trail and the page title to the template, since postDispatch() is called prior to the automatic view renderer displaying the template.

Listing 6-2 shows the updated version of CustomControllerAction.php, which now instantiates Breadcrumbs and assigns it to the template.

Listing 6-2. *Instantiating and Assigning the Breadcrumbs Class (CustomControllerAction.php)*

```php
<?php
    class CustomControllerAction extends Zend_Controller_Action
    {
```

```
    public $db;
    public $breadcrumbs;

    public function init()
    {
        $this->db = Zend_Registry::get('db');

        $this->breadcrumbs = new Breadcrumbs();
        $this->breadcrumbs->addStep('Home', '/');
    }

    // ... other code

    public function postDispatch()
    {
        $this->view->breadcrumbs = $this->breadcrumbs;
        $this->view->title = $this->breadcrumbs->getTitle();
    }
}
?>
```

Note When we add the title of the current page to the trail, we don't need to add its URL, since the user is already on this page and doesn't need to navigate to it.

Generating URLs

Before we go any further, we need to consider how to generate URLs for each step we add to the breadcrumbs. For example, if we wanted to link to the account login page, the URL would be /account/login. In this instance, the controller name is account and the action name is login.

The simplest solution is to hard-code this URL both in the PHP code (when creating the breadcrumbs) and in the template (when creating hyperlinks). However, hard-coding URLs doesn't give you any flexibility to change the format of the URL. For example, if you decide to move your web application to a subdirectory of your server instead of the root directory, all of your hard-coded URLs would be incorrect.

Tip If you did decide to use a subdirectory, you would call $controller->setBaseUrl('/path/to/base') in the index.php bootstrap file. This could then be retrieved by calling $request->getBaseUrl() when inside a controller action, as you will see shortly.

Generating URLs in Controller Actions

We now need to write a function that generates a URL based on the controller and action names passed to it. To help us with URL generation, we will use the Url helper that comes with Zend_Controller. The only thing to be aware of is that this helper will not prefix the generated URL with a slash, or even with the base URL (as mentioned in the preceding tip). Because of this, we must make a slight modification by extending this helper—we will create a new function called getUrl().

Listing 6-3 shows the getUrl() function we will add to CustomControllerAction.php. This code uses the Url helper to generate the URL, and then prepends the base URL and a slash at the start. The other change made in this file modifies the home link that is generated so it calls the new getUrl() function, rather than hard-coding the slash.

Listing 6-3. *Creating a Function to Generate Application URLs (CustomControllerAction.php)*

```php
<?php
    class CustomControllerAction extends Zend_Controller_Action
    {
        // ... other code

        public function init()
        {
            // ... other code

            $this->breadcrumbs->addStep('Home', $this->getUrl(null, 'index'));
        }

        public function getUrl($action = null, $controller = null)
        {
            $url  = rtrim($this->getRequest()->getBaseUrl(), '/') . '/';
            $url .= $this->_helper->url->simple($action, $controller);

            return $url;
        }

        // ... other code
    }
?>
```

■Note The call to rtrim() is included because the base URL may end with a slash, in which case the URL would have // at the end.

Now within each controller action we can call $this->getUrl() directly. For example, if we wanted to generate the URL for the login page, we would call $this->getUrl('login', 'account').

■**Note** This code uses the `simple()` method on the `Url` helper, which is used to generate a URL from an action and a controller. In later chapters we will define custom routes, which means the format of URLs is more complex. This helper also provides a method called `url()`, which is used to generate URLs based on the defined routes.

Generating URLs in Smarty Templates

Before we go any further, we must also cater for URL generation within our templates. To achieve this, we will implement a Smarty plug-in called `geturl`. Doing so will allow us to generate URLs by using {geturl} in templates. For instance, we could generate a URL for the login page like this:

```
{geturl action='login' controller='account'}
```

Additionally, we will allow the user to omit the `controller` argument, meaning that the current controller would be used.

■**Tip** The preceding code is an example of a Smarty function call. The three main types of plug-ins are functions, modifiers, and blocks. Modifiers are functions that are applied to strings that are being output (making a string uppercase with {$myString|upper}, for example) while blocks are used to define output that wraps whatever is between the opening and closing tags (such as {rounded_box} Inner content. {/rounded_box}). In the case of `geturl`, we will use a Smarty *function* in order to perform a specific operation based on the provided arguments; that function isn't being applied to an existing string, so it is not a modifier.

A Smarty plug-in is created by defining a PHP function called smarty_*type_name*(), where type is either function, modifier, or block. In our case, since the plug-in is called geturl, the function is called smarty_function_geturl().

■**Tip** There are other plug-in types available, such as output filters (which modify template output after it has been generated), compiler functions (which change the behavior of the template compiler), pre and post filters (which modify template source prior to or immediately after compilation), and resources (which load templates from a source other than the defined template directory). These could be the subject of their own book, so I can't cover them all here, but this section will at least give you a good idea of how to implement your own function plug-ins.

All plug-ins should be stored in one of the registered Smarty plug-in directories. Smarty comes with its own set of plug-ins, and in Chapter 2 we created our own directory in which to store custom plug-ins (./include/Templater/plugins). The filename of plug-ins follows the format *type*.*name*.php, so in our case the file is named function.geturl.php. Smarty will automatically load the plug-in as soon as we try to access it in a template.

The code for the geturl plug-in is shown in Listing 6-4. It should be written to ./include/Templater/plugins/function.geturl.php.

Listing 6-4. *The Smarty geturl Plug-In That Uses the Zend_Controller URL Helper (function.geturl.php)*

```php
<?php
    function smarty_function_geturl($params, $smarty)
    {
        $action     = isset($params['action']) ? $params['action'] : null;
        $controller = isset($params['controller']) ? $params['controller'] : null;

        $helper = Zend_Controller_Action_HelperBroker::getStaticHelper('url');

        $request = Zend_Controller_Front::getInstance()->getRequest();

        $url  = rtrim($request->getBaseUrl(), '/') . '/';
        $url .= $helper->simple($action, $controller);

        return $url;
    }
?>
```

All function plug-ins in Smarty retrieve an array of parameters as the first argument and the Smarty object as the second argument. The array of parameters is generated using the arguments specified when calling the function. In other words, calling the geturl function using {geturl action='login' controller='account'} will result in the $params array being the same as if you used the following PHP code:

```php
<?php
    $params = array(
        'action'     => 'login',
        'controller' => 'account'
    );
?>
```

The function must do its own initialization and checking of the specified parameters. This is why the code in Listing 6-4 checks for the existence of the action and controller parameters in the first two lines of the function.

Next the Url helper and the current request are retrieved using the provided functions. You will notice that the code we use to generate the actual URL is almost identical to that in the CustomControllerAction class.

Finally, the URL is returned to the template, meaning it is output directly. This allows us to use it inside forms and hyperlinks (such as <form action="{geturl …}">).

■**Tip** The function in Listing 6-4 returns the generated URL so it is output directly to the template. You may prefer to write it to a variable in your template so you can reuse the URL as required. The convention for this in Smarty is to pass an argument called `assign`, whose value is then used as the variable name. For instance, you could call the function using `{geturl action='login' controller='account' assign='myUrl'}`. By including `$smarty->assign($params['assign'], $url)` in the plug-in instead of returning the value, you can then access `$myUrl` from within your template. Typically you would check for the existence of `assign` and output the value normally if it is not specified.

Now, if you need to link to another controller action within a template, you should be using the {geturl} plug-in. This may be a normal hyperlink, or it may be a form action.

■**Note** At this point I make the assumption that existing templates have been updated to use the {geturl} plug-in. Try updating the existing templates for registration, login, and updating details (located in the `./templates/account` directory) that we created in Chapter 4 so the forms and any other links in the page use {geturl}. Alternatively, the downloadable source code for this and remaining chapters will use {geturl} wherever it should.

Setting the Title and Trail for Each Controller Action

We now have the ability to set the page title and breadcrumb trail for all pages in our web application, so we must update the `AccountController` class we created in Chapter 3 to use these features.

First, we want all action handlers in this controller to have a base breadcrumb trail of "Home: Account", with additional steps depending on the action. To add the "Account" breadcrumb step automatically, we will define the `init()` method in this class, which calls the `Breadcrumbs::addStep()` method.

We must also call `parent::init()`, because the `init()` method in `CustomControllerAction` sets up other important data. In fact, this parent method instantiates `Breadcrumbs`, so it must be called before adding the breadcrumbs step.

By automatically adding the "Account" step for all actions in this controller, we are effectively naming the index action for this controller `Account`. This means that in the `indexAction()` function we don't need to set a title, as `Breadcrumbs::getTitle()` will work this out for us automatically.

Listing 6-5 shows the changes we must make to the `AccountController` class to set up the trail for the `register` and `registercomplete` actions. No change is required for the `index` action. Note that we also set the base URL for the controller in the `init()` method and change the redirect URL upon successful registration.

Listing 6-5. *Defining the Page Titles and Trails for the Index and Registration Actions (AccountController.php)*

```php
<?php
```

```php
class AccountController extends CustomControllerAction
{
    public function init()
    {
        parent::init();
        $this->breadcrumbs->addStep('Account', $this->getUrl(null, 'account'));
    }

    public function indexAction()
    {
        // nothing to do here, index.tpl will be displayed
    }

    public function registerAction()
    {
        $request = $this->getRequest();

        $fp = new FormProcessor_UserRegistration($this->db);

        if ($request->isPost()) {
            if ($fp->process($request)) {
                $session = new Zend_Session_Namespace('registration');
                $session->user_id = $fp->user->getId();
                $this->_redirect($this->getUrl('registercomplete'));
            }
        }

        $this->breadcrumbs->addStep('Create an Account');
        $this->view->fp = $fp;
    }

    public function registercompleteAction()
    {
        // ... other code here

        $this->breadcrumbs->addStep('Create an Account',
                                    $this->getUrl('register'));
        $this->breadcrumbs->addStep('Account Created');

        $this->view->user = $user;
    }

    // ... other code here

}
?>
```

■**Note** You can try adding titles to each of the other actions in this controller (although the logout action will not require it), or you can simply download the source for this chapter, which will be fully updated to use the breadcrumbs system.

Because we define the title of the section in the controller's init() method, we typically don't need to define a title in indexAction(), since the title added in init() will be adequate. Next, we specify the title as "Create an Account" in the registerAction() function. This string is added to the trail as well as being assigned to the template as $title (this is done in CustomControllerAction's postDispatch() method, as we saw in Listing 6-2).

Creating a Smarty Plug-In to Output Breadcrumbs

The breadcrumb trail has been assigned to templates as is, meaning that we can call the getTrail() method to return an array of all of the trail steps. The problem with this is that it clutters the template, especially when you consider some of the options that can be used.

Instead, we will create another Smarty plug-in: a function called breadcrumbs. With this function, we will be able to output the trail based on a number of different options. This function is reusable, and you'll be able to use it for other sites you create with Smarty. This should always be a goal when developing code such as this.

Listing 6-6 shows the contents of function.breadcrumbs.php, which is stored in the ./include/Templater/plugins directory. This code basically loops over each step in the breadcrumb trail and generates a hyperlink and a displayable title. Since it is optional for steps to have a link, a title is only generated if no link is included. The same class and file naming conventions apply as in the geturl plug-in discussed previously (in the "Generating URLs in Smarty Templates" section), and as before it is best to initialize all parameters at the beginning of the function.

Listing 6-6. *A Custom Smarty Plug-In Used to Output the Breadcrumb Trail (function.breadcrumbs.php)*

```php
<?php
    function smarty_function_breadcrumbs($params, $smarty)
    {
        $defaultParams = array('trail'     => array(),
                               'separator' => ' &gt; ',
                               'truncate'  => 40);

        // initialize the parameters
        foreach ($defaultParams as $k => $v) {
            if (!isset($params[$k]))
                $params[$k] = $v;
        }

        // load the truncate modifier
        if ($params['truncate'] > 0)
```

```
        require_once $smarty->_get_plugin_filepath('modifier', 'truncate');


    $links = array();
    $numSteps = count($params['trail']);
    for ($i = 0; $i < $numSteps; $i++) {
        $step = $params['trail'][$i];

        // truncate the title if required
        if ($params['truncate'] > 0)
            $step['title'] = smarty_modifier_truncate($step['title'],
                                              $params['truncate']);

        // build the link if it's set and isn't the last step
        if (strlen($step['link']) > 0 && $i < $numSteps - 1) {
            $links[] = sprintf('<a href="%s" title="%s">%s</a>',
                            htmlSpecialChars($step['link']),
                            htmlSpecialChars($step['title']),
                            htmlSpecialChars($step['title']));
        }
        else {
            // either the link isn't set, or it's the last step
            $links[] = htmlSpecialChars($step['title']);
        }
    }

    // join the links using the specified separator
    return join($params['separator'], $links);
    }
?>
```

After the array of links has been built in this function, we create a single string to be returned by joining on the separator option. The default value for the separator is >, which we preescape. It is preescaped because some characters you might prefer to use aren't typable, so you can specify the preescaped version when calling the plug-in. An example of this is the » symbol, which we can use by calling {breadcrumbs separator=' » '}.

When we generate the displayable title for each link, we make use of the Smarty truncate modifier. This allows us to restrict the total length of each breadcrumb link by specifying the maximum number of characters in a given string. If the string is longer than that number, it is chopped off at the end of the previous word and "..." is appended. For instance, if you were to truncate "The Quick Brown Fox Jumped over the Lazy Dog" to 13 characters, it would become "The Quick...". This is an improvement over the PHP substr() function, since substr() will simply perform a hard break in the middle of a word (so the example string would become "The Quick Bro").

■Tip In a Smarty template, you would use {$string|truncate}, but we can use the truncate modifier directly in our PHP code by first loading the modifier (using $smarty->_get_plugin_filepath() to retrieve the full path of the plug-in and then passing the plug-in type and name as the arguments) and then calling smarty_modifier_truncate() on the string.

The final thing to note in this function is that the URLs and titles are escaped as required when adding elements to the $links array. This ensures that valid HTML is generated and also prevents cross-site scripting (XSS) and cross-site request forgery (CSRF). This is explained in more detail in Chapter 7.

Displaying the Page Title

The final step is to display the title and breadcrumbs in the site templates, and to update the links to use the geturl plug-in. Listing 6-7 shows the changes to be made to header.tpl, where we now display the page title within the <title> tag as well as within an <h1> tag. Additionally, we use the new {breadcrumbs} plug-in to easily output the breadcrumb trail.

Listing 6-7. *Outputting the Title and Breadcrumbs in the Header Template (header.tpl)*

```
<!DOCTYPE html
    PUBLIC "-//W3C//DTD XHTML 1.0 Strict//EN"
    "http://www.w3.org/TR/xhtml1/DTD/xhtml1-strict.dtd">
<html xmlns="http://www.w3.org/1999/xhtml" lang="en" xml:lang="en">
    <head>
        <title>{$title|escape}</title>
        <meta http-equiv="Content-Type" content="text/html; charset=iso-8859-1" />
    </head>
    <body>
        <div>
            <a href="{geturl controller='index'}">Home</a>
            {if $authenticated}
                | <a href="{geturl controller='account'}">Your Account</a>
                | <a href="{geturl controller='account'
                            action='details'}">Update Your Details</a>
                | <a href="{geturl controller='account'
                            action='logout'}">Logout</a>
            {else}
                | <a href="{geturl controller='account'
                            action='register'}">Register</a>
                | <a href="{geturl controller='account'}">Login</a>
            {/if}

            <hr />

            {breadcrumbs trail=$breadcrumbs->getTrail()}
```

```
{if $authenticated}
    <hr />
    <div>
        Logged in as
        {$identity->first_name|escape} {$identity->last_name|escape}
        (<a href="{geturl controller='account'
                          action='logout'}">logout</a>)
    </div>
{/if}

<hr />

<h1>{$title|escape}</h1>
```

Figure 6-1 shows the page, now that it includes the page title and breadcrumbs.

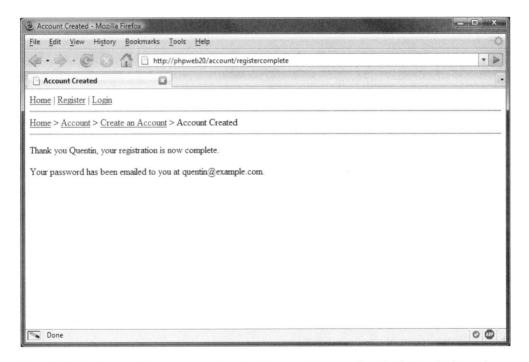

Figure 6-1. *The Account Created page, showing the page title as well as the full trail of how the page was reached*

Integrating the Design into the Application

We are now at the stage where we can create the application layout by using a more formal design in the header and footer templates and styling it using Cascading Style Sheets (CSS). In this section, we will first determine which elements we want to include on pages, and then create a static HTML file (allowing us to see a single complete page), which we will break up into various parts that can be integrated into the site templates.

Creating the Static HTML

Figure 6-2 shows the design we will use for the web application (including CSS, which we will integrate in the next section), as viewed in Firefox. The layout developed in this chapter has been tested with Firefox 2, Internet Explorer 6 and 7, and Safari.

■**Note** It is worth mentioning here that this book is devoted to the development side of web applications, not the design side. As such, the look and feel we use for the web application will be straightforward in comparison to what a professional web designer would come up with. Hopefully, though, the techniques here can help you in marking up a professional design into HTML and CSS.

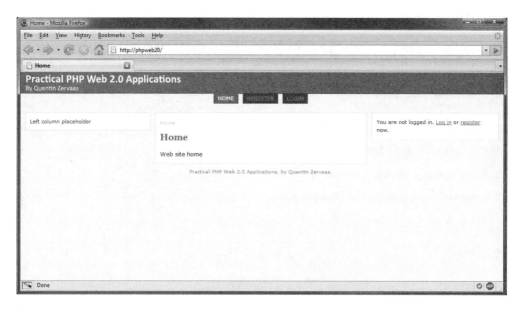

Figure 6-2. *The web page design we will use for the web application: a cross-browser, fluid, table-free layout*

The key elements of this layout include:

- Three columns with a fluid middle column and fixed-size left and right columns

- No tables to set the columns

- A header area (for a logo), which can also be expanded to include other elements (such as advertising)

- A tabbed navigation system that allows users to see which section of the site they are in

- A breadcrumb trail and page title

It is actually somewhat difficult to get a multiple-column layout with a single fluid central column without using tables. This cross-browser solution is adapted from Matthew Levine's Holy Grail technique from "A List Apart" (http://www.alistapart.com/articles/holygrail).

The following HTML code shows the basic structure of how our main site template will be structured. We will integrate this into our templates shortly.

```html
<html>
    <head>
    </head>
    <body>
        <div id="header">
        </div>

        <div id="nav">
        </div>

        <div id="content-container" class="column">
        </div>

        <div id="left-container" class="column">
        </div>

        <div id="right-container" class="column">
        </div>

        <div id="footer">
        </div>
    </body>
</html>
```

As you can see in this HTML code, the center column (#content-container) appears before the other columns. This helps with search engine optimization, as the core page content is earlier in the file, and is therefore treated as being of greater priority in the document.

■**Note** Placing the center column first is also an accessibility feature, since users who rely on screen readers will reach the relevant content sooner.

The preceding code simply demonstrates at the most basic level how the elements of the page piece together. Let's now take a look at the full markup before we integrate it into the templates. Listing 6-8 shows the HTML code that we will be splitting up for use in the templates. We must also include calls to the Smarty plug-ins we created in order to generate links and for displaying breadcrumbs. For now though, we just include placeholders for these, which we will replace with Smarty code in Listing 6-9.

Note If you're anything like me—a programmer rather than a designer—it can be useful to see a site design statically before it is integrated into the application. Typically when I build a new web site or web application, I work from either prebuilt HTML templates such as this or from a Photoshop design which I then convert into static HTML with corresponding CSS.

Listing 6-8. *The Complete HTML Code Used in Figure 6-2 (listing-6.8.html)*

```html
<!DOCTYPE html
    PUBLIC "-//W3C//DTD XHTML 1.0 Strict//EN"
    "http://www.w3.org/TR/xhtml1/DTD/xhtml1-strict.dtd">

<html xmlns="http://www.w3.org/1999/xhtml" lang="en" xml:lang="en">
    <head>
        <title>Sample HTML Layout</title>
        <meta http-equiv="Content-Type" content="text/html; charset=iso-8859-1" />
        <link rel="stylesheet" href="/css/styles.css" type="text/css" media="all" />
    </head>
    <body>
        <div id="header">
        </div>

        <div id="nav">
            <ul>
                <li class="active"><a href="#">Home</a></li>
                <li><a href="#">Menu Item 1</a></li>
                <li><a href="#">Menu Item 2</a></li>
                <li><a href="#">Menu Item 3</a></li>
            </ul>
        </div>

        <div id="content-container" class="column">
            <div id="content">

                <div id="breadcrumbs">
                    <a href="#" title="Home">Home</a> &raquo;
                    Sample HTML Layout
                </div>

                <h1>Sample HTML Layout</h1>

                <p>
                    Center column
                </p>
            </div>
        </div>
```

```
        <div id="left-container" class="column">
            <div class="box">
                Left column box 1
            </div>

            <div class="box">
                Left column box 2
            </div>
        </div>

        <div id="right-container" class="column">
            <div class="box">
                Right column box
            </div>
        </div>

        <div id="footer">
            Practical Web 2.0 Application Development With PHP, by Quentin Zervaas.
        </div>
    </body>
</html>
```

In this code, we first create the #header block, which is left empty. We will display the logo in this block by using a CSS background image. Of course, you could choose to include the logo here using an <img> tag—I have left it blank here because we will be using this block to include a "print-only" logo (which we will cover in the "Creating a Print-Only Style Sheet" section in this chapter).

Next, we use an unordered list (<ul>) to display the web site navigation. You could argue that this list is in fact in order, so the <ol> tag may be used instead. In any case, the correct semantics involve using an HTML list.

Tip Using an unordered (or ordered) list lends itself to scalability very well. For example, if you were using JavaScript and CSS to build a drop-down navigation system (one that expands the navigation on mouseover), using nested <ul> tags would work perfectly. Additionally, if the user's web browser doesn't render a JavaScript menu solution, they could easily navigate the site because the links would be structured for them.

After defining the main content area, we populate the left and right columns. The content that appears in these columns will be split up into separate boxes, so we give the divs within these columns a class of .box to easily define that structure. We will define this style shortly in the style sheet.

Let's now take a look at how this markup is rendered in Firefox with no styles defined. Figure 6-3 demonstrates how everything gets rendered from top to bottom exactly as it is defined in the HTML. Additionally, you can see how the navigation is displayed horizontally, which we will also fix in the CSS.

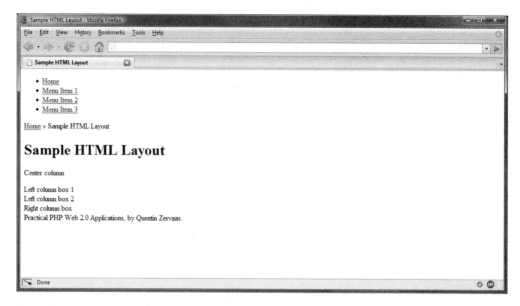

Figure 6-3. *The web page design we will use for the web application before it has had styles applied to it*

Moving the HTML Markup into Smarty Templates

The next step in styling our web application is to integrate the HTML from Listing 6-8 into our existing templates. This primarily involves modifying the `header.tpl` and `footer.tpl` files, but there are also some minor changes that need to be made to other templates.

In this section, we will go over all of the changes required to integrate this design. The steps are as follows:

- Copy the top half of the HTML file into `header.tpl`.

- Copy the bottom half of the HTML file into `footer.tpl`.

- Keep the dynamic variables in place in the header (namely the browser title, page title, and breadcrumbs).

- Highlight the active section in the navigation based on a variable passed in from the action templates, and modify the action templates to tell `header.tpl` which section to highlight in the navigation.

Note The "top half" of the design referred to in the preceding list is all markup prior to the content for the body of each controller action, while the "bottom half" is all markup after the end of the controller action content. In Listing 6-8, the top half is all code from the start of the file until the breadcrumbs (including the breadcrumbs). Everything else inside the #content element will be defined in each action's template.

One other thing to note is that we don't yet have content to place in either of the side columns, so we will use the right column to display the details of the currently logged-in user, and we will simply leave a place marker in the left column until these columns are populated.

If you haven't done so already, copy the `logo.gif` and `logo-print.gif` files into the `images` directory from the book's source code. We will create the `styles.css` file that is loaded in the header later in this chapter.

Modifying header.tpl

To make the necessary changes to `header.tpl`, we can just copy some of the HTML in Listing 6-8 into this file—from the beginning of the listing down to where the page heading is displayed. We then include the calls to {breadcrumbs} and {geturl} where appropriate.

Listing 6-9 shows the new version of `header.tpl` (in the `./templates` directory). This version loads the external style sheet and uses variables for the breadcrumbs and title unlike the static values in Listing 6-8. This code should replace the code previously in the `header.tpl` file.

Listing 6-9. *Integrating the Design into the Header Template (header.tpl)*

```
<!DOCTYPE html
    PUBLIC "-//W3C//DTD XHTML 1.0 Strict//EN"
    "http://www.w3.org/TR/xhtml1/DTD/xhtml1-strict.dtd">

<html xmlns="http://www.w3.org/1999/xhtml" lang="en" xml:lang="en">
  <head>
    <title>{$title|escape}</title>
    <meta http-equiv="Content-Type" content="text/html; charset=iso-8859-1" />
    <link rel="stylesheet" href="/css/styles.css" type="text/css" media="all" />
  </head>
  <body>
    <div id="header">
    </div>

    <div id="nav">
      <ul>
        <li{if $section == 'home'} class="active"{/if}>
            <a href="{geturl controller='index'}">Home</a>
        </li>
      {if $authenticated}
        <li{if $section == 'account'} class="active"{/if}>
          <a href="{geturl controller='account'}">Your Account</a>
        </li>
        <li><a href="{geturl controller='account' action='logout'}">Logout</a></li>
      {else}
        <li{if $section == 'register'} class="active"{/if}>
          <a href="{geturl controller='account' action='register'}">Register</a>
        </li>
        <li{if $section == 'login'} class="active"{/if}>
          <a href="{geturl controller='account' action='login' }">Login</a>
```

```
      </li>
    {/if}
    </ul>
</div>

<div id="content-container" class="column">
    <div id="content">
        <div id="breadcrumbs">
            {breadcrumbs trail=$breadcrumbs->getTrail() separator=' &raquo; '}
        </div>

        <h1>{$title|escape}</h1>
```

There are a few things to notice in this template:

- The site navigation has been modified so the geturl plug-in is used to generate the links, while the "Update Details" link has been removed (we will include this in the right column in footer.tpl).

- The value of the $section variable is checked to determine which navigation item should be highlighted. To highlight the item, the CSS class .active is applied. We must define the $section variable when we load the header.tpl template.

- The breadcrumbs separator is specified as » (which has the entity name ») for a slightly fancier look. Spaces must also be included on either side of this character.

- The "Logged in as…" information is removed. This will also move to the right column (in footer.tpl).

- We no longer bother to check the $section variable for the logout link because after logging out a user is directed right back to the login page.

Modifying footer.tpl

In order to finish integrating this template, we must add the corresponding section of markup from Listing 6-8 to the site footer. Listing 6-10 shows the code that will replace the code in the footer.tpl file (in the ./templates directory). Note that this code includes details about the currently logged-in user in a box in the right column, and it includes a link to "Update details".

Listing 6-10. *Integrating the Design into the Site Footer (footer.tpl)*

```
      </div>
</div>

<div id="left-container" class="column">
  <div class="box">
    Left column placeholder
  </div>
</div>
```

```
    <div id="right-container" class="column">
      <div class="box">
      {if $authenticated}
        Logged in as
        {$identity->first_name|escape} {$identity->last_name|escape}
        (<a href="{geturl controller='account' action='logout'}">logout</a>).
        <a href="{geturl controller='account' action='details'}">Update details</a>.
      {else}
        You are not logged in.
        <a href="{geturl controller='account' action='login'}">Log in</a> or
        <a href="{geturl controller='account' action='register'}">register</a> now.
      {/if}
      </div>
    </div>

    <div id="footer">
      Practical PHP Web 2.0 Applications, by Quentin Zervaas.
    </div>
  </body>
</html>
```

■Tip If you haven't yet tried, you should be able to validate the generated markup with no warnings or errors using the W3C validator at `http://validator.w3.org`. In fact, you could have done so prior to this chapter, as we are developing standards-compliant code. It is important when developing your CSS and templates to check the validity of both your HTML/XHTML and your CSS (using `http://jigsaw.w3.org/css-validator`), as it is easy to accidentally put something in your code that breaks the validation. Chris Pederick's Web Developer toolbar for Firefox (`http://chrispederick.com/work/web-developer`) has quick-access links to validate HTML and CSS code.

Highlighting the Active Navigation Section

The new `header.tpl` in Listing 6-9 includes code to check the value of the `$section` variable to determine which section to highlight. We must now update each of the controller action templates so each one defines the `$section` variable. This is done when including the header template.

For example, to highlight the "Home" link, the following code would be used to include `header.tpl`:

```
{include file='header.tpl' section='home'}
```

Note that we don't use $ in front of `section` when using a variable name as the attribute value in Smarty, but we do use it when referring to the variable in `header.tpl`.

Listing 6-11 shows the updated version of `index.tpl`, which now highlights the corresponding entry in the main navigation. Note that there may be situations where no item is selected.

Listing 6-11. *Highlighting the "Home" Link in the Header Template (index.tpl)*

```
{include file='header.tpl' section='home'}

Web site home

{include file='footer.tpl'}
```

■**Note** Try updating each of the other controller action templates so the correct section is highlighted. You can check what the value needs to be by checking the `header.tpl` file. Specifically, you will need to update each of the files in the `./templates/account` directory to use `{include file='header.tpl' section='account'}` rather than `{include file='header.tpl'}`. This is fairly simple to test, since you only need to visit each page and check that the navigation is highlighted properly. Alternatively, you can download the source code for this chapter.

Constructing the CSS

Now that we've integrated the HTML markup into our Smarty templates, we can incorporate the CSS so the page displays nicely as the three-column layout we discussed. All styles will be stored in a file called `styles.css`, which will reside in the `css` directory of the web site (`/var/www/phpweb20/htdocs/css`).

■**Note** There's no particular reason for choosing this directory, other than that it keeps the files organized. You may find that an internal section of your web site may require its own CSS file—for example, it might require a large number of custom styles that you don't want to include in the main site's CSS file (why slow down the loading of the home page with extra styles that aren't required?). Creating a separate directory for your CSS files will help you keep the files organized, just as you might organize images.

Specifying Media Types and Loading the CSS File

Later in this chapter we will look at creating a print-only style sheet, so we must keep in mind that we need to provide styles for different media types. There are two different ways of telling the browser which media type is being used: the `@media` rule and the `media` attribute (used when loading the CSS file with a `<link>` tag). For our application, we will use the `@media` CSS rule, but we will look at them both here first.

■**Note** I'm not necessarily advocating using `@media` over loading a separate style sheet with `<link>`; however, using `@media` is my personal preference in most cases, since it means fewer files are loaded when a user visits the site, reducing page-load time and server overhead.

To load separate style sheets for the screen and for printing, you could use the following HTML code:

```
<link rel="stylesheet" href="screen.css" type="text/css" media="screen" />
<link rel="stylesheet" href="print.css" type="text/css" media="print" />
```

Alternatively, if you wanted to use the @media rule, you could load a single style sheet and separate the media types within that file. First, you would load the file specifying media="all" so this style sheet would be used regardless of what type of device is viewing the page:

```
<link rel="stylesheet" href="styles.css" type="text/css" media="all" />
```

Next, you would use the @media rule to separate the media types. Within styles.css, you would use the following:

```
.some-css-item { color : #000; }

@media screen {
    .some-css-item { color : #f00; }
}

@media print {
    .some-css-item { color : #00f; }
}
```

In this example, the global styles for .some-css-item would use the color black, while red (#f00) would be used for screen, and blue (#00f) would be used when printing.

Other media types you might use include aural (for screen-reading software) and hand-held (for handheld devices, such as a phone with a small screen and limited capabilities).

Tip According to the Apple Developer Connection web site at http://developer.apple.com/iphone /designingcontent.html, you can specify a style sheet specifically for the Apple iPhone by using the only keyword in combination with the screen media type. Other devices will ignore the only keyword and therefore not use the style sheet. For example, to load the iphone.css file only for people viewing on an iPhone you can use <link rel="stylesheet" href="iphone.css" type="text/css" media="only screen and (max-device-width: 480px)" />.

Creating the Application CSS

The next step is to create the first CSS code in our web application. In this section I will briefly describe the custom CSS that is used. The Holy Grail technique mentioned earlier is explained by Matthew Levine at http://www.alistapart.com/articles/holygrail. The entire CSS file is listed at the end of this section so you can see how it all fits together.

Creating the Three-Column Layout

Since the Holy Grail article describes how the fluid three-column layout works, I will not describe those techniques here. The important thing to note is that we are setting both of the side columns to be 300 pixels wide. If you want to use a different size, you will need to modify the values in the code accordingly.

```
body { margin : 0; padding : 0 300px; min-width : 600px; }


#header, #footer, #nav { margin : 0 -300px 0 -300px; }


.column            { float : left; position : relative; }
#content-container { width : 100%;  padding : 0; }
#left-container    { width : 300px; margin-left : -100%; right : 300px; }
#right-container   { width : 300px; margin-right : -300px; }


#footer { clear : both; }


* html #left-container { left : 300px; }
```

If you were to view the HTML code from Listing 6-8 using only the preceding CSS, the display in Firefox would be similar to the screen in Figure 6-4. The bottom half of this figure shows the Firebug console as it integrates into Firefox.

■**Tip** Firebug is arguably the most powerful web development plug-in available for Firefox. While the Web Developer toolbar has been around for longer and is also very useful, the CSS and DOM inspection capabilities, as well as the ability to debug subrequests made with XMLHttpRequest, make it a must-have plug-in. You can download Firebug from http://www.getfirebug.com.

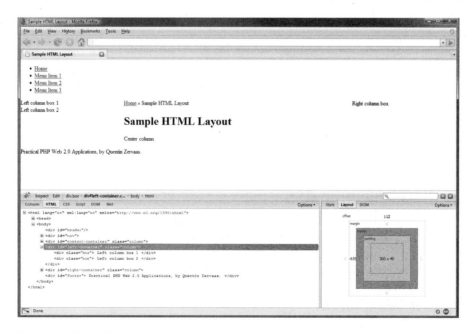

Figure 6-4. *Using Firebug to see the layout properties of the three-column layout*

Styling the Page Header

In Figure 6-2, there was a logo displayed in a header block that hasn't appeared in subsequent figures. To include this logo, we must set the background to use an image in the CSS. This allows us to include other code in #header as we need. For instance, when we implement printer-friendly styles later in this chapter, we will include a printer-friendly logo in this area, since CSS backgrounds typically aren't included when people print web pages.

Here is the code used to style the #header div:

```
#header {
    background    : url(../images/logo.gif) no-repeat 5px center #f22;
    height        : 45px;
    border-bottom : 1px solid #922;
}
```

We first set the background properties. The path used in url() is relative to the CSS file, not to the HTML document that loads the CSS file. By using no-repeat, we tell the browser to include the background image only once. The image is also positioned 5 pixels from the left of the div and centered vertically. Finally, the background color is set to a shade of red (to match the background color of logo.gif).

Next, we set the height of the div to 45 pixels, which is slightly taller than the image. Since #header is empty, we must give it a height so the browser will make it big enough for the background image to appear.

Finally, we add a dark red border to the bottom of the div. We will also be using this color when we join the navigation to the header.

Styling the Tabbed Navigation Bar

The navigation bar consists of horizontal tabs created as an unordered list. In order to make the unordered list horizontal, we set the display property of list items (<li>) to be inline. Additionally, we need to consider browser defaults for unordered lists: Internet Explorer uses a margin, and Firefox uses padding on the left of each element. We remove this by setting both the padding and margin to 0. Additionally, each list item will display a bullet point, which we can remove by using list-style : none.

■**Tip** A useful way to deal with browsers that have different default styles is to use a "reset" style sheet. This is an extra style sheet that you load in your pages to give all elements the same style across all browsers (where relevant). The Yahoo Developer Network provides a reset style sheet that you can use (http://developer.yahoo.com/yui/reset), although Eric Meyer has developed his own, which he based on Yahoo's. You can find his latest reset style sheet at http://meyerweb.com/eric/thoughts/2007/05/01/reset-reloaded, or his original article at http://meyerweb.com/eric/thoughts/2007/04/12/reset-styles. One thing to be aware of is that using an extra style sheet may result in extra page-load time. You may prefer to just include your own reset styles as you need them to keep your CSS file smaller.

The following code styles the navigation bar. This code defines not only the layout of the navigation (making the list horizontal), but also the style of links in the navigation. The .active class highlights the navigation item that represents the section of the user's current page. We use this style when we check for the $section variable in header.tpl.

```
#nav {
    margin-top      : -1px;
    margin-bottom   : 20px;
    font-size       : 0.9em;
    text-transform  : uppercase;
}

#nav ul {
    margin     : 0;
    padding    : 4px 0;
    text-align : center;
}

#nav li {
    list-style      : none;
    padding         : 0;
    margin          : 0;
    display         : inline;
}

#nav a {
    background      : #922;
    color           : #aaa;
    text-decoration : none;
    padding         : 4px 8px;
    text-align      : center;
    border          : 1px solid #922;
    border-top      : none;
    margin          : 0 3px;
}

#nav a:hover {
    color           : #fff;
    text-decoration : underline;
}

#nav li.active a {
    color       : #fff;
    background  : #f22;
    font-weight : bold;
}
```

Setting the Global Styles

In addition to setting styles for specific containers or areas on a page, we must also define a set of global styles. They are called *global* styles because each selector applies to every occurrence in a page of its respective element(s).

The following code sets the heading style, the text font and size, and the style for links. Take the img style as an example. Every time an image is used in the page, it will have no border—even if it is hyperlinked. Each global style can be overridden on a case-by-case basis.

```
body {
    color      : #333;
    background : #fafafa;
    font-family : Verdana, Arial, Helvetica, sans-serif;
    font-size  : 0.75em;
}

h1 { font-size : 1.7em; margin-top : 0; }
h2 { font-size : 1.5em; }
h3 { font-size : 1.3em; }
h4 { font-size : 1.1em; }
h5 { font-size : 1.0em; }
h1, h2, h3, h4, h5 { font-family : Georgia, serif; color : #f22; }

img  { border : 0; }
form { margin : 0; }

a       { color : #f22; background : none; text-decoration : underline; }
a:hover { color : #fff; background : #f22; text-decoration : none; }
```

In this code, we set the base font size to 0.75em. While the specific value used here isn't important, the fact that we use ems is. A single unit of em (1 em) is the width of the "m" character in the current font family and size. In other words, you could interpret a font-size directive inside the body as saying "set the font size to 75 percent of the browser's default size." Using ems allows the browser to scale fonts as required (most noticeably when a user selects "increase font size" or "decrease font size" in their browser).

Note We could also use ems instead of pixels for other measurements in the style sheet, such as for the column widths or border sizes. However, I have chosen not to in order to have more precise control over the on-screen layout.

Styling the Page Content

The remaining page areas to be styled are the content areas of the three columns. This includes creating the .box class, since all side-column content will appear inside various divs using this style.

The following styles format the various content areas of the page, including the page footer and the breadcrumb trail:

```
#content-container { background : #fff; }

#content {
    border      : 1px solid #eee;
    padding     : 10px;
    line-height : 1.8em;
}

#breadcrumbs {
    font-size : 0.8em;
    color     : #ccc;
}

#breadcrumbs a { color : #aaa; }
#breadcrumbs a:hover { background : #aaa; color : #fff; }

#left-container .box, #right-container .box {
    margin      : 0 10px 10px 10px;
    padding     : 10px;
    border      : 1px solid #eee;
    background  : #fff;
    font-size   : 0.9em;
    line-height : 1.6em;
}

#footer {
    color      : #999;
    font-size  : 0.8em;
    padding    : 10px;
    text-align : center;
}
```

This concludes the selectors for setting up global styles and styling the screen media type according to the design in Figure 6-2. We will add further elements as we require them throughout the book (including later in this chapter for styling forms), but the base styles defined here will suffice in most situations.

Creating a Print-Only Style Sheet

Many web sites offer a "print this page" link on their pages. Traditionally, this will link to another page on the site that repeats the content while stripping out all of the elements that have no relevance when printed (such as site navigation or a search form). By using print-only style sheets, we can mimic this behavior without the need for a secondary page of the same content. All we need to do is define styles for the print media type, as we saw earlier.

Before we do this, we should at least compare the two methods: using a secondary page as opposed to using a print style sheet. The advantages of using a print style sheet are as follows:

- The user doesn't need to navigate to another page in order to print content.

- You, as the developer, don't need to code in extra functionality to serve a stripped-down page (you will have to create a style sheet for this page anyway).

- The server does not have to serve an extra page, reducing server load and bandwidth use.

- Your web site statistics will be more accurate (although this isn't much of a problem, since you could always filter these extra entries out).

On the other hand, the advantages of using a secondary print page instead of a print style sheets are as follows:

- It will make more sense to users, as they will be able to see that the content is indeed stripped down.

- Users are more used to this method.

- Users might want to print the page exactly as it appears on screen, but a print style sheet won't allow them to do this (unless they use an advanced tool, which will allow them to block certain style sheets).

- Users probably won't rely on there being a print style sheet, because most developers don't provide one.

Note that the advantages of using secondary print pages stem from the fact that people are more used to using them. Ultimately, you must decide how you want to do this; since this is a book on Web 2.0 development, we will follow the CSS standard and implement code as it was intended. After all, adhering to standards was one of the aspects of Web 2.0 I defined in Chapter 1.

Modifying the Screen Style Sheet

There are essentially two key things we want to do in creating a print style sheet for our web application. The first is to hide elements that don't need to be printed, which in this case means the navigation and left and right columns. The second is to add a header that will be printed on all pages.

Typically, web browsers will strip out background colors and images when printing pages (users can generally change this setting, but most won't). To deal with this, we will place a printer-friendly image in our HTML. This forces the browser to print the logo; however, we must then alter the screen style sheet so this image isn't normally displayed on the screen.

Listing 6-12 shows how we can add the printer-friendly logo to the header.tpl template.

Listing 6-12. *Including a Printer-Friendly Logo in the Header Template (header.tpl)*

```
<!-- // ... other code -->

<div id="header">
```

```
    <img src="/images/logo-print.gif" alt="" />
</div>
```

```
<!-- // ... other code -->
```

We then just need to add a rule to the screen media-type section of the style sheet that hides this logo when the user views the page in their browser.

We also need to add rules to the print media-type section of the style sheet to hide the elements that we don't want to print (the side columns and the navigation). The following code shows how this is achieved (ignoring the remainder of the style sheet for now).

```
@media screen {
    #header img { display : none; }
}

@media print {
    #nav, #left-container, #right-container { display : none; }
}
```

Figure 6-5 shows how the page will look if you use the print preview tool in Firefox, compared to how the page normally looks in the browser. As an exercise, you may want to add extra styles to the print style sheet so the printable page has a nicer layout.

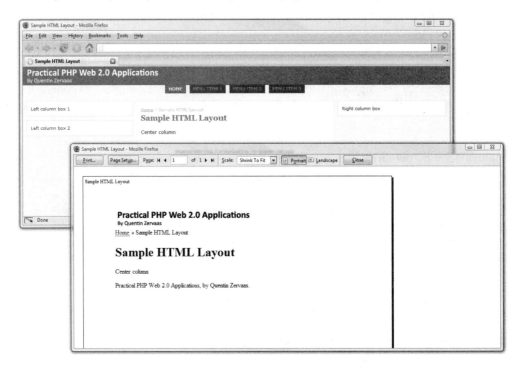

Figure 6-5. *Comparing the screen and print styles of the same page*

As a final note on this topic, you can easily add sections you want to include when printing, yet don't want to include when viewed on screen. This is just the opposite of how we hid the navigation and side columns; simply include them in the HTML markup, and then hide them in the screen section of the style sheet. This is effectively the same thing we did with the print-only logo.

The Full Application Style Sheet

Now that we have looked at all of the sections that make up the style sheet (including global styles, screen-only styles, and print-only styles), we can see how it all pieces together. Listing 6-13 shows the full CSS file with all the styles we have looked at in this chapter. This code should be written to the styles.css file in ./htdocs/css.

Listing 6-13. *The CSS Used to Implement the Three-Column Layout (styles.css)*

```
@media screen {

    /**
     * Global elements
     */

    body {
        color       : #333;
        background  : #fafafa;
        font-family : Verdana, Arial, Helvetica, sans-serif;
        font-size   : 0.75em;
    }

    h1 { font-size : 1.7em; margin-top : 0; }
    h2 { font-size : 1.5em; }
    h3 { font-size : 1.3em; }
    h4 { font-size : 1.1em; }
    h5 { font-size : 1.0em; }
    h1, h2, h3, h4, h5 { font-family : Georgia, serif; color : #f22; }

    img { border : 0; }
    form { margin : 0; }

    a       { color : #f22; background : none; text-decoration : underline; }
    a:hover { color : #fff; background : #f22; text-decoration : none; }


    /**
     * Setup the 3 column layout
     */
```

```css
body { margin : 0; padding : 0 300px; min-width : 300px; }

#header, #footer, #nav { margin : 0 -300px 0 -300px; }

.column            { float : left; position : relative; }
#content-container { width : 100%;  padding : 0; }
#left-container    { width : 300px; margin-left : -100%; right : 300px; }
#right-container   { width : 300px; margin-right : -300px; }

#footer { clear : both; }

* html #left-container { left : 300px; }


/**
 * Style the main page areas
 */
#header {
    background    : url(../images/logo.gif) no-repeat 5px center #f22;
    height        : 45px;
    border-bottom : 1px solid #922;
}
#header img { display : none; }

#content-container { background : #fff; }

#content {
    border      : 1px solid #eee;
    padding     : 10px;
    line-height : 1.8em;
}

#breadcrumbs {
    font-size : 0.8em;
    color         : #ccc;
    margin-bottom : 10px;
}

#breadcrumbs a { color : #aaa; }
#breadcrumbs a:hover { background : #aaa; color : #fff; }

#left-container .box, #right-container .box {
    margin      : 0 10px 10px 10px;
    padding     : 10px;
    border      : 1px solid #eee;
    background  : #fff;
```

```css
    font-size   : 0.9em;
    line-height : 1.6em;
}

#footer {
    color      : #999;
    font-size  : 0.8em;
    padding    : 10px;
    text-align : center;
}

/**
 * Tabbed navigation
 */

#nav {
    margin-top     : -1px;
    margin-bottom  : 20px;
    font-size      : 0.9em;
    text-transform : uppercase;
}

#nav ul {
    margin     : 0;
    padding    : 4px 0;
    text-align : center;
}

#nav li {
    list-style : none;
    padding    : 0;
    margin     : 0;
    display    : inline;
}

#nav a {
    background      : #922;
    color           : #aaa;
    text-decoration : none;
    padding         : 4px 8px;
    text-align      : center;
    border          : 1px solid #922;
    border-top      : none;
    margin          : 0 3px;
}
```

```
    #nav a:hover {
        color            : #fff;
        text-decoration : underline;
    }

    #nav li.active a {
        color        : #fff;
        background   : #f22;
        font-weight : bold;
    }
}

@media print {

    /**
     * Elements to hide
     */
    #nav, #left-container, #right-container { display : none; }
}
```

Styling the Application Web Forms

In Chapter 4 we created three forms for the user system: a registration form, a login form, and a fetch-password form. Since forms play such an important part in interactive web sites, we must make our forms easy for users to understand and use. Let's look at how to style these forms. Each form should meet the following requirements:

- Elements must be clearly labeled.

- Errors that occur should be highlighted.

- A submit button must be included.

In Chapter 4 we used a Smarty template called error.tpl to output errors. This template outputs a div regardless of whether an error has occurred, since this allows us to use it as a placeholder for JavaScript-generated errors. As such, we must hide this div if no error has occurred.

First, we style the .error div. This div will have a red background with white text so it stands out. Additionally, we will add a rule so that if the error div occurs inside the .row class (the container we use to hold each form element), we will shrink the font slightly.

```
div.error {
    background : #a00;
    padding    : 5px;
    margin     : 5px 0;
    color      : #fff;
}
```

```
form .row div.error {
    font-size : 0.8em;
    line-height : 1em;
}
```

Next, we will style the `.row` class, which holds each element. We will add a margin to the top and bottom of each `.row`, and then float the label left (allowing us to set its `display` type to `block` instead of the default of `inline`) and give it a width of `150px`. If you set the width when its display type is `inline`, this will be ignored.

```
form .row { margin : 10px 0; clear : both; }
form .row label {
    width       : 150px;
    float       : left;
    display     : block;
    font-weight : bold;
}
```

Next, we set the default widths of text inputs, using the following CSS:

```
form .row input[type=text] { width : 230px; }
form .row input[type=password] { width : 230px; }
```

Be aware that Internet Explorer 6 does not understand CSS selectors based on element attribute values (although Internet Explorer 7 does). An alternative would be to simply use `.row input`, but this would affect check boxes and radio buttons (and any other type of `<input>`). The other alternative is to explicitly set a class name on the input, and then style that class accordingly.

Finally, we will set the CAPTCHA image to align with the other input elements by setting its left margin, and then we'll create a simple style to hold submit buttons.

```
form .captcha { margin-left : 150px; }
form .submit {
    padding : 5px;
    margin-top : 10px;
    background : #eee;
}
```

Listing 6-14 shows how this new CSS code fits into the `styles.css` file. I have omitted the parts not relevant to display forms.

Listing 6-14. *The Application Style Sheet Including Styling of Forms and Errors (styles.css)*

```
@media screen {
    /* ... other code */

    /**
     * Forms
     */
```

```css
div.error {
    background : #a00;
    padding    : 5px;
    margin     : 5px 0;
    color      : #fff;
}

form .row div.error {
    font-size : 0.8em;
    line-height : 1em;
}

form .row { margin : 10px 0; clear : both; }

form .row label {
    width       : 150px;
    float       : left;
    display     : block;
    font-weight : bold;
}

form .row input[type=text] { width : 230px; }
form .row input[type=password] { width : 230px; }

form .captcha { margin-left : 150px; }

form .submit {
    padding : 5px;
    margin-top : 10px;
    background : #eee;
}

/* ... other code */
}
```

Note that these are all somewhat generic styles, and while they will work fine for most situations, they may not suit every type of form you create—you may need to create new form styles in some situations. However, these styles do work well for the registration form, the login form, and the fetch-password form, as you can see in Figure 6-6.

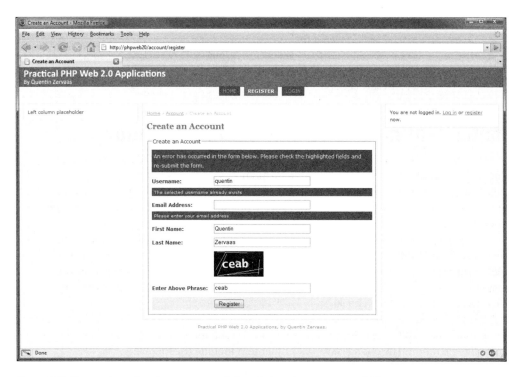

Figure 6-6. *The registration form, now styled and showing errors usefully*

Loading Prototype and Scriptaculous

In Chapter 5 we took a look at the Prototype and Scriptaculous JavaScript libraries, which we will make heavy use of in later chapters. Since the examples used in that chapter were independent of the application we are developing, we did not actually load these libraries for our application. We will now update the header.tpl template to automatically load these libraries in the <head> section of the template. For more discussion on loading each of these libraries, refer to Chapter 5.

Listing 6-15 shows the lines we will add to header.tpl to load Prototype and Scriptaculous. The lines not listed here that we added earlier in this chapter remain the same.

Listing 6-15. *Loading Prototype and Scriptaculous Automatically (header.tpl)*

```
<!DOCTYPE html
    PUBLIC "-//W3C//DTD XHTML 1.0 Strict//EN"
    "http://www.w3.org/TR/xhtml1/DTD/xhtml1-strict.dtd">

<html xmlns="http://www.w3.org/1999/xhtml" lang="en" xml:lang="en">
    <head>
        <title>{$title|escape}</title>
        <meta http-equiv="Content-Type" content="text/html; charset=iso-8859-1" />
        <link rel="stylesheet" href="/css/styles.css" type="text/css" media="all" />
```

```
<script type="text/javascript" src="/js/prototype.js"></script>
<script type="text/javascript"
        src="/js/scriptaculous/scriptaculous.js"></script>

<!-- // ... other code -->
```

Implementing Client-Side Form Validation

Now that we have looked at how Prototype and Scriptaculous work and have added styles to the site, we can revisit the user registration form. In this section, we will add client-side form validation to the user registration form using JavaScript and Ajax. Adding client-side validation improves usability since the user will receive feedback about any invalid form values more quickly.

Specifically, we will check that each of the form fields contain valid values when the user clicks the submit button to register. If everything appears correct, we will allow the form to be sent to the server. Note that we will still have our server-side validation in place (as implemented in Chapter 4), so even if the user doesn't have JavaScript enabled, they cannot circumvent any of the data checks.

Rather than duplicating the server-side validation we already have in place, we will make some small changes to the existing code so it can be used for Ajax validation in addition to the normal registration. The changes we will implement include the following:

- Modifying the `FormProcessor_UserRegistration` class so we have the option of validating form data without actually creating the user if no errors occur

- Changing the way the `registerAction()` method of `AccountController` works so that if the action is requested via Ajax, a JSON response is sent containing any errors that occurred

- Creating a JavaScript class to trigger the form validation, as well as submitting the form once all values have been verified

In actual fact, the form validation we are implementing here still uses the server in that it submits the data to the server for validation. We could add simple validation (such as checking for empty fields) without communicating with the server, but more complicated checks such as determining whether or not a username is already in use require server interaction. Although the client-side validation still uses the server for validation, it is quicker than doing a normal post-back since the page doesn't need to be reloaded.

Note In this particular example, all validation is done using the `FormProcessor_UserRegistration` class. The client-side code we will implement is really just a proxy to this class. This means we can easily expand the form-processing capabilities in the future by modifying `FormProcessor_UserRegistration`— the JavaScript we develop in this section will scale automatically.

Adding JSON Support to CustomControllerAction

In Chapter 5 we briefly looked at JSON (JavaScript Object Notation), which can be used to easily send data between client and server in Ajax requests. Implementing this form validator gives us our first chance of using JSON in this application.

In order to return JSON data from controller actions, we will add a new method to the `CustomControllerAction` class. Since we need to send a certain content type HTTP header for JSON data, it is much simpler to add this method once rather than sending the header manually each time we need to send JSON data.

Listing 6-16 shows the `sendJson()` method we will add to the `CustomControllerAction.php` file in `./include`.

Listing 6-16. *A Utility Method to Send JSON Data from Controller Actions (CustomControllerAction.php)*

```php
<?php
    class CustomControllerAction extends Zend_Controller_Action
    {
        // ... other code

        public function sendJson($data)
        {
            $this->_helper->viewRenderer->setNoRender();

            $this->getResponse()->setHeader('content-type', 'application/json');
            echo Zend_Json::encode($data);
        }
    }
?>
```

The first thing that we do here is disable autorendering of the view, since we're not outputting with a template. For more discussion of how the automatic view rendering in `Zend_Controller` works, refer to Chapter 2.

Next, we must send the appropriate `content-type` header. By default, PHP will send a content type of `text/html`, which will work in this case, but it is not technically correct. According to RFC 4627 (which can be found at `http://www.ietf.org/rfc/rfc4627.txt`), the official MIME type for JSON data is `application/json`.

Finally, we can call `Zend_Json::encode()` to encode the $data array.

Modifying the Form Processor

The next step in implementing client-side form validation is to add an extra option to the `FormProcessor_UserRegistration` class so form data can be checked without actually creating a new user account. We do this so the JavaScript code can determine whether the form data is correct before submitting the actual form.

To achieve this, we will add a new method to this class called `validateOnly()`. If this method is called with an argument value of `true`, the form will be processed, but even if there are no errors, the new user database row will not be created.

Listing 6-17 shows the changes we need to make to the UserRegistration.php file in the ./include/FormProcessor directory.

Listing 6-17. *Adding the Ability to Only Validate the Registration Form (UserRegistration.php)*

```php
<?php
    class FormProcessor_UserRegistration extends FormProcessor
    {
        protected $db = null;
        public $user = null;
        protected $_validateOnly = false;

        public function __construct($db)
        {
            // ... other code
        }

        public function validateOnly($flag)
        {
            $this->_validateOnly = (bool) $flag;
        }

        public function process(Zend_Controller_Request_Abstract $request)
        {
            // ... other code

            // if no errors have occurred, save the user
            if (!$this->_validateOnly && !$this->hasError()) {
                $this->user->save();
                unset($session->phrase);
            }

            // return true if no errors have occurred
            return !$this->hasError();
        }
    }
?>
```

Modifying the Registration Controller Action

In order to make use of the validation-only mode of the form processor, as well as to return a JSON response of any errors, we must now make some changes to the registerAction() method of the AccountController class. If the request was submitted using Ajax, we want the method just to validate the form and return any errors by calling the sendJson() method we just created. Conversely, if the request wasn't submitted using Ajax, we want this method to behave as normal—that is, to process the user registration and then redirect the confirmation page once complete.

Detecting Ajax Requests

Using Zend_Controller we can easily determine whether a request came from an Ajax subrequest by calling the isXmlHttpRequest() method on the request object that is available inside controller actions. Internally, this method looks for the presence of the X-Requested-With HTTP header. If the value of this header is XMLHttpRequest, this method returns true.

This header is not automatically set when using XMLHttpRequest to initiate HTTP subrequests, but Prototype will set this header automatically. This means the Prototype Ajax.Request class is compatible with the isXmlHttpRequest() method from the Zend_Controller_Request_Http class.

Returning Form Errors Using JSON

Now that you know how to detect Ajax requests, we can make the necessary changes to the registerAction() method in the AccountController class. If the request was initiated using XMLHttpRequest, we will call the validateOnly() method we just implemented and send back any errors using JSON. Note that we can call the getErrors() method on the form processor to retrieve an array of all errors (this will be an empty array if there are no errors).

Listing 6-18 shows the changes to the AccountController.php file in ./include/Controllers.

Listing 6-18. *Adding Form Validation for Ajax Requests (AccountController.php)*

```php
<?php
    class AccountController extends CustomControllerAction
    {
        // ... other code

        public function registerAction()
        {
            $request = $this->getRequest();

            $fp = new FormProcessor_UserRegistration($this->db);
            $validate = $request->isXmlHttpRequest();

            if ($request->isPost()) {
                if ($validate) {
                    $fp->validateOnly(true);
                    $fp->process($request);
                }
                else if ($fp->process($request)) {
                    $session = new Zend_Session_Namespace('registration');
                    $session->user_id = $fp->user->getId();
                    $this->_redirect($this->getUrl('registercomplete'));
                }
            }

            if ($validate) {
                $json = array(
```

```
                'errors' => $fp->getErrors()
            );
            $this->sendJson($json);
        }
        else {
            $this->breadcrumbs->addStep('Create an Account');
            $this->view->fp = $fp;
        }
    }

    // ... other code
    }
?>
```

To gain an understanding of what the return JSON data may look like, let's look at a quick example. According to the FormProcessor_UserRegistration class, if the user enters a username that is already in use, the following line is executed:

```
$this->addError('username', 'The selected username already exists');
```

If this were the only error to occur, the following JSON data would be generated:

```
{"errors":{"username":"The selected username already exists"}}
```

This means that if you assigned this JSON data to a JavaScript variable called json, you could access the error using json.errors.username, like this:

```
var json = {
    "errors" : {
        "username" : "The selected username already exists"
    }
}

alert(json.errors.username);
```

Creating the JavaScript Form Validator

Now that we have added the necessary PHP code to implement client-side validation, we can implement the client-side portion of code. To do this, we will create a JavaScript class called UserRegistrationForm to trigger validation of the form and to display errors. Then we will attach this class to the existing HTML form.

This class essentially performs the following steps:

1. Observes the existing HTML form so that when it is submitted, the JavaScript validation is triggered.

2. Clears any existing errors that are being displayed (just in case the user already submitted the form).

3. Submits the form data to the server for validation using Ajax.

4. Accepts the response, which contains any errors that occurred.

- If there are no errors, tells the browser to submit the form normally.

- If there are errors, loops over them and displays each one on the form.

Because all of the error containers are already in place on the form, it is a simple matter to write the error message to the error container and then call the show() method on it (this is a method Prototype adds to all HTML elements, as we saw in Chapter 5). For more discussion of how to create JavaScript classes using Prototype, refer to Chapter 5.

Initializing the UserRegistrationForm JavaScript Class

To begin this class, we will first declare the class and then implement its constructor (the initialize() method). In this constructor, we will store the form as a property of the class, and then observe the onsubmit event on it. We'll complete the constructor by calling the resetErrors() method (which we will look at next) to ensure no errors are being shown.

Listing 6-19 shows the declaration and constructor of the UserRegistrationForm class. This code should be written to a file called UserRegistrationForm.class.js in the ./htdocs/js directory.

Listing 6-19. *Initializing the Registration Form Validation Class (UserRegistrationForm.class.js)*

```
UserRegistrationForm = Class.create();

UserRegistrationForm.prototype = {

    form    : null,

    initialize : function(form)
    {
        this.form = $(form);
        this.form.observe('submit', this.onSubmit.bindAsEventListener(this));

        this.resetErrors();
    },
```

Hiding Form Errors

Next, we will implement a utility method to help us clear any error messages. Whenever the form is submitted, we want to call this method to clear errors from any previous attempt—if a user attempts to submit the form multiple times, a different set of errors may occur. Since all errors on the form are contained within elements that have the .error class, we can simply find all of those elements and hide them.

Listing 6-20 shows the code we need to add to UserRegistrationForm.class.js to clear all errors. This code first uses the Prototype getElementsBySelector() method to find the elements and then calls the invoke() enumerator method to hide each of them.

Listing 6-20. *Clearing All Form Errors with resetErrors() (UserRegistrationForm.class.js)*

```
resetErrors : function()
{
    this.form.getElementsBySelector('.error').invoke('hide');
},
```

Displaying Form Errors

To complement the hiding of form errors, we also need the ability to show errors. We will implement the showError() method, which takes the name of the error's form field as the first argument and the error message as the second argument.

The biggest challenge in this method is to locate the error container that corresponds to the given form field. To find this element, we use the Prototype DOM traversal functions (up() and down()) to locate the element. We make the assumption that the error container is within the same parent element as the form input. Therefore, we can find the parent element of the form element and look within that parent for an element with the class name .error.

Listing 6-21 shows the code for the showError() method, which also goes in UserRegistrationForm.class.js.

Listing 6-21. *Writing the Error Message to a Form Element's Error Container (UserRegistrationForm.class.js)*

```
showError : function(key, val)
{
    var formElement = this.form[key];
    var container = formElement.up().down('.error');

    if (container) {
        container.update(val);
        container.show();
    }
},
```

Handling the Form Submission

In Listing 6-19 we observed the onsubmit event on the user registration form. This means that when the form is submitted, the onSubmit() method in the UserRegistrationForm class is called.

The goal of onSubmit() is to initiate an Ajax request that submits the form data to the registerAction() method of the AccountController class. Since this request will be initiated using Ajax, the changes we made in Listing 6-18 will come into play (that is, processing the form but not creating the user if there are no errors).

The onSubmit() method begins by calling Event.stop(). This means that the browser won't submit the form as usual once this method has been called. This allows us to control the submission of the form (we will submit it once we ensure no errors have occurred in the form). Additionally, we make a call to resetErrors() so that any errors from a previous submission attempt are removed.

Listing 6-22 shows the code for the onSubmit() method in the UserRegistrationForm.class.js file.

Listing 6-22. *Submitting the Form Data for Validation via Ajax (UserRegistrationForm.class.js)*

```
onSubmit : function(e)
{
    Event.stop(e);

    var options = {
        parameters : this.form.serialize(),
        method     : this.form.method,
        onSuccess  : this.onFormSuccess.bind(this)
    };

    this.resetErrors();
    new Ajax.Request(this.form.action, options);
},
```

We make use of the original form method and action based on the values in the HTML code. This means that if we ever change the URL for the registration form, we don't need to make any changes to this JavaScript code.

Additionally, we can easily scale the form, since we call the serialize() method on it to retrieve all form values. This method is provided by Prototype.

Handling the Form Validation Response

In Listing 6-22 we specified that a method called onFormSuccess() would be used to handle the response from the form validation. In this JSON data, we are expecting an array called errors that holds all of the errors that occurred in the form validation. We can decode this data using the evalJSON() method.

If this array contains one or more values, then an error has occurred. In that case, we must loop over each of these errors and call showError() for each error. Note that we also must look for the first element within the form with the class .error, since we have a global error message container at the top of the form (as discussed in Chapter 4). This line of code in our JavaScript makes this global error message appear.

If the errors array is empty, we can assume the form values were all valid and tell the browser to submit the form by calling the submit() method on the form element.

Listing 6-23 shows the code for the onFormSuccess() method, and the closing of the UserRegistrationForm class.

Listing 6-23. *Handling the Form Validation Response (UserRegistrationForm.class.js)*

```
onFormSuccess : function(transport)
{
    var json = transport.responseText.evalJSON(true);
    var errors = $H(json.errors);

    if (errors.size() > 0) {
```

```
            this.form.down('.error').show();
            errors.each(function(pair) {
                this.showError(pair.key, pair.value);
            }.bind(this));
        }
        else {
            this.form.submit();
        }
    }
};
```

> **Note** When calling `each()` on the `errors` array, we call `bind()` on the function so `this` refers to the `UserRegistrationForm` object. For further discussion on binding JavaScript class methods using Prototype, refer to Chapter 5.

Loading the UserRegistrationForm Class

Finally, we must make use of the JavaScript class we just implemented. To do so, we will load the JavaScript file in the registration form template and then instantiate the class. Since this class relies on Prototype, make sure you have added the code to load `prototype.js` as instructed earlier in this chapter.

Listing 6-24 shows the changes to `register.tpl` in `./templates/account`. In addition to loading the JavaScript, we also give an ID to the form so we can refer to it when instantiating the `UserRegistrationForm` class.

Listing 6-24. *Loading and Instantiating the Form Validation Class (register.tpl)*

```
{include file='header.tpl' section='register'}

<form method="post"
      action="{geturl action='register'}"
      id="registration-form">

    <!-- // form elements go here -->

</form>

<script type="text/javascript" src="/js/UserRegistrationForm.class.js"></script>
<script type="text/javascript">
    new UserRegistrationForm('registration-form');
</script>

{include file='footer.tpl'}
```

This completes the client-side form validation. If you now try to submit a form with invalid values, you will be shown the error messages as before; however, the page isn't reloaded and the response is displayed much more quickly.

Summary

In this chapter we created a basic web design for our Web 2.0 application and integrated it into the existing Smarty templates. This included creating a fluid table-free layout that works well in all major browsers. We then revisited the forms we created in Chapter 2 and set up styles for them so they would be formatted nicely and display errors in a way that is easy to understand.

Following this, we changed the site header template so Prototype and Scriptaculous would be automatically loaded. We immediately made use of Prototype by adding client-side form validation to the user registration form. We implemented this using Ajax and JSON.

While the content in this chapter didn't include much Web 2.0 content, it was still very important, as we started to bring together the look and feel of the site, while keeping the HTML markup to a minimum. This sets a solid base for integrating JavaScript code that will run efficiently, as well as being accessible and easy to maintain. This will also help in the loading speed of the site, which in turn improves the experience of users while keeping the load of your server (and the bandwidth it uses) to a minimum.

In Chapter 7 we will start to build the blogging system of our web application. This will set the basis for the remainder of the book, as all features following on from here tie into this system. It also means we can really start to look at the features that define a Web 2.0 application.

CHAPTER 7

■ ■ ■

Building the Blogging System

Now that users can register and log in to the web application, it is time to allow them to create their own blogs. In this chapter, we will begin to build the blogging functionality for our Web 2.0 application. We will implement the tools that will permit each user to create and manage their own blog posts.

In this chapter, we will be adding the following functionality to our web application:

- **Enable users to create new blog posts.** A blog post will consist of a title, the date submitted, and the content (text or HTML) relating to the post. We will implement the form (and corresponding processing code) that allows users to enter this content, and that correctly filters submitted HTML code so JavaScript-based attacks cannot occur. This form will also be used for editing existing posts.

- **Permit users to preview new posts.** This simple workflow system will allow users to double-check a post before sending it live. When a user creates a new post, they will have an option to either preview the post or send it live immediately. When previewing a post, they will have the option to either send it live or to make further changes.

- **Notify users of results.** We will implement a system that notifies the user what has happened when they perform an action. For instance, when they choose to publish one of their blog posts, the notification system will flash a message on the screen confirming this action once it has happened.

There are additional features we will be implementing later in this book (such as tags, images, and web feeds); in this chapter we will simply lay the groundwork for the blog.

There will be some repetition of Chapter 3 in this chapter when we set up database tables and classes for modifying the database, but I will keep it as brief as possible and point out the important differences.

Because there is a lot of code to absorb in developing the blog management tools, Chapter 8 also deals with implementing the blog manager. In this chapter we will primarily deal with creating and editing blog posts; in the next chapter we will implement a what-you-see-is-what-you-get (WYSIWYG) editor to help format blog posts.

Creating the Database Tables

Before we start on writing the code, we must first create the database tables. We are going to create one table to hold the main blog post information and a secondary table to hold extra properties for each post (this is much like how we stored user information). This allows us to expand the data stored for blog posts in the future without requiring significant changes to the code or the database table. This is important, because in later chapters we will be expanding upon the blog functionality, and there will be extra data to be stored for each post.

Let's now take a look at the SQL required to create these tables in MySQL. The table definitions can be found in the schema-mysql.sql file (in the /var/www/phpweb20 directory). The equivalent definitions for PostgreSQL can be found in the schema-pgsql.sql file. Listing 7-1 shows the SQL used to create the blog_posts and blog_posts_profile tables.

Listing 7-1. *SQL to Create the blog_posts Table in MySQL (schema-mysql.sql)*

```
create table blog_posts (
    post_id         serial          not null,
    user_id         bigint unsigned not null,

    url             varchar(255)    not null,
    ts_created      datetime        not null,
    status          varchar(10)     not null,

    primary key (post_id),
    foreign key (user_id) references users (user_id)
) type = InnoDB;

create index blog_posts_url on blog_posts (url);

create table blog_posts_profile (
    post_id         bigint unsigned not null,
    profile_key     varchar(255)    not null,
    profile_value   text            not null,

    primary key (post_id, profile_key),
    foreign key (post_id) references blog_posts (post_id)
) type = InnoDB;
```

In blog_posts we link (using a foreign key constraint) to the users table, as each post will belong to a single user. We also store a timestamp of the creation date. This is the field we will primarily be sorting on when displaying blog posts, since a blog is essentially a journal that is organized by the date of each post.

We will use the url field to store a permanent link for the post, generated dynamically based on the title of the post. Additionally, since we will be using this field to load blog posts (as you will see in Chapter 9), we create an index on this field in the database to speed up SQL select queries that use this field.

The other field of interest here is the status field, which we will use to indicate whether or not a post is live. This will help us implement the preview functionality.

The blog_posts_profile table is almost a duplicate of the users_profile table, but it links to the blog_posts table instead of the users table.

■**Note** As discussed in Chapter 3, when using PostgreSQL we use `timestamptz` instead of `datetime` for creating timestamp fields. Additionally, we use `int` for a foreign key to a `serial` (instead of `bigint unsigned`). Specifying the InnoDB table type is MySQL-specific functionality so constraints will be enforced.

Setting Up DatabaseObject and Profile Classes

In this section, we will add new *models* to our application that allow us to control data in the database tables we just created. We do this the same way we managed user data in Chapter 3. That is, we create a DatabaseObject subclass to manage the data in the blog_posts table, and we create a Profile subclass to manage the blog_posts_profile table.

It may appear that we're duplicating some code, but the DatabaseObject class makes it very easy to manage a large number of database tables, as you will see. Additionally, we will add many functions to the DatabaseObject_BlogPost class that aren't relevant to the DatabaseObject_User class.

Creating the DatabaseObject_BlogPost Class

Let's first take a look at the DatabaseObject_BlogPost class. Listing 7-2 shows the contents of the BlogPost.php file, which should be stored in the ./include/DatabaseObject directory.

Listing 7-2. *Managing Blog Post Data (BlogPost.php in ./include/DatabaseObject)*

```php
<?php
    class DatabaseObject_BlogPost extends DatabaseObject
    {
        public $profile = null;

        const STATUS_DRAFT = 'D';
        const STATUS_LIVE  = 'L';

        public function __construct($db)
        {
            parent::__construct($db, 'blog_posts', 'post_id');

            $this->add('user_id');
            $this->add('url');
            $this->add('ts_created', time(), self::TYPE_TIMESTAMP);
            $this->add('status', self::STATUS_DRAFT);

            $this->profile = new Profile_BlogPost($db);
        }

        protected function postLoad()
        {
            $this->profile->setPostId($this->getId());
```

```
        $this->profile->load();
    }

    protected function postInsert()
    {
        $this->profile->setPostId($this->getId());
        $this->profile->save(false);
        return true;
    }

    protected function postUpdate()
    {
        $this->profile->save(false);
        return true;
    }

    protected function preDelete()
    {
        $this->profile->delete();
        return true;
    }
    }
?>
```

■**Caution** This class relies on the `Profile_BlogPost` class, which we will be writing shortly, so this class will not work until we add that one.

This code is somewhat similar to the `DatabaseObject_User` class in that we initialize the `$_profile` variable, which we eventually populate with an instance of `Profile_BlogPost`. Additionally, we use callbacks in the same manner as `DatabaseObject_User`. Many of the utility functions in `DatabaseObject_User` were specific to managing user data, so they're obviously excluded from this class.

The key difference between `DatabaseObject_BlogPost` and `DatabaseObject_User` is that here we define two *constants* (using the `const` keyword) to define the different statuses a blog post can have. Blog posts in our application will either be set to *draft* or *live* (D or L).

We use constants to define the different statuses a blog post can have because these values never change. Technically you could use a static variable instead; however, static variables are typically used for values that are set once only, at runtime.

Additionally, by using constants we don't need to concern ourselves with the actual value that is stored in the database. Rather than hard-coding a magic value of D every time you want to refer to the draft status, you can instead refer to `DatabaseObject_BlogPost::STATUS_DRAFT` in your code. Sure, it's longer in the source code, but it's much clearer when reading the code, and the internal cost of storage is the same.

Creating the Profile_BlogPost Class

The Profile_BlogPost class that we use to control the profile data for each post is almost identical to the Profile_User class. The only difference between the two is that we name the utility function setPostId() instead of setUserId().

The code for this class is shown in Listing 7-3 and is to be stored in BlogPost.php in the ./include/Profile directory.

Listing 7-3. *Managing Blog Post Profile Data (BlogPost.php in ./include/Profile)*

```php
<?php
    class Profile_BlogPost extends Profile
    {
        public function __construct($db, $post_id = null)
        {
            parent::__construct($db, 'blog_posts_profile');

            if ($post_id > 0)
                $this->setPostId($post_id);
        }

        public function setPostId($post_id)
        {
            $filters = array('post_id' => (int) $post_id);
            $this->_filters = $filters;
        }
    }
?>
```

Creating a Controller for Managing Blog Posts

In its current state, our application has three MVC controllers: the index, account, and utility controllers. In this section, we will create a new controller class called BlogmanagerController specifically for managing blog posts.

This controller will handle the creation and editing of blog posts, the previewing of posts (as well as sending them live), as well as the deletion of posts. This controller will not perform any tasks relating to displaying a user's blog publicly (either on the application home page or on the user's personal page); we will implement this functionality in Chapter 9.

Extending the Application Permissions

Before we start creating the controller, we must extend the permissions in the CustomControllerAclManager class so only registered (and logged-in) users can access it. The way we do this is to first deny all access to the blogmanager controller, and then allow access for the member user role (which automatically also opens it up for the administrator user type, because administrator inherits from member). We must also add blogmanager as a resource before access to it can be controlled.

In the constructor of the CustomerControllerAclManager.php file (located in ./include/Controllers), we will add the following three lines in this order:

```
$this->acl->add(new Zend_Acl_Resource('blogmanager'));
$this->acl->deny(null, 'blogmanager');
$this->acl->allow('member', 'blogmanager');
```

Listing 7-4 shows how you should add them to this file.

Listing 7-4. *Adding Permissions for the Blog Manager Controller (CustomControllerAclManager.php)*

```php
<?php
    class CustomControllerAclManager extends Zend_Controller_Plugin_Abstract
    {
        // ... other code

        public function __construct(Zend_Auth $auth)
        {
            $this->auth = $auth;
            $this->acl = new Zend_Acl();

            // add the different user roles
            $this->acl->addRole(new Zend_Acl_Role($this->_defaultRole));
            $this->acl->addRole(new Zend_Acl_Role('member'));
            $this->acl->addRole(new Zend_Acl_Role('administrator'), 'member');

            // add the resources we want to have control over
            $this->acl->add(new Zend_Acl_Resource('account'));
            $this->acl->add(new Zend_Acl_Resource('blogmanager'));
            $this->acl->add(new Zend_Acl_Resource('admin'));

            // allow access to everything for all users by default
            // except for the account management and administration areas
            $this->acl->allow();
            $this->acl->deny(null, 'account');
            $this->acl->deny(null, 'blogmanager');
            $this->acl->deny(null, 'admin');

            // add an exception so guests can log in or register
            // in order to gain privilege
            $this->acl->allow('guest', 'account', array('login',
                                                        'fetchpassword',
                                                        'register',
                                                        'registercomplete'));

            // allow members access to the account management area
            $this->acl->allow('member', 'account');
```

```
        $this->acl->allow('member', 'blogmanager');

        // allow administrators access to the admin area
        $this->acl->allow('administrator', 'admin');
    }

    // ... other code
    }
?>
```

Refer back to Chapter 3 if you need a reminder of how Zend_Acl works and how we use it in this application.

The BlogmanagerController Actions

Let's now take a look at a skeleton of the BlogmanagerController class, which at this stage lists each of the different action handlers we will be implementing in this chapter (except for indexAction(), which will be implemented in Chapter 8). Listing 7-5 shows the contents of BlogmanagerController.php, which we will store in the ./include/Controllers directory.

Listing 7-5. *The Skeleton for the BlogmanagerController Class (BlogmanagerController.php)*

```php
<?php
    class BlogmanagerController extends CustomControllerAction
    {
        public function init()
        {
            parent::init();
            $this->breadcrumbs->addStep('Account', $this->getUrl(null, 'account'));
            $this->breadcrumbs->addStep('Blog Manager',
                                    $this->getUrl(null, 'blogmanager'));

            $this->identity = Zend_Auth::getInstance()->getIdentity();
        }

        public function indexAction()
        {

        }

        public function editAction()
        {

        }

        public function previewAction()
        {
```

```
            }

            public function setstatusAction()
            {

            }
        }
    ?>
```

As part of the initial setup for this controller, I've added in the calls to build the appropriate breadcrumb steps. Additionally, since all of the actions we will add to this controller will require the user ID of the logged-in user, I've also provided easy access to the user identity data by assigning it to an object property.

There are four controller action methods we must implement to complete this phase of the blog management system:

- indexAction(): This method will be responsible for listing all posts in the blog. At the top of this page, a summary of each of the current month's posts will be shown. Previous months will be listed in the left column, providing access to posts belonging to other months. This will be implemented in Chapter 8.

- editAction(): This action method is responsible for creating new blog posts and editing existing posts. If an error occurs, this action will be displayed again in order to show these errors.

- previewAction(): When a user creates a new post, they will have the option of previewing it before it is sent live. This action will display their blog post to them, giving them the option of making further changes or publishing the post. This action will also be used to display a complete summary of a single post to the user.

- setstatusAction(): This method will be used to update the status of a post when a user decides to publish it live. This will be done by setting the post's status from DatabaseObject_BlogPost::STATUS_DRAFT to DatabaseObject_BlogPost::STATUS_LIVE. Once it has been sent live, previewAction() will show a summary of the post and confirm that it has been sent live. The setstatusAction() method will also allow the user to send a live post back to draft or to delete blog posts. A confirmation message will be shown after a post is deleted, except the user will be redirected to indexAction() (since the post will no longer exist, and they cannot be redirected back to the preview page).

Linking to Blog Manager

Before we start to implement the actions in BlogmanagerController, let's quickly create a link on the account home page to the blog manager. Listing 7-6 shows the new lines we will add to the index.tpl file from the ./templates/account directory.

Listing 7-6. *Linking to the Blog Manager from the Account Home Page (index.tpl)*

```
{include file='header.tpl' section='account'}

Welcome {$identity->first_name}.

<ul>
    <li><a href="{geturl controller='blogmanager'}">View all blog posts</a></li>
    <li><a href="{geturl controller='blogmanager'
                        action='edit'}">Post new blog entry</a></li>
</ul>

{include file='footer.tpl'}
```

The other link we will add is in the main navigation across the top of the page. This item will only be shown to logged-in users. Listing 7-7 shows the new lines in the header.tpl navigation (in ./templates), which creates a new list item labeled "Your Blog".

Listing 7-7. *Linking to the Blog Manager in the Site Navigation (header.tpl)*

```
<!-- // ... other code -->
<div id="nav">
  <ul>
    <li{if $section == 'home'} class="active"{/if}>
      <a href="{geturl controller='index'}">Home</a>
    </li>
    {if $authenticated}
      <li{if $section == 'account'} class="active"{/if}>
        <a href="{geturl controller='account'}">Your Account</a>
      </li>
      <li{if $section == 'blogmanager'} class="active"{/if}>
        <a href="{geturl controller='blogmanager'}">Your Blog</a>
      </li>
      <li><a href="{geturl controller='account' action='logout'}">Logout</a></li>
    {else}
      <!-- // ... other code -->
    {/if}
  </ul>
  <!-- // ... other code -->
```

At this point, there is no template for the indexAction() method of BlogmanagerController, meaning that if you click the new link from this listing, you will see an error. Listing 7-8 shows the code we need to write to the ./templates/blogmanager/index.tpl file as an intermediate solution—we will build on this template in Chapter 8. You will need to create the ./templates/ blogmanager directory before writing this file since it's the first template we've created for this controller.

Listing 7-8. *The Blog Manager Index (index.tpl)*

```
{include file='header.tpl' section='blogmanager'}

<form method="get" action="{geturl action='edit'}">
    <div class="submit">
        <input type="submit" value="Create new blog post" />
    </div>
</form>

{include file='footer.tpl'}
```

Now when a user is logged in to their account, they will see a link in the main navigation allowing them to visit the blog post management area. At this stage, when they visit this page they will only see a button allowing them to create a new blog post. We will now implement this blog post creation functionality.

Creating and Editing Blog Posts

We will now implement the functionality that will allow users to create new blog posts and edit existing posts. To avoid duplication, both the creating and editing of posts use the same code. Initially, we will implement this action using a `<textarea>` as the input method for users to enter their blog posts. In Chapter 8, we will implement a what-you-see-is-what-you-get (WYSIWYG) editor to replace this text area.

The fields we will be prompting users to complete are as follows:

- **A title for the post entry.** This is typically a short summary or headline of the post. Later in development, all blog posts will be accessible via a friendly URL. We will generate the URL based on this title.

- **The submission date for the post.** For new posts, the current date and time will be selected by default, but we will allow members to modify this date.

- **The blog post content.** Users will be able to enter HTML tags in this field. We will write code to correctly filter this HTML to prevent unwanted tags or JavaScript injection. As mentioned previously, we will use a text area for this field, to be replaced with a WYSIWYG editor in Chapter 8.

We will first create a form that users will use to create new or edit existing blog posts. Next, we will implement the `editAction()` method for the `BlogmanagerController` class. Finally, we will write a class to process the blog post submission form (`FormProcessor_BlogPost`).

Creating the Blog Post Submission Form Template

The first step in creating the form for submitting or editing blog posts is to create the form template. The structure of this template is very similar to the registration form, except that the form fields differ slightly.

Listing 7-9 shows the first part of the `edit.tpl` template, which is stored in the `./templates/blogmanager` directory. Note that the form action includes the `id` parameter, which means that when an existing post is submitted, the form updates that post in the database and doesn't create a new post.

Listing 7-9. *The Top Section of the Blog Post Editing Template (edit.tpl)*

```
{include file='header.tpl' section='blogmanager'}

<form method="post" action="{geturl action='edit'}?id={$fp->post->getId()}">

{if $fp->hasError()}
    <div class="error">
        An error has occurred in the form below. Please check
        the highlighted fields and resubmit the form.
    </div>
{/if}


<fieldset>
    <legend>Blog Post Details</legend>

    <div class="row" id="form_title_container">
        <label for="form_title">Title:</label>
        <input type="text" id="form_title"
                name="username" value="{$fp->title|escape}" />
        {include file='lib/error.tpl' error=$fp->getError('title')}
    </div>
```

Next, we must display date and time drop-down boxes. We will use the {html_select_date} and {html_select_time} Smarty functions to simplify this. These plug-ins generate form elements to select the year, month, date, hour, minute, and second. (You can read about these plug-ins at http://smarty.php.net/manual/en/language.custom.functions.php.)

We can customize how each of these plug-ins work by specifying various parameters. In both functions, we will specify the prefix argument. This value is prepended to the name attribute of each of the generated form elements. Next, we will specify the time argument. This is used to set the preselected date and time. If this value is null (as it will be for a new post), the current date and time are selected.

By default, the year drop-down will only include the current year, so to give the user a wider range of dates for their posts, we will specify the start_year and end_year attributes. These can be either absolute values (such as 2007), or values relative to the current year (such as –5 or +5).

■**Note** The {html_select_date} function is clever in that if you specify a date in the time parameter that falls outside of the specified range of years, Smarty will change the range of years to start (or finish) at the specified year.

We will customize the time drop-downs by setting the display_seconds attribute to false (so only hours and minutes are shown), as well as setting use_24_hours to false. This changes the range of hours from 0–23 to 1–12 and adds the meridian drop-down.

Listing 7-10 shows the middle section of the edit.tpl template, which outputs the date and time drop-downs as well as an error container for the field.

Listing 7-10. *Outputting the Date and Time Drop-Downs in the Template (edit.tpl)*

```
<div class="row" id="form_date_container">
    <label for="form_date">Date of Entry:</label>

    {html_select_date prefix='ts_created'
                      time=$fp->ts_created
                      start_year=-5
                      end_year=+5}

    {html_select_time prefix='ts_created'
                      time=$fp->ts_created
                      display_seconds=false
                      use_24_hours=false}

    {include file='lib/error.tpl' error=$fp->getError('date')}
</div>
```

We will complete this template by outputting the text area used for entering the blog post, as well as the form submit buttons. This text area is the one we will eventually replace with a WYSIWYG editor.

When displaying the submit buttons, we will include some basic logic to display user-friendly messages that relate to the context in which the form is used. For new posts, we will give the user the option to send the post live or to preview it. For existing posts that are already live, only the option to save the new details will be given. If the post already exists but is not yet published, we will give the user the same options as for new posts.

We will include the name="preview" attribute in the submit button used for previews. This is the value we will check in the form processor to determine whether or not to send a post live immediately. If the other submit button is clicked, the preview value is not included in the form.

■**Tip** Using multiple submit buttons on a form is not often considered by developers but it is very useful for providing users with multiple options for the same data. If there are multiple submit buttons, the browser only uses the value of the button that was clicked, and not any of the other submit buttons. Thus, by giving each button a different name, you can easily determine which button was clicked within your PHP code.

Listing 7-11 shows the remainder of the edit.tpl file. Note that if you view the blog manager edit page in your browser now, you will see an error, since the $fp variable isn't yet defined.

Listing 7-11. *The Remainder of the Post Submission Template (edit.tpl)*

```
<div class="row" id="form_content_container">
    <label for="form_content">Your Post:</label>
    <textarea name="content">{$fp->content|escape}</textarea>
    {include file='lib/error.tpl' error=$fp->getError('content')}
</div>
</fieldset>

<div class="submit">
    {if $fp->post->isLive()}
        {assign var='label' value='Save Changes'}
    {elseif $fp->post->isSaved()}
        {assign var='label' value='Save Changes and Send Live'}
    {else}
        {assign var='label' value='Create and Send Live'}
    {/if}

    <input type="submit" value="{$label|escape}" />
    {if !$fp->post->isLive()}
        <input type="submit" name="preview" value="Preview This Post" />
    {/if}
</div>

</form>

{include file='footer.tpl'}
```

In this template, we use the {assign} Smarty function to set the label for the submit buttons. This function allows you to create template variables on the fly. Using it has the same effect as assigning variables from your PHP code. The name argument is the name the new variable will have in the template, while the value argument is the value to be assigned to this variable.

Note Be careful not to overuse {assign}; you may find yourself including application logic in your templates if you use it excessively. In this instance, we are only using it to help with the display logic—we are using it to create temporary placeholders for button labels so we don't have to duplicate the HTML code used to create submit buttons.

Instantiating FormProcessor_BlogPost in editAction()

The next step in being able to create or edit blog posts is to implement editAction() in the BlogmanagerController class. We will use the same controller action for displaying the edit form and for calling the form processor when the user submits the form. This allows us to easily display any errors that occurred when processing the form, since the code will fall through to display the template again if an error occurs.

Since we are using this action to edit posts as well as create new posts, we need to check for the id parameter in the URL, as this is what will be passed in to the form processor as the third argument if an existing post is to be edited.

We then fetch the user ID from the user's identity and instantiate the FormProcessor_BlogPost class, which we will implement shortly. The form processor will try to load an existing blog post for that user based on the ID passed in the URL. If it is unable to find a matching record for the ID, it behaves as though a new post is being created.

The next step is to check whether the action has been invoked by submitting the blog post submission form. If so, we need to call the process() method of the form processor. If the form is successfully processed, the user will be redirected to the previewAction() method. If an error occurs, the code falls through to creating the breadcrumbs and displaying the form (just as it would when initially viewing the edit blog post page).

Note that the breadcrumbs include a check to see whether an existing post is being edited (which is done by checking if the $fp->post object has been saved). If it is, we include a link back to the post preview page in the breadcrumb trail.

Listing 7-12 shows the full contents of editAction() from the BlogmanagerController.php file, which concludes by assigning the $fp object to the view so it can be used in the template we created previously.

Listing 7-12. *The editAction() Method, Which Displays and Processes the Form (BlogmanagerController.php)*

```php
<?php
    class BlogmanagerController extends CustomControllerAction
    {
        // ... other code

        public function editAction()
        {
            $request = $this->getRequest();
            $post_id = (int) $this->getRequest()->getQuery('id');

            $fp = new FormProcessor_BlogPost($this->db,
                                             $this->identity->user_id,
                                             $post_id);

            if ($request->isPost()) {
                if ($fp->process($request)) {
                    $url = $this->getUrl('preview') . '?id=' . $fp->post->getId();
                    $this->_redirect($url);
                }
            }

            if ($fp->post->isSaved()) {
                $this->breadcrumbs->addStep(
                    'Preview Post: ' . $fp->post->profile->title,
                    $this->getUrl('preview') . '?id=' . $fp->post->getId()
                );
```

```
            $this->breadcrumbs->addStep('Edit Blog Post');
        }
        else
            $this->breadcrumbs->addStep('Create a New Blog Post');

        $this->view->fp = $fp;
    }

    // ... other code
    }
?>
```

> **Note** Regardless of whether the user chooses to preview the post or to send the post live straight away, they are still redirected to the post preview page after a post has been saved. The difference between sending a post live and previewing it is the status value that is stored with the post, which determines whether or not other people will be able to read the post.

Implementing the FormProcessor_BlogPost Class

Finally, we need to implement the FormProcessor_BlogPost class, which is used to process the blog post edit form. Just as we did for user registration, we are going to extend the FormProcessor class to simplify the tasks of sanitizing form values and storing errors. Because we're using the same class for both creating new posts and editing existing posts, we need to handle this in the constructor.

Listing 7-13 shows the constructor for the FormProcessor_BlogPost class, which accepts the database connection and the ID of the user creating the post as the first two arguments. The third argument is optional, and if specified is the ID of the post to be edited. Omitting this argument (or passing a value of 0, since our primary key sequence only generates values greater than 0) indicates a new post will be created. This code should be written to a file called BlogPost.php in the ./include/FormProcessor directory.

Listing 7-13. *The Constructor for FormProcessor_BlogPost (BlogPost.php)*

```php
<?php
    class FormProcessor_BlogPost extends FormProcessor
    {
        protected $db = null;
        public $user = null;
        public $post = null;

        public function __construct($db, $user_id, $post_id = 0)
        {
            parent::__construct();

            $this->db = $db;
```

```php
        $this->user = new DatabaseObject_User($db);
        $this->user->load($user_id);

        $this->post = new DatabaseObject_BlogPost($db);
        $this->post->loadForUser($this->user->getId(),
                                 $post_id);

        if ($this->post->isSaved()) {
            $this->title = $this->post->profile->title;
            $this->content = $this->post->profile->content;
            $this->ts_created = $this->post->ts_created;
        }
        else
            $this->post->user_id = $this->user->getId();
    }

    public function process(Zend_Controller_Request_Abstract $request)
    {
        // ... other code
    }
    }
?>
```

The purpose of the constructor of this class is to try to load an existing blog post based on the third argument. If the blog post can be loaded, the class is being used to edit an existing post; otherwise it is being used to process the form for a new blog post.

An important feature of this code is that we use a new method called loadForUser(), which is a custom loader method for DatabaseObject_BlogPost. This ensures that the loaded post belongs to the corresponding user. If we didn't check this, it would be possible for a user to edit the posts of any other user simply by manipulating the URL.

Listing 7-14 shows the code for loadForUser(), which we will add to DatabaseObject_BlogPost. In order to write a custom loader for DatabaseObject, we simply need to create an SQL select query with the desired conditions (where statements) that retrieves all of the columns in the table, and pass that query to the internal _load() method.

We will use the helper function getSelectFields() to retrieve an array of the columns to fetch in the custom loader SQL (the values in this array are determined by the columns specified in the class constructor). There is also a small optimization at the start of the function that bypasses performing the SQL if invalid values are specified for $user_id and $post_id.

This function should be added to the BlogPost.php file in the ./include/DatabaseObject directory.

Listing 7-14. *A Custom Loader for DatabaseObject_BlogPost (BlogPost.php)*

```php
<?php
    class DatabaseObject_BlogPost extends DatabaseObject
    {
        // ... other code
```

```php
    public function loadForUser($user_id, $post_id)
    {
        $post_id = (int) $post_id;
        $user_id = (int) $user_id;

        if ($post_id <= 0 || $user_id <= 0)
            return false;

        $query = sprintf(
            'select %s from %s where user_id = %d and post_id = %d',
            join(', ', $this->getSelectFields()),
            $this->_table,
            $user_id,
            $post_id
        );

        return $this->_load($query);
    }

    // ... other code
}
?>
```

Looking back to the constructor for the form processor in Listing 7-13, if an existing blog post was successfully loaded, we initialize the form processor with the values of the loaded blog post. This is so that those existing values will be shown in the form. If an existing post wasn't loaded, we set the user_id property to be that of the loaded user. This means that when the post is saved in the process() method (as we will shortly see), the user_id property has already been set.

Next, we must process the submitted form by implementing the process() method in FormProcessor_BlogPost. The steps involved in processing this form are as follows:

1. Check the title and ensure that a value has been entered.

2. Validate the date and time submitted for the post.

3. Filter unwanted HTML out of the blog post body.

4. Check whether or not the post should be sent live immediately.

5. Save the post to the database.

First, to check the title we need to initialize and clean the value using the sanitize() method we first used in Chapter 3. To restrict the length of the title to a maximum of 255 characters (the maximum length of the field in our database schema), we pass the value through substr(). If you try to insert a value into the database longer than the field's definition, the database will simply truncate the variable anyway. We then check the title's length, recording an error if the length is zero.

Note that this isn't very strict checking at all. You may want to extend this check to ensure that at least some alphanumeric characters have been entered. Listing 7-15 shows the code that initializes and checks the title value.

Listing 7-15. *Validating the Blog Post Title (BlogPost.php)*

```php
<?php
    class FormProcessor_BlogPost extends FormProcessor
    {
        // ... other code

        public function process(Zend_Controller_Request_Abstract $request)
        {
            $this->title = $this->sanitize($request->getPost('username'));
            $this->title = substr($this->title, 0, 255);

            if (strlen($this->title) == 0)
                $this->addError('title', 'Please enter a title for this post');

            // ... other code
        }
    }
?>
```

Next, we need to process the submitted date and time to ensure that the specified date is real. We don't really mind what the date and time are, as long as it is a real date (so November 31, for instance, would fail).

To simplify the interface, we showed users a 12-hour clock (rather than a 24-hour clock), so we need to check the meridian ("am/pm") value and adjust the submitted hour accordingly. We will also use the max() and min() functions to ensure the hour is a value from 1 to 12 and the minute is a value from 0 to 59.

Finally, once the date and time have been validated, we will use the mktime() function to create a timestamp that we can pass to DatabaseObject_BlogPost.

■**Note** Beginning in PHP 5.2.0 there is a built-in DateTime class available, which can be used to create and manipulate timestamps. It remains to be seen how popular this class will be. I have chosen to use existing date manipulation functions that most users will already be familiar with.

The code used to initialize and validate the date and time is shown in Listing 7-16. Once we create the timestamp, we must store it in the form processor object so the value can be used when outputting the form again if an error occurs.

Listing 7-16. *Initializing and Processing the Date and Time (BlogPost.php)*

```php
<?php
    class FormProcessor_BlogPost extends FormProcessor
    {
        // ... other code

        public function process(Zend_Controller_Request_Abstract $request)
        {
            // ... other code

            $date = array(
                            'y' => (int) $request->getPost('ts_createdYear'),
                            'm' => (int) $request->getPost('ts_createdMonth'),
                            'd' => (int) $request->getPost('ts_createdDay')
                        );

            $time = array(
                            'h' => (int) $request->getPost('ts_createdHour'),
                            'm' => (int) $request->getPost('ts_createdMinute')
                        );

            $time['h'] = max(1, min(12, $time['h']));
            $time['m'] = max(0, min(59, $time['m']));

            $meridian = strtolower($request->getPost('ts_createdMeridian'));
            if ($meridian != 'pm')
                $meridian = 'am';

            // convert the hour into 24 hour time
            if ($time['h'] < 12 && $meridian == 'pm')
                $time['h'] += 12;
            else if ($time['h'] == 12 && $meridian == 'am')
                $time['h'] = 0;


            if (!checkDate($date['m'], $date['d'], $date['y']))
                $this->addError('ts_created', 'Please select a valid date');

            $this->ts_created = mktime($time['h'],
                                        $time['m'],
                                        0,
                                        $date['m'],
                                        $date['d'],
                                        $date['y']);

            // ... other code
        }
    }
?>
```

Next, we must initialize the blog post body. Since we are allowing a limited set of HTML to be used by users, we must filter the data accordingly. We will write a method called cleanHtml() to do this.

Listing 7-17 shows how we will retrieve the content value from the form, as well as the method we use to filter it (cleanHtml()). This method has been left blank for now, but in the next section we will look more closely at filtering the HTML, which is a very important aspect of securing web-based applications.

Listing 7-17. *Initializing and Processing the Blog Post Content (BlogPost.php)*

```php
<?php
    class FormProcessor_BlogPost extends FormProcessor
    {
        // ... other code

        public function process(Zend_Controller_Request_Abstract $request)
        {
            // ... other code

            $this->content = $this->cleanHtml($request->getPost('content'));

            // ... other code
        }

        // temporary placeholder
        protected function cleanHtml($html)
        {
            return $html;
        }
    }
?>
```

> **■Tip** You may want to specify a maximum length for blog posts (such as a maximum of 5000 characters), although users will likely find this restrictive and annoying. If you were to do this, you could create a new configuration setting in the settings.ini file that defines the maximum length. Note that you would also need to take the HTML tags into consideration. For instance, even though we are allowing some HTML tags, you might want to strip all tags before determining the length of a post.

At this point in the code, the submitted form data will have been read from the form and validated. However, before we save the post, we must determine whether the user wants to preview the post or send it live straight away. We do this by checking for the presence of the preview variable in the submitted form. Since we are using two submit buttons on the form, we must name the buttons differently so we can determine which one was clicked. We named the preview button preview (see Listing 7-12), so if the preview value is set in the form, we know the user clicked that button. (This test can be seen in Listing 7-19.)

In order to make the post live, we must set the status value of the blog post to STATUS_LIVE (since a post is marked as preview initially by default). We will create a new method called sendLive() in the DatabaseObject_BlogPost class to help us with this—it is shown in Listing 7-18.

Listing 7-18. *Easily Setting a Blog Post to Live Status (BlogPost.php)*

```php
<?php
    class DatabaseObject_BlogPost extends DatabaseObject
    {
        public $profile = null;

        const STATUS_DRAFT = 'D';
        const STATUS_LIVE  = 'L';

        // ... other code

        public function sendLive()
        {
            if ($this->status != self::STATUS_LIVE) {
                $this->status = self::STATUS_LIVE;
                $this->profile->ts_published = time();
            }
        }

        public function isLive()
        {
            return $this->isSaved() && $this->status == self::STATUS_LIVE;
        }
    }
?>
```

In the preceding code, we also set a profile variable (that is, a value that is written to the blog_posts_profile table) called ts_published, which stores a timestamp of when the post was set live. Note that the post still needs to be saved after calling this function. The ts_published variable is only set if the status value is actually being changed. In order to check whether or not a post is live, we also add a helper method called isLive() to this class, which returns true if the status value is self::STATUS_LIVE.

In Listing 7-19 we continue implementing the form processor. We first check whether or not any errors have occurred by using the hasError() method. If no errors have occurred, we set the values of the DatabaseObject_BlogPost object and then mark the post as published if required. Finally, we save the database record and return from process().

Listing 7-19. *Saving the Database Record and Returning from the Processor (BlogPost.php)*

```php
<?php
    class FormProcessor_BlogPost extends FormProcessor
    {
        // ... other code

        public function process(Zend_Controller_Request_Abstract $request)
        {
            // ... other code

            // if no errors have occurred, save the blog post
            if (!$this->hasError()) {
                $this->post->profile->title = $this->title;
                $this->post->ts_created = $this->ts_created;
                $this->post->profile->content = $this->content;

                $preview = !is_null($request->getPost('preview'));
                if (!$preview)
                    $this->post->sendLive();

                $this->post->save();
            }

            // return true if no errors have occurred
            return !$this->hasError();
        }

        // ... other code
    }
?>
```

We are nearly at the stage where we can create new blog posts. However, before the form we have created will work, we must perform one final step: create a unique URL for each post. We will now complete this step.

Generating a Permanent Link to a Blog Post

One thing we have overlooked so far is the setting of the url field we created in the blog_posts table. Every post in a user's blog must have a unique value for this field, as the value is used to create a URL that links directly to the respective blog post.

We will generate this value automatically, based on the title of the blog post (as specified by the user when they create the post). We can automate the generation of this value by using the preInsert() method in the DatabaseObject_BlogPost class. This method is called immediately prior to executing the SQL insert statement when creating a new record.

■**Note** Generating the URL automatically when creating the blog post doesn't give users the opportunity to change the URL. If they were able to change this value, it would somewhat defeat the purpose of a permanent link. However, if the user chooses to change the title of their post, the URL will no longer be based on the title. You may want to add an option to the form to let users change the URL value—to simplify matters, I have not included this option.

There are four steps to generating a unique URL:

1. Turn the title value into a string that is URL friendly. To do this, we will ensure that only letters, numbers, and hyphens are included. Additionally, we will make the entire string lowercase for uniformity. We will make the string a maximum of 30 characters, which should be enough to ensure uniqueness. For example, a title of "Went to the movies" could be turned into `went-to-the-movies`. Note that these rules aren't hard and fast—you can adapt them as you please.

2. Check whether or not the generated URL already exists for this user. If it doesn't, proceed to step 4.

3. If the URL already exists, create a unique one by appending a number to the end of the string. So if `went-to-the-movies` already existed, we would make the URL `went-to-the-movies-2`. If this alternate URL already existed, we would use `went-to-the-movies-3`. This process can be repeated until a unique URL is found.

4. Set the URL field in the blog post to the generated value.

Listing 7-20 shows the `generateUniqueUrl()` method, which we will now add to the `BlogPost.php` file in `./include/DatabaseObject`. This method accepts a string as its value and returns a unique value to be used as the URL. The listing also shows the `preInsert()` method, which calls `generateUniqueUrl()`. Remember that `preInsert()` is automatically called when the `save()` method is called for new records.

Listing 7-20. *Automatically Setting the Permanent Link for the Post (BlogPost.php)*

```php
<?php
    class DatabaseObject_BlogPost extends DatabaseObject
    {
        // ... other code

        protected function preInsert()
        {
            $this->url = $this->generateUniqueUrl($this->profile->title);
            return true;
        }
```

```php
// ... other code already in this class

protected function generateUniqueUrl($title)
{
    $url = strtolower($title);

    $filters = array(
        // replace & with 'and' for readability
        '/&+/' => 'and',

        // replace non-alphanumeric characters with a hyphen
        '/[^a-z0-9]+/i' => '-',

        // replace multiple hyphens with a single hyphen
        '/-+/'          => '-'
    );


    // apply each replacement
    foreach ($filters as $regex => $replacement)
        $url = preg_replace($regex, $replacement, $url);

    // remove hyphens from the start and end of string
    $url = trim($url, '-');

    // restrict the length of the URL
    $url = trim(substr($url, 0, 30));

    // set a default value just in case
    if (strlen($url) == 0)
        $url = 'post';


    // find similar URLs
    $query = sprintf("select url from %s where user_id = %d and url like ?",
                     $this->_table,
                     $this->user_id);

    $query = $this->_db->quoteInto($query, $url . '%');
    $result = $this->_db->fetchCol($query);


    // if no matching URLs then return the current URL
    if (count($result) == 0 || !in_array($url, $result))
        return $url;
```

```
        // generate a unique URL
        $i = 2;
        do {
            $_url = $url . '-' . $i++;
        } while (in_array($_url, $result));

        return $_url;
    }
  }
?>
```

■Note The position of these functions in the file is not important, but I tend to keep the callbacks near the top of the classes and put other functions later on in the code.

At the beginning of generateUniqueUrl(), we apply a series of regular expressions to filter out unwanted values and to clean up the string. This includes ensuring the string only has letters, numbers, and hyphens in it, as well as ensuring that multiple hyphens don't appear consecutively in the string. We also trim any hyphens from the start and end of the string. As a final touch to make the string nicer, we replace the & character with the word and.

■Tip As an exercise, you may want to change this portion of the function to use a custom filter that extends from Zend_Filter. To do this, you would create a class called Zend_Filter_CreateUrl (or something similar) that implements the filter() method.

Next, we check the database for any other URLs belonging to the current user that begin with the URL we have just generated. This is done by fetching other URLs that were previously generated from the same value, and then looping until we find a new value that isn't in the database.

At this stage, the code is sufficiently developed that you will be able to use the form at http://phpweb20/blogmanager/edit to create a new blog post. However, we will continue to develop the blog management area in this chapter.

Filtering Submitted HTML

In this application, we allow anybody that signs up (using the registration form created earlier) to submit their own content. Because of this, we need to protect against malicious users whose goal is to attack the web site or its users. This is crucial to ensuring the security of web applications such as this one, where any user can submit data. In situations where only trusted users will be submitting data, filtering data is not as critical, but when anybody can sign up, it is extremely important.

The primary thing we want to protect against is a malicious user submitting JavaScript in one of their posts, which is then executed by another user who views their blog. There are several common ways a malicious user might try to inject JavaScript code into their postings:

- **Inserting `<script>` tags into the submitted data.** A script tag can either load an external JavaScript file (by specifying the `src` attribute), or it can contain any number of commands inline that perform malicious actions.

- **Adding DOM event handlers to other nonmalicious tags.** Manipulating other tags, such as hyperlinks or images, to include JavaScript can be just as effective as using `<script>` tags directly. An example would be adding a mouseover event to an image, such as `<img src="/some-image.jpg" onmouseover="doSomethingEvil()" />`.

■**Note** This hasn't been a problem in earlier user-submitted data we have processed because we have passed it to the `sanitize()` method of `FormProcessor`, which strips all tags from the data. Additionally, when we have outputted this data, we have used the Smarty `escape` modifier, which means that even if an HTML tag such as `<script>` were to get through our processing, it would be output to screen as `&lt;script&gt;`, meaning that any code included would not be treated as JavaScript by the browser.

Why Filter Embedded JavaScript?

You may wonder what it matters if a user manages to inject JavaScript code into one of their posts. After all, how bad could it possibly be if somebody makes a pop-up window appear on somebody else's screen?

■**Note** Making a pop-up window appear is one of the simplest and least harmful attacks that can be achieved.

The biggest problem occurs when another authenticated user views the malicious post. Some examples of the damage that could occur are as follows:

- The JavaScript could dynamically send the user's cookies to some third-party web site. This could potentially allow the malicious user to hijack the victim's session, since session IDs are usually stored in cookies. The malicious user could then masquerade as an authenticated user on the web site. This is known as a cross-site scripting (XSS) attack.

- The JavaScript could submit a form or visit some other URL on the current web site that deletes a post in the victim's blog, or that updates their password. This is called a cross-site request forgery (CSRF) attack.

Types of Filtering

There are two ways we can filter out HTML tags from submitted data:

- Define a *white list* of tags that users are allowed to use. We then strip out every other tag.

- Define a *black list* of tags that are not allowed to be used. We then strip out only these tags and allow the rest.

Whether you use a white list or a black list comes down to personal preference and how the system will be used in the future. I prefer the white list in this situation, since there are so many HTML tags and a white list allows you to fully control what can be used. For example, if a browser introduced a new tag called <doSomethingMalicious> (as an extreme example), a white list would automatically prevent the use of this, while a black list would allow it until we added it to the list.

This is the white list of tags and attributes we will use:

- Allow the <a>, <img>, <b>, <strong>, <em>, <i>, <ul>, <li>, <ol>, <p>, and <br> tags.

- For the <a> tag, allow the href, target, and name attributes.

- For the <img> tag, allow the src and alt attributes.

This automatically rules out the use of any event attributes in tags (such as onmouseover or onclick).

You could potentially choose to allow the style attribute, since you might not care how users choose to manipulate the styles and colors. However, if you're going to display posts from a number of different users on a single page, you will want to be a bit fussier about how they are displayed.

Implementing the cleanHtml() Method

Now that we have defined which tags and attributes are acceptable, we must implement the cleanHtml() method in FormProcessor_BlogPost, which we created in Listing 7-17.

Thankfully, the Zend_Filter component of the Zend Framework provides a filter called Zend_Filter_StripTags, which gives us some flexibility in setting our tag and attribute requirements. We can either pass an array of allowed tags and an array of allowed attributes, or we can pass a single array where the key is the allowed tag and the element is an array of allowed attributes for that tag.

Note, though, that there is a special case we must deal with: the href attribute value for hyperlinks. Browsers will execute inline JavaScript code if it begins with javascript:. The simplest test case for this is to create a link as follows:

```
<a href="javascript:alert('Oh no!')">Open alert box</a>
```

To deal with this special case, we will simply replace any occurrences of javascript: that occur within any tags. This can be achieved easily using preg_replace().

■**Caution** Be aware of tags similar to `<a>` that aren't in our white list, such as `<area>` (used in image maps), which also define an `href` attribute. Web browsers will also allow JavaScript to be embedded using `javascript:` so you must also filter these tags if you decide to use them.

Listing 7-21 shows the code for `cleanHtml()`, which defines the list of allowed tags and attributes we covered above, and then filters the passed-in HTML and returns it to be inserted into the database. The highlighted code should be included in the `BlogPost.php` file in the `./include/FormProcessor` directory.

Listing 7-21. *Using Zend_Filter_StripTags to Clean Submitted HTML (BlogPost.php)*

```php
<?php
    class FormProcessor_BlogPost extends FormProcessor
    {
        static $tags = array(
            'a'      => array('href', 'target', 'name'),
            'img'    => array('src', 'alt'),
            'b'      => array(),
            'strong' => array(),
            'em'     => array(),
            'i'      => array(),
            'ul'     => array(),
            'li'     => array(),
            'ol'     => array(),
            'p'      => array(),
            'br'     => array()
        );

        // ... other code

        protected function cleanHtml($html)
        {
            $chain = new Zend_Filter();
            $chain->addFilter(new Zend_Filter_StripTags(self::$tags));
            $chain->addFilter(new Zend_Filter_StringTrim());

            $html = $chain->filter($html);

            $tmp = $html;
            while (1) {
                // Try and replace an occurrence of javascript:
                $html = preg_replace('/(<[^>]*)javascript:([^>]*>)/i',
                                     '$1$2',
                                     $html);
```

```
            // If nothing changed this iteration then break the loop
            if ($html == $tmp)
                break;

            $tmp = $html;
        }

        return $html;
    }
}
?>
```

The regular expression in Listing 7-21 looks for an occurrence of the string javascript: within the < and > characters (thereby allowing the term to be written in the normal blog post text). Whatever is matched before javascript: in the string is held in $1 for the replacement, and the text afterwards is held in $2.

Because this pattern only replaces one instance of javascript: at a time, we need to keep looping until all instances have been found. We do this by checking whether the string returned from preg_replace() is different from the one returned on the previous call. If these strings are the same, all instances of javascript: have been removed.

Consider a string such as the following:

```
<a href="javascript:alert('Oh no!')">javascript: is bad!</a>
```

After this string is processed by preg_replace(), it becomes

```
<a href="alert('Oh no!')">javascript: is bad!</a>
```

This version of the string is perfectly safe and won't result in any JavaScript being executed when the link is clicked (the link however, is invalid, and will likely result in an error).

Creating a New Blog Post

Aside from including the WYSIWYG editor, the form for submitting new blog posts and the corresponding form processor are now complete, meaning that users can now create new blog posts by logging in to their accounts and either clicking the "Post new blog entry" link or browsing to the blog manager (using the main navigation) and clicking the button labeled "Create new blog post". The URL of the form we just created is http://phpweb20/blogmanager/edit.

Figure 7-1 shows how the form looks when viewed in Firefox. As you can see, the text area holding the post is somewhat small and almost unusable. If you would prefer not to use a WYSIWYG editor, you could add a style to the CSS file to make this field larger (such as form .row textarea { width : 230px; height : 60px; }); however, since we will be replacing this in the next chapter, I have not worried about it.

> ■**Note** The WYSIWYG editor we will integrate in Chapter 8 will automatically display a text area if the user's browser is unable to show the "proper" version. Additionally, it will size the text area to the size the WYSIWYG editor would have been.

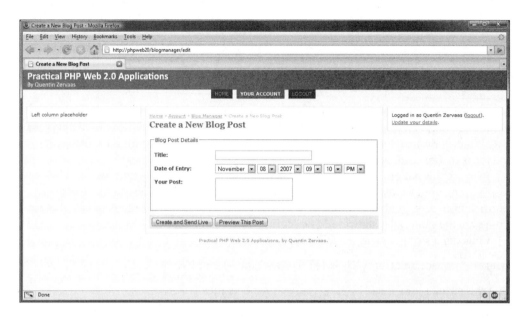

Figure 7-1. *Creating a new blog post*

If you try to submit this form, you will be redirected to the preview action of the controller after successful completion, which we have not yet implemented. Additionally, although the form has the ability to update existing blog posts, there is not yet any way for users to view their existing posts, meaning that they cannot reach this form to edit their posts. We will add the list of existing posts in Chapter 8.

Previewing Blog Posts

The next step in implementing blog management tools is to provide a preview of each post to the user. We will implement the previewAction() method of BlogmanagerController, which is used to show a single post to a user, giving them options to either publish or unpublish the post (depending on its existing status). Additionally, users will be able to edit or delete their posts using the buttons we will add to this page, and we will expand these options in the future to include tag management (Chapter 10), image management (Chapter 11), and location management (Chapter 13).

Creating the Preview Action

The previewAction() method will display the details of the post, while also giving the user the option to edit or delete the post. Additionally, the user will be able to make draft posts live, or to unpublish posts that are already live.

These options will be handled by the setstatusAction() method that we will implement in the next section, but for now we will implement the previewAction() method and its associated template.

Listing 7-22 shows the content we will add to BlogmanagerController.php (in ./include/Controllers). If the selected post is unable to be loaded for the logged-in user, the user is redirected back to the blog manager index page. You could choose to display a "post not found" message, but since they could only access such a URL by manually typing it, this extra level of user friendliness is simply overkill.

Listing 7-22. *Loading a Blog Post for Preview (BlogmanagerController.php)*

```php
<?php
    class BlogmanagerController extends CustomControllerAction
    {
        // ... other code

        public function previewAction()
        {
            $post_id = (int) $this->getRequest()->getQuery('id');

            $post = new DatabaseObject_BlogPost($this->db);
            if (!$post->loadForUser($this->identity->user_id, $post_id))
                $this->_redirect($this->getUrl());

            $this->breadcrumbs->addStep('Preview Post: ' . $post->profile->title);

            $this->view->post = $post;
        }

        // ... other code
    }
?>
```

Implementing the Preview Template

Now we will look at the preview.tpl template, which we will use to show a blog post to its owner. Listing 7-23 shows the first half of this template, which we will store in the ./templates/blogmanager directory. We will enhance this template using JavaScript (created in Listing 7-26).

Listing 7-23. *The First Half of the Preview Template (preview.tpl)*

```
{include file='header.tpl' section='blogmanager'}

<script type="text/javascript" src="/js/blogPreview.js"></script>

<form method="post"
      action="{geturl controller='blogmanager' action='setstatus'}"
      id="status-form">

<div class="preview-status">
    <input type="hidden" name="id" value="{$post->getId()}" />
    {if $post->isLive()}
        <div class="status live">
            This post is live on your blog. To unpublish
            it click the <strong>Unpublish post</strong> button below.
            <div>
                <input type="submit" value="Unpublish post"
                       name="unpublish" id="status-unpublish" />
                <input type="submit" value="Edit post"
                       name="edit" id="status-edit" />
                <input type="submit" value="Delete post"
                       name="delete" id="status-delete" />
            </div>
        </div>
```

Note This template won't work until we complete it below—we're currently in the middle of an {if} statement.

In the preceding code, the status box that is created is for live listings only. This is determined by calling the isLive() method on the post. Listing 7-24 shows the remainder of this template, which shows similar code for unpublished listings.

Listing 7-24. *The Second Half of the Preview Template (preview.tpl)*

```
    {else}
        <div class="status draft">
            This post is not yet live on your blog. To publish
            it on your blog, click the button below.
            <div>
                <input type="submit" value="Publish post"
                       name="publish" id="status-publish" />
                <input type="submit" value="Edit post"
                       name="edit" id="status-edit" />
```

```
                <input type="submit" value="Delete post"
                        name="delete" id="status-delete" />
            </div>
        </div>
    {/if}
</div>

</form>

<div class="preview-date">
    {$post->ts_created|date_format:'%x %X'}
</div>

<div class="preview-content">
    {$post->profile->content}
</div>

{include file='footer.tpl'}
```

As you can see, after the if/else statement is closed, we output the date and time of the post, as well as the content of the post. To output the date and time, we use the date_format modifier, which uses the same arguments as the PHP strftime() function. We use the %x switch to output the current date and %X for the current time, both using the preferred representation for the current locale.

Next we need to add some new styles to format the status box and the date and time. We will show the status box in green for published posts and in orange for unpublished posts. Listing 7-25 shows the new styles we will add to the ./htdocs/css/styles.css file.

Listing 7-25. *New Styles Used to Format the Blog Post Preview (styles.css)*

```
@media screen {

    /* ... other code */

    /**
     * Status boxes
     */

    div.status {
        padding    : 5px;
        margin     : 5px 0;
    }

    .status.live {
        color      : #fff;
        background : #070;
    }
```

```css
.status.draft {
    color      : #fff;
    background : #fa0;
}



/**
 * Previewing of blog posts
 */

.preview-status form { margin-top : 5px; }
.preview-status { margin-bottom : 10px; }
.preview-date {
    font-size : 0.9em;
    color     : #999;
}
}

/* ... other code */
```

Tip To apply styles to elements with multiple class names (as we did with `<div class="status live">`), you simply include both class names without spacing in the CSS file. So, in this case, we can apply styles to `.status.live`. Note that the support of this functionality in Internet Explorer 6 is somewhat unpredictable, and the order of the classes can sometimes affect how the markup is rendered (so in IE6 `.live.status` may behave differently than `.status.live`), depending on the makeup of other styles in the style sheet.

Requesting Confirmation for User Actions

Finally, as a way to improve the interface, we will display a confirmation box when a user tries to publish (or unpublish) a blog post, as well as when they try to delete a post. To help with this, we will now create a new JavaScript file in which we observe the `click` events on each of those buttons. For further details on how Prototype's `Event.observe()` works, refer to Chapter 5.

Listing 7-26 shows the code we will add to the `./htdocs/js/blogPreview.js` file (this file was loaded by the code in Listing 7-23). In this code, we check that each element exists before trying to observe the `click` event, since the publish button won't be shown for posts that are already published, and the unpublish button won't be shown for draft posts.

Listing 7-26. *Attaching Click Events to the Post Preview Buttons (blogPreview.js)*

```javascript
Event.observe(window, 'load', function() {

    var publishButton   = $('status-publish');
```

```
    var unpublishButton = $('status-unpublish');
    var deleteButton    = $('status-delete');

    if (publishButton) {
        publishButton.observe('click', function(e) {
            if (!confirm('Click OK to publish this post'))
                Event.stop(e);
        });
    }

    if (unpublishButton) {
        unpublishButton.observe('click', function(e) {
            if (!confirm('Click OK to unpublish this post'))
                Event.stop(e);
        });
    }

    if (deleteButton) {
        deleteButton.observe('click', function(e) {
            if (!confirm('Click OK to permanently delete this post'))
                Event.stop(e);
        });
    }
});
```

■Note This code goes inside the window `onload` event to ensure that the button elements exist in the DOM when this code is executed.

In the preceding code we want to stop the form from being submitted if the user clicks cancel in any of the confirmation boxes. To achieve this, we call the `Event.stop()` method.

■Note You may be more familiar with returning `false` from links or forms to prevent the browser from proceeding. In Prototype's event handling, this does not apply—to prevent an event from propagating (that is, from following the link or submitting the form) after the event has been handled, you must call `Event.stop()`. This is covered in more detail in Chapter 5.

Figure 7-2 shows the preview page for a post that has not yet been published. Note that the buttons will not work until we implement the `setstatus` action.

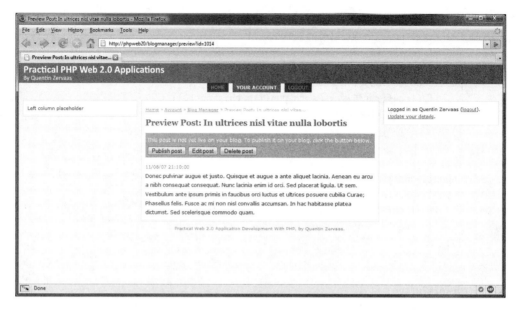

Figure 7-2. *Previewing a blog post that is not yet live*

Updating the Status of a Blog Post

In Listings 7-23 and 7-24 we created a form to update the status of a blog post. We must now implement the controller action to handle the processing of this form. In addition to changing the status or deleting the post, we also added an option to edit posts. If the user clicks the edit button, we need to redirect them to the edit action we created earlier.

Completing setstatusAction()

Since the earlier version of setstatusAction() we created was empty, we will complete the method with the code shown in Listing 7-27.

Listing 7-27. *Handling the Different Types of Status Updates (BlogmanagerController.php)*

```php
<?php
    class BlogmanagerController extends CustomControllerAction
    {
        // ... other code

        public function setstatusAction()
        {
            $request = $this->getRequest();
            $post_id = (int) $request->getPost('id');

            $post = new DatabaseObject_BlogPost($this->db);
            if (!$post->loadForUser($this->identity->user_id, $post_id))
```

```php
        $this->_redirect($this->getUrl());

        // URL to redirect back to
        $url = $this->getUrl('preview') . '?id=' . $post->getId();

        if ($request->getPost('edit')) {
            $this->_redirect($this->getUrl('edit') . '?id=' . $post->getId());
        }
        else if ($request->getPost('publish')) {
            $post->sendLive();
            $post->save();

        }
        else if ($request->getPost('unpublish')) {
            $post->sendBackToDraft();
            $post->save();

        }
        else if ($request->getPost('delete')) {
            $post->delete();

            // Preview page no longer exists for this page so go back to index
            $url = $this->getUrl();

        }

        $this->_redirect($url);
    }

    // ... other code
}
?>
```

Once again, as in previewAction(), we initialize the post ID and try to load the record based on that value and the user ID of the logged-in user. Since we are accessing the request variables several times in the method, it makes the code somewhat more readable to assign the request to $request.

Next, we define the return URL. This is where the user will be redirected to after the current action has completed (apart from the edit and delete actions). This URL is simply the preview page for the given blog post.

To determine which action to take, we simply need to check for the presence of the appropriate variable in the request post data. For example, if the user clicks the publish button, publish will be set in the post data, but the other buttons won't be.

In order to unpublish a live blog post, we will use a helper function called sendBackToDraft(), which does nothing more than set the status value of the post to DatabaseObject_BlogPost:: STATUS_DRAFT. The function—which we will add to ./include/DatabaseObject/BlogPost.php—is provided more for completeness than anything, since we already have the sendLive() function. The sendBackToDraft() function is shown in Listing 7-28.

Listing 7-28. *The sendBackToDraft() Function (BlogPost.php)*

```php
<?php
    class DatabaseObject_BlogPost extends DatabaseObject
    {
        // ... other code

        public function sendBackToDraft()
        {
            $this->status = self::STATUS_DRAFT;
        }

        // ... other code
    }
?>
```

Referring back to Listing 7-27, you can see that it's simply a matter of calling the delete()
method on the DatabaseObject_BlogPost object to delete the post. Since the preview page for
this post will no longer be valid (since the post doesn't exist), we will change the URL to redirect the user back to the blog manager index page.

■**Note** If you look closely at setstatusAction(), you will notice that if you pass in a valid post ID but not
a valid action, all that occurs is that the user is redirected to the post preview page. You can take advantage
of this if you want to provide a submit button to reach the preview page.

Notifying the User

As the code stands now, the user isn't informed when a change is made. For example, when a
post is deleted, the user is simply redirected back to the blog manager index page and is not
told that the post was actually deleted. While this is not a huge problem when sending a post
live (or changing it back to draft) due to the colored box we use to display the status, it is still
good practice to inform them of the change that was made. It is also important after updating
an existing post to notify the user that the changes have been saved.

To achieve this, we are going to display a message to the user after they arrive on the
"next" page (that is, the page we redirect them to after competing the chosen action). One
thing to be aware of is that the new page needs to know about the status message somehow.
To do this, we will store the message in the user's session, and then remove it from the session
once they have viewed it (to prevent it from continually being shown).

Fortunately, Zend_Controller provides us with functionality to achieve this. The
FlashMessenger action helper class (in no way related to Adobe's Flash technology) allows us
to easily do exactly this. It is instantiated automatically by Zend Controller when we try to
access it.

The other change we will make to our code is to assign all messages found in the flash
messenger object to the template. In the template, we will then check whether there are any
messages, and if so we can output them accordingly.

■**Note** This flash message container will integrate nicely with any real-time operations we perform using Ajax. We can reuse this same container to display any messages that are generated dynamically with JavaScript. As we implement Ajax features in this book, we will use this container.

Adding FlashMessenger to CustomControllerAction

We are going to create the flash messenger in the init() function of CustomControllerAction, which means it will be created for every single request that takes place on our site. This makes it very useful, as we can then use it not only to tell logged-in users about updates to their blog posts, but also to give any notification to any user (whether authenticated or not).

To instantiate the flash messenger, we simply access it from the _helper object, which is an internal property of Zend_Controller_Action (the class which CustomControllerAction extends from). If $this->_helper doesn't find the flash messenger, it will automatically create it for us.

Listing 7-29 shows the code we will add to the CustomControllerAction.php file (in the ./include directory), which includes not only additions to init(), but also assigns any messages that may be stored in the messenger to the template.

Listing 7-29. *Creating the Flash Messenger and Assigning Its Messages to the Template (CustomControllerAction.php)*

```php
<?php
    class CustomControllerAction extends Zend_Controller_Action
    {
        public $db;
        public $breadcrumbs;
        public $messenger;

        public function init()
        {
            // ... other code

            $this->messenger = $this->_helper->_flashMessenger;
        }

        // ... other code

        public function postDispatch()
        {
            // ... other code

            $this->view->messages = $this->messenger->getMessages();
        }
    }
?>
```

Writing Messages to FlashMessenger

The next step is to write messages to the flash messenger as required. In the case of updating the status of blog posts, we will write a message when a post is sent live, when a post is unpublished, and when a post is deleted. We will make further use of the messenger in other parts of this web application.

To add a message, we simply call $this->messenger->addMessage('The message'). Effectively, all this does is write a message to the current session, which will automatically be deleted on the subsequent page request (meaning it is retrieved for display in the next request and then immediately deleted).

Listing 7-30 shows a new version of the setstatusAction() function for BlogmanagerController, which now adds messages to the $this->messenger object as required.

Listing 7-30. *Adding Messages to the Messenger As Required (BlogmanagerController.php)*

```php
<?php
    class BlogmanagerController extends CustomControllerAction
    {
        // ... other code

        public function setstatusAction()
        {
            $request = $this->getRequest();
            $post_id = (int) $request->getPost('id');

            $post = new DatabaseObject_BlogPost($this->db);
            if (!$post->loadForUser($this->identity->user_id, $post_id))
                $this->_redirect($this->getUrl());

            // URL to redirect back to
            $url = $this->getUrl('preview') . '?id=' . $post->getId();

            if ($request->getPost('edit')) {
                $this->_redirect($this->getUrl('edit') . '?id=' . $post->getId());
            }
            else if ($request->getPost('publish')) {
                $post->sendLive();
                $post->save();

                $this->messenger->addMessage('Post sent live');
            }
            else if ($request->getPost('unpublish')) {
                $post->sendBackToDraft();
                $post->save();

                $this->messenger->addMessage('Post unpublished');
            }
            else if ($request->getPost('delete')) {
```

```
            $post->delete();

            // Preview page no longer exists for this page so go back to index
            $url = $this->getUrl();

            $this->messenger->addMessage('Post deleted');
        }

        $this->_redirect($url);
    }

    // ... other code
    }
?>
```

Outputting FlashMessenger Messages on the Web Site

Finally, we must output any existing messages to the template. In order for messages to be displayed regardless of where the user is in the site (in other words, so we can use it in other areas aside from managing blog posts), we add the display code to the footer.tpl template, because we will be displaying messages in the right column.

Just like the error containers we created for form errors, we will reuse this message container for similar messages we generate from Ajax requests. To achieve this, we check how many messages there are available to be written. If there are none, we apply the display: none style so the message container does not appear. Later, when we add Ajax functionality, we can simply unhide this element as required. If there is more than one message, we will use an unordered list (<ul>) to output the messages.

Listing 7-31 shows the changes we will make to footer.tpl (in the ./templates directory), which checks the $messages array for any messages to output. Note that if there's only one message, the $messages array contains only one element, so we use $messages.0 in Smarty to access this array element.

Listing 7-31. *Outputting Status Messages to the Template (footer.tpl)*

```
        </div>
    </div>

    <div id="left-container" class="column">
        <!-- // ... other code -->
    </div>

    <div id="right-container" class="column">
        {if $messages|@count > 0}
            <div id="messages" class="box">
                {if $messages|@count == 1}
                    <strong>Status Message:</strong>
                    {$messages.0|escape}
                {else}
```

```
                    <strong>Status Messages:</strong>
                    <ul>
                        {foreach from=$messages item=row}
                            <li>{$row|escape}</li>
                        {/foreach}
                    </ul>
                {/if}
            </div>
        {else}
            <div id="messages" class="box" style="display:none"></div>
        {/if}

        <!-- // ... other code -->
    </div>

    <!-- // ... other code -->
    </body>
</html>
```

Note I have chosen to display status messages in the right column of the web site. You may prefer to use a different location, such as between the breadcrumbs and page title in the main area of the page. You may also want to add a close button to the `#messages` div to allow the user to hide the status message window immediately. To do so, you would use `Event.observe()` on that close button, which would call `$('messages').hide()`. When we reuse this status box later in this chapter for Ajax notifications, we will set the box to auto-hide after a short delay.

This is all that is required to get the flash messenger working; however, it doesn't stand out for users very well. In order to make it stand out more, we will use the Scriptaculous `Highlight` effect. To apply this effect (with the default colors and time delay), the only code we have to use is as follows:

```
<script type="text/javascript">
    new Effect.Highlight('messages');
</script>
```

In an effort to keep the page markup as clean as possible (and also to ensure that this code doesn't run until the Scriptaculous files have all loaded), we will make this effect run once the page has loaded.

To do so, we will create a new file called `scripts.js`, which we will store in `./htdocs/js`. This file will contain any custom JavaScript we will use globally in our application (that is, on all pages). For now, though, all we are going to do is create a function that runs once the page has loaded. This is the equivalent of writing HTML like `<body onload="someFunc()">`, but we are going to do it the "Web 2.0 way" using Prototype (that is, observing the `window.onload` event properly and not cluttering up the page HTML).

Listing 7-32 shows the contents of the scripts.js file, which begins by creating a hash called settings that we can use to hold any required settings (making the JavaScript code more maintainable). For starters, we define the ID of the element that holds messages. Next, we define a function that will run on page load, which currently finds the #messages element and applies the Effect.Highlight class to it. Finally, we observe the onload event. The Event.observe() call follows the function definition of init(), because the function would be undefined at run time if it were the other way around.

Note that we first check that #messages is visible using the Prototype function isVisible(), as we still include the element on the page (as a hidden element) even if there are no messages. Internally, Effect.Highlight actually checks this for you, but it's still good to be explicit in your own code as to how you want it to function.

Listing 7-32. *Highlighting the Messages Div after the Page Has Loaded (scripts.js)*

```
var settings = {
    messages : 'messages'
};

function init(e)
{
    // check if the messages element exists and is visible,
    // and if so, apply the highlight effect to it
    var messages = $(settings.messages);

    if (messages && messages.visible()) {
        new Effect.Highlight(messages);
    }
}

Event.observe(window, 'load', init);
```

Note Because Effect.Highlight is a class and not a function, you must remember to use the new keyword when applying the effect. Otherwise a JavaScript error will occur. This applies to other effects in Scriptaculous too.

Finally, we must make the scripts.js file load from header.tpl. This file must be included after the inclusion of both Prototype and Scriptaculous. Listing 7-33 shows the updated version of header.tpl that loads scripts.js.

Listing 7-33. *Loading scripts.js in the Web Site Header (header.tpl)*

```
<!DOCTYPE html
    PUBLIC "-//W3C//DTD XHTML 1.0 Strict//EN"
    "http://www.w3.org/TR/xhtml1/DTD/xhtml1-strict.dtd">
```

```
<html xmlns="http://www.w3.org/1999/xhtml" lang="en" xml:lang="en">
    <head>
        <!-- // ... other code -->
        <script type="text/javascript" src="/js/prototype.js"></script>
        <script type="text/javascript"
                src="/js/scriptaculous/scriptaculous.js"></script>
        <script type="text/javascript" src="/js/scripts.js"></script>
    </head>
    <body>
        <!-- // ... other code -->
```

Figure 7-3 shows how status messages are displayed on a typical page in our web application. This message is a result of clicking the Publish Post button on the preview page for a post.

Figure 7-3. *Displaying the status message after a blog post has been sent live*

Summary

In this chapter we began the implementation of the blogging functionality of our Web 2.0 application. Specifically, we added the ability to create, edit, and delete posts. We also implemented a simple publishing system that allows users to preview a blog post before they publish it. The blog posts aren't actually published anywhere yet—we will do this in Chapter 9.

The key concepts we covered in this chapter include the following:

- Extending the permissions system as required.

- Cross-site scripting (XSS) and cross-site request forgery (CSRF) attacks and how they can occur.

- Preventing such attacks by correctly filtering user-submitted data. We achieved this by defining a white list of allowed HTML tags and attributes, and stripping out everything else.

- Implementing a simple notification system using the Zend_Controller flash messenger and Scriptaculous, so users know what (if any) action has been performed.

In Chapter 8 we will continue to build on the blogging system by adding greater functionality to the blog manager. This will include an Ajax-powered blog post listing to help users manage their blogs, as well a WYSIWYG editor so users can format their posts more easily.

CHAPTER 8

■■■

Extending the Blog Manager

In Chapter 7 we began implementing the blogging functionality in our web application, which included giving users the ability to add, edit, and delete posts, as well as allowing them to preview posts prior to sending them live.

In this chapter, we will continue to implement these blog management tools, building on what we started in the previous chapter. The features we will implement include the following:

- **Retrieving multiple posts.** So far in the blog manager we load only one blog post database record at a time. We will look at how to effectively retrieve large amounts of data from the database in a single operation.

- **Displaying existing blog posts.** Using the functions we create to retrieve multiple blog posts, we will create an index page used to list a user's posts so they can preview or edit them as required. We will make this post index Ajax-powered to help users quickly access their previous posts.

- **Integrating a WYSIWYG editor.** We will implement FCKeditor, an open source What You See Is What You Get (WYSIWYG) editor. This will allow users to easily format their blog posts with HTML using the provided toolbar.

Once you have completed this chapter, the blog management tools will be in a sufficient state to allow users to quickly and easily post new entries to their blogs. This will allow users to move on (in Chapter 9) to publishing their blog so other users can view it.

Listing Blog Posts on the Blog Manager Index

Currently users are able to create new blog posts using the tools created in Chapter 7, but there is no way to return to existing posts to edit them. For users to easily manage their blog posts, we will now add a list of all their posts on the blog manager index page (http://phpweb20/blogmanager).

We'll display their posts so all of their posts from the current month are displayed at the top of the page (with a short teaser summary of each post), with a monthly summary to the side of this list, in the left column. The user will be able to click a month to reload the page with the selected month's posts showing.

Once we have completed this functionality, we will improve this code to use Ajax to fetch a list of the selected month's post, meaning the page will not have to be reloaded. Initially we are creating the "non-Ajax" version of the blog manager index, which is provided for accessibility and for browsers that don't support JavaScript.

The process for achieving this is as follows:

1. Retrieving the posts for the specified month (this will default to the current month)

2. Retrieving a list of the other months that contain posts, as well as the number of posts belonging to that month

3. Outputting the selected month's posts with a brief summary of the post

4. Outputting the summary of months, linking back to the indexAction() method to list those posts

Fetching Blog Posts from the Database

Before we can do anything else, we must allow multiple records to be accessed at one time in the DatabaseObject_BlogPost class. So far, we have only ever loaded one record at a time; however, now we want to load multiple records.

To do this, we'll write four separate static methods that we can use in this chapter, as well as in other parts of the application (when displaying blog posts in other areas of the site):

- GetPosts(): This method will retrieve an array of posts based on the options passed in. This includes the ability to set the offset and limit of the returned results for multipaged data. It will return an array of DatabaseObject_BlogPost objects.

- GetPostsCount(): This method will return the total number of posts that match the passed-in criteria. Since GetPosts() will be able to return multipaged data (in that we can specify the offset and limit), we will need to know the total number of posts so the number of pages can be determined.

- GetMonthlySummary(): Similar to GetPostsCount(), this method is used to return the number of posts found for each month in the specified date range. If no date range is specified, then all months with posts will be included.

- _GetBaseQuery(): This private method will be used by each of the previous functions to build a query for the specified options. This is purely used to prevent code duplication. For instance, if you wanted to add a new option to how posts are retrieved in GetPosts(), you would want this same functionality in GetPostsCount() so an accurate count is returned.

Creating the _GetBaseQuery() Method

Since GetPosts(), GetPostsCount(), and GetMonthlySummary() will all rely on _GetBaseQuery(), I'll cover the _GetBaseQuery() method first. We'll use the Zend_Db_Select class that comes with the Zend_Db component of the Zend Framework. This class is used to build SQL select queries.

It provides methods to easily add the various parts that make up such a query. For example, the where() method is called to add a where clause. For more information on this class, you can read the Zend Framework manual entry at http://framework.zend.com/manual/en/zend.db.select.html.

To instantiate Zend_Db_Select, you can use new Zend_Db_Select($db) (where $db is the database connection), or you can call $db->select() to retrieve a new instance.

Listing 8-1 shows the complete _GetBaseQuery() function as it fits into the DatabaseObject_ BlogPost class.

Listing 8-1. *The _GetBaseQuery() Function, Used to Build a SQL Select Statement (BlogPost.php)*

```php
<?php
    class DatabaseObject_BlogPost extends DatabaseObject
    {
        // ... other code

        private static function _GetBaseQuery($db, $options)
        {
            // initialize the options
            $defaults = array(
                'user_id' => array(),
                'from'    => '',
                'to'      => ''
            );

            foreach ($defaults as $k => $v) {
                $options[$k] = array_key_exists($k, $options) ? $options[$k] : $v;
            }

            // create a query that selects from the blog_posts table
            $select = $db->select();
            $select->from(array('p' => 'blog_posts'), array());


            // filter the records based on the start and finish dates
            if (strlen($options['from']) > 0) {
                $ts = strtotime($options['from']);
                $select->where('p.ts_created >= ?', date('Y-m-d H:i:s', $ts));
            }

            if (strlen($options['to']) > 0) {
                $ts = strtotime($options['to']);
                $select->where('p.ts_created <= ?', date('Y-m-d H:i:s', $ts));
            }

            // filter results on specified user ids (if any)
            if (count($options['user_id']) > 0)
                $select->where('p.user_id in (?)', $options['user_id']);

            return $select;
        }
    }
?>
```

The first thing this method does is define an array of default options. At this stage, the only options are the user_id parameter (to specify which user to filter returned data on) and the from and to parameters, which define the date range of returned posts.

Next we loop over these defaults to initialize all of these values in the $options array, so we know they will exist when we try to access them in the remainder of the method.

The next step is to instantiate Zend_Db_Select by calling $db->select(). Typically the first thing you should do with your new instance of Zend_Db_Select is to define the tables to select from and to define which fields to select from those tables. Each table to select from can be specified using the from() method (you must call it once for each table).

The first argument to from() is the name of the table. You can use either a string or an array for this argument. Using an array allows you to give an alias to the table name for later use in the query. This array consists of one element: the value is the name of the table, while its key is the table alias.

We will be using the blog_posts table, which we will give an alias of p. Hence, the first argument to from() is array('p' => 'blog_posts').

The second argument to from() is the fields you want to select. You can select one field by specifying a single string, or you can select multiple fields by using an array (where each element corresponds to a column from the table). In our case, we use an empty array since _GetBaseQuery() is used only to build the base options for the query. In the other methods that call _GetBaseQuery(), we will specify which fields to select.

Next we check for the presence of the from and to parameters, which are used to filter the posts by the date and time stored in the ts_created column of the blog_posts table. If the options are empty, we ignore them, but if they have been specified, we add where clauses to restrict the dates based on these timestamps.

The next thing we to do is add where clauses to filter the results on the user_id column. The Zend_Db class takes care of quoting the values. This is extremely important since this helps to prevent malicious users who try to attack your applications using SQL injection.

When calling the where() method, the first argument is the where clause, which can include a question mark to indicate a placeholder for a value that should be substituted into the clause. The second (optional) argument is the value that should be substituted in for the question mark.

When Zend_Db quotes values, it checks their types so values are included correctly. For example, if an array is specified (as in our case), each value is quoted accordingly (and then joined by a comma). This allows us to pass in multiple values in the $options['user_id'] value, meaning we can filter on multiple users at once if we want to do so.

■**Note** Using an array as the value is designed for using in rather than an equals sign. So if $options['user_id'] were defined as array(1, 2, 3, 4), the generated SQL would read user_id in (1, 2, 3, 4).

Finally, we return the Zend_Db_Select object. This allows GetPosts() and GetPostsCount() to make further additions to the query if required (which they will, as you will now see). Note that the query generated thus far is unusable since we haven't specified any fields to select (as noted earlier in the discussion of the from() method).

Creating the GetPostsCount() Function

Next we define the GetPostsCount() method, which returns the total number of results that
would be returned for the passed-in criteria (that is, the number of rows that GetPosts()
would return if no limit were specified). Just like in _GetBaseQuery(), we accept an array called
$options that holds the required options for the database query. There are no options specific
to GetPostsCount(), so it simply passes on the array to _GetBaseQuery().

Listing 8-2 shows the GetPostsCount() method, which belongs in the BlogPost.php file in
the ./include/DatabaseObject directory. Since we already specified the table to select from
in _GetBaseQuery(), we pass null as the argument to from() and include only which column
to fetch—in this case count(*), since we are counting the number of rows. It then uses the
fetchOne() function to return the first element of the first returned row, which in this case will
be the total number of rows found.

Listing 8-2. *The GetPostsCount() Method, Which Determines the Total Number of Rows That
Would Be Returned (BlogPost.php)*

```php
<?php
    class DatabaseObject_BlogPost extends DatabaseObject
    {
        // ... other code

        public static function GetPostsCount($db, $options)
        {
            $select = self::_GetBaseQuery($db, $options);
            $select->from(null, 'count(*)');

            return $db->fetchOne($select);
        }

        private static function _GetBaseQuery($db, $options)
        {
            // ... other code
        }
    }
?>
```

Creating the GetPosts() Function

Now that we have a good idea of how _GetBaseQuery() and GetPostsCount() work, we
can write the GetPosts() function. The idea in this function is to build the query with
_GetBaseQuery() and then add the required fields to select.

The other important task we do here and not in _GetBaseQuery() is to set the offset, limit,
and ordering options. Since these options don't apply to GetPostsCount(), they must be done
here instead of in _GetBaseQuery().

I have split this function up into three parts so we can easily dissect it. Listing 8-3 shows
the first part of the function.

Listing 8-3. *The First Third of the GetPosts() Function (BlogPost.php)*

```php
<?php
    class DatabaseObject_BlogPost extends DatabaseObject
    {
        // ... other code

        public static function GetPosts($db, $options = array())
        {
            // initialize the options
            $defaults = array(
                'offset' => 0,
                'limit'  => 0,
                'order'  => 'p.ts_created'
            );

            foreach ($defaults as $k => $v) {
                $options[$k] = array_key_exists($k, $options) ? $options[$k] : $v;
            }

            $select = self::_GetBaseQuery($db, $options);

            // set the fields to select
            $select->from(null, 'p.*');

            // set the offset, limit, and ordering of results
            if ($options['limit'] > 0)
                $select->limit($options['limit'], $options['offset']);

            $select->order($options['order']);
```

■**Note** Using `Zend_Db_Select` helps make queries that work on different database servers. For example, MySQL uses `LIMIT x, y` or `LIMIT y OFFSET x` to limit the returned results, while PostgreSQL uses `OFFSET x LIMIT y` (where x is the offset and y is the limit).

The next step is to perform the database query and build an array of DatabaseObject_ BlogPost objects that we can return. We use the $db->fetchAll() method to retrieve all the database data and write it to an array. Since a single instance of the DatabaseObject subclass (such as DatabaseObject_BlogPost) corresponds to a single database record, we need multiple instances of this class: one for each row returned from the SQL we have just created.

To help us create this array, we use the static BuildMultiple() helper method of DatabaseObject. We pass the name of the class (DatabaseObject_BlogPost, which we can use __CLASS__ to dynamically generate) to this method as well as the data we're using to build the array of objects. Listing 8-4 shows this process. The key of each element in the array corresponds to its post_id value.

Listing 8-4. *Creating an Array of DatabaseObject_BlogPost Objects (BlogPost.php)*

```
// fetch post data from database
$data = $db->fetchAll($select);

// turn data into array of DatabaseObject_BlogPost objects
$posts = self::BuildMultiple($db, __CLASS__, $data);
$post_ids = array_keys($posts);

if (count($post_ids) == 0)
    return array();
```

The process of creating the database data for GetPosts() is nearly done; however, when we have previously used an instance of DatabaseObject_BlogPost, the object has also had a Profile_BlogPost object attached to it as the $profile property. Since all of the important data of the post (such as the title and content) is stored in the profile, we must load the profile for each of the blog posts.

When a record is normally loaded with DatabaseObject, the postLoad() method is automatically called. Since this would result in an SQL query for every row (in order to load the profile), we need a more efficient solution. Instead, we are going to use a method that is included with my Profile class that is used to create multiple Profile instances. Doing this means only a single SQL statement is executed internally, rather than one for each blog post for which we're loading the profile.

We use the BuildMultiple() method of the Profile class to retrieve an array of Profile_BlogPost objects. The first argument is the database connection, the second is the Profile subclass to use, while the third argument consists of the IDs of the posts to load. This is effectively the same as calling $profile = new Profile_BlogPost($db, $post_id) once for every blog post.

Finally, we must match up each Profile_BlogPost object with the corresponding DatabaseObject_BlogPost object. In both the $profiles and $posts arrays, the key corresponds to the post_id of the element.

To assign each profile to its corresponding blog post, we loop over each post and look for a matching profile record. If one isn't found, we simply make sure we call setPostId() so we can write to the profile if required (the profile property is set to be an instance of Profile_BlogPost in the DatabaseObject_BlogPost constructor).

Listing 8-5 shows the conclusion of the GetPosts() method. Once again, this code belongs in the BlogPost.php file in ./include/DatabaseObject.

Listing 8-5. *Loading the Profile Data for Each Blog Post (BlogPost.php)*

```
// load the profile data for loaded posts
$profiles = Profile::BuildMultiple(
    $db,
    'Profile_BlogPost',
    array('post_id' => $post_ids)
);

foreach ($posts as $post_id => $post) {
```

```
            if (array_key_exists($post_id, $profiles)
                    && $profiles[$post_id] instanceof Profile_BlogPost) {

                $posts[$post_id]->profile = $profiles[$post_id];
            }
            else {
                $posts[$post_id]->profile->setPostId($post_id);
            }
        }

        return $posts;
    }

    // ... other code
    }
?>
```

Retrieving a Monthly Summary of Posts

As an extra utility function, we will now implement a function called GetMonthlySummary(),
which returns a summary of the number of posts in each month. Once again we use the
$options array that we pass on to _GetBaseQuery(), allowing us to easily extend the capabili-
ties of the function in the future.

This function is slightly different from GetPosts() and GetPostsCount(), since we will be
grouping the results by the year and month of each post.

Listing 8-6 shows the code for GetMonthlySummary(), which builds the query once again
using Zend_Db_Select and then calls fetchPairs() to create an array that uses the first column
(the year and month) as the key and the second column (the number of posts) as the value.

Listing 8-6. *Building the SQL Query and Fetching the Post Data (BlogPost.php)*

```
<?php
    class DatabaseObject_BlogPost extends DatabaseObject
    {
        // ... other code

        public static function GetMonthlySummary($db, $options)
        {
            if ($db instanceof Zend_Db_Adapter_Pdo_Mysql)
                $dateString = "date_format(p.ts_created, '%Y-%m')";
            else
                $dateString = "to_char(p.ts_created, 'yyyy-mm')";

            // initialize the options
            $defaults = array(
                'offset' => 0,
                'limit'  => 0,
                'order'  => $dateString . ' desc'
```

```
        );

        foreach ($defaults as $k => $v) {
            $options[$k] = array_key_exists($k, $options) ? $options[$k] : $v;
        }

        $select = self::_GetBaseQuery($db, $options);
        $select->from(null,
                    array($dateString . ' as month',
                        'count(*) as num_posts'));

        $select->group($dateString);

        $select->order($options['order']);

        return $db->fetchPairs($select);
    }

    // ... other code
    }
?>
```

After calling _GetBaseQuery(), we add the fields we require to the statement. To execute the query, we call fetchPairs(). This method returns an array of the rows returned from the SQL query. It uses the first selected column as the array key and the second selected column as the array element.

In this code, we use the timestamp as the array key and the number of posts for that month as the array value. The format string we pass to MySQL's date_format() function will generate a timestamp in the format of YYYY-MM, so in the case of November 2007, the returned month column would have the value 2007-11.

■Note The date_format() function is specific to MySQL and will not work in other database servers. Other servers such as PostgreSQL use the to_char() function instead, which is why we check the type of database adapter being used in Listing 8-6.

Next we must group the data by the year/month value, before setting the ordering options.

Note In MySQL, if you give a column alias to a function call (as we did by using `date_format()` as month), you can then refer directly to the `month` pseudocolumn in other parts of the statement (in this case in `group by` and `order by`). In other database servers, this syntax is not allowed—the function call must be used explicitly in each required place. This is the reason we assigned the function call to the variable in the PHP code (`$dateString`).

Assigning Recent Posts and the Monthly Summary to the Template

Since we have just written code to retrieve posts from the database, we can now fetch all the data we need to display on the blog manager index. We are going to retrieve two different items:

- The posts for the selected month using the `GetPosts()` function (using the current month as the default).

- The total number of posts by the logged-in user using the `GetPostsCount()` function.

To display data that we retrieve from `GetMonthlySummary()`, we are going to create a Smarty plug-in, which we will look at shortly.

Listing 8-7 shows the code we add to the `indexAction()` method in the `BlogmanagerController.php` file in order to fetch a summary of the blog posts for the current user.

Listing 8-7. *Calling the New Post Retrieval Functions from indexAction() (BlogManagerController.php)*

```php
<?php
    class BlogmanagerController extends CustomControllerAction
    {
        // ... other code

        public function indexAction()
        {
            // initialize the month
            $month = $this->getRequest()->getQuery('month');
            if (preg_match('/^(\d{4})-(\d{2})$/', $month, $matches)) {
                $y = $matches[1];
                $m = max(1, min(12, $matches[2]));
            }
            else {
                $y = date('Y'); // current year
                $m = date('n'); // current month
            }

            $from = mktime(0, 0, 0, $m,    1, $y);
```

```
$to    = mktime(0, 0, 0, $m + 1, 1, $y) - 1;

$options = array(
    'user_id' => $this->identity->user_id,
    'from'    => date('Y-m-d H:i:s', $from),
    'to'      => date('Y-m-d H:i:s', $to),
    'order'   => 'p.ts_created desc'
);

$recentPosts = DatabaseObject_BlogPost::GetPosts($this->db,
                                                  $options);

// get the total number of posts for this user
$totalPosts = DatabaseObject_BlogPost::GetPostsCount(
    $this->db,
    array('user_id' => $this->identity->user_id)
);

$this->view->month       = $from;
$this->view->recentPosts = $recentPosts;
$this->view->totalPosts  = $totalPosts;
    }

    // ... other code
  }
?>
```

The first thing we do in this action is initialize the selected month and year. By default, the current month and year is selected, but if a valid string (in the form of YYYY-MM) is specified, then the month and year in that string are used instead.

Once we have the month and year, we can define the from and to parameters for GetPosts(). We use mktime() to generate the start of the month, and then we find the start of the next month and subtract 1 to find the last second in the selected month. Another way would be to use mktime(23, 59, 59, date('n', $from), date('t', $from), date('Y', $from), since the t parameter returns the number of days in a given month. I think the first way is simpler.

In each of the $options arrays defined in this code, the key parameter is the user_id parameter. If this isn't specified, then posts will be returned for all users, not just the current user.

The final step in this method is to assign the returned data to the template.

■**Note** You could assign these values directly to the template (that is, $this->view->recentPosts = DatabaseObject_BlogPost::GetPosts(…)), but I prefer to group all the template assignments together at the end of the method so I can quickly see exactly which data will be available in the template just by looking at the end of the method.

Displaying Recent Posts in the Template

We now have all of the recent posts (if any) assigned to template, as well as a timestamp of the month they are from. We can now write a template to output these posts. Rather than outputting them directly to the ./templates/blogmanager/index.tpl template (that is, the template for the indexAction() method of BlogmanagerController), we'll create a helper template to output the necessary HTML. We will then include this template from index.tpl.

The reason we do this is so we can easily add some Ajax functionality to this page, which we will be doing later in the "Ajaxing the Blog Monthly Summary" section. By creating a separate template, we can generate HTML in the background HTTP request (which uses XMLHttpRequest) and directly display the output. Let's forget about the Ajax part for now, though; we will add that functionality later in this chapter.

As I mentioned, I like to store helper templates in a directory called lib, which then separates them from the main controller action templates. Listing 8-8 shows the contents of the month-preview.tpl template, which we store in the ./templates/blogmanager/lib directory. Since this template is specific to the blog manager, I have created a separate lib directory in ./templates/blogmanager rather than using the "global" lib directory.

Listing 8-8. *A Basic Template to Output All the Posts for a Single Month (month-preview.tpl)*

```
<h2>{$month|date_format:'%B %Y'}</h2>

{if $posts|@count == 0}
    <p>
        No posts found for this month.
    </p>
{else}
    <dl>
        {foreach from=$posts item=post}
            <dt>
                {$post->ts_created|date_format:'%a, %e %b'}:
                <a href="{geturl action='preview'}?id={$post->getId()}">
                    {$post->profile->title|escape}
                </a>
                {if !$post->isLive()}
                    <span class="status draft">not published</span>
                {/if}
            </dt>

            <dd>
                {$post->getTeaser(100)|escape}
            </dd>
        {/foreach}
    </dl>
{/if}
```

This template is fairly straightforward in that it assumes a timestamp called $month is assigned, as well as an array of DatabaseObject_BlogPost objects called $posts. The template loops over each post and outputs it inside a definition list (<dl>). The <dl> HTML tag serves our needs well, because we want to output the date and title of the blog (using the definition title tag <dt>), followed by a brief summary of the content (using the definition description tag <dd>).

To include a short summary (also known as a *teaser*) of the blog post, we call the getTeaser() method from the DatabaseObject_BlogPost class. Listing 8-9 shows the code for this method, which we add to the BlogPost.php file in ./include/DatabaseObject.

To ensure the preview of the content fits on a single line, we apply the PHP strip_tags() function as a modifier. Additionally, we use the Smarty truncate modifier to restrict the total length to 100 characters.

Listing 8-9. *Generating a One-Line Summary of a Blog Post (BlogPost.php)*

```php
<?php
    class DatabaseObject_BlogPost extends DatabaseObject
    {
        // ... other code

        public function getTeaser($length)
        {
            require_once('Smarty/plugins/modifier.truncate.php');

            return smarty_modifier_truncate(strip_tags($this->profile->content),
                                            $length);
        }

        // ... other code
    }
?>
```

To use the month-preview.tpl template created in Listing 8-8, we must now include it (using Smarty's {include} function) in the index.tpl template from the ./templates/blogmanager directory. Listing 8-10 shows the changes to this template (which we started in Chapter 7).

Listing 8-10. *Displaying a Summary of the User's Blog and Outputting the Assigned Posts (index.tpl)*

```
{include file='header.tpl' section='blogmanager'}

{if $totalPosts == 1}
    <p>
        There is currently 1 post in your blog.
    </p>
```

```
{else}
    <p>
        There are currently {$totalPosts} posts in your blog.
    </p>
{/if}

<form method="get" action="{geturl controller='blogmanager' action='edit'}">
    <div class="submit">
        <input type="submit" value="Create new blog post" />
    </div>
</form>

<div id="month-preview">
    {include file='blogmanager/lib/month-preview.tpl'
            month=$month
            posts=$recentPosts}
</div>

{include file='footer.tpl'}
```

At the start of this template we include some basic introductory text that uses the $totalPosts variable. Note that we change the language depending on the number of posts. This is simple to do, yet if you look closely at many computer or web applications, developers often seem to miss this (have you ever noticed text along the lines of "1 blog posts found"?).

The only thing to do now is to add a few extra styles to tidy up this output. We will make the date and title appear in bold, as well as making the status text for unpublished posts a bit smaller and not bold. Listing 8-11 shows these styles, which should be added to the styles.css file (in ./htdocs/css).

Listing 8-11. *Styling the Blog Post Summary (styles.css)*

```css
#month-preview .status {
    font-weight : normal;
    font-size   : 0.9em;
}

#month-preview dt {
    font-weight : bold;
}
```

If you now visit http://phpweb20/blogmanager after logging in to the web application, you should see a display similar to Figure 8-1. The posts for the current month are now being displayed, although there's no way to navigate to past months. We will add this to the template in the next section.

Figure 8-1. *Displaying a summary of posts from the current month*

Displaying the Monthly Summary

Now that we are displaying a summary of posts from the current month, we need a way to display posts from the other months. In Listing 8-6 we created the GetMonthlySummary() method, which gives us an array of months and the number of posts belonging to that month.

We will now create a Smarty plug-in to retrieve this data and assign it to the template. We could have generated this data in the indexAction() method and then assigned it directly; however, the problem with this occurs when we want to show the same data on another page. We would have to retrieve and assign the data on every page on which we wanted to display it. This means if we decided to change the layout of the pages, we would need to make changes to the PHP code, not just the templates. Using a Smarty plug-in allows us to get the data whenever we like.

To bring the data from GetMonthlySummary(), we are going to use Smarty code as follows:

```
{get_monthly_blog_summary user_id=$identity->user_id assign=summary}
```

Effectively what this code means is that we are going to create a custom Smarty function called get_monthly_blog_summary. This function will take two arguments: the ID of the user the summary is being fetched for and the name of the template variable to assign the summary to (meaning we will be able to access the $summary variable in the template after this function has been called).

Listing 8-12 shows the code for this plug-in. We save this code to a file called function.get_monthly_blog_summary.php, which we store in the ./include/Templater/plugins directory.

Listing 8-12. *A Custom Smarty Plug-in to Retrieve the Blog Summary (function.get_monthly_blog_summary.php)*

```php
<?php
    function smarty_function_get_monthly_blog_summary($params, $smarty)
    {
        $options = array();

        if (isset($params['user_id']))
            $options['user_id'] = (int) $params['user_id'];

        $db = Zend_Registry::get('db');

        $summary = DatabaseObject_BlogPost::GetMonthlySummary($db, $options);

        if (isset($params['assign']) && strlen($params['assign']) > 0)
            $smarty->assign($params['assign'], $summary);
    }
?>
```

The first thing this plug-in does is to check for the user_id parameter. If it is set, it adds it to the $options array. We must fetch the $db object from the application registry because it is required to make the call to GetMonthlySummary().

Finally, we determine the variable name to use for assigning the data back to the template. As you saw earlier, we'll use a variable called $summary. After calling get_monthly_blog_summary, we can simply loop over the $summary array in the template as we would with any other array.

Calling the Smarty Plug-in in the Side Columns

We are now going to use the plug-in we just created to output the monthly summary in the left column of the site template. By using the plug-in, we have made it very easy to include this data on other pages also. The one problem we now run into is that to add content to either of the side columns, we must alter the footer.tpl template.

Since we don't want to include this data site-wide, we must make some enhancements to our template structure to allow us to include these additions to the left column only when required.

To do this, we'll pass two optional parameters when we include the footer.tpl template. The first parameter will specify a template to use to generate content for the left column, while the second parameter will specify a template for generating content in the right column.

First, let's create the template that calls the get_monthly_blog_summary plug-in and outputs its data. This is the template we will pass to footer.tpl to output. Listing 8-13 shows the left-column.tpl template, which we store in the ./templates/blogmanager/lib directory. Note that we use the class name .box, because this is the class we defined earlier for styling content areas in the side columns.

Listing 8-13. *Outputting the Data from the get_monthly_blog_summary Plug-in (left-column.tpl)*

```
{get_monthly_blog_summary user_id=$identity->user_id assign=summary}

{if $summary|@count > 0}
    <div id="preview-months" class="box">
        <h3>Your Blog Archive</h3>
        <ul>
            {foreach from=$summary key=month item=numPosts}
                <li>
                    <a href="{geturl controller='blogmanager'}?month={$month}">
                        {$month|date_format:'%B %Y'}
                    </a>
                    ({$numPosts} post{if $numPosts != 1}s{/if})
                </li>
            {/foreach}
        </ul>
    </div>
{/if}
```

Second, we must modify the index.tpl template (from ./templates/blogmanager) to tell footer.tpl to use this template. Listing 8-14 shows the change we make to the bottom {include} call.

Listing 8-14. *Specifying the Template to Use in the Left Column of the Site (index.tpl)*

```
{include file='header.tpl' section='blogmanager'}

{if $totalPosts == 1}
    <p>
        There is currently 1 post in your blog.
    </p>
{else}
    <p>
```

```
        There are currently {$totalPosts} posts in your blog.
    </p>
{/if}

<form method="get" action="{geturl controller='blogmanager' action='edit'}">
    <div class="submit">
        <input type="submit" value="Create new blog post" />
    </div>
</form>

<div id="month-preview">
    {include file='blogmanager/lib/month-preview.tpl'
            month=$month
            posts=$recentPosts}
</div>

{include file='footer.tpl'
        leftcolumn='blogmanager/lib/left-column.tpl'}
```

You should also make the same change to the edit.tpl and preview.tpl templates from the blog manager controller.

The final change is to make footer.tpl recognize the $leftcolumn and $rightcolumn parameters and include the templates accordingly. Listing 8-15 shows the new version of footer.tpl, which now includes the left and right templates if required. Note that for the left column we can use the else block to display some default content. I haven't worried about this for the right column, since there is always authentication data shown (whether logged in or not).

Listing 8-15. *Including the Template to Generate Left and Right Column Content (footer.tpl)*

```
            </div>
        </div>

        <div id="left-container" class="column">
            {if isset($leftcolumn) && $leftcolumn|strlen > 0}
                {include file=$leftcolumn}
            {else}
                <div class="box">
                    Left column placeholder
                </div>
            {/if}
        </div>

        <div id="right-container" class="column">
            <!--
                // ... status messages box
                // ... authentication box
            -->
```

```
            {if isset($rightcolumn) && $rightcolumn|strlen > 0}
                {include file=$rightcolumn}
            {/if}
        </div>

        <div id="footer">
            <!-- // ... other code -->
        </div>
    </body>
</html>
```

Including Additional Data in the Side Column Sometimes

In certain instances you will want different combinations of data included in the side columns. For example, you might want to show the blog summary and the authentication data in the same column—but only on a particular page.

To achieve this, you would make a new template that outputs this data accordingly and then pass this new template in as the value to $leftcolumn or $rightcolumn.

The recommended way to do this is to not include multiple content boxes in a single template but to keep them all in separate templates and then to create an additional wrapper template to bring them together.

For example, you might store the monthly blog summary in blog-summary-box.tpl, and you might keep authentication data in authentication-box.tpl. You would then create another template called some-template.tpl that might look as follows:

```
{include file='blog-summary-box.tpl'}
{include file='authentication-box.tpl'}
```

You would then use some-template.tpl as the value for $leftcolumn. To keep the code relatively simple, I have chosen not to break up the templates to this degree.

Ajaxing the Blog Monthly Summary

In the previous section, we wrote code to output blog posts in the blog manager for the selected month, with a list of all months that have posts in the side column. The way it works now is that if a month is clicked by the user, the page reloads, displaying the posts from that month.

We'll now enhance this system. Instead of reloading the page for the newly selected month, we'll make the blog manager index page fetch the posts in the background using Ajax and then display them on the page.

This code will still be accessible for non-JavaScript users, because the solution we have already implemented does not rely on JavaScript. This new functionality will be built on top of the existing functionality, meaning those who use it will have an improved experience but those who don't will not suffer.

The only other consideration we must make is that we're also listing the monthly summary on the edit and preview pages. If one of the months is clicked from these pages, we will not use Ajax to fetch the new page content but instead navigate normally to the page as we would without this Ajax functionality.

Creating the Ajax Request Output

Before we add any JavaScript code, we will create the necessary changes to generate the Ajax request data. We can reuse the indexAction() method from BlogmanagerController.php without any changes to code. All we need to do is to change its corresponding template so the page header and footer aren't included when the controller action is requested via Ajax.

To help with this, we'll make a minor addition to the CustomControllerAction class. In Chapter 6 we discussed how the isXmlHttpRequest() method worked with the Zend_Controller_Request_Http class. This method is a simple way to determine whether the current request was initiated using XMLHttpRequest. We'll assign the value of this function call to all templates.

Listing 8-16 shows the changes we make to the CustomControllerAction.php file in the ./include directory.

Listing 8-16. *Adding Ajax Request Detection to Templates (CustomControllerAction.php)*

```php
<?php
    class CustomControllerAction extends Zend_Controller_Action
    {
        // ... other code

        public function postDispatch()
        {
            // ... other code

            $this->view->isXmlHttpRequest = $this->getRequest()->isXmlHttpRequest();
        }

        // ... other code
    }
?>
```

Next we modify the template for the BlogmanagerController's indexAction() method. All we do in this template now is check the value of the $isXmlHttpRequest variable that is automatically assigned. If this value is false, then the template will generate output as previously, whereas if it's true, then we won't include the page header and footer.

Listing 8-17 shows the changes we make to the index.tpl file in ./templates/blogmanager.

Listing 8-17. *Altering the Output for Ajax Requests (index.tpl)*

```
{if $isXmlHttpRequest}
    {include file='blogmanager/lib/month-preview.tpl'
            month=$month
            posts=$recentPosts}
{else}
    {include file='header.tpl' section='blogmanager'}

    {if $totalPosts == 1}
        <p>
```

```
            There is currently 1 post in your blog.
        </p>
    {else}
        <p>
            There are currently {$totalPosts} posts in your blog.
        </p>
    {/if}

    <form method="get" action="{geturl controller='blogmanager' action='edit'}">
        <div class="submit">
            <input type="submit" value="Create new blog post" />
        </div>
    </form>

    <div id="month-preview">
        {include file='blogmanager/lib/month-preview.tpl'
                month=$month
                posts=$recentPosts}
    </div>

    {include file='footer.tpl'
            leftcolumn='blogmanager/lib/left-column.tpl'}
{/if}
```

The BlogMonthlySummary JavaScript Class

To initiate the background HTTP request to fetch the monthly summary data (using XMLHttpRequest), we need to attach some JavaScript code to each of the links in the month listing. To do this, we'll create a JavaScript class called BlogMonthlySummary.

This class will be loaded and instantiated automatically when we include the left-column.tpl template we created earlier this chapter, as you will see shortly.

Using some of the Prototype techniques you learned in Chapter 5, we can create a class to encapsulate all the functionality we need. The general algorithm for this class is as follows:

1. Check for the existence of the link container (where the month links are listed) and the content container (where the blog posts are listed). If either one doesn't exist, stop execution (meaning clicking the month links will just load the respective page as normal).

2. Observe the click event for each of the links found in the link container.

3. When a link is clicked, initiate an Ajax request using the Ajax.Updater class. This class is built on top of the Ajax.Request class and is used specifically to update an element with the results from XMLHttpRequest.

4. Cancel the click event so the browser doesn't follow the link href. We use the Event.stop() method in the event handler to achieve this.

Listing 8-18 shows the contents of the BlogMonthlySummary.class.js file, which we store in the ./htdocs/js directory.

Listing 8-18. *The BlogMonthlySummary JavaScript Class (BlogMonthlySummary.class.js)*

```javascript
BlogMonthlySummary = Class.create();

BlogMonthlySummary.prototype = {

    container     : null,
    linkContainer : null,

    initialize : function(container, linkContainer)
    {
        this.container     = $(container);
        this.linkContainer = $(linkContainer);

        if (!this.container || !this.linkContainer)
            return;

        this.linkContainer.getElementsBySelector('a').each(function(link) {
            link.observe('click', this.onLinkClick.bindAsEventListener(this));
        }.bind(this));
    },

    onLinkClick : function(e)
    {
        var link = Event.element(e);

        var options = {
        };

        new Ajax.Updater(this.container,
                         link.href,
                         options);

        Event.stop(e);
    }
};
```

After creating the class using Prototype's Class.create() function, we define the constructor for the class (the initialize() method), which accepts the content container as the first argument and the link container as the second argument.

If both of these containers are found to exist, the code continues to add the click event handler to each of the links. This results in the onLinkClick() method being called if any of the links are clicked.

■**Note** Chapter 6 discusses the Prototype event handling mechanism. You'll also see how the bind() and bindAsEventListener() functions work in that chapter.

We begin the onLinkClick() method by determining exactly which link was clicked. This is achieved by calling the Event.element() function with the event object passed to onLinkClick(). We will use the href attribute of the link as the URL to pass to Ajax.Updater.

Currently there are no extra options we need to pass to this Ajax request; however, we still define the options hash since we will be using it later in this chapter.

The onLinkClick() method concludes by calling Event.stop(). This is to ensure the browser doesn't follow the link, thereby defeating the point of using Ajax.

Installing the BlogMonthlySummary Class

Now we must update the left-column.tpl template to load and instantiate the BlogMonthlySummary JavaScript class.

Listing 8-19 shows the updated version of left-column.tpl, which now loads and instantiates this JavaScript class. Once you reload your page, clicking these links while on the blog manager index will refresh the middle container without reloading the whole page!

Listing 8-19. *Instantiating the BlogMonthlySummary Class (left-container.tpl)*

```
{get_monthly_blog_summary user_id=$identity->user_id assign=summary}

{if $summary|@count > 0}
    <div id="preview-months" class="box">
        <h3>Your Blog Archive</h3>
        <ul>
            {foreach from=$summary key=month item=numPosts}
                <li>
                    <a href="{geturl controller='blogmanager'}?month={$month}">
                        {$month|date_format:'%B %Y'}
                    </a>
                    ({$numPosts} post{if $numPosts != 1}s{/if})
                </li>
            {/foreach}
        </ul>
    </div>

    <script type="text/javascript" src="/js/BlogMonthlySummary.class.js"></script>
    <script type="text/javascript">
        new BlogMonthlySummary('month-preview', 'preview-months');
    </script>
{/if}
```

Notifying the User About the Content Update

Although the code we have just implemented works well and updates the page as it should, the only problem with it is that it doesn't give any feedback to the user. To fix this, we will use the messages container we created in Chapter 7 to notify the user that new content is being loaded.

In this section, we will create two new functions: message_write(), which we use to write a new message to the message container (and then make the container appear if hidden), and message_clear(), which hides the message container.

We will then update the BlogMonthlySummary JavaScript class to use these functions so the user knows when page content has been updated.

Managing Message Containers

The first thing we need to do is to create a new setting for the settings hash in the scripts.js file. When we implement the message_clear() function next, we'll add a delay so the message is cleared only after the specified interval. This ensures the user has time to read the message before it disappears.

Listing 8-20 shows the messages_hide_delay setting we add to scripts.js in ./htdocs/js. This value is the number of seconds before the message container is hidden.

Listing 8-20. *Adding the Delay Setting to the Application JavaScript Settings (scripts.js)*

```
var settings = {
    messages           : 'messages',
    messages_hide_delay : 0.5
};
```

Next we define the message_write() and message_clear() functions, which can go after the Event.observe() call in the scripts.js file. Listing 8-21 shows these functions.

Listing 8-21. *Setting and Clearing Site Status Messages (scripts.js)*

```
function message_write(message)
{
    var messages = $(settings.messages);
    if (!messages)
        return;

    if (message.length == 0) {
        messages.hide();
        return;
    }

    messages.update(message);
    messages.show();
    new Effect.Highlight(messages);
}

function message_clear()
{
    setTimeout("message_write('')", settings.messages_hide_delay * 1000);
}
```

The message_write() function works by first checking the length of the message to show. If it is an empty string, the messages container is hidden. If the string isn't empty, then the content of the container is updated to show the message. Finally, the container is shown, and the Scriptaculous highlight effect is once again applied.

The message_clear() function simply calls the message_write() function with an empty string after the specified delay time. Note that to be consistent with Scriptaculous, I specified the delay time in seconds, while setTimeout() accepts milliseconds (1/1000th of a second). This is why we multiply the value by 1,000.

Updating the Messages Container with BlogMonthlySummary

Finally, we must modify the BlogMonthlySummary JavaScript class to use the message_write() and message_clear() functions.

We'll call message_write() in the link click event handler (onLinkClick()), and we will then call message_clear() once the Ajax request has completed. We do this by calling message_clear() in the onSuccess callback option for Ajax.Updater.

Listing 8-22 shows the new version of the onLinkClick() event handler in BlogMonthlySummary.class.js (in the ./htdocs/js directory).

Listing 8-22. *Updating the Message Container When Loading Blog Posts (BlogMonthlySummary.class.js)*

```
BlogMonthlySummary = Class.create();

BlogMonthlySummary.prototype = {

    // ... other code

    onLinkClick : function(e)
    {
        var link = Event.element(e);

        var options = {
            onComplete : message_clear
        };

        message_write('Loading blog posts...');

        new Ajax.Updater(this.container,
                         link.href,
                         options);

        Event.stop(e);
    }
};
```

In Figure 8-2 you can see how the blog manager index page now looks after an archive link in the left column has been clicked. Note the status message at the top of the right of the picture, while at the bottom Firebug shows that a background request is running.

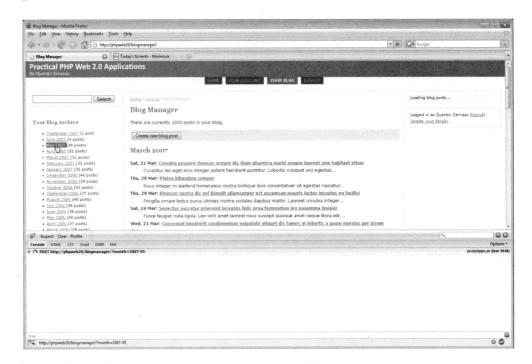

Figure 8-2. *The blog manager index when an archive link is clicked*

We have now completed the Ajax functionality on the blog manager monthly summary page. The way we have implemented it works very well, because of the following reasons:

- **It is easy to maintain.** We are using the same Smarty template for both the non-Ajax and Ajax versions, meaning to change the layout we need to modify only this one file.

- **The code is clean.** There is almost no clutter in our HTML code for the extensive JavaScript code that is used. The only code is a single call to instantiate the BlogMonthlySummary class.

- **The page is accessible.** If the user doesn't have a JavaScript-enabled browser (or disables JavaScript), they are not restricted from using this section in any way. It is simply enhanced for users who do use JavaScript.

- **The page is scalable.** An alternative method to loading the posts by Ajax would be to preload them and place them in hidden containers on the page. This works fine for a small number of posts, but once you hit a larger number, the page takes much longer to load and uses more memory on your computer.

- **It tells the users what is happening.** By adding the message container, the user knows that something is happening when they click an archive link, even though the browser doesn't start to load another page.

- **The code is cross-browser compatible.** Because we used the Prototype library, we were easily able to make code that works across all major browsers. Using Prototype cuts down on development time, because only a single solution needs to be implemented— not one for each browser.

Integrating a WYSIWYG Editor

The final step in implementing the blog management tools we created in Chapter 7 and this chapter is to add "what you see is what you get" functionality. This allows users to easily format their blog posts without requiring any real knowledge of HTML.

The WYSIWYG editor we will be using is called FCKeditor, named so after its creator, Frederico Caldeira Knabben. It is a very powerful and lightweight editor, and it doesn't require installation of any programs on the client's computer (aside from their web browser, that is).

More important, it is highly customizable. These are some of the customization features it contains:

- It is easy to change the toolbar buttons available to users.

- Custom plug-ins can be written, allowing the developer to create their own toolbar buttons.

- It contains a built-in file browser that allows users to upload files to the server in real-time. Additionally, it allows custom-made *connectors*, which are scripts written in a server-side language (such as PHP) that handle uploads through the file browser. The connector can save the file wherever or however it needs to, and it can send back the list of files to the FCKeditor file browser as required.

- The editor can be reskinned. In other words, the color scheme and look and feel of the buttons can be changed.

- It provides the ability to define custom templates that can be easily inserted into the editor (not to be confused with the Smarty templates in our application).

Figure 8-3 shows the default layout of FCKeditor, with all the toolbar buttons.

Other features that make FCKeditor a popular choice for content management systems include the following:

- It generates valid XHTML code (subject to how the user chooses to manipulate the HTML).

- Users can paste in content from Microsoft Word, which will automatically be cleaned up by the editor.

- It is cross-browser compatible. Currently it is not compatible with Safari because of some restrictions in that browser, but it works on other major browsers. Mac OS users can use Firefox as an alternative. Users of Safari are shown a plain textarea instead of the editor.

In the following sections, we will download, install, and integrate FCKeditor into our web application. We will make some basic customizations to the editor, including restricting the toolbar buttons so only the HTML tags listed earlier this chapter will be generated.

Figure 8-3. *An example of editing content in FCKeditor*

Additionally, we will develop a Smarty plug-in that allows us to easily load the WYSIWYG in our templates when required.

Downloading and Installing FCKeditor

At time of writing, the current version of FCKeditor is version 2.4.3. This can be downloaded from http://www.fckeditor.net/download. We will be storing the code in the ./htdocs/js directory, just as we did with Prototype and Scriptaculous.

Once you have the FCKeditor_2.4.3.tar.gz file, extract it to that directory. I have assumed you downloaded the file to /var/www/phpweb20/htdocs/js.

```
# cd /var/www/phpweb20/htdocs/js
# tar -zxf FCKeditor_2.4.3.tar.gz
# rm FCKeditor_2.4.3.tar.gz
# cd fckeditor/
# ls
_documentation.html    fckeditor.afp     fckeditor.php       fckstyles.xml
_samples/               fckeditor.asp     fckeditor.pl        fcktemplates.xml
_upgrade.html           fckeditor.cfc     fckeditor.py        htaccess.txt
_whatsnew.html          fckeditor.cfm     fckeditor_php4.php  license.txt
editor/                 fckeditor.js      fckeditor_php5.php
fckconfig.js            fckeditor.lasso   fckpackager.xml
```

The first thing I usually like to do is go through and clean out the unnecessary files in the distribution. I will leave all these items for now, but you may consider deleting the following:

- Loader classes for other languages (the `fckeditor.*` files in the main directory, aside from the `fckeditor_php5.php` file, which we will use shortly).

- The file browser and upload connectors that aren't being used. These can be found within the `./htdocs/js/fckeditor/editor/filemanager` directory.

Configuring FCKeditor

Next we must configure the way FCKeditor works. We do this by modifying `fckconfig.js` in the main directory. Most of the settings we won't need to touch, but we will need to customize the toolbars and then disable the connectors that are enabled by default.

First we'll define a new toolbar that contains only buttons for the list of tags we defined in Chapter 7. These tags are `<a>`, `<img>`, `<b>`, `<strong>`, `<em>`, `<i>`, `<ul>`, `<li>`, `<ol>`, `<p>`, and `<br>`.

On line 94 in `fckconfig.js` a toolbar called `Default` is defined, which contains a wide range of buttons, which is directly followed by a simpler toolbar called `Basic`. We will leave these two toolbars in this file and define a new toolbar called `phpweb20` that is a combination of these toolbars. The primary reason for leaving them in is to use them as a reference for the other buttons that can be added.

Listing 8-23 shows the JavaScript array we use to create a new toolbar. This can be placed in `fckconfig.js` directly after the other toolbars. Note that the `'-'` element renders a separator in the toolbar.

Listing 8-23. *The Custom FCKeditor Toolbar (fckconfig.js)*

```
FCKConfig.ToolbarSets["phpweb20"] = [
    ['Bold','Italic','-','OrderedList','UnorderedList','-',
     'Link','Unlink','-','Image']
];
```

Note Technically speaking, Listing 8-23 actually defines a *toolbar set*, not a toolbar. In other words, one or more toolbars makes up a toolbar set. This code creates an array of arrays, where the internal arrays are the actual toolbars.

The only other change we need to make in this configuration file is to disable the file manager and upload connectors, since we aren't allowing users to upload files. Disabling them removes the respective options from the user interface.

Listing 8-24 shows the new lines for `fckconfig.js`, all of which set the listed values to `false`. You can find at the bottom of the `fckconfig.js` file where each of these variables is defined as `true` and update them accordingly.

Listing 8-24. *Disabling the File Browser and Upload Connectors (fckconfig.js)*

```
FCKConfig.LinkBrowser = false;
```

```
FCKConfig.ImageBrowser = false;
FCKConfig.FlashBrowser = false;
FCKConfig.LinkUpload = false;
FCKConfig.ImageUpload = false;
FCKConfig.FlashUpload = false;
```

Loading FCKeditor in the Blog Editing Page

Finally, we need to load the editor in the blog post's editing form. First we will write a Smarty plug-in that outputs HTML code to load. There is a PHP class bundled with FCKeditor to facilitate the generation of the HTML.

The FCKeditor class is located in the fckeditor_php5.php file in the main FCKeditor directory (./htdocs/js/fckeditor). To keep our own code organized, we will copy this class to the application include directory. Additionally, we will rename the file to FCKeditor.php to be consistent with our application file naming. This also means it can be autoloaded with Zend_Loader.

```
# cd /var/www/phpweb20/htdocs/js/fckeditor
# cp fckeditor_php5.php /var/www/phpweb20/include/FCKeditor.php
```

Now we create a new Smarty plug-in called wysiwyg, which we can call in our template using {wysiwyg}. Listing 8-25 shows the contents of function.wysiwyg.php, which we store in ./include/Templater/plugins.

Listing 8-25. *A Smarty Plug-in to Create the FCKeditor in a Template (function.wysiwyg.php)*

```php
<?php
    function smarty_function_wysiwyg($params, $smarty)
    {
        $name = '';
        $value = '';

        if (isset($params['name']))
            $name = $params['name'];

        if (isset($params['value']))
            $value = $params['value'];

        $fckeditor = new FCKeditor($name);
        $fckeditor->BasePath = '/js/fckeditor/';
        $fckeditor->ToolbarSet = 'phpweb20';
        $fckeditor->Value = $value;

        return $fckeditor->CreateHtml();
    }
?>
```

When we call this Smarty function in the template, we provide two arguments: the name parameter and the value parameter. The name parameter defines the name of the form element the user's HTML is submitted in. The `value` parameter sets the default value to be shown in the WYSIWYG editor.

After initializing these parameters, we instantiate the `FCKeditor` class. Next we must tell the `$fckeditor` object where the editor code is stored relative to the web root (we stored it in `http://phpweb20/js/fckeditor`). Next we must tell it to use the new toolbar we just created (phpweb20) rather than the default toolbar (`Default`). We then pass in the default value to the class. Finally, we call the `CreateHtml()` method to generate the FCKeditor HTML code, and we return it to the template.

Note You can also set the width and height of the editor. By default, a width of 100 percent and a height of 200 pixels are used. To change the height to 300 pixels, you would use `$fckeditor->Height = 300;`.

The only thing left to do now is to call `{wysiwyg}` in the `edit.tpl` template in the `./templates/blogmanager` directory. Listing 8-26 shows the changes we make to this template. I've moved the WYSIWYG editor out of the fieldset to make the form look a little nicer. Additionally, I've wrapped it in a `div` with a class name of `.wysiwyg`, allowing us to add a new CSS class that adds some extra spacing around the editor.

This new code replaces the `textarea` that was in the template previously.

Listing 8-26. *Loading the WYSIWYG in the Template*

```
<!-- // ... other code -->

<fieldset>
    <legend>Blog Post Details</legend>

    <!-- // ... other code -->
</fieldset>

<div class="wysiwyg">
    {wysiwyg name='content' value=$fp->content}
    {include file='lib/error.tpl' error=$fp->getError('content')}
</div>

<!-- // ... other code -->
```

Finally, we add an extra style to `styles.css` (in `./htdocs/css`) to add some extra spacing around the editor, as shown in Listing 8-27.

Listing 8-27. *Adding Spacing Around the WYSIWYG Editor (styles.css)*

```
.wysiwyg { margin : 10px 0; }
```

By creating a Smarty plug-in to help with loading the WYSIWYG editor, it is extremely simple to load the editor, and we manage to keep the template code very clean. Additionally, you can easily define new parameters for the plug-in that you can then use with the FCKeditor class as required.

Summary

In this chapter, we extended the blog post management tools that we began in Chapter 7. We first looked at how to select large amounts of data from the database in an efficient manner before using this data to help users manage their blogs.

Next we extended the capabilities of the blog post listing so it is Ajax-powered, thereby making it easier to use (since each page will load more quickly). One of the biggest advantages of our implementation is that it will automatically fall back to a non-Ajax solution if the user wasn't using JavaScript.

The final step in this chapter was to implement FCKeditor, an open source WYSIWYG editor that allows users to easily format their blog posts using HTML.

In the next chapter, we will focus on creating a public home page for each user that lists all of their live blog posts. When we do this, we will also update the application home page so it displays blog posts from all users that choose to have their posts included.

CHAPTER 9

■■■

Personalized User Areas

In Chapters 7 and 8 we created the necessary forms and tools for users to manage their blogs, allowing them to create, edit, and delete posts. In this chapter we will be extending the web application further by creating a public home page for each user, which will be used to display their blog posts.

In addition to creating a home page for each user, we will populate the main home page of the web application. The home page will consist of blog posts from all users who choose to have their posts included. They will be able to make this choice by using the options we will add to the "Your Account Details" page in this chapter.

One key technique we will be looking at in this chapter is defining a custom URL scheme, instead of using the /controller/action method used previously. The address of a user's home page will be defined by their username, and we will manipulate the request handling of Zend_Controller_Front so that http://phpweb20/user/username will be used as the unique address to a user's page. Combining this with the URL field we defined for blog posts, we will also create a unique permanent URL for every blog post that exists in the database.

Controlling User Settings

The first thing we're going to do in this chapter is implement a settings-management system for users. This will allow them to control the way their blog behaves. These are the settings we want users to be able to control:

- **Whether or not posts are shown on the application home page.** In the last section of this chapter we will change the application so it displays blog posts from all registered users on the home page if they choose to. By default, we will not include a user's posts on the home page, but if they want to allow it, they will be able to change this setting.

- **The number of posts displayed on their own home page.** When we set up the user home page, we will list the most recent posts on the this page. This setting will let the user control how many posts are shown on their home page. To see further posts, visitors will be able to click on a month to view all posts from that month.

When we created the database tables for managing user data in Chapter 3, we created two tables: users and users_profile. The users_profile table was designed to allow us to easily expand the amount of data stored for each user account. We will use this table to store the settings we add in this section.

Because of how this system is designed, you will be able to expand on it in the future if you want to give users more control over how their accounts or public home pages work.

■**Note** Since we have also created a profile table for blog posts (blog_posts_profile), we could even add per-post settings. You could use this in a number of different scenarios. For example, if you had allowed visitors to post comments on your blog posts, you could use per-post settings to disable commenting on a single post. An appropriate place to add these settings to the interface would be in the "Edit Blog Post" form that we added in Chapter 7.

Presenting Customizable Settings to Users

To give users control over these settings, we will add them to the "Your Account Details" page. This involves adding the necessary HTML elements to the template for this page, as well as updating the class that processes this form (FormProcessor_UserDetails).

■**Note** The code used to update user details was introduced at the end of Chapter 4. We didn't actually implement this code in the book, so you will need to first download the source code to implement the functionality in this section. This includes the UserDetails.php file in ./include/FormProcessor, the detailsAction() and detailscompleteAction() methods in ./include/Controllers/ AccountController.php, and the details.tpl and detailscomplete.tpl templates in ./templates/ account.

To implement settings management, the first thing we will do is add the settings described previously to the "Your Account Details" template. Listing 9-1 shows the HTML code we will add to the ./templates/account/details.tpl template. This code also includes several variables from the form processor. We will add these to the form processor shortly.

Listing 9-1. *Allowing Users to Configure Settings When Updating Their Account Details (details.tpl)*

```
{include file='header.tpl' section='account'}

<form method="post" action="{geturl action='details'}">

<fieldset>
    <legend>Update Your Details</legend>

    <!-- // ... other code -->

</fieldset>

<fieldset>
    <legend>Account Settings</legend>

    <dl>
```

```
    <dt>
        How many blog posts would you like to show on your home page?
    </dt>
    <dd>
        <input type="text" name="num_posts" value="{$fp->num_posts}" />
    </dd>

    <dt>
        Would you like to display your blog posts on the web site home page?
    </dt>
    <dd>
        <select name="blog_public">
            <option value="0"
              {if !$fp->blog_public} selected="selected"{/if}>No</option>

            <option value="1"
              {if $fp->blog_public} selected="selected"{/if}>Yes</option>
        </select>
    </dd>
  </dl>
</fieldset>

<div class="submit">
    <input type="submit" value="Save New Details" />
</div>

</form>

{include file='footer.tpl'}
```

■Tip To create standards-compliant XHTML, we must use `selected="selected"` to choose the prese-lected value in a `<select>` element. This is a change from the HTML 4.01 specification, which says Boolean values such as this should be specified using `selected` without an attribute value. Similarly, when prese-lecting the state of a check box (`<input type="checkbox" … />`), `checked="checked"` should be used. For more information about this, refer to the "Attribute Minimization" section at `http://www.w3.org/TR/xhtml1/#h-4.5`.

This form can be viewed by logged-in users at `http://phpweb20/account/details`.

Processing Changes to User Settings

The next change we will make is to the form processor that processes the `details.tpl` tem-plate. First, we will retrieve the existing settings from the user profile so that they can be used in the form. Then we will process the submitted values and save them to the user profile.

Listing 9-2 shows the changes we will make to the UserDetails.php file in ./include/
FormProcessor.

Listing 9-2. *Changes to the User Details Form Processor (UserDetails.php)*

```php
<?php
    class FormProcessor_UserDetails extends FormProcessor
    {
        // ... other code

        public function __construct($db, $user_id)
        {
            // ... other code

            $this->blog_public  = $this->user->profile->blog_public;
            $this->num_posts    = $this->user->profile->num_posts;
        }

        public function process(Zend_Controller_Request_Abstract $request)
        {
            // ... other code

            // process the user settings
            $this->blog_public = (bool) $request->getPost('blog_public');
            $this->num_posts   = max(1, (int) $request->getPost('num_posts'));

            $this->user->profile->blog_public = $this->blog_public;
            $this->user->profile->num_posts   = $this->num_posts;

            // if no errors have occurred, save the user
            if (!$this->hasError()) {
                $this->user->save();
            }

            // return true if no errors have occurred
            return !$this->hasError();
        }
    }
?>
```

It is now possible for users to update their settings by submitting the form shown in
Figure 9-1.

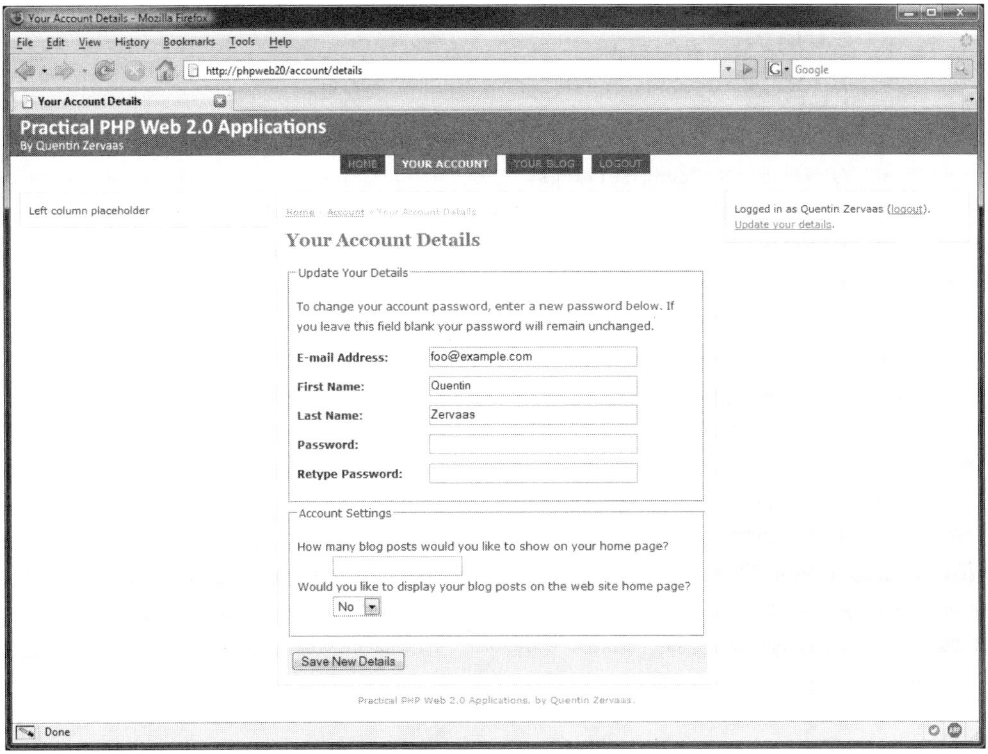

Figure 9-1. *Allowing users to update account settings*

Creating Default User Settings

If you were paying close attention to Figure 9-1, you might have noticed that the num_posts setting is empty. In other words, this setting won't be set until the form has been submitted. It would be better to include some default value so the user has some reference point for changing the setting when they use this form.

In order to assign default settings to a new user account, we will modify the preInsert() method on the DatabaseObject_User class. This method is automatically called prior to a new user record being saved to the database—we used this method previously to create the password for a new account.

Listing 9-3 shows the changes we will make to the User.php file in ./include/DatabaseObject. I have set the default value for num_posts to be 10, and I chose false as the default setting for blog_public. You may prefer different values.

Listing 9-3. *Assigning Default Settings for Users (User.php)*

```
<?php
    class DatabaseObject_User extends DatabaseObject
    {
        // ... other code
```

```
        protected function preInsert()
        {
            $this->_newPassword = Text_Password::create(8);
            $this->password = $this->_newPassword;

            // default account settings
            $this->profile->blog_public = false;
            $this->profile->num_posts = 10;

            return true;
        }

        // ... other code
    }
?>
```

■**Note** You could present these settings to users when they register, thereby not requiring any defaults to be set here. However, you typically want to encourage people to register, so you want to make the process as simple as possible and allow them to further customize their account once they log in.

To test that this functionality works correctly, try registering as a new user in the application. Once you have done so, you can either check the users_profile table in the database to see which values have been saved, or you can log in with the new account and visit the "Your Account Details" form we just modified to see if the setting values are prepopulated correctly.

The UserController Class

The next thing we will do is create a new controller for Zend_Controller_Front to display the public page. We will call it UserController. In this class, we will implement three main actions:

- indexAction(): This method will be used to generate the home page for each user, accessible from http://phpweb20/user/*username*. On this page, we will list the most recent posts on the given user's blog. The number of posts to be shown is controlled by the num_posts setting we added in the previous section.

- archiveAction(): This method will be used to generate a list of all posts for a single month (which I refer to as a monthly archive). The output will be basically the same as that of indexAction(). By default, the current month will be selected.

- viewAction(): This method will be used to display a single blog post. The posts listed on the indexAction() and monthAction() methods will link to this method.

In the left column of each of these pages, a list of months that have blog posts will be shown, much like in the blog manager. The key difference is that this list is for visitors to view the blog archive, while the one in the blog manager allows the blog owner to access their posts to update them.

In addition to these three main actions, we will also implement two methods called userNotFoundAction() and postNotFoundAction(), the first being used when a nonexistent username is present in the URL, while the second when trying to display a nonexistent blog post.

Routing Requests to UserController

For all the other controllers we have created so far, the access URL has been in the format http://phpweb20/*controller*/*action*; for example, the edit action of the blogmanager controller has a URL of http://phpweb20/blogmanager/edit. If no action is specified, index is the default action used for a controller. So in the case of blogmanager, the index action can be accessed using either http://phpweb20/blogmanager or http://phpweb20/blogmanager/index.

In UserController, we will be altering the way URLs work, since all actions in this controller will relate to a particular user. In order to specify the user, we will change the URL scheme to be http://phpweb20/user/*username*/*action*. As you can see, we have inserted the username between the controller name (user) and the action.

To achieve this, we must modify the *router* for our front controller. The router—an instance of Zend_Controller_Router—is responsible for determining the controller and action that should handle a user's request based on the request URL. When Zend_Controller_Front is instantiated in our bootstrap index.php file, a set of default routes is automatically created to route requests using the http://phpweb20/*controller*/*action* scheme. We want to keep these routes intact for all other requests, but for the UserController we want an extra route. To do this, we must define the route, and then inject it into the front controller's router.

Creating a New Route

To create a new route, there are three Zend_Controller classes that can be used (or you can develop your own). These are the existing classes:

- Zend_Controller_Router_Route: This is the standard route used by Zend_Controller, allowing a combination of static and dynamic variables in a URL. A dynamic variable is indicated by preceding the variable name with a colon, such as :controller. The route we have used in this application so far has been /:controller/:action. For example, in http://phpweb20/blogmanager/edit, blogmanager is assigned to the controller request variable, while edit is assigned to the action request variable.

- Zend_Controller_Router_Route_Static: In some cases, the URL you want to use doesn't require any dynamic variables, and you can use this static route type. For example, if you wanted a URL such as http://phpweb20/sitemap, which internally was handled by a controller action called sitemapAction() in one of your controllers, you could route this URL accordingly, using /sitemap as the static route.

- Zend_Controller_Router_Route_Regex: This type of route allows you to route URLs based on regular expression matches. For example, if you wanted to route all requests such as http://phpweb20/*1234* (where 1234 could be any number), you could match the route using /([0-9]+). When used in combination with the default routes, any request that didn't match this regular expression would be routed using the normal /:controller/:action route.

We will now create a new route to match a URL scheme of http://phpweb20/user/*username*/*action*. Since this route will only be used for the UserController class we will be implementing shortly, we will hard-code the controller name (user), while the username and action values will be determined dynamically. If the action isn't specified in the URL (as in the URL http://phpweb20/user/*username*), the action will default to index, just as it has previously.

The route we will use is user/:username/:action/*. Since we are only using this route for UserController, we don't include :controller in the string. When instantiating Zend_ Controller_Router_Route, the first argument is this string, while the second argument is an array that specifies the default parameters for the request. Since we know the controller for this request is user, we can specify this. We can also specify index as the default action. Therefore, the code we use to create this new route is as follows:

```
$route = new Zend_Controller_Router_Route(
    'user/:username/:action/*',
    array('controller' => 'user',
          'action'     => 'index')
);
```

Injecting the Route into the Router

Once the route has been created, it must be injected into the router so subsequent user requests will be matched against the route (in addition to any existing routes).

The route is added by calling the addRoute() method on the Zend_Controller router, which can be accessed from the front controller by calling getRouter(). The first argument to addRoute() is a unique name to identify the route—it does not actually affect the behavior of the route.

Listing 9-4 shows the code we will add to ./htdocs/index.php in order to create this route. The route should be added just prior to dispatching the request with $controller->dispatch().

Listing 9-4. *Defining a New Route for User Home Pages (index.php)*

```
<?php
    // ... other code

    // setup the route for user home pages
    $route = new Zend_Controller_Router_Route('user/:username/:action/*',
                                        array('controller' => 'user',
                                              'action'     => 'index'));

    $controller->getRouter()->addRoute('user', $route);

    $controller->dispatch();
?>
```

■Note An alternative solution to the route we have created in this section could be to create URLs like
`http://phpweb20/`*`username`* without including the `user` controller name in the URL. While this is relatively
easy to achieve, it requires some other changes in coding. For example, when users enter a username on
the registration form, you would need to ensure that the entered username doesn't conflict with an existing
controller name (or file or directory name). You would also need to be wary of any future controllers you may
want to create, as they will not be able to conflict with an existing username.

Once this route has been added, you will be able to access the `username` parameter of the
URL inside any of the actions in `UserController` by calling `$request->getUserParam('username')`.

Dynamically Generating URLs for Custom Routes

When we implemented the `{geturl}` Smarty plug-in—as well as the `getUrl()` method in the
`CustomControllerAction` class—in Chapter 6, we used the `Url` helper. We used the `simple()`
method from this class to generate a URL based on the controller and action name. This
helper also provides a method called `url()`, which can be used to generate more complex
URLs based on custom routes, such as the one we added in Listing 9-4. We will now use this
method to generate the URL to the home page of each user.

To generate a link using the `url()` method of the `Url` helper, you pass the route parameters (in our case, the name of the action and the username) as the first parameter, and the
name of the route it is being built for as the second argument. The URL helper will then recon-
struct a URL based on these parameters.

Let's now look at a specific example. In Listing 9-4, the name of the route we created was
called `user`. Thus, if we wanted to generate a link to the home page of the user with a username of `qz`, the following code would be used:

```
$helper = Zend_Controller_Action_HelperBroker::getStaticHelper('url');

$url = $helper->url(
    array('username' => 'qz'),
    'user'
);
```

This code would generate the following string:

```
/user/qz/
```

We want to make use of this functionality in our own code, not only for the actions we will
add in this chapter, but also for other actions we will add to this controller later in this book.
To do this, we will add a new function to the `CustomControllerAction.php` file in `./include`.

Listing 9-5 shows the code for the `getCustomUrl()` method, which accepts the URL
parameters as the first argument and the name of the route as the second argument. As
described in Chapter 6, we can access the helper using `$this->_helper->url` from within a
controller.

Listing 9-5. *Building Complex URLs for Custom Routes (CustomControllerAction.php)*

```php
<?php
    class CustomControllerAction extends Zend_Controller_Action
    {
        // ... other code

        public function getUrl($action = null, $controller = null)
        {
            $url  = rtrim($this->getRequest()->getBaseUrl(), '/') . '/';
            $url .= $this->_helper->url->simple($action, $controller);

            return $url;
        }

        public function getCustomUrl($options, $route = null)
        {
            return $this->_helper->url->url($options, $route);
        }

        // ... other code
    }
?>
```

In order to generate URLs with this helper from within our templates, we will also make some changes to the {geturl} Smarty plug-in. We will modify this plug-in so that if a parameter called route is specified, we will use the url() method of the Url helper; otherwise we will revert back to the previous method of generating URLs (using simple()).

For instance, to generate a URL back to the home page of the qz user from within a template, we will be able to use the following code in the template:

```
{geturl route='user' username='qz'}
```

Listing 9-6 shows the changes we will make to the function.geturl.php file in ./include/Templater/plugins.

Listing 9-6. *Extending the geturl Smarty Plug-In to Support Custom Routes (function.geturl.php)*

```php
<?php
    function smarty_function_geturl($params, $smarty)
    {
        $action     = isset($params['action']) ? $params['action'] : null;
        $controller = isset($params['controller']) ? $params['controller'] : null;
        $route      = isset($params['route']) ? $params['route'] : null;

        $helper = Zend_Controller_Action_HelperBroker::getStaticHelper('url');

        if (strlen($route) > 0) {
            unset($params['route']);
```

```
            $url = $helper->url($params, $route);
        }
        else {
            $request = Zend_Controller_Front::getInstance()->getRequest();
            $url = rtrim($request->getBaseUrl(), '/') . '/';
            $url .= $helper->simple($action, $controller);
        }

        return $url;
    }
?>
```

■**Note** The url() method of the Url helper will automatically prepend the Zend_Controller base URL, but the simple() method does not. This is why we manually do this only for the simple() call in this code.

Generating Other Required Routes

In addition to the route added in Listing 9-4, we will add two more routes: one for displaying individual blog posts, and one for displaying the monthly archives of a user's blog.

When we implemented the blog-management tools in Chapters 7 and 8, we included a url field with each blog post. The value for this field is unique for every post in a single user's blog. We will now use this value to create URLs for individual blog posts. Each blog post will have a URL in the form of /user/*username*/view/*blog-post-url*. The controller action that will handle requests to this route will be called viewAction()—we will implement this method later in this chapter.

In this particular case, the controller and action name are hard-coded in the URL; it's the username and blog post URL that are unique. Thus, we can use the following code to generate this new route:

```
$route = new Zend_Controller_Router_Route(
    'user/:username/view/:url/*',
    array('controller' => 'user',
          'action'     => 'view')
);
```

For example, if I created a blog post with the title "My Holiday", this would generate a unique URL of my-holiday. The full URL to this blog post (remembering that my username is qz) would be /user/qz/view/my-holiday.

If I wanted to generate a link to this post from within a Smarty template, I could use the {geturl} plug-in we modified in Listing 9-6 as follows:

```
{geturl user='qz' url='my-holiday' route='post'}
```

■**Note** This assumes that when we inject the preceding route into the router, we use a name of post. We will do this shortly.

Similarly, we can now create another route to handle blog post archives. The URL format for blog archives will be /user/*username*/archive/*year*/*month*. So to view my blog's archive for, say, November 2007, the URL would be /user/qz/archive/2007/11.

Once this route has been added (with a name of archive), we will be able to generate a link to this particular page in Smarty like this:

```
{geturl user='qz' year=2007 month=11 route='archive'}
```

The code we use to create this route is as follows:

```
$route = new Zend_Controller_Router_Route(
    'user/:username/archive/:year/:month/*',
    array('controller' => 'user',
          'action'     => 'archive')
);
```

Listing 9-7 shows the changes we need to make to the bootstrap file (./htdocs/index.php) in order to create these new routes and add them to the router.

Listing 9-7. *Adding the Post and Archive Routes to the Router (index.php)*

```
<?php
    // ... other code

    // set up the route for user home pages
    $route = new Zend_Controller_Router_Route(
        'user/:username/:action/*',
        array('controller' => 'user',
              'action'     => 'index')
    );

    $controller->getRouter()->addRoute('user', $route);

    // set up the route for viewing blog posts
    $route = new Zend_Controller_Router_Route(
        'user/:username/view/:url/*',
        array('controller' => 'user',
              'action'     => 'view')
    );

    $controller->getRouter()->addRoute('post', $route);

    // set up the route for viewing monthly archives
    $route = new Zend_Controller_Router_Route(
```

```
        'user/:username/archive/:year/:month/*',
        array('controller' => 'user',
              'action'      => 'archive')
    );

    $controller->getRouter()->addRoute('archive', $route);

    $controller->dispatch();
?>
```

Handling Requests to UserController

Despite the fact that we have changed the routing rules for this particular controller, we still create actions in the same way as the other controllers. The only difference is that for all actions in this controller, there will be a request parameter called username available.

Since each method in the controller is used to present data for a particular user, we want to load that user's database record in every action. To aid with this, we will add code to UserController's preDispatch() method, which is called automatically prior to the controller action method being called. Loading the user details in preDispatch() means the user data will be available to all actions in UserController. If the user record cannot be loaded (such as if we have an invalid username), we will forward control to a method we will implement shortly called userNotFoundAction().

Listing 9-8 shows the initial code for the UserController.php file, which is stored in the ./include/Controllers directory.

Listing 9-8. *Loading the Requested User Automatically for All Actions (UserController.php)*

```php
<?php
    class UserController extends CustomControllerAction
    {
        protected $user = null;

        public function preDispatch()
        {
            // call parent method to perform standard predispatch tasks
            parent::preDispatch();

            // retrieve request object so we can access requested user and action
            $request = $this->getRequest();

            // check if already dispatching the user not found action. if we are
            // then we don't want to execute the remainder of this method
            if (strtolower($request->getActionName()) == 'usernotfound')
                return;

            // retrieve username from request and clean the string
            $username = trim($request->getUserParam('username'));
```

```php
        // if no username is present, redirect to site home page
        if (strlen($username) == 0)
            $this->_redirect($this->getUrl('index', 'index'));

        // load the user, based on username in request. if the user record
        // is not loaded then forward to notFoundAction so a 'user not found'
        // message can be shown to the user.

        $this->user = new DatabaseObject_User($this->db);

        if (!$this->user->loadByUsername($username)) {
            $this->_forward('userNotFound');
            return;
        }

        // Add a link to the breadcrumbs so all actions in this controller
        // link back to the user home page
        $this->breadcrumbs->addStep(
            $this->user->username . "'s Blog",
            $this->getCustomUrl(
                array('username' => $this->user->username,
                      'action'   => 'index'),
                'user'
            )
        );

        // Make the user data available to all templates in this controller
        $this->view->user = $this->user;
    }

    public function userNotFoundAction()
    {
        $username = trim($this->getRequest()->getUserParam('username'));

        $this->breadcrumbs->addStep('User Not Found');
        $this->view->requestedUsername = $username;
    }

    public function indexAction()
    {

    }

    public function viewAction()
    {

    }
```

```
        public function postNotFoundAction()
        {

        }

        public function archiveAction()
        {

        }
    }
?>
```

The first thing we do in this class is define the $user property, which holds an instance of DatabaseObject_User (created in Chapter 3). This variable will be automatically assigned to all templates in this controller (this is done on the final line of preDispatch()).

We begin the preDispatch() method by first calling the parent preDispatch() method, as this contains code that we need executed for all actions (such as initializing the breadcrumbs trail and flash messenger created in Chapter 6). After this we must check whether the current action is the user-not-found action. If we don't do this, the code will enter a recursive loop that cannot be broken (since it will continually redirect back to the userNotFoundAction() method).

The preDispatch() method continues by initializing the username parameter from the request. If the string is empty (as will be the case if a URL of http://phpweb20/user is used), we ignore the request by just redirecting back to the home page.

Note We could have used getParam() instead of getUserParam() on the request, but this would fall back to check "get" and "post" variables if an internal parameter was not found. This means that if you used http://phpweb20/user?username=validUser, the user record would be loaded. Typically, you don't want people to be able to manipulate your applications in a way that wasn't intended.

If the string isn't empty, we try to load a DatabaseObject_User record based on the username value. To do this, we implement a loader function called loadByUsername() in the DatabaseObject_User class, which is shown shortly in Listing 9-9.

If the user record doesn't load, we instantly forward the request to the userNotFound action and return from the current function.

Tip Normally when you call _forward() in the Zend_Controller_Front controller, the current action is completed before calling the action to which you're forwarding. If you call _forward() in preDispatch(), however, the original action is completely skipped and only the new action is executed. In Listing 9-8, we must still return after calling _forward() because the remainder of the code in preDispatch() will still be executed otherwise.

Next, we add a new step to the breadcrumb trail—one that will be automatically added to the trail for all actions in this controller. We use the getCustomUrl() method we added in Listing 9-5.

Finally, we write the $this->user object to the view so it is available for all actions within this controller.

As mentioned previously, we also need to implement a new record in the DatabaseObject_User class to allow us to load a user record based on their username (previously we have used the record's unique ID to load a record when using DatabaseObject). Listing 9-9 shows the code for the loadByUsername() method we will add to User.php in ./include/DatabaseObject. For a further description of how custom loader methods for DatabaseObject work, refer to the example in Chapter 7 (Listing 7-14).

Listing 9-9. *The loadByUsername() and getUrl() Functions for DatabaseObject_User (User.php)*

```php
<?php
    class DatabaseObject_User extends DatabaseObject
    {
        // ... other code

        public function loadByUsername($username)
        {
            $username = trim($username);
            if (strlen($username) == 0)
                return false;

            $query = sprintf('select %s from %s where username = ?',
                             join(', ', $this->getSelectFields()),
                             $this->_table);

            $query = $this->_db->quoteInto($query, $username);

            return $this->_load($query);
        }

        // ... other code
    }
?>
```

We will finish off UserController.php for now by creating the userNotFoundAction() method. In order to tell the user specifically which username could not be found in the template, we will initialize it once again from the request and assign it to the template.

Listing 9-10 shows a template you can use for userNotFoundAction(). This code belongs in the usernotfound.tpl template in ./templates/user.

Listing 9-10. *A Sample Template That Can Be Used When an Invalid User Is Specified in the URL (usernotfound.tpl).*

```
{include file='header.tpl'}

<p>
    The user "{$requestedUsername|escape}" could not be found.
</p>

{include file='footer.tpl'}
```

Displaying the User's Blog

Now that we know which user's blog is being requested when the UserController class is invoked, we can load the relevant blog posts and display them. This works much like the blog index in the blog manager controller we created in Chapter 6. The key difference is in the presentation:

- Only approved blog posts will ever be included in this controller. This applies to all actions, not just the index action.

- The index page will only show recent blog posts (determined by the num_posts setting we implemented earlier in this chapter). All posts from previous months will be accessible using the archive links. Each month in the archive will have a unique URL.

- Rather than seeing edit and delete buttons, users will see a link to view the full blog post.

Displaying the Blog Index Page

On the blog index page, we want to show recent posts, although this differs from the blog manager in that we must be wary of the following:

- If we only show posts from the current month, there may be no content to display. This is especially true when a new month begins.

- If we show all content from the current month, there may be too much content to display. If the user has been extremely active in the month, there could be 30 or 40 posts, which could result in a long loading time for the page.

- If we don't show all of the posts from the current month, the viewer may not be able to access posts from earlier in the month.

We are going to solve each of these problems by displaying only a limited number of posts on the user's home page (based on the num_posts setting) and providing a link to the monthly archives.

Implementing the indexAction() Method

The first change we will make is to the indexAction() method in the UserController class. We created a placeholder for this method earlier in this chapter, but we will now implement it by retrieving the relevant posts using the GetPosts() method from DatabaseObject_BlogPost.

This method begins by determining the number of posts to retrieve. We first check for the num_posts setting (making sure the value is at least 1 by using max()). If this setting isn't found in the user profile, a default value of 10 is used.

Next, we will build an array of options to pass to DatabaseObject_BlogPost::GetPosts(). In this array, we will include the $limit variable just created, and we'll specify that only live blog posts should be loaded (by using the DatabaseObject_BlogPost::STATUS_LIVE constant).

Listing 9-11 shows the code we will add to the indexAction() of the UserController.php file (in ./include/Controllers).

Listing 9-11. *Loading the Most Recent Posts in the Index Action (UserController.php)*

```php
<?php
    class UserController extends CustomControllerAction
    {
        // ... other code

        public function indexAction()
        {
            if (isset($this->user->profile->num_posts))
                $limit = max(1, (int) $this->user->profile->num_posts);
            else
                $limit = 10;

            $options = array(
                'user_id' => $this->user->getId(),
                'status'  => DatabaseObject_BlogPost::STATUS_LIVE,
                'limit'   => $limit,
                'order'   => 'p.ts_created desc'
            );

            $posts = DatabaseObject_BlogPost::GetPosts($this->db,
                                                        $options);

            $this->view->posts = $posts;
        }

        // ... other code
    }
?>
```

The preceding code includes a parameter called status that we use to ensure that only live posts are returned; however, the _GetBaseQuery() method in DatabaseObject_BlogPost doesn't yet allow for this option. Listing 9-12 shows how we can make changes to the available options in _GetBaseQuery(), so that the changes are also available in other functions such as GetPosts() and GetPostsCount(). These changes are made in the BlogPost.php file in ./include/DatabaseObject.

Listing 9-12. *Filtering Posts Based on the Status Field (BlogPost.php)*

```php
<?php
    class DatabaseObject_BlogPost extends DatabaseObject
    {
        // ... other code

        private static function _GetBaseQuery($db, $options)
        {
            // initialize the options
            $defaults = array(
                'user_id' => array(),
                'status'  => '',
                'from'    => '',
                'to'      => ''
            );

            // ... other code

            // filter results based on post status
            if (strlen($options['status']) > 0)
                $select->where('status = ?', $options['status']);

            return $select;
        }
    }
?>
```

Displaying Blog Posts on the User Home Page

To output the posts retrieved in indexAction() of UserController, we will make a template called index.tpl, which we will store in the ./templates/user directory.

Just as in the blog manager, this template will loop over each post and then call another template in the loop to control the actual output. This is done so we can reuse this template when outputting the monthly archives. Listing 9-13 shows the code for index.tpl.

Listing 9-13. *Outputting the Most Recent Posts on the User's Blog (index.tpl)*

```
{include file='header.tpl'}

{if $posts|@count == 0}
    <p>
        No blog posts were found for this user.
    </p>
{else}
    {foreach from=$posts item=post name=posts}
        {include file='user/lib/blog-post-summary.tpl' post=$post}
    {/foreach}
{/if}

{include file='footer.tpl'
        leftcolumn='user/lib/left-column.tpl'}
```

This code first checks whether any posts are in the $posts array. If there are none, it is safe to assume there are no approved posts in the user's blog. We then loop over the $posts array, including the blog-post-summary.tpl template for each iteration. Using a separate template to output the blog post allows us to reuse the same code on other pages.

■**Note** By naming the {foreach} loop (that is, specifying the name parameter), we can access the {$smarty.foreach.*name*.last} parameter, which is a Boolean value that is true only for the last iteration of the loop. Similarly, Smarty makes the $smarty.foreach.*name*.first value available (among others). For more details, refer to the Smarty manual page at http://smarty.php.net/manual/en/language.function.foreach.php.

Next, we need to create the blog-post-summary.tpl template, which is stored in ./templates/default/user/lib. This template is shown in Listing 9-14.

Listing 9-14. *Displaying a Single Blog Post Teaser (blog-post-summary.tpl)*

```
{capture assign='url'}{geturl username=$user->username
                              url=$post->url
                              route='post'}{/capture}

<div class="teaser">
    <h3>
        <a href="{$url|escape}" class="entry-title" rel="bookmark">
            {$post->profile->title}
        </a>
    </h3>

    <div class="teaser-date">
```

```
        {$post->ts_created|date_format:'%b %e, %Y %l:%M %p'}
    </div>

    <div class="teaser-content summary">
        {$post->getTeaser(500)}
    </div>

    <div class="teaser-links">
        <a href="{$url|escape}">Read More...</a>
    </div>
</div>
```

At the beginning of this template, we generate a URL to the full page for the blog post. By doing this once at the start of the template, we can reuse the $url variable in this template, rather than having to call {geturl} for every spot we want to include the URL.

Because {geturl} returns the generated URL to the template directly, we can use the {capture} Smarty plug-in (built into Smarty) to trap the output and assign it to the $url variable. This plug-in works similarly to output buffering in PHP.

The remainder of the template simply outputs a summary of the blog post. In order to style this output, we can add several styles to the ./htdocs/css/styles.css file, as shown in Listing 9-15.

Listing 9-15. *Styling the Blog Post Preview (styles.css)*

```css
.teaser {
    border-top  : 1px dashed #eee;
    padding     : 5px 0;
    margin      : 10px 0;
}

.teaser h3 {
    margin      : 0;
}

.teaser-date {
    font-size   : 0.8em;
    color       : #666;
    margin      : 0 0 10px 0;
}

.teaser-links {
    font-size   : 0.9em;
    background  : #f7f7f7;
    padding     : 5px;
    line-height : 1em;
    margin-top  : 5px;
    clear       : both;
}
```

After creating these templates and making the changes to the style sheet, you should be able to view a user's home page, as shown in Figure 9-2.

Figure 9-2. *Displaying posts on a user's public home page*

■**Caution** The template created in Listing 9-13 uses the `left-column.tpl` template, which we have not yet created. In order to emulate Figure 9-2, you can either remove this from the code temporarily or create the `./templates/user/lib/left-column.tpl` file. We will implement this template later in this chapter.

Displaying Individual Blog Posts

In the previous section, we created the `indexAction()` method, which displayed a list of the most recent blog posts, each with a link to view the full details. We will now implement `viewAction()`, which will display the full details of the post.

For now, all the page will show is the title, timestamp, and body content of the post, but we will expand this page in later chapters when we add more functionality to the blogging system (such as tags, images, and maps).

Because of the custom route we added earlier in this chapter, the `viewAction()` method will be accessed using a URL of `http://phpweb20/user/`*username*`/view/`*blogposturl*. This means that in order to access the requested blog post URL, we must fetch the url user param-eter using $request->getUserParam('url'). We can then load the blog post that corresponds to this URL value for the current user.

Loading Live Blog Posts Using the URL

To load a blog post based on the loaded user record and the blog post URL, we must implement another loader method in the DatabaseObject_BlogPost class, similar to the loadForUser() method, but this time using the post URL instead of the post ID. Additionally, we must ensure that only live records are loaded and not blog posts that are still in draft.

Listing 9-16 shows the code for the loadLivePost() method, which we will add to the BlogPost.php file in ./include/DatabaseObject.

Listing 9-16. *Loading Live Blog Posts Based on the URL (BlogPost.php)*

```php
<?php
    class DatabaseObject_BlogPost extends DatabaseObject
    {
        // ... other code

        public function loadLivePost($user_id, $url)
        {
            $user_id = (int) $user_id;
            $url     = trim($url);

            if ($user_id <= 0 || strlen($url) == 0)
                return false;

            $select = $this->_db->select();

            $select->from($this->_table, $this->getSelectFields())
                   ->where('user_id = ?', $user_id)
                   ->where('url = ?', $url)
                   ->where('status = ?', self::STATUS_LIVE);

            return $this->_load($select);
        }

        // ... other code
    }
?>
```

Implementing the viewAction() Method

Now that we have the ability to load a live blog post based on its URL, we will implement viewAction()—the method responsible for calling loadLivePost() and then displaying a blog post's details.

Listing 9-17 shows the code we will add to the UserController.php file in ./include/ Controllers. I have also included the code for postNotFoundAction(), which is used if a blog post that isn't found (or that isn't live) is requested.

Listing 9-17. *Implementing the viewAction() and postNotFoundAction() Methods (UserController.php)*

```php
<?php
    class UserController extends CustomControllerAction
    {
        // ... other code

        public function viewAction()
        {
            $request = $this->getRequest();
            $url = trim($request->getUserParam('url'));

            // if no URL was specified, return to the user home page
            if (strlen($url) == 0) {
                $this->_redirect($this->getCustomUrl(
                    array('username' => $this->user->username,
                          'action'   => 'index'),
                    'user'
                ));
            }

            // try and load the post
            $post = new DatabaseObject_BlogPost($this->db);
            $post->loadLivePost($this->user->getId(), $url);

            // if the post wasn't loaded redirect to postNotFound
            if (!$post->isSaved()) {
                $this->_forward('postNotFound');
                return;
            }

            // build options for the archive breadcrumbs link
            $archiveOptions = array(
                'username' => $this->user->username,
                'year'     => date('Y', $post->ts_created),
                'month'    => date('m', $post->ts_created)
            );

            $this->breadcrumbs->addStep(
                date('F Y', $post->ts_created),
                $this->getCustomUrl($archiveOptions, 'archive')
            );
            $this->breadcrumbs->addStep($post->profile->title);
```

```
            // make the post available to the template
            $this->view->post = $post;
        }

        public function postNotFoundAction()
        {
            $this->breadcrumbs->addStep('Post Not Found');
        }

        // ... other code
    }
?>
```

This method begins by retrieving the url parameter from the request. If this value is empty (if, for example, the URL http://phpweb20/user/*username*/view was requested), the visitor is redirected to the user's home page.

Next, the code attempts to load a live record based on the url parameter. If the record was not loaded, the request is forwarded to the postNotFoundAction() method, used to show a simple error message to the user. This would typically occur if a visitor bookmarked a blog post that was either deleted or changed from live to draft.

We then add steps to the breadcrumb trail so the user can navigate to a list of other posts in the month of the current post. We use the getCustomUrl() method of CustomControllerAction to generate these URLs. Although we haven't yet implemented the archiveAction() method, we added the archive route to the router earlier in this chapter.

Finally, the post is assigned to the template so we can output it to the viewer.

Displaying the Blog Post Details

The next step is to make the template that will output the blog post details. In this template, we will output the timestamp of the blog and the blog post content. The title is displayed automatically, since we added it to the breadcrumb trail. When we add other features to the blog (such as images, tags, and maps) we will expand on this template to display those new elements.

Listing 9-18 shows the code for view.tpl, which we write to the ./templates/user directory.

Listing 9-18. *Outputting a Single Blog Post in Full (view.tpl)*

```
{include file='header.tpl'}

<div class="post-date">
    {$post->ts_created|date_format:'%b %e, %Y %l:%M %p'}
</div>

<div class="post-content">
    {$post->profile->content}
</div>

{include file='footer.tpl'
        leftcolumn='user/lib/left-column.tpl'}
```

To style the date, we will add the styles shown in Listing 9-19 to the `./htdocs/css/styles.css` file.

Listing 9-19. *Formatting the Display of the Blog Post Date (styles.css)*

```
.post-date {
    font-size   : 0.8em;
    color       : #666;
    margin      : 0 0 10px 0;
}
```

Creating the Template for postNotFoundAction()

Finally, we need to create a template to notify the visitor that the requested blog post couldn't be found. This template will be shown if a visitor bookmarks a blog post that has subsequently been deleted or sent back to draft.

Listing 9-20 shows the `postnotfound.tpl` template, which is stored in the `./templates/user` directory.

Listing 9-20. *Displaying a "Post not Found" Template (postnotfound.tpl)*

```
{include file='header.tpl'}

<p>
    The selected post could not be found.
</p>

<p>
    <a href="{geturl username=$user->username route='user'}">
        Return to {$user->username|escape}'s blog
    </a>
</p>

{include file='footer.tpl'
         leftcolumn='user/lib/left-column.tpl'}
```

Generating Blog Archive Links

Next, we must provide links to each of the months in a user's blog so all previous posts can easily be accessed. Thankfully, we already implemented this in Chapter 8 when creating the blog manager.

We will be adding these links in the side column, once again using the {get_monthly_blog_summary} Smarty plug-in we created in Chapter 8. In order to use this plug-in, we must make one modification to it, which is to add an extra parameter to indicate that only live blog posts should be included. Listing 9-21 shows the changes we will make to the `function.get_monthly_blog_summary.php` file in `./include/Templater/plugins`.

Listing 9-21. *Modifying the Plug-In to Only Include Live Posts (function.get_monthly_blog_summary.php)*

```php
<?php
    function smarty_function_get_monthly_blog_summary($params, $smarty)
    {
        $options = array();

        if (isset($params['liveOnly']) && $params['liveOnly'])
            $options['status'] = DatabaseObject_BlogPost::STATUS_LIVE;

        // ... other code
    }
?>
```

We can now create a new template to display content in the left column, just like in the blog manager. We will call this template `left-column.tpl` and save it in the `./templates/user/lib` directory. This file is shown in Listing 9-22. The templates we created earlier in this chapter use this template (`view.tpl`, `usernotfound.tpl`, and `postnotfound.tpl`). Note that this template is similar to the corresponding blog manager file (`./templates/blogmanager/lib/left-column.tpl`), except that the user ID is specified using `$user->getId()` instead of `$identity->user_id` (since we want the user ID of the blog, not of the logged-in user).

Listing 9-22. *Displaying the Monthly Summary for the Current Blog (left-column.tpl)*

```
{get_monthly_blog_summary user_id=$user->getId() assign=summary liveOnly=true}

{if $summary|@count > 0}
    <div id="preview-months" class="box">
        <h3>{$user->username|escape}'s Blog Archive</h3>
        <ul>
            {foreach from=$summary key=month item=numPosts}
                <li>
                    <a href="{geturl username=$user->username
                                route='archive'
                                year=$month|date_format:'%Y'
                                month=$month|date_format:'%m'}">
                        {$month|date_format:'%B %Y'}
                    </a>
                    ({$numPosts} post{if $numPosts != 1}s{/if})
                </li>
            {/foreach}
        </ul>
    </div>
{/if}
```

■Note An interesting aspect of this template is in the `year` and `month` arguments of the call to `{geturl}`. Here we use modifiers on a function argument, whereas previously we've only used modifiers when outputting a variable directly.

Once you have implemented this template, you will now be able to view a blog post as well as have links to all the months in your blog. This is shown in Figure 9-3.

Figure 9-3. *Viewing the details for a single blog post*

Displaying the Monthly Archive

The next step is to create a page that displays all posts for a single month. This is the page that the links generated in Listing 9-22 link to. To do this, we will implement the `archiveAction()` method of `UserController`. This is the method used by the `archive` route we created earlier in this chapter.

Implementing the archiveAction() Method

The `archiveAction()` method that we use to display all the posts for a single month is somewhat trivial to implement. All of the pieces are already in place to retrieve this data (`DatabaseObject_BlogPost::GetPosts()`) and to display it (the `blog-post-summary.tpl` template)—we just now need to glue the pieces together.

Listing 9-23 shows the code for archiveAction() as it appears in the UserController.php file in ./include/Controllers. Note that unlike the blog manager, where we manually parsed the month and year, we can now simply fetch them out of the request because of the new route that was created in Listing 9-7.

Listing 9-23. *Retrieving All Posts for a Single Month (UserController.php)*

```php
<?php
    class UserController extends CustomControllerAction
    {
        // ... other code

        public function archiveAction()
        {
            $request = $this->getRequest();

            // initialize requested date or month
            $m = (int) trim($request->getUserParam('month'));
            $y = (int) trim($request->getUserParam('year'));

            // ensure month is in range 1-12
            $m = max(1, min(12, $m));

            // generate start and finish timestamp for the given month/year
            $from = mktime(0, 0, 0, $m,     1, $y);
            $to   = mktime(0, 0, 0, $m + 1, 1, $y) - 1;


            // get live posts based on timestamp with newest posts listed first
            $options = array(
                'user_id' => $this->user->getId(),
                'from'    => date('Y-m-d H:i:s', $from),
                'to'      => date('Y-m-d H:i:s', $to),
                'status'  => DatabaseObject_BlogPost::STATUS_LIVE,
                'order'   => 'p.ts_created desc'
            );
            $posts = DatabaseObject_BlogPost::GetPosts($this->db,
                                                       $options);

            $this->breadcrumbs->addStep(date('F Y', $from));

            // assign the requested month and the posts found to the template
            $this->view->month = $from;
            $this->view->posts = $posts;
        }

        // ... other code
    }
?>
```

Finally, we will implement the `archive.tpl` template, which we will store in the `./templates/user` directory. This is shown in Listing 9-24. It is very similar to the `./templates/user/index.tpl` template we implemented earlier in this chapter.

Listing 9-24. *Outputting the Monthly Archive (archive.tpl)*

```
{include file='header.tpl'}

{if $posts|@count == 0}
    <p>
        No blog posts were found for this month.
    </p>
{else}
    {foreach from=$posts item=post name=posts}
        {include file='user/lib/blog-post-summary.tpl' post=$post}
    {/foreach}
{/if}

{include file='footer.tpl'
        leftcolumn='user/lib/left-column.tpl'}
```

Populating the Application Home Page

Now that we have created a home page for each user on the site, we will implement the main application home page. This will work similarly to the user home page, except that it will combine blog posts from all users on the site instead of just displaying posts for one user at a time.

When we implemented settings management earlier in this chapter, one of the settings users could customize was the `blog_public` setting. If this value is set to `true`, the user's posts will be included on the home page.

In this section, we will first make some changes to the `GetPosts()` method in `DatabaseObject_BlogPost` so we can select posts only for users who have public posts. Then we will implement the `indexAction()` method of the `IndexController` class. This is the method that handles the application home page. Finally, we will change the template for this method so the blog posts are displayed.

Loading Recent Public Posts

The first thing we will do is extend the `_GetBaseQuery()` method in the `DatabaseObject_BlogPost` class. We do this so that when we call `GetPosts()` we are able to return posts only for users who have set the `blog_public` setting to `true`.

Listing 9-25 shows the changes we must make to the `BlogPost.php` file in `./include/DatabaseObject`.

Listing 9-25. *Selecting Posts Only for Users Who Have Public Blogs (BlogPost.php)*

```
<?php
    class DatabaseObject_BlogPost extends DatabaseObject
    {
```

```
    // ... other code

    private static function _GetBaseQuery($db, $options)
    {
        // initialize the options
        $defaults = array(
            'user_id' => array(),
            'public_only' => false,
            'status'  => '',
            'from'    => '',
            'to'      => ''
        );

        // ... other code

        if ($options['public_only']) {
            $select->joinInner(array('up' => 'users_profile'),
                               'p.user_id = up.user_id',
                               array())
                   ->where("profile_key = 'blog_public'")
                   ->where('profile_value = 1');
        }

        return $select;
    }

    // ... other code
    }
?>
```

These changes work by joining against the users_profile table if the public_only option is set to true. It joins using the user_id column that exists in both the blog_posts and users_profile table, using the profile_key value of blog_public. Note that the Profile class (introduced in Chapter 3) stores Boolean values as integers. Thus, true is stored as 1 and false as 0.

Implementing the Application Home Page

The next step is to implement the application home page. The action handler for this page is the indexAction() method of the IndexController class. This is the very first controller we created in this book (see Chapter 2).

Our goal in this method is to retrieve the latest blog posts (we will use the 20 most recent) and assign them to the template. We will use the GetPosts() method from DatabaseObject_BlogPost to achieve this, specifying the public_only option we created in Listing 9-25.

The other thing we need to do in this method is load the corresponding DatabaseObject_User record for each post that is returned. We do this so that when we list each post on the home page we can link back to each users' home page.

Loading Multiple User Records

In order to fetch the multiple user records, as just described, we need to implement a method that allows us to do so. We will do this in a similar manner to the GetPosts() method we implemented in Chapter 8. The main difference is that we are now selecting data from the users table instead of the blog_posts table.

Listing 9-26 shows the code for the GetUsers(), GetUsersCount(), and _GetBaseQuery() methods we will add to the User.php file in ./include/DatabaseObject. For a detailed description on how these methods work, you can refer to the "Fetching Blog Posts from the Database" section in Chapter 8.

Listing 9-26. *Adding the Ability to Retrieve Multiple User Records at Once (User.php)*

```php
<?php
    class DatabaseObject_User extends DatabaseObject
    {
        // ... other code

        public static function GetUsers($db, $options = array())
        {
            // initialize the options
            $defaults = array(
                'offset' => 0,
                'limit'  => 0,
                'order'  => 'u.username'
            );

            foreach ($defaults as $k => $v) {
                $options[$k] = array_key_exists($k, $options) ? $options[$k] : $v;
            }

            $select = self::_GetBaseQuery($db, $options);

            // set the fields to select
            $select->from(null, 'u.*');

            // set the offset, limit, and ordering of results
            if ($options['limit'] > 0)
                $select->limit($options['limit'], $options['offset']);

            $select->order($options['order']);

            // fetch user data from database
            $data = $db->fetchAll($select);

            // turn data into array of DatabaseObject_User objects
            $users = parent::BuildMultiple($db, __CLASS__, $data);

            if (count($users) == 0)
                return $users;
```

```php
        $user_ids = array_keys($users);

        // load the profile data for loaded posts
        $profiles = Profile::BuildMultiple($db,
                                    'Profile_User',
                                    array('user_id' => $user_ids));

        foreach ($users as $user_id => $user) {
            if (array_key_exists($user_id, $profiles)
                    && $profiles[$user_id] instanceof Profile_User) {

                $users[$user_id]->profile = $profiles[$user_id];
            }
            else {
                $users[$user_id]->profile->setUserId($user_id);
            }
        }

        return $users;
    }

    public static function GetUsersCount($db, $options)
    {
        $select = self::_GetBaseQuery($db, $options);
        $select->from(null, 'count(*)');

        return $db->fetchOne($select);
    }

    private static function _GetBaseQuery($db, $options)
    {
        // initialize the options
        $defaults = array('user_id' => array());

        foreach ($defaults as $k => $v) {
            $options[$k] = array_key_exists($k, $options) ? $options[$k] : $v;
        }

        // create a query that selects from the users table
        $select = $db->select();
        $select->from(array('u' => 'users'), array());


        // filter results on specified user ids (if any)
        if (count($options['user_id']) > 0)
            $select->where('u.user_id in (?)', $options['user_id']);

        return $select;
    }
}
?>
```

Retrieving the Latest Posts for the Home Page

We can now retrieve the latest posts for users who have public blogs, as well as retrieving their user records so we can correctly link back to their blogs when we output their posts. Listing 9-27 shows the code we will add to the IndexController.php file in ./include/Controllers to do this.

Listing 9-27. *Retrieving the Latest Public Posts for the Home Page (IndexController.php)*

```php
<?php
    class IndexController extends CustomControllerAction
    {
        public function indexAction()
        {
            // define the options for retrieving blog posts
            $options = array(
                'status'      => DatabaseObject_BlogPost::STATUS_LIVE,
                'limit'       => 2,
                'order'       => 'p.ts_created desc',
                'public_only' => true
            );

            // retrieve the blog posts
            $posts = DatabaseObject_BlogPost::GetPosts($this->db, $options);

            // determine which users' posts were retrieved
            $user_ids = array();
            foreach ($posts as $post)
                $user_ids[$post->user_id] = $post->user_id;

            // load the user records
            if (count($user_ids) > 0) {
                $options = array(
                    'user_id' => $user_ids
                );

                $users = DatabaseObject_User::GetUsers($this->db, $options);
            }
            else
                $users = array();

            // assign posts and users to the template
            $this->view->posts = $posts;
            $this->view->users = $users;
        }
    }
?>
```

This method begins by defining the options to be passed to the GetPosts() method. Unlike when we used GetPosts() to retrieve posts for the user home page (see Listing 9-11), we don't specify which `user_id` value to filter the results on. Instead, we use the new `public_only` parameter, which will then make use of all public user blogs. We can then call `GetPosts()` to retrieve an array of blog posts to display on the home page.

The next step is to determine which users' blog posts were used. We do this by looping over the posts and adding the `user_id` field to the `$user_ids` array. Using the ID as the key is a little trick used to prevent duplication in the array (in case one user has multiple posts on the home page).

We can then retrieve an array of user records, which we write to the `$users` template variable (along with the blog posts in `$posts`).

Creating the Application Home Page Template

Finally, we can create the template used to output the blog posts that were retrieved in Listing 9-27. Once again, we will make use of the `blog-post-summary.tpl` template to output the template teaser. We will make a slight change to this template now, so that in addition to linking to the blog post it represents, it will also link back to the post owner's home page.

Listing 9-28 shows the changes we will make to the `blog-post-summary.tpl` template in `./templates/user/lib`. In this template, we now check for the `$linkToBlog` variable. If this variable is set to `true`, we will provide a link back to the user's home page.

Listing 9-28. *Linking Back to a User's Home Page (blog-post-summary.tpl)*

```
<!-- // ... other code -->

<div class="teaser-links">
    <a href="{$url|escape}">Read More...</a>
    {if $linkToBlog}
        |
        <a href="{geturl username=$user->username route='user'}">
            Published by {$user->username|escape}
        </a>
    {/if}
</div>
</div>
```

Next, we implement the home page template. Since `blog-post-summary.tpl` expects a variable called `$user` (which has been automatically assigned in previous methods where we've used this template), we must retrieve the correct user object from the `$users` array assigned in Listing 9-27. Additionally, we specify the `$linkToBlog` variable. Listing 9-29 shows the code for the `index.tpl` template, which is stored in the `./templates/index` directory.

Listing 9-29. *Displaying Posts on the Application Home Page (index.tpl)*

```
{include file='header.tpl' section='home'}

{if $posts|@count == 0}
    <p>
        No blog posts were found!
    </p>
```

```
{else}
    {foreach from=$posts item=post name=posts}
        {assign var='user_id' value=$post->user_id}
        {include file='user/lib/blog-post-summary.tpl'
                post=$post
                user=$users.$user_id
                linkToBlog=true}
    {/foreach}
{/if}

{include file='footer.tpl'}
```

In the preceding code, we assign the `user_id` value to a temporary variable in the template called `$user_id`. This is done so that we can retrieve the correct value from the `$users` array. Smarty syntax doesn't allow us to use `$users[$post->user_id]`.

Once you have added the code in this section, your application home should now list recent posts from all users who have chosen to have a public home page, as shown in Figure 9-4.

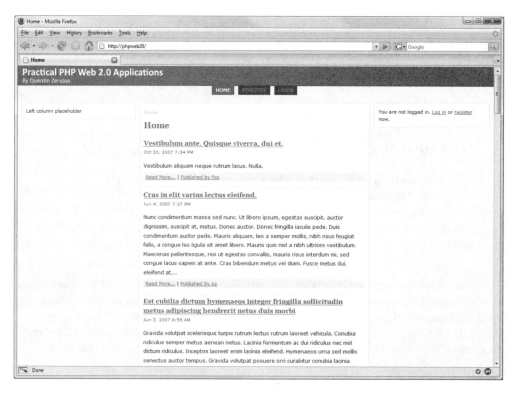

Figure 9-4. *The application home page, showing posts from all users with public blogs*

Summary

In this chapter, we primarily focused on creating a public page for each user that has registered in our web application. In order to create friendly URLs for user pages, we looked at how to create new request routes for `Zend_Controller_Front`. This meant that not only does each user have a short and simple URL for their home page, but each post within their blog has a short and simple URL also.

Prior to doing this, we gave registered users the ability to customize various account settings. This was done in a manner that easily scales, since new settings can be added with only minor changes to code and no changes to the database. We also looked at how to set default account settings.

After creating user home pages, we then implemented the application home page functionality. On this page we included posts that were recently submitted by all users who chose to have a public blog (using the settings-management system we implemented).

In the next chapter, we will continue to expand the blog by implementing a number of Web 2.0 features, including adding tags to blog posts, formatting HTML using microformats, and creating web feeds for user blogs.

CHAPTER 10

■■■

Implementing Web 2.0 Features

Up until now in this book, we have looked at various techniques of using Ajax (that is, the `XMLHttpRequest` object with the help of Prototype) to manipulate data in the web application we are developing.

Some examples of this include updating the HTML content on a web page dynamically, validating forms, and using JSON as a means to exchange data between the client and the server.

Although these techniques are very useful and somewhat straightforward to implement, they are not the only features that define a web site as being "Web 2.0." In this chapter, we will look at some of the other features of Web 2.0, which include the following:

- **Tags.** A tag is typically one or two words used to describe some arbitrary item. Because a tag is usually very concise, it is used as a way to categorize said items. One item can have multiple tags, and if used properly, one tag will belong to multiple items.

- **Web feeds.** A web feed is a stream of a web site's content provided by the site's owner in order to allow other publishers to display that data. This is often done using the Atom or RSS standard, although other formats are available.

- **Microformats.** A microformat is a simple data format used to formally structure certain kinds of HTML data. For instance, whenever you want to list a person's contact details on a web page, you would mark it up in HTML according to the hCard microformat (which we will look at later in this chapter). You can still style and lay out the contact details however you'd like in your CSS, but by marking it up in this way a microformat reader can recognize this data easily as a person's contact details. For more information about microformats, visit `http://microformats.org`.

In this chapter, we will extend the capabilities of the blogging system we have created to allow users to assign tags to posts. We will then change the output of their home page to categorize their blog posts based on the assigned tags.

Next we will take a look at web feeds by creating an Atom feed of a user's blog using the `Zend_Feed` component of the Zend Framework.

Finally, we will look at microformats and how to consume them using the Operator plug-in for Firefox. We will use the rel-tag microformat on the tagging system we create, as well as extend user accounts to allow a public profile. We will then display the created profile using the hCard microformat, allowing contact details to be easily exported to other programs.

Tags

Tags are used as a way to categorize items on a web site. The type of item being tagged can be anything really, such as a news article, an image, a product, or a link. By assigning a series of keywords to that item (that is, tags), it is easy to find related items based on the keyword of choice.

Let's look at a practical example of how tagging could be used. If you were to categorize this book, you could say it is about *PHP*, *Web 2.0*, *Ajax*, and *MySQL*, among other things. Each of the italicized terms would be perfectly acceptable as tags. Now consider if you had a web site that listed a catalog of books. Each book would have its own relevant set of tags, just like the tags we just mentioned. To find every book that had something to do with PHP (assuming it had been tagged correctly), you could simply search for all books with a tag of *PHP*.

We will be implementing a system like this, but instead of tagging books in a library or catalog, we will be tagging blog posts. Technically speaking, we won't be tagging posts—we will provide the blog owner with the tools to tag their own posts.

Additionally, we will then provide the means to filter posts by one or more tags. We will implement this on a per-user basis by listing each of a user's unique tags in a list on their public home page.

In Chapter 12, we will extend the tagging functionality we create here to allow users to search for tags.

Implementing Tagging

To implement a tagging system, we must first create a database table in which to store tags. Since each blog post can have multiple tags, we create a table with two columns: one to indicate the post ID and another to store the actual tag, as shown in Listing 10-1. This means if two posts share the same tag, each post will have its own record in this table for that tag.

Listing 10-1. *Database Table to Store Blog Post Tags In (schema-mysql.sql)*

```
create table blog_posts_tags (
    post_id         bigint unsigned not null,
    tag             varchar(255)    not null,

    primary key (post_id, tag)
) type = InnoDB;
```

Next we must create some tag management functions in the DatabaseObject_BlogPost class. The functions we will create are as follows:

- getTags(): Retrieves all tags for a blog post

- hasTag(): Checks whether a blog post has the specified tag

- addTags(): Adds one or more tags to a blog post

- deleteTags(): Deletes one or more tags from a blog post

- deleteAllTags(): Deletes all tags from a blog post

Listing 10-2 shows the getTags() method, which returns an array of all tags that belong to the loaded post. This code (along with the other four methods) belongs in the BlogPost.php file in the ./include/DatabaseObject directory.

Listing 10-2. *Retrieving All Tags Belonging to a Post with getTags() (BlogPost.php)*

```php
<?php
    class DatabaseObject_BlogPost extends DatabaseObject
    {
        // ... other code

        public function getTags()
        {
            if (!$this->isSaved())
                return array();

            $query = 'select tag from blog_posts_tags where post_id = ?';

            // sort tags alphabetically
            $query .= ' order by lower(tag)';

            return $this->_db->fetchCol($query, $this->getId());
        }
```

This method starts by ensuring the post has been loaded before trying to retrieve the tags. In the SQL query we sort the retrieved tags alphabetically. In MySQL, this sort is not case-sensitive, but by using the lower() function, tags will be returned correctly in other database servers such as PostgreSQL that are case-sensitive.

Next we look at hasTag(), which we use to check whether a blog post has a specific tag. Listing 10-3 shows this method.

Listing 10-3. *Checking Whether a Post Has a Specific Tag (BlogPost.php)*

```php
        public function hasTag($tag)
        {
            if (!$this->isSaved())
                return false;

            $select = $this->_db->select();
            $select->from('blog_posts_tags', 'count(*)')
                    ->where('post_id = ?', $this->getId())
                    ->where('lower(tag) = lower(?)', trim($tag));

            return $this->_db->fetchOne($select) > 0;
        }
```

Here we use the Zend_Db_Select class that we first used in Chapter 8. For short queries such as in Listing 10-2, I tend not to bother using this class, but when the query gets longer as in this listing, it is definitely worth using. This query retrieves the number of rows for the current blog that have the given tag (this value should be only 1 or 0 since the same tag can't be used more than once for a post). This method returns true if the count is greater than zero.

The next function we'll look at is addTags(), which is shown in Listing 10-4. This function begins once again by making sure the record is loaded and then continues by cleaning the tags that have been passed in using the $tags argument. This function will accept either a string or an array of strings to use as the tags.

Listing 10-4. *Adding One or More Tags to a Post Using addTags() (BlogPost.php)*

```php
public function addTags($tags)
{
    if (!$this->isSaved())
        return;

    if (!is_array($tags))
        $tags = array($tags);

    // first create a clean list of tags
    $_tags = array();
    foreach ($tags as $tag) {
        $tag = trim($tag);
        if (strlen($tag) == 0)
            continue;

        $_tags[strtolower($tag)] = $tag;
    }

    // now insert each into the database, first ensuring
    // it doesn't already exist for the current post
    $existingTags = array_map('strtolower', $this->getTags());

    foreach ($_tags as $lower => $tag) {
        if (in_array($lower, $existingTags))
            continue;

        $data = array('post_id' => $this->getId(),
                      'tag'     => $tag);

        $this->_db->insert('blog_posts_tags', $data);
    }
}
```

As part of this function, we must first ensure that no duplicates have been passed to the function. We are ignoring case in the tags (so AJAX and Ajax would be treated as the same tag).

Additionally, to ensure that no duplicate tags are inserted, we retrieve all tags using getTags() and then make them all lowercase using array_map(). Finally, each tag is inserted into the database. We could instead use hasTag() to check whether the new tag already exists, but this would result in one lookup query for each tag, whereas doing it this way requires only one lookup query.

The next function we implement is deleteTags(), which we use to remove one or more tags from a blog post, as shown in Listing 10-5.

Listing 10-5. *Deleting One or More Blog Post Tags with deleteTags() (BlogPost.php)*

```
public function deleteTags($tags)
{
    if (!$this->isSaved())
        return;

    if (!is_array($tags))
        $tags = array($tags);

    $_tags = array();
    foreach ($tags as $tag) {
        $tag = trim($tag);
        if (strlen($tag) > 0)
            $_tags[] = strtolower($tag);
    }

    if (count($_tags) == 0)
        return;

    $where = array('post_id = ' . $this->getId(),
                    $this->_db->quoteInto('lower(tag) in (?)', $tags));

    $this->_db->delete('blog_posts_tags', $where);
}
```

Just as when inserting tags, we must clean up the tags that are passed in (which can be either a single tag or an array of tags). Once this has been done, we can use the Zend_Db's delete() method to remove the matching rows.

Finally, we include the deleteAllTags() method, which takes no arguments and removes every tag associated with a single post, as shown in Listing 10-6. This is primarily used in the preDelete() method, which will we update shortly.

Listing 10-6. *Deleting All of a Post's Tags (BlogPost.php)*

```
public function deleteAllTags()
{
    if (!$this->isSaved())
        return;
```

```
            $this->_db->delete('blog_posts_tags', 'post_id = ' . $this->getId());
        }

        // ... other code
    }
?>
```

As mentioned, we must call this function in the preDelete() method of DatabaseObject_ BlogPost, which is called automatically prior to a blog post being deleted. This is shown in Listing 10-7. We do this so prior to a blog post being deleted, the associated tags are deleted, ensuring that the foreign key constraints don't prevent the post from being deleted.

Listing 10-7. *Deleting All Tags for a Post When a Post Is Deleted (BlogPost.php)*

```php
<?php
    class DatabaseObject_BlogPost extends DatabaseObject
    {
        // ... other code

        protected function preDelete()
        {
            $this->profile->delete();
            $this->deleteAllTags();
            return true;
        }

        // ... other code
    }
?>
```

Managing Blog Post Tags

The next step in implementing tagging is to add it to the blog manager interface. We will add a simple form to the blog post preview page that lists all existing tags and includes a form to add a tag to the given post.

First, we add a new action handler to the BlogmanagerController class to add or remove tags. We call this method tagsAction(), as shown in Listing 10-8. This method expects three items in the HTTP post data: the ID of the of the blog post, the presence of an add or delete variable (defined by the form submit buttons), and the tag being either added or deleted.

Listing 10-8. *Adding and Removing Tags from Blog Posts (BlogmanagerController.php)*

```php
<?php
    class BlogmanagerController extends CustomControllerAction
    {
        // ... other code

        public function tagsAction()
```

```
        {
            $request = $this->getRequest();

            $post_id = (int) $request->getPost('id');

            $post = new DatabaseObject_BlogPost($this->db);
            if (!$post->loadForUser($this->identity->user_id, $post_id))
                $this->_redirect($this->getUrl());

            $tag = $request->getPost('tag');

            if ($request->getPost('add')) {
                $post->addTags($tag);
                $this->messenger->addMessage('Tag added to post');
            }
            else if ($request->getPost('delete')) {
                $post->deleteTags($tag);
                $this->messenger->addMessage('Tag removed from post');
            }

            $this->_redirect($this->getUrl('preview') . '?id=' . $post->getId());
        }
    }
?>
```

After a tag is added or removed, an appropriate message is written to the flash messenger, and then the user is redirected back to the preview page.

Next we must list the existing tags in the `preview.tpl` template (found in `./templates/blogmanager`), as well as the form used to add a new tag. This is shown in Listing 10-9, fitting in between the post status and its date and time.

Listing 10-9. *Showing the Tags on the Blog Post Preview Page (preview.tpl)*

```
<!-- // other code -->

<fieldset id="preview-tags">
    <legend>Tags</legend>
    <ul>
        {foreach from=$post->getTags() item=tag}
            <li>
                <form method="post" action="{geturl action='tags'}">
                    <div>
                        {$tag|escape}
                        <input type="hidden" name="id" value="{$post->getId()}" />
                        <input type="hidden" name="tag" value="{$tag|escape}" />
                        <input type="submit" value="Delete" name="delete" />
                    </div>
                </form>
```

```
                </li>
            {foreachelse}
                <li>No tags found</li>
            {/foreach}
        </ul>

        <form method="post" action="{geturl action='tags'}">
            <div>
                <input type="hidden" name="id" value="{$post->getId()}" />
                <input type="text" name="tag" />
                <input type="submit" value="Add Tag" name="add" />
            </div>
        </form>
</fieldset>

<!-- // other code -->
```

Finally, in order to display these tags in a user-friendly manner, we add some extra styles to the site CSS file. By using display : inline, the list items are shown horizontally instead of vertically. Listing 10-10 shows the new styles added to styles.css.

Listing 10-10. *Displaying the Tag Management Area in a User-Friendly Manner (styles.css)*

```css
#preview-tags {
    background   : #f7f7f7;
    padding      : 5px;
}

#preview-tags input {
    font-size    : 0.95em;
}

#preview-tags a {
    font-size    : 0.95em;
}

#preview-tags ul {
    margin       : 0;
    padding      : 0;
}

#preview-tags li {
    margin       : 0;
    padding      : 0 5px;
    display      : inline;
}
```

```
#preview-tags form, #preview-tags div {
    display : inline;
}
```

To generate valid XHTML, form elements cannot exist directly inside a `<form>` tag, which is why we wrapped them in `<div>` tags in Listing 10-9. Because we want all existing tags to appear next to each other, we must change the `form` and `div` elements to display `inline` instead of `block`.

Figure 10-1 shows what the preview page looks like now with the tags displayed. It is very straightforward for a user to add or remove tags.

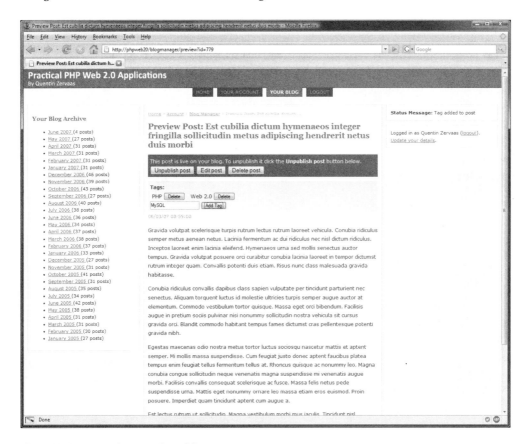

Figure 10-1. *Managing tags for a blog post*

Note that you could use Ajax to control this form, but in all honesty, it won't make much difference to the user's experience at all; you shouldn't necessarily use Ajax just for the sake of it if it isn't really needed.

If instead you wanted more advanced functionality (such as allowing the user to order tags themselves rather than alphabetically), then you may instead choose to use Ajax for adding, removing, and reordering tags.

Displaying a User's Tags on Their Blog

The next step in implementing a tagging system is to display the tags to the people who use the site. We will do this simply by listing all tags in the side column with a count of the number of posts that use that tag in the blog.

When one of these tags is clicked, the user will be taken to a page listing all posts with that tag. The URL of this page will be in the format http://phpweb20/user/*username*/tag/*tagname*.

■**Note** Such a page is called a *tag space*. The microformats rel-tag specification (http://microformats. org/wiki/rel-tag#Tag_Spaces) defines a tag space as a well-defined URI from which an embedded tag can be mechanically extracted. Specifically, the last segment of a path (after the final slash) denotes that tag (not taking into account any URL parameters or anchors). So, in the case of the URL mentioned earlier, *tagname* is the last segment and therefore denotes the tag of that tag space. We will look at the rel-tag microformat later in this chapter.

To generate the list of tags and the number of posts that have that tag, we must write another new function for DatabaseObject_BlogPost, which we call GetTagSummary(). To retrieve the number of posts for each tag, we must use the following SQL statement:

```
SELECT count(*) as count, t.tag
    FROM blog_posts_tags t
    INNER JOIN blog_posts p ON p.post_id = t.post_id
    WHERE p.user_id = [user id]
    AND p.status = 'L'
    GROUP BY t.tag
```

The only problem with this query is that it differentiates between uppercase and lowercase versions of the same tag, whereas we don't want it to do so. To deal with this, we add some extra processing to GetTagSummary(). Listing 10-11 shows the full function to go in ./include/DatabaseObject/BlogPost.php.

Listing 10-11. *Retrieving a Summary of All Tags for a Single User (BlogPost.php)*

```php
<?php
    class DatabaseObject_BlogPost extends DatabaseObject
    {
        // ... other code

        public static function GetTagSummary($db, $user_id)
        {
            $select = $db->select();
            $select->from(array('t' => 'blog_posts_tags'),
                        array('count(*) as count', 't.tag'))
                    ->joinInner(array('p' => 'blog_posts'),
                        'p.post_id = t.post_id',
```

```
                              array())
                ->where('p.user_id = ?', $user_id)
                ->where('p.status = ?', self::STATUS_LIVE)
                ->group('t.tag');

        $result = $db->query($select);
        $tags = $result->fetchAll();

        $summary = array();

        foreach ($tags as $tag) {
            $_tag = strtolower($tag['tag']);

            if (array_key_exists($_tag, $summary))
                $summary[$_tag]['count'] += $tag['count'];
            else
                $summary[$_tag] = $tag;
        }

        return $summary;
    }
}
?>
```

Next we write a Smarty plug-in that calls this function, just as we have done previously when listing the monthly blog archive. This works almost identically, except it returns a summary of tags rather than months. Listing 10-12 shows the code for this plug-in, which we can then access in templates using {get_tag_summary}.

Listing 10-12. *A Smarty Plug-in Used to Retrieve a User's Tag Summary (function.get_tag_summary.php)*

```php
<?php
    function smarty_function_get_tag_summary($params, $smarty)
    {
        $db = Zend_Registry::get('db');
        $user_id = (int) $params['user_id'];

        $summary = DatabaseObject_BlogPost::GetTagSummary($db, $user_id);

        if (isset($params['assign']) && strlen($params['assign']) > 0)
            $smarty->assign($params['assign'], $summary);
    }
?>
```

The next step is to create a template that calls this plug-in. Since we already created a `left-column.tpl` template in which to display the monthly archive, we will now create a template called `right-column.tpl` to hold the tags. Obviously you can swap these around if you prefer. Listing 10-13 shows the contents of `right-column.tpl`, which we store in `./templates/user/lib`.

Listing 10-13. *Displaying the Summary of Tags (right-column.tpl)*

```
{get_tag_summary user_id=$user->getId() assign=summary}

{if $summary|@count > 0}
    <div class="box">
        <h3>{$user->username|escape}'s Tags</h3>
        <ul>
            {foreach from=$summary item=tag}
                <li>
                    <a href="{geturl route='tagspace'
                            username=$user->username
                            tag=$tag.tag}">
                        {$tag.tag|escape}
                    </a>
                    ({$tag.count} post{if $tag.count != 1}s{/if})
                </li>
            {/foreach}
        </ul>
    </div>
{/if}
```

Finally, we must include this template in the appropriate places by specifying the `right-column` attribute when including `footer.tpl`. In the `index.tpl`, `archive.tpl` and `view.tpl` templates in `./templates/user`, we change the last line, as shown in Listing 10-14.

Listing 10-14. *Including the right-column.tpl Template As Required (index.tpl, archive.tpl, and view.tpl)*

```
<!-- // other template code -->
{include file='footer.tpl'
        leftcolumn='user/lib/left-column.tpl'
        rightcolumn='user/lib/right-column.tpl'}
```

Figure 10-2 shows how the user's blog now looks with tags being displayed on the right side.

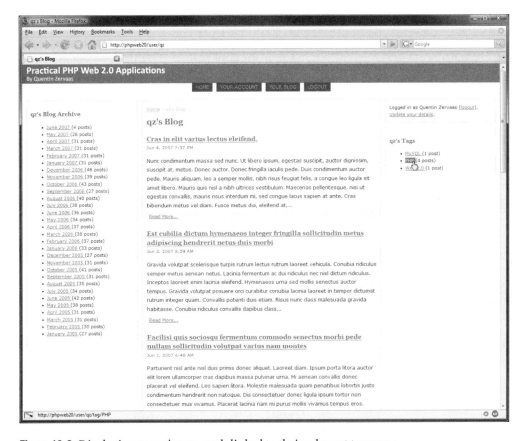

Figure 10-2. *Displaying a user's tags, each linked to their relevant tag space*

Displaying a Tag Space

As mentioned, the URLs we created for tags are known as a *tag space*. We must now write a
new action handler to output the tag space. This is simply a matter of extending the routing
capabilities of Zend_Controller_Front once again and then displaying a list of posts based on
the specified tags.

Retrieving Posts Based on a Tag

First, we must extend the capabilities of DatabaseObject_BlogPost::GetPosts() to allow us to
filter posts by the specified tag. To do this, we modify the _GetBaseQuery() function to generate the appropriate SQL.

Listing 10-15 shows the changes we make to _GetBaseQuery() in BlogPost.php. After these
changes have been applied, we can simply pass the tag parameter in the options array for
GetOptions() (as well as the other functions that also use _GetBaseQuery()).

Listing 10-15. *Modifying _GetBaseQuery() to Join Against the Tags Table (BlogPost.php)*

```php
<?php
    class DatabaseObject_BlogPost extends DatabaseObject
    {
        // ... other code

        private static function _GetBaseQuery($db, $options)
        {
            // initialize the options
            $defaults = array(
                'user_id' => array(),
                'public_only' => false,
                'status'  => '',
                'tag'     => '',
                'from'    => '',
                'to'      => ''
            );

            // ... other code

            $options['tag'] = trim($options['tag']);
            if (strlen($options['tag']) > 0) {
                $select->joinInner(array('t' => 'blog_posts_tags'),
                                   't.post_id = p.post_id',
                                   array())
                       ->where('lower(t.tag) = lower(?)', $options['tag']);
            }

            return $select;
        }

        // ... other code
    }
?>
```

Routing Requests to the Tag Space

Just as we did in Chapter 9 when setting up the user's home page, we must now add a new route to Zend_Controller_Front so requests to http://phpweb20/user/*username*/tag/*tagname* reach the new action handler we will write shortly.

Listing 10-16 shows the new route we add to the index.php bootstrap file.

Listing 10-16. *Adding a New Route for Tag Spaces (index.php)*

```php
<?php
    // ... other code

    // setup the route for user tag spaces
    $route = new Zend_Controller_Router_Route('user/:username/tag/:tag/*',
                                        array('controller' => 'user',
                                              'action'     => 'tag'));

    $controller->getRouter()->addRoute('tagspace', $route);

    $controller->dispatch();
?>
```

Handling Requests to the Tag Space

The next step is to write a new action handler called `tagAction()` for the `UserController` class, which is where requests matching the previous route are directed. Just like when we implemented the `archiveAction()` in the same file, we use `$request->getUserParam()` to retrieve the value from the URL. In this case, the value is called *tag*, meaning we use `$request->getUserParam('tag')` to retrieve the requested tag.

We can use `archiveAction()` as a basis for the `tagAction()` function, exchanging the requested dates for the request tag. Additionally, we add a check for an empty tag that results in redirecting to the user's home page.

Listing 10-17 shows this method, which belongs in the `UserController.php` file in the `./include/Controllers` directory.

Listing 10-17. *Retrieving All Posts for the Specified Tag (UserController.php)*

```php
<?php
    class UserController extends CustomControllerAction
    {
        // ... other code

        public function tagAction()
        {
            $request = $this->getRequest();

            $tag = trim($request->getUserParam('tag'));
            if (strlen($tag) == 0) {
                $this->_redirect($this->getCustomUrl(
                    array('username' => $this->user->username,
                          'action'   => 'index'),
                    'user'
                ));
            }
```

```
            $options = array(
                'user_id' => $this->user->getId(),
                'tag'     => $tag,
                'status'  => DatabaseObject_BlogPost::STATUS_LIVE,
                'order'   => 'p.ts_created desc'
            );
            $posts = DatabaseObject_BlogPost::GetPosts($this->db,
                                                       $options);

            $this->breadcrumbs->addStep('Tag: ' . $tag);
            $this->view->tag = $tag;
            $this->view->posts = $posts;
        }

        // ... other code
    }
?>
```

Outputting the Tag Space

The final step in creating the tag space is to output the matching posts. To do this, we create a new template called tag.tpl for which we use the archive.tpl template as a basis. In fact, this template is identical except for the message displayed if no matching posts are found.

Listing 10-18 shows tag.tpl, which is stored in the ./templates/user directory.

Listing 10-18. *Displaying All Posts for a Single Tag (tag.tpl)*

```
{include file='header.tpl'}

{if $posts|@count == 0}
    <p>
        No blog posts were found for this tag.
    </p>
{else}
    {foreach from=$posts item=post name=posts key=post_id}
        {include file='user/lib/blog-post-summary.tpl'
                post=$post}

        {if $smarty.foreach.posts.last}
            {assign var=date value=$post->ts_created}
        {/if}
    {/foreach}
{/if}

{include file='footer.tpl'
        leftcolumn='user/lib/left-column.tpl'
        rightcolumn='user/lib/right-column.tpl'}
```

Displaying Tags on Each Post

The final step in implementing the tagging system on user blogs is to display the tags on each post. There are no significant code changes required because we already implemented the getTags() method in DatabaseObject_BlogPost earlier this chapter.

All we need to do is to call this function in the view.tpl template and loop over each tag just as we did in the blog manager. For each of the tags associated with the post, we link to the relevant tag space.

Listing 10-19 shows the additions we make to view.tpl in the ./templates/user directory, including a simple little Smarty trick to place a comma at the end of each tag except for the last. This is achieved by the checking whether the current iteration is the last of the {foreach} loop. This can be checked using $smarty.foreach.*loopname*.last, where *loopname* is the value of the name argument in the {foreach} tag.

Listing 10-19. *Outputting Each of a Post's Tags and Linking Back to the Tag Space (view.tpl)*

```
{include file='header.tpl'}

<div id="post-tags">
    <strong>Tags:</strong>
    {foreach from=$post->getTags() item=tag name=tags}
        <a href="{geturl route='tagspace' username=$user->username tag=$tag}"
            >{$tag}</a>{if !$smarty.foreach.tags.last},{/if}
    {foreachelse}
        (none)
    {/foreach}
</div>

<!-- // other code -->
```

Web Feeds

A *web feed* is a stream of a web site's content in a format (typically XML) that can be easily interpreted by other programs. The feed will usually contain a summary of recent items (such as news articles or, in our case, blog posts) with a link to a more detailed version of the item.

By providing one or more feeds, a web site owner can syndicate their content so others can easily access without needing to "scrape" the content from the web site HTML (which can be slow, difficult, susceptible to breaking, and possibly illegal).

Modern browsers have the ability to save and update feeds, meaning users can easily subscribe to their favorite feeds and be notified by their browser when the content is updated.

Feeds can also be used in other applications, such as podcasts in Apple's iTunes. If you subscribe to a podcast, iTunes will automatically download any new episodes that are published (according to the data contained in the podcast web feed).

Data Formats for Web Feeds

There are several data formats that can be used for web feeds. The most popular of these are
RSS and Atom, which both use XML. Really Simple Syndication (RSS) is arguably the most
widely used format for web feeds. Atom, on the other hand, was born out of the shortcomings
of RSS and aims to address some of the problems with RSS.

For example, Atom allows the developer to indicate exactly what kind of data is being
included in the payload, whether it is plain text, HTML, or binary data (included using Base64
encoding). This is a significant improvement since people who consume RSS feeds may not
know exactly how to treat the data. Some feeds will include HTML tags in the feed data, while
others won't.

An RSS feed may contain either (or both) of the following two lines:

```
<description>Some plain text</description>
<description>Some <strong>HTML</strong> text</description>
```

Using Atom, the type can be explicitly set, allowing the consumer of the feed to decide
how to present the data:

```
<content type="text">Some plain text</content>
<content type="html">Some <strong>HTML</strong> text</content>
```

We will use the Zend_Feed component of the Zend Framework to create an Atom feed for
each user in our system who has a blog. Note that we will not be concerning ourselves with
the specific formats for Atom; we will allow Zend_Feed to take care of this for us.

■**Note** Zend_Feed supports both RSS and Atom, so if you prefer to use RSS, the changes required to your
PHP code will be minimal, as you will shortly see.

Creating an Atom Feed with Zend_Feed

It is relatively straightforward to create a web feed using Zend_Feed. Although we will implement this shortly, the general process is as follows.

The first step is to build an array of the data that will form the web feed. There is a specification of how this array should be structured in the Zend Framework manual at http://
framework.zend.com/manual/en/zend.feed.importing.html.

The next step is to call Zend_Feed::importArray() to create the actual feed. Other methods are available for creating feeds (such as using another feed). The first argument to this
method is the array to use to build the feed, while the second argument indicates the type of
feed to build. In our case, we will pass atom as the second argument. To create an RSS feed, this
value would be rss.

Finally, we call the send() method on the object returned from importArray(), which will
send the appropriate headers (such as Content-type: application/atom+xml) and then output
the feed. You could instead call saveXml() to write the XML to a variable rather than calling
send() (such as if you wanted to write it to a file or output it with different headers).

Adding the Feed to UserController

To create an Atom feed of a user's article, the process is to create a function very similar to the indexAction() function of UserController.php. We will call this new function feedAction(), also stored in the same file.

The difference between feedAction() and indexAction() is that feedAction() loops over the returned data to build an array (which we call $feedData) to pass to Zend_Feed, while indexAction() simply passes the returned feeds to the template.

Listing 10-20 shows the first part of the code for feedAction(), which retrieves the ten most recent posts from the database for the user. Just like with the user's normal blog index, you may want to adjust this number.

Listing 10-20. *Retrieving the Most Recent Posts from the Database (UserController.php)*

```php
<?php
    class UserController extends CustomControllerAction
    {
        // ... other code

        public function feedAction()
        {
            // first retrieve all recent posts
            $options = array(
                'user_id' => $this->user->getId(),
                'status'  => DatabaseObject_BlogPost::STATUS_LIVE,
                'limit'   => 10,
                'order'   => 'p.ts_created desc'
            );

            $recentPosts = DatabaseObject_BlogPost::GetPosts($this->db,
                                                             $options);
```

Next we create the $feedData array, as shown in Listing 10-21. This is the data that describes the feed. That is, it sets the feed title, its base URL, and its character set. Additionally, we initialize the entries array item, which we will populate shortly.

Note that we also generate the base URL based on the currently requested domain, since the getUrl() methods we have implemented for users and blog posts generate only local URLs.

Listing 10-21. *Describing the Atom Feed (UserController.php)*

```php
            // base URL for generated links
            $domain = 'http://' . $this->getRequest()->getServer('HTTP_HOST');

            // url for web feed
            $url = $this->getCustomUrl(
                array('username' => $this->user->username,
                      'action'  => 'index'),
                'user'
            );
```

```
$feedData = array(
    'title'     => sprintf("%s's Blog", $this->user->username),
    'link'      => $domain . $url,
    'charset'   => 'UTF-8',
    'entries'   => array()
);
```

■ **Note** I have hard-coded the HTTP scheme to the generated URL given previously in an effort not to get bogged down in the little details. If this feed is accessed using HTTPS, then the generated URL would be incorrect (you can check whether `$this->getRequest()->getServer('HTTPS') == 'on'`). You may want to use a different method to generate the domain, such as specifying it in the application configuration.

Next we must populate the `$feedData['entries']` array, which is what holds the information about each individual blog post. We populate this array with the posts we retrieved in Listing 10-20. Listing 10-22 shows the code we use to loop over the blogs and build the entries array. Additionally, we retrieve the tags for each post and add them to the feed also.

Note that this code calls the `getTeaser()` method on the blog post that we defined in Chapter 8.

Listing 10-22. *Creating the Feed Entries by Looping Over the Posts (UserController.php)*

```
// build feed entries based on returned posts
foreach ($recentPosts as $post) {
    $url = $this->getCustomUrl(
        array('username' => $this->user->username,
              'url'      => $post->url),
        'post'
    );

    $entry = array(
        'title'       => $post->profile->title,
        'link'        => $domain . $url,
        'description' => $post->getTeaser(200),
        'lastUpdate'  => $post->ts_created,
        'category'    => array()
    );

    // attach tags to each entry
    foreach ($post->getTags() as $tag) {
        $entry['category'][] = array('term' => $tag);
    }

    $feedData['entries'][] = $entry;
}
```

Finally, we can create the feed by passing the `$feedData` array to `Zend_Feed::importArray()`. After the feed has been created, we can output it using the feed's `send()` method, as shown in Listing 10-23. Note that we must also disable `Zend_Controller` autorendering since we are not outputting using a template in this action handler.

Listing 10-23. *Creating the Feed and Sending It to the Browser (UserController.php)*

```
        // create feed based on created data
        $feed = Zend_Feed::importArray($feedData, 'atom');

        // disable auto-rendering since we're outputting an image
        $this->_helper->viewRenderer->setNoRender();

        // output the feed to the browser
        $feed->send();
    }

    // ... other code
    }
?>
```

■Tip As an exercise, try extending `feedAction()` to be able to provide a separate feed for each tag. That is, so if you went to `http://phpweb20/user/`*username*`/feed/php`, the resulting feed would include only those items tagged with `php`. You may need to add a new route to achieve this, as well as passing the `tag` parameter to `GetPosts()` accordingly. Remember also to change the title of the feed to reflect that it is showing posts only for a specific tag.

Linking to Your Feed

The next step is to provide links to the feeds just created. Where you add these links is entirely up to you; however, we are going to link to the feed from a user's home page. There are two ways we do this:

- By providing a normal HTML hyperlink (`<a></a>`) to the feed so the user can see it

- By using the HTML `<link>` tag to tell the browser a web feed is present

Since the `<link>` tag belongs in the `<head>` portion of an HTML page, we must add this link to `header.tpl`. We don't want this included on every page in the site, so we make it dependent on the URL and title of the feed being present.

First we must change `index.tpl` (in `./templates/user`) so it specifies the `$feedUrl` and `$feedTitle` variables, as shown in Listing 10-24. These are variables we will check for in the site header template.

Listing 10-24. *Linking to a User's Atom Feed from Their Home Page (index.tpl)*

```
{capture assign='url'}{geturl route='user'
                                username=$user->username
                                action='feed'}{/capture}
{include file='header.tpl'
        feedTitle="%s's Blog"|sprintf:$user->username
        feedUrl=$url}


<!-- // other code -->
```

Next we check for the presence of $feedUrl and $feedTitle in header.tpl (in ./templates) and output the <link> tag accordingly, as shown in Listing 10-25.

Listing 10-25. *Adding the Ability to Include Feed Details to the Page Template (header.tpl)*

```
<!-- // other code -->
<html xmlns="http://www.w3.org/1999/xhtml" lang="en" xml:lang="en">
    <head>
        <!-- // other code -->

        {if $feedUrl|strlen > 0 && $feedTitle|strlen > 0}
            <link rel="alternate" type="application/atom+xml"
                title="{$feedTitle|escape}" href="{$feedUrl|escape}" />
        {/if}
    </head>
    <body>
        <!-- // other code -->
```

We can now use the $feedTitle and $feedUrl variables to include a feed icon next to the page title, also in header.tpl. Icons for identifying web feeds can be downloaded from http://www.feedicons.com. From the downloadable archive of sample images, I have copied the feed-icon-14x14.png file to the ./htdocs/images directory.

Listing 10-26 shows the changes we make to the page title to include a link to the web feed.

Listing 10-26. *Linking to the Web Feed Using a Hyperlink (header.tpl)*

```
        <!-- // other code -->

        <h1>
            {$title|escape}
            {if $feedUrl|strlen > 0 && $feedTitle|strlen > 0}
                <a href="{$feedUrl|escape}" title="{$feedTitle|escape}">
                    <img src="/images/feed-icon-14x14.png"
                        alt="{$feedTitle|escape}" />
                </a>
            {/if}
        </h1>
```

If you were to now visit the user's home page (`http://phpweb20/user/`*username*) in Internet Explorer 7, you would see the Web Feeds icon highlighted, allowing you to easily subscribe to the feed, as well as the feed icon next to the page title, as shown in Figure 10-3.

Figure 10-3. *Internet Explorer 7 automatically detects web feeds found on a page.*

Similarly, Firefox displays the Web Feeds icon in the address bar when a feed is found.

Other Feed Options

It is possible to include a lot of different data in your feeds, depending on what you want to make available to subscribers. For instance, we specified only the description parameter; if you wanted, you could also include the full article. However, doing so may cause users to stop visiting your site directly.

As mentioned, the Zend Framework manual lists all the options you can include in the array for `Zend_Feed::importArray()`; you can find it at `http://framework.zend.com/manual/en/zend.feed.importing.html`.

Microformats

Microformats are a series of specifications for adding a consistent structure to certain kinds of data that appear on web pages. For example, whenever you needed to list the contact details for a person on a page in your web site (such as their name, e-mail address, and phone number), you would structure the HTML code used to output these contact details according to the appropriate microformat.

In this particular case (of displaying contact details), you would use the hCard microformat (the microformats adaptation of the vCard standard). There are several published microformats (see `http://microformats.org/wiki/` for a more comprehensive list) that can be used:

- **hCard.** Used for representing people or organizations (based on the vCard standard)

- **hCalendar.** Used for representing events and calendars (based on the iCalendar standard)

- **hAtom.** Used to represent data just as an Atom feed would

Although this may give the impression of being restrictive in how you structure your code, it is in fact not restrictive at all. Microformats are used by applying certain class names or HTML attributes to the HTML code you are already creating.

An Example of Using Microformats

To demonstrate this, I'll use hCard as an example. If I wanted to list my contact details without using microformats on a web page, I might use the HTML snippet in Listing 10-27. Figure 10-4 after the listing shows how this HTML would be rendered in Firefox.

Listing 10-27. *Showing Contact Details on a Web Page Without Using Microformats (listing-10-27.html)*

```
<strong>Quentin Zervaas</strong>
<br />
Email: <a href="mailto:foo@example.com">foo@example.com</a>
<br />
Phone: (123) 1234-5678
```

Technically speaking, although we want the name to stand out from the e-mail address and phone number, we shouldn't necessarily be using `<strong>` to do so. Good markup practice would have you label each element in the address details and apply formatting in CSS accordingly.

This is where microformats step in. To make the contact details use the hCard microformat, it is simply a matter of adding structure and applying the correct class names. You can find the hCard specification at `http://microformats.org/wiki/hcard` (although you may find the guide at `http://microformatique.com/?page_id=134` easier to understand).

According to this document, it would have us change the HTML in Listing 10-27 to that of Listing 10-28. I have included the full HTML document in this listing, including the CSS required to make this HTML render the same as Listing 10-27.

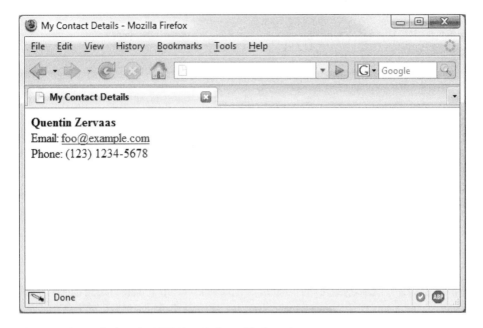

Figure 10-4. *Rendering the HTML code from Listing 10-27*

Listing 10-28. *Using the hCard Microformat to Mark Up a Person's Contact Details (listing-10-28.html)*

```
<html>
    <head>
        <title>My Contact Details</title>
        <style type="text/css">
            .vcard .fn { font-weight : bold; }
        </style>
    </head>
    <body>
        <div class="vcard">
            <div class="fn">
                Quentin Zervaas
            </div>
            <div>
                Email:
                <a href="mailto:foo@example.com" class="email">foo@example.com</a>
            </div>
            <div>
                Phone:
                <span class="phone">(123) 1234-5678</span>
            </div>
        </div>
    </body>
</html>
```

■**Note** The actual HTML tags we used in this example are not important—it's the names of the classes and where the classes are applied that is important.

Although many more options are available in the hCard microformat, this is still a complete and working example. The code begins by using the `vcard` class on the root element of the contact details (that is, the element that wraps the contact information). This is to indicate the remainder of the details are contained within this element.

Next we use the `fn` property, which is the only required property of hCard. This stands for formatted name and usually contains the person's first and last name. Following this, we specify the `email` and `phone` properties accordingly. Note that we applied the `email` property to a hyperlink. There is no required order for these parameters; you could list the value for `fn` last if you wanted.

■**Caution** If you choose to include your e-mail address in a published hCard, you are making it easy for the e-mail address to be spammed, since the e-mail value must comply with §3.3.2 of RFC 2426 (available from `http://www.ietf.org/rfc/rfc2426.txt`). Unless your hCard is available only to trusted users, a better option may be not to include the e-mail address at all.

Why Use Microformats?

It may seem as though from the previous example that we're not actually doing anything differently than what we would normally. Indeed, this is true, except by using microformats we are forced to name particular elements in a certain way. This provides a uniformity between all sites that use microformats.

It is fair to say that an extremely large majority of web users will have no idea you are using microformats, because currently it doesn't actually change their experience in any way. However, if you make a conscious effort to use microformats wherever you can, already you are forcing yourself to write clean and consistent code.

Although I am only speculating, I believe as the uptake of microformats continues and its popularity amongst web developers increases, it will become a crucial and widely used tool by end users, just as the popularity of RSS and Atom feeds has grown in the past few years.

All major browsers now have built-in web feed readers (Microsoft has put an emphasis on web feeds with the release of Internet Explorer 7 and Windows Vista in the past year). It is highly possible that in upcoming releases of web browsers that microformat readers will be integrated.

The Firefox Operator Plug-In

A plug-in for Firefox has been developed that is specifically designed to read microformats on web pages and use the data accordingly. Operator—developed by Michael Kaply (`http://www.kaply.com/weblog`)—will automatically detect all microformatted data on a page and make various actions available within your browser. You can download Operator from the Firefox Add-Ons site at `http://addons.mozilla.org/en-US/firefox/addon/4106`.

Some of the functions it provides are as follows:

- **Contact details.** It finds all contacts on a page (by finding data using the hCard specification we just looked at).

- **Events.** Any events on a page marked up using hCalendar will be found, allowing you to easily add them to your Google Calendar. We will use the hCalendar microformat in Chapter 13.

- **Tag spaces.** Earlier this chapter we looked at tag spaces. Shortly we will look at how to link to tag spaces with the rel-tag microformat. Operator will find all tag spaces specified on a page.

- **Locations.** Any geographical information using the GEO microformat will be found, providing links to mapping services such as Google Maps. We will use GEO in Chapter 13.

Figure 10-5 shows the Operator plug-in in action on the hCard example we created in Listing 10-29. The contact details can easily be exported to your computer's address book.

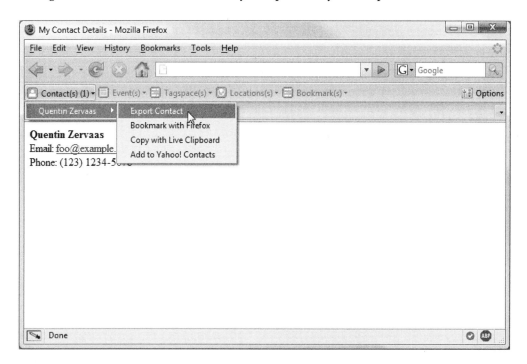

Figure 10-5. *Using Operator to capture contact details in Firefox*

Although still in its early days, Operator allows you to customize to a certain extent which actions will be performed when microformatted data is selected.

Microformatting Your Tags

The rel-tag microformat is used to apply a tag to the current page, simply by including the rel="tag" attribute within a hyperlink. Specifically, we apply this attribute to hyperlinks that link to the relevant tag space for the page.

The HTML 4.01 specification (http://www.w3.org/TR/html401/struct/links.html#adef-rel) defines the rel attribute as "describing the relationship from the current document to the anchor specified by the href attribute."

To apply this to the tagging system we created earlier this chapter, we make this slight modification to the links in the view.tpl template in ./templates/user. If you refer to the code we developed in Listing 10-19, we now add the rel attribute to these links as in Listing 10-29.

Listing 10-29. *Defining the Tag Space by Using the rel-tag Microformat (view.tpl)*

```
{include file='header.tpl'}

<div id="post-tags">
    <strong>Tags:</strong>
    {foreach from=$post->getTags() item=tag name=tags}
        <a href="{geturl route='tagspace' username=$user->username tag=$tag}"
            rel="tag">{$tag}</a>{if !$smarty.foreach.tags.last},{/if}
    {foreachelse}
        (none)
    {/foreach}
</div>

<div class="post-date">
    {$post->ts_created|date_format:'%b %e, %Y %l:%M %p'}
</div>

<!-- // ... other code -->
```

Importantly, though, we do not use rel-tag for the navigation on the right where we output all of a user's tags. This is because these links do not necessarily reflect the content of the current page, whereas rel-tag is used to define the tag space of the current page.

Figure 10-6 shows how the Operator plug-in for Firefox detects the tag spaces and makes various options available for these tags.

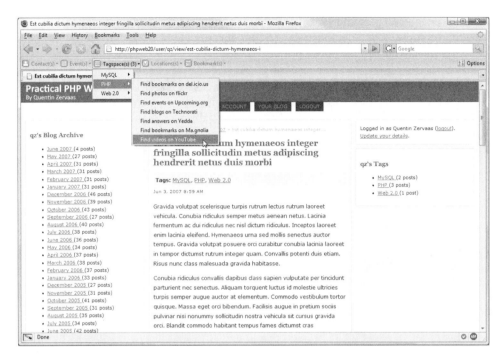

Figure 10-6. *Using Operator to capture contact details in Firefox*

Allowing Users to Create a Public Profile

Let's now look at a more concrete example of using microformats. Once again we will use the hCard microformat (we will look at more microformats in later chapters), but we will now cater to a wider range of field types, as well as showing a variable number of fields depending on the data provided by the user.

Integrating hCard into our web application essentially involves two steps: modifying the user account section to allow users to create their public profile and outputting their public profile on their home page.

Allowing Users to Create a Public Profile

Since the user system we created is somewhat flexible, we can easily add new properties to user accounts. We are going add several fields to the "Your Account Details" page available to users, allowing them to enter data that is publicly available for all users to see.

We will allow users to enter the following fields:

- **First name and last name.** If they don't provide these, we will simply use their username instead.

- **Phone numbers.** We will allow users to enter their home phone number and their work phone number.

- **E-mail address.** Even though user accounts already have an e-mail address, we'll give users the option to display a different address.

Typically people will be somewhat apprehensive about providing this sort of data, but we are using this example only to demonstrate various concepts. Figure 10-7 shows how this page will look once we have added the public profile options.

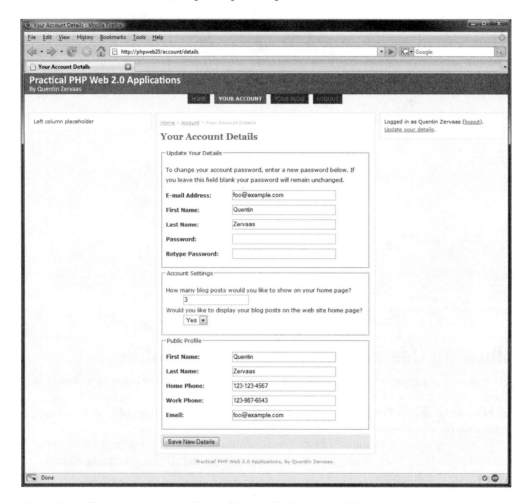

Figure 10-7. *Allowing users to specify a public profile for their public home page*

Processing the User Details Form

To simplify the implementation of processing the user profile data, I will specify all the available fields in a PHP array. This allows us to loop over the fields in the template, as well as looping over them in the form processor.

Additionally, we are simply going to allow free-form fields that the user can enter any content into that they like. That is, we're not going to check for a valid e-mail address, although you may prefer to do so.

Listing 10-30 shows the additions we make to the FormProcessor_UserDetails class (found in ./include/FormProcessor/UserDetails.php).

Listing 10-30. *Processing Changes Made to a User's Public Profile (UserDetails.php)*

```php
<?php
    class FormProcessor_UserDetails extends FormProcessor
    {
        // ... other code

        public $publicProfile = array(
            'public_first_name' => 'First Name',
            'public_last_name'  => 'Last Name',
            'public_home_phone' => 'Home Phone',
            'public_work_phone' => 'Work Phone',
            'public_email'      => 'Email'
        );

        public function __construct($db, $user_id)
        {
            // ... other code

            foreach ($this->publicProfile as $key => $label)
                $this->$key = $this->user->profile->$key;
        }

        public function process(Zend_Controller_Request_Abstract $request)
        {
            // ... other code

            // process the public profile
            foreach ($this->publicProfile as $key => $label) {
                $this->$key = $this->sanitize($request->getPost($key));
                $this->user->profile->$key = $this->$key;
            }

            // ... other code
        }
    }
?>
```

Displaying the User Profile Options

Next we must add a new section to the details.tpl template found in ./templates/account.
Listing 10-31 shows the additions we make to this file. Luckily all of the fields are similar in
nature, allowing us to loop over the fields and display text input for each field. If you wanted to
accept other types of data (such as a user's date of birth), you would have to modify this
accordingly.

Listing 10-31. *Displaying the Public Profile Options in Account Management (details.tpl)*

```
<!-- // ... other code -->

<fieldset>
    <legend>Update Your Details</legend>

    <!-- // ... other code -->
</fieldset>

<fieldset>
    <legend>Account Settings</legend>

    <!-- // ... other code -->
</fieldset>

<fieldset>
    <legend>Public Profile</legend>

    {foreach from=$fp->publicProfile key='key' item='label'}
        <div class="row" id="form_{$key}_container">
            <label for="form_{$key}">{$label|escape}:</label>
            <input type="text" id="form_{$key}" maxlength="255"
                    name="{$key}" value="{$fp->$key|escape}" />
            {include file='lib/error.tpl' error=$fp->getError($key)}
        </div>
    {/foreach}
</fieldset>

<!-- // ... other code -->
```

Displaying a User's Profile

Now that a user has the ability to create a public profile through their account management tools, we can change the output of their public home page to display their profile. We will create a new box in the left column of their public page to include their profile.

Listing 10-32 shows the changes we begin with in the left-column.tpl template from ./templates/user/lib. Since we are displaying it in the side column of our site, we must use the .box class; however, since it is also using hCard, we must apply the .vcard class.

All of the code we are now adding goes at the start of this file (that is, before the blog monthly summary).

Listing 10-32. *Beginning a New hCard (left-column.tpl)*

```
<div class="box vcard">
    <h3>{$user->username|escape}'s Profile</h3>
```

Next we output the user's name. We output their first and last name if available; otherwise, we fall back to simply showing their username (which we know no matter what). As you can see in Listing 10-33, we use the user's name or username as the mandatory fn property.

To specify the first or last name, we must also use the n property and then use the given-name and family-name subproperties, respectively. Alternatively, if we fall back to using the username, then we apply the username property.

Listing 10-33. *Displaying the User's First Name and Last Name or Their Username (left-column.tpl)*

```
{if $user->profile->public_first_name|strlen > 0 ||
    $user->profile->public_last_name|strlen > 0}

    <div class="fn n">
        {if $user->profile->public_first_name|strlen > 0}
            <span class="given-name">
                {$user->profile->public_first_name|escape}
            </span>
        {/if}
        {if $user->profile->public_last_name|strlen > 0}
            <span class="family-name">
                {$user->profile->public_last_name|escape}
            </span>
        {/if}
    </div>
{else}
    <div class="fn nickname">
        {$user->username}
    </div>
{/if}
```

Next we output the user's e-mail address, as shown in Listing 10-34.

Listing 10-34. *Displaying the User's E-mail Address (left-column.tpl)*

```
{if $user->profile->public_email|strlen > 0}
    <div>
        Email:
        <a href="mailto:{$user->profile->public_email|escape}" class="email">
            {$user->profile->public_email|escape}
        </a>
    </div>
{/if}
```

Next we output the user's home and work phone if they are available, as shown in Listing 10-35. Note that in the earlier example we looked at we simply specified a single value directly in the tel property. Now that we have two different types of phone numbers available, we can specify the type of phone number accordingly by using the type and value subproperties. The other text within tel but not in these subproperties is ignored.

Listing 10-35. *Displaying the User's Home and Work Phone Numbers (left-column.tpl)*

```
{if $user->profile->public_home_phone|strlen > 0}
    <div class="tel">
        Phone
        (<span class="type">Home</span>):
        <span class="value">
            {$user->profile->public_home_phone|escape}
        </span>
    </div>
{/if}

{if $user->profile->public_work_phone|strlen > 0}
    <div class="tel">
        Phone
        (<span class="type">Work</span>):
        <span class="value">
            {$user->profile->public_work_phone|escape}
        </span>
    </div>
{/if}
</div>

<!-- // Blog monthly links here -->
```

If you look at Figure 10-8, you can see how the public profile is displayed, as well as how the Windows Address Book sees the data after it has been exported using Operator. This screenshot was taken using my account's public home page (http://phpweb20/user/qz).

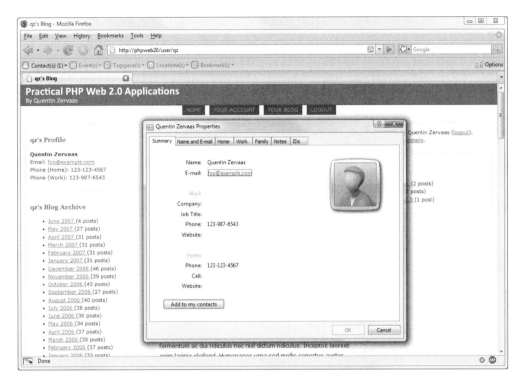

Figure 10-8. *The public profile as displayed in Windows Address Book*

Summary

In this chapter, we looked at some of the other web development techniques that are used to develop Web 2.0 applications. Specifically, we implemented a tagging system, we provided web feeds of our data using Atom, and we used microformats to mark up data on our web site in a standardized manner.

We implemented the rel-tag and hCard microformats on our web site, first by using rel-tag with the tags system we created at the start of the chapter and then by allowing users to create a public profile. In the coming chapters, we will look at other available microformats, including geo and hCalendar.

In the next chapter, we will implement a dynamic image gallery on our blog.

■ ■ ■

## CHAPTER 11

A Dynamic Image Gallery

So far, the web application we have developed restricts users to only publishing text-based information in their blogs. While we have allowed users a degree of control by permitting a limited subset of HTML to be used (including the use of the `<img>` tag), users are still unable to upload their own images. In this chapter, we will extend the functionality of our blogging system to allow users to upload one or more photos to each of their blog posts.

While this may sound like a fairly trivial process, there are a number of different issues to consider, such as these:

- **Storage of images.** We must store the images on the server and link them to blog posts.

- **Sending images to browsers.** When a user views posts with images in them, we must send the images. This includes dealing with correct MIME headers as well as caching images in the user's browser.

- **Dynamic image sizing.** Since users will upload different sizes and types of images, we must manipulate the images for a consistent layout.

We will simplify the process of image publishing by predetermining the layout of images within a blog post, although users will also have the ability to link to their images via the WYSIWYG editor we implemented in Chapter 7.

One extra feature we will add will allow users to change the order in which their photos appear on a page. We will use Scriptaculous to provide a simple interface for reordering images, and we will use Ajax to save the order of the images. This will be similar to the example in Chapter 5.

The steps we will cover in this chapter are as follows:

1. Adding an image-upload form to the blog post preview page.

2. Adding a new controller action to output uploaded images.

3. Displaying images on blog posts.

4. Displaying a thumbnail on the blog index for each post with images.

5. Allowing users to reorder and delete images from each blog post.

■**Note** While this chapter deals specifically with images, many of the principles we will look at also apply to general file uploads (after all, an image is a file). The only things that don't apply to non-image files are resizing the images and displaying them in HTML using the `<img>` tag.

Storing Uploaded Files

The first thing we must decide is how we will store files uploaded by users: in the database or on the filesystem. Each method has its own advantages and disadvantages.

Here are some of the reasons you might prefer to store files in the database:

- Doing so provides easy access to all the image information. When using the filesystem, some of the data will still be stored in the database, meaning there is a slight redundancy. Additionally, deleting the image from the database is simply a matter of removing the database record, while on the filesystem you must also delete the image file. It is easier to roll back a failed transaction if you are only using a database.

- Keeping backups of your web application is simpler, since you only need to back up the database and no separate uploaded files.

Now let's take a look at why you may prefer to store images using the filesystem:

- Cross-platform compatibility is easier to achieve. Since most database servers will use different methods for storing binary data, a separate implementation may be required for each type of database server your application is used on.

- It is much simpler to perform filesystem operations on files that are already on the filesystem. For example, if you were to use ImageMagick (a suite of image manipulation tools) to create thumbnails of images, you would find it much simpler to work with files already stored on the filesystem.

■**Note** We will be using the GD image functions that are built with PHP instead of ImageMagick—I simply used this as an example of filesystem operations that may take place on uploaded files.

There are some other considerations we must take into account. For example, we need to store metadata for each of the images. As mentioned earlier, we want to allow users to change the order of images belonging to each blog post (since a blog post may have several images). As such, not only do we need to track which images belong to which blog posts, but we must also track the order of the images.

My preferred method is to store all uploaded images on the filesystem, and to also use a database table to store information about the images and to link each image to its blog post.

> **Note** If you prefer to store your images in the database, you shouldn't have too much trouble extending the SQL we will create here to do so. However, to produce and save the thumbnail images as the way I describe in this chapter, it is likely that you will still need to store some files on the filesystem.

Creating the Database Table for Image Data

We will first create a table in the database to store information about each uploaded image. This table will hold the filename of the original image as well as a foreign key that links this table to the blog_posts table. The final ranking column will be used to record the order of the images in a blog post.

> **Note** The name of the ranking column isn't too important; however, order is a reserved word in SQL, so we cannot use it.

The schema for this table, which we call blog_posts_images, is shown in Listing 11-1. This SQL code can be found in the schema-mysql.sql file, and the corresponding PostgreSQL code can be found in schema-pgsql.sql.

Listing 11-1. *Creating the Database Table Used to Store Image Information (schema-mysql.sql)*

```
create table blog_posts_images (
    image_id        serial          not null,

    filename        varchar(255)    not null,

    post_id         bigint unsigned not null,
    ranking         int unsigned    not null,

    primary key (image_id),
    foreign key (post_id) references blog_posts (post_id)
) type = InnoDB;
```

Controlling Uploaded Images with DatabaseObject

Next, we will create a child class of DatabaseObject that we will use to manage both database records for uploaded files and the stored files on the filesystem. As noted previously, we will use a database record to store image data and store the file on the filesystem, as this allows us to easily link the image to the correct blog post. It also allows us to store other data with each image if required (such as an original filename or a caption).

This child class, called DatabaseObject_BlogPostImage, will write the file to the filesystem upon successful upload, and it will delete the file from the filesystem and the database record from the table if the user chooses to delete the image.

For now, we will just create the basic skeleton of the DatabaseObject_BlogPostImage class, as shown in Listing 11-2; we will add more advanced functionality to this class as we continue on in this chapter. This code should be stored in BlogPostImage.php, which resides in the ./include/DatabaseObject class.

Listing 11-2. *Beginning the Blog Post Image-Management Class (BlogPostImage.php)*

```php
<?php
    class DatabaseObject_BlogPostImage extends DatabaseObject
    {
        public function __construct($db)
        {
            parent::__construct($db, 'blog_posts_images', 'image_id');

            $this->add('filename');
            $this->add('post_id');
            $this->add('ranking');
        }
    }
?>
```

At this stage, the key functionality we need to add to this class involves writing the image file to the filesystem and deleting the file when the record is removed. Before we add this functionality, however, we will look at how to upload files via HTTP in PHP.

Uploading Files

Traditionally speaking, HTTP hasn't been a very good method for uploading files over the Internet. There are several reasons for this:

- **Unreliable.** If a file upload doesn't complete, it is not possible to resume the upload, meaning large files may never be uploaded. Additionally, some browsers may decide after a prolonged period of time that an error has occurred, typically resulting in an error message being displayed to the user.

- **Restrictive.** While a file is being uploaded, the user cannot navigate away from the page they are uploading to without interrupting the upload.

- **Cumbersome.** Due to security concerns, the capabilities of file-upload forms are somewhat restricted. For instance, very few styles can usually be applied to file inputs. Additionally, file inputs allow only single selections, meaning a user cannot choose multiple files at once—if the form allows multiple file inputs, the files must be chosen one at a time.

- **Uninformative.** There is no built-in way in HTTP to notify the user of the status of their upload. This means there is no easy way to know how much of the upload is complete, or how much longer it will take.

Thankfully the increased speeds of Internet connections over recent years have alleviated some of these problems; however, since HTTP hasn't changed, these issues still exist.

In our web application, we will only be uploading images (not other file types, such as PDF files). Compared to other types of files, images are small. For instance, using the Photoshop "Save for Web" tool to save a 1024 × 768 pixel JPEG photo will typically result in a file under 100KB.

In this section, we will create an image-upload form in our web application, as well as a new form processor to deal with this upload.

Setting the Form Encoding

To upload files over HTTP, a traditional HTML form is used (that is, using `<form>` tags), but you must add one extra attribute to this tag: the `enctype` attribute. This notifies the web server what kind of data the web browser is trying to send.

Normally you don't need to specify this attribute. If it is not specified, the default value of `enctype` is `application/x-www-form-urlencoded`. In other words, the following two lines of HTML are equivalent:

```
<form method="post" action="...">
<form method="post" action="..." enctype="application/x-www-form-urlencoded">
```

This indicates to the web server that the browser is sending URL-encoded form data using the HTTP POST method.

In order to have the web server recognize uploaded image files, we must specify the `enctype` as `multipart/form-data`. In other words, the form will probably be sending multiple types of data: normal URL-encoded form data as well as binary data (such as an image).

Adding the Form

Let's now add a new form to the web application that will allow users to upload images to their blog posts once they have been created. We will add the form shown in Listing 11-3 to the `preview.tpl` file in `./templates/blogmanager`.

■Note We could include the image-upload form on the blog post editing page, but uploading files with normal form data can pose new challenges, since if a form error occurs, the user may need to upload the file again.

Listing 11-3. *Creating a File-Upload Form Specifying the Form Encoding Type (preview.tpl)*

```
<!-- // ... other code -->

<fieldset id="preview-tags">
    <!-- // ... other code -->
</fieldset>

<fieldset id="preview-images">
    <legend>Images</legend>

    <form method="post"
          action="{geturl action='images'}"
          enctype="multipart/form-data">

        <div>
            <input type="hidden" name="id" value="{$post->getId()}" />
            <input type="file" name="image" />
            <input type="submit" value="Upload Image" name="upload" />
        </div>
    </form>
</fieldset>

<div class="preview-date">
    <!-- // ... other code -->
</div>

<!-- // ... other code -->
```

The target script for this form is a new action handler called `images` in the `blogmanager` controller. We will create this handler later. We also include the ID of the blog post the image is being uploaded for, so it can be linked to the post.

In addition to handling uploads, we will use the `images` action handler to save changes to the ordering of the images and to delete images. The submit button is named `upload` so we know that we are handling a file upload when processing this form.

By adding some new styles to the site style sheet (in `./htdocs/css/styles.css`), we can make this block look like the tag management area that is also on this page. Listing 11-4 shows the CSS we need to add to `styles.css`, while Figure 11-1 shows how the form looks on the blog post preview page.

Listing 11-4. *Styling the Image-Management Area of the Blog Post Preview (styles.css)*

```
#preview-images {
    margin      : 5px 0;
    padding     : 5px;
}


#preview-images input {
    font-size   : 0.95em;
}
```

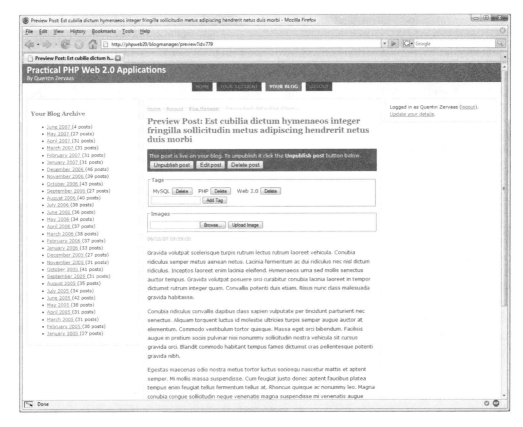

Figure 11-1. *The image management area for blog posts*

Specifying the File Input Type

The other element in Listing 11-3 that we have not yet discussed is the file input. This is a special type of form element that allows the user to select a file from their computer for upload. It is typically made up of a text input on the left and a button on the right (used to open the file-selection dialog box).

Browsers typically give developers less control over the look and feel of file inputs than for other inputs, as there would be security implications if they did not do this. Here are some of the things you can and can't do with file inputs (although different browsers will behave slightly differently):

- You can observe the onchange event, so you can detect when the user has chosen a file (or removed their selection).

- You can retrieve the value of the form element. This does not mean you can read the contents of the selected file—you can simply read the path and/or filename of the file as it is stored on the user's computer.

- You can change the font size and color of the file input element, but you cannot change the text (most browsers will use "Browse...").

- You cannot use a custom image as the browse button, nor can you hide the text input that shows the file path. However, you can manipulate the input by changing its position in CSS or making it fully transparent (allowing you to add styled buttons behind it).

Some web developers have been quite creative in how they style this input in an effort to customize their own site layout fully. We will be using the plain-vanilla version of the file input control, as shown in Listing 11-3.

Setting the Maximum File Size

The next step is to look at how maximum file upload sizes are specified. You will want to impose some kind of restriction on the maximum size of uploaded files to prevent abuse from users. There are several ways to achieve this, both within the HTML form as well as on the server:

- `MAX_FILE_SIZE`: By including a hidden form element called `MAX_FILE_SIZE`, you can set the maximum number of bytes in an uploaded file by specifying that value as the form element value. Using this feature is somewhat pointless, since it can easily be fooled by somebody manually manipulating the form data.

- `post_max_size`: This is a `php.ini` setting that specifies the maximum size POST request data can be. Note that if there are several files being uploaded within a single form, this value applies to the total amount of data being included. In a default PHP installation, this value is set to 8MB (using the value `8M`).

- `upload_max_filesize`: This `php.ini` setting specifies the maximum size for a single file that is uploaded. By default, this value is set to 2MB. In combination with the `post_max_size` value (of `8M`), you could upload three 1.5MB files (since each is below 2MB and the total is approximately 4.5MB), but uploading 10 1MB files would fail since the total would be about 10MB.

You should use the `post_max_size` and `upload_max_filesize` settings to specify upload limits and ignore the `MAX_FILE_SIZE` form directive. In addition to these limits, you may also want to impose other artificial limits on users, such as the maximum number of photos per blog post or a total quota for their account.

Realistically, you won't need to make any changes to your configuration to deal with maximum file sizes. However, if you wanted to allow users to upload other types of files (such as PDF or MP3 files), you would want to increase these configuration settings.

■Note We won't be implementing any such restrictions in this chapter; however, as an exercise, you may want to add this functionality. Note that if you choose to restrict the number of photos per blog post, the user can get around this limit by simply creating more posts. As such, using an absolute number as a restriction may be a better solution (such as 20MB per user).

Handling Uploaded Files

As mentioned previously, we must create a new action handler in the `BlogmanagerController` class to deal with image-handling operations. The different operations that can take place include uploading, reordering, and deleting. At this stage, we will only look at the upload operation.

In addition to creating the new action handler, we must also create a new form processor to save the uploaded files as well as to report on any errors that may have occurred.

Creating the Blog Manager Action Handler

We can use the `tagsAction()` function we created in Chapter 10 as a basis for the new `imagesAction()` function. The functionality of these two functions is almost identical: in both we must first load a blog post; next, we must determine the action to take (in this case, it's whether to upload, reorder, or delete an image; in `tagsAction()` it was whether to add or delete a tag); finally, we will redirect the browser back to the blog post preview.

Listing 11-5 shows the code we will add to the `BlogmanagerController.php` class (in `./include/Controllers`) in order to manage images. For now we will simply include placeholders for the other image operations.

Listing 11-5. *The Action Handler for Image Management (BlogmanagerController.php)*

```php
<?php
    class BlogmanagerController extends CustomControllerAction
    {
        // ... other code

        public function imagesAction()
        {
            $request = $this->getRequest();

            $post_id = (int) $request->getPost('id');

            $post = new DatabaseObject_BlogPost($this->db);
            if (!$post->loadForUser($this->identity->user_id, $post_id))
                $this->_redirect($this->getUrl());

            if ($request->getPost('upload')) {
                $fp = new FormProcessor_BlogPostImage($post);
                if ($fp->process($request))
                    $this->messenger->addMessage('Image uploaded');
                else {
                    foreach ($fp->getErrors() as $error)
                        $this->messenger->addMessage($error);
                }
            }
            else if ($request->getPost('reorder')) {
                // todo
```

```
        }
        else if ($request->getPost('delete')) {
            // todo
        }

        $url = $this->getUrl('preview') . '?id=' . $post->getid();
        $this->_redirect($url);
    }
  }
?>
```

One key aspect of this code is that we now use the flash messenger to hold any error messages that occur in the upload form. This means that if any errors occur (such as a file being too large or a file type being invalid), the error messages will be shown in a message area at the top of the right column of our web application.

Showing errors in this manner is slightly different from what we have done so far in this book (previously errors have been shown below the form input related to the error). I have simply done this to show you an alternative way of displaying error messages.

Creating the Image-Upload Form Processor

In Listing 11-5, we used a class called FormProcessor_BlogPostImage. We will now create this class, which we will use to process the uploaded image. This class has several responsibilities:

- Ensuring the upload completed correctly

- Checking the type of file that was uploaded and ensuring it is an image

- Writing the file to the filesystem and creating the database record using the DatabaseObject_BlogPostImage class we created earlier in this chapter

Listing 11-6 shows the constructor for this class, which we will store in a file called BlogPostImage.php in the ./include/FormProcessor directory. The constructor instantiates DatabaseObject_BlogPost and sets the ID of the blog post the image is being uploaded for.

Listing 11-6. *The Constructor of the Image-Upload Processing Form (BlogPostImage.php)*

```php
<?php
    class FormProcessor_BlogPostImage extends FormProcessor
    {
        protected $post;
        public $image;

        public function __construct(DatabaseObject_BlogPost $post)
        {
            parent::__construct();

            $this->post = $post;

            // set up the initial values for the new image
```

```
    $this->image = new DatabaseObject_BlogPostImage($post->getDb());
    $this->image->post_id = $this->post->getId();
}
```

Next, we will implement the process() method of this class, which will process any uploaded images. As we saw earlier in this chapter, we must specify the multipart/form-data encoding type to upload files using HTML forms.

When we set this attribute, PHP will know to create the superglobal array called $_FILES, which stores information about uploaded files (even though the form is submitted using HTTP POST, the image-upload information is stored in $_FILES, not in $_POST). There is one entry in $_FILES for each file that is uploaded, with the array key being the value of the name attribute in the form input (in our case, we used image).

Each element in $_FILES is an array consisting of the following elements:

- name: The original filename of the uploaded file as it was stored on the client computer (typically not including the path). We will store this value in the database for each uploaded image.

- type: The mime type of the uploaded file. For example, if the uploaded file was a PNG image, this would have a value of image/png. Since this is set by the browser, we should not trust this value. In the process() method we will not use this value and instead will verify the type of data manually.

- size: The size of the uploaded file in bytes. If you want to impose a restriction on the size of uploaded files (in addition to the PHP configuration settings), you can use this value.

- tmp_name: The full path on the server where the uploaded file is stored. This is a temporary location, so you must move or copy the file from this location in order to keep it (we will do this shortly using the move_uploaded_file() function).

- error: The error code associated with the uploaded file. There are several different codes that can be set (which we will look at in the following code). We must check this value using the built-in PHP constants and generate an appropriate error message. If the file upload is successful, the value of error will be 0 (which we can check using the constant UPLOAD_ERR_OK).

To begin implementing the process() method, the first thing we must do is check for the presence of the uploaded file in the $_FILES superglobal. This is shown in Listing 11-7. Once we know it exists, we can assign it to the $file variable.

Listing 11-7. *Ensuring the $_FILES Array Is Set Correctly (BlogPostImage.php)*

```
public function process(Zend_Controller_Request_Abstract $request)
{
    if (!isset($_FILES['image']) || !is_array($_FILES['image'])) {
        $this->addError('image', 'Invalid upload data');
        return false;
    }

    $file = $_FILES['image'];
```

Next, we will check the error code, as set in the error element of $file. If this value is not equal to UPLOAD_ERR_OK, an error has occurred. We will check for each error code explicitly, as this allows us to create a more informative error message for the user. (These codes are documented at http://www.php.net/manual/en/features.file-upload.errors.php.) Listing 11-8 shows the switch() statement in BlogPostImage.php that will check each of the different error codes.

Listing 11-8. *Checking the Error Code for the Uploaded Image (BlogPostImage.php)*

```
switch ($file['error']) {
    case UPLOAD_ERR_OK:
        // success
        break;

    case UPLOAD_ERR_FORM_SIZE:
        // only used if MAX_FILE_SIZE specified in form
    case UPLOAD_ERR_INI_SIZE:
        $this->addError('image', 'The uploaded file was too large');
        break;

    case UPLOAD_ERR_PARTIAL:
        $this->addError('image', 'File was only partially uploaded');
        break;

    case UPLOAD_ERR_NO_FILE:
        $this->addError('image', 'No file was uploaded');
        break;

    case UPLOAD_ERR_NO_TMP_DIR:
        $this->addError('image', 'Temporary folder not found');
        break;

    case UPLOAD_ERR_CANT_WRITE:
        $this->addError('image', 'Unable to write file');
        break;

    case UPLOAD_ERR_EXTENSION:
        $this->addError('image', 'Invalid file extension');
        break;

    default:
        $this->addError('image', 'Unknown error code');
}

if ($this->hasError())
    return false;
```

In this code, note that if an error has occurred, we return from the `process()` function immediately, since there's nothing else to do. The remainder of the code relies on a file being successfully uploaded.

Next, we must ensure that the uploaded file is in fact an image. Since we cannot rely on the mime type specified by the user's web browser, we must check the data manually. This is fairly straightforward for images, since PHP has the `getImageSize()` function, which returns an array of information about image files. This function will return `false` if the file is not an image.

The `getImageSize()` function supports a wide range of image types, but since we only want to allow JPEG, GIF, and PNG files (since these are the three types of files commonly supported in web browsers), we must first check the type of image. The `getImageSize()` function returns an array: the first and second elements are the width and height of the image, and the third element (index of 2) specifies the image type.

Listing 11-9 shows the code we will add to fetch the image information and check its type. We will use built-in constants to check for JPEG, GIF, and PNG images.

Listing 11-9. *Ensuring the Uploaded File Is a JPEG, GIF, or PNG Image (BlogPostImage.php)*

```
$info = getImageSize($file['tmp_name']);
if (!$info) {
    $this->addError('type', 'Uploaded file was not an image');
    return false;
}

switch ($info[2]) {
    case IMAGETYPE_PNG:
    case IMAGETYPE_GIF:
    case IMAGETYPE_JPEG:
        break;

    default:
        $this->addError('type', 'Invalid image type uploaded');
        return false;
}
```

At this point in the code, we can assume a valid file was uploaded and that it is a JPEG, GIF, or PNG image (it doesn't matter to us which one). Now we must write the file to the filesystem (it is currently stored in a temporary area) and save the database record.

To move the file from the temporary area, we will call the `uploadFile()` method, which we will implement shortly. Additionally, we will set the filename of the uploaded file and save the database record, as shown in Listing 11-10.

Listing 11-10. *Saving the Image File and the Database Record (BlogPostImage.php)*

```
// if no errors have occurred, save the image
if (!$this->hasError()) {
    $this->image->uploadFile($file['tmp_name']);
    $this->image->filename = basename($file['name']);
    $this->image->save();
```

```
            }

            return !$this->hasError();
        }
    }
?>
```

Note Be sure to use `basename()` on the value in `$file['name']`, since this value is supplied by the browser. The `basename()` method is used to strip out the path from a full filesystem path (so `/path/to/foo.jpg` becomes `foo.jpg`). As mentioned earlier, most browsers will not include the full path, but you should still call `basename()` just in case.

Writing Files to the Filesystem

Now that we have completed the action handler and the form processor, we must make the necessary changes to the `DatabaseObject_BlogPostImage` class to save the uploaded image. There are a number of functions we must write, including the `uploadFile()` function we briefly looked at in Listing 11-10.

The first function we will write is one that returns the path on the filesystem where we will be storing the uploaded images. In Chapter 1 we created a directory called `uploaded-files` in the `./data` directory—this is where the uploaded images will be stored. Listing 11-11 shows `GetUploadPath()`, a static function we will call to determine where files will be stored.

Listing 11-11. *Determining the Base Location for Uploaded Files (BlogPostImage.php)*

```php
<?php
    class DatabaseObject_BlogPostImage extends DatabaseObject
    {
        // ... other code

        public static function GetUploadPath()
        {
            $config = Zend_Registry::get('config');

            return sprintf('%s/uploaded-files', $config->paths->data);
        }
    }
?>
```

Next, we will write a function to determine the full path where an uploaded file is stored for a particular database record. To simplify this process, rather than storing files with the names they used on the client's computer, we will store them in the uploaded file directory using their database ID. If we need to refer back to their original filenames, we can get this information from the database record.

Listing 11-12 shows the getFullpath() function, which returns the full path to the uploaded file. This basically just combines the GetUploadPath() function with the record ID.

Listing 11-12. *Retrieving the Full Filesystem Path of an Uploaded File (BlogPostImage.php)*

```php
<?php
    class DatabaseObject_BlogPostImage extends DatabaseObject
    {
        // ... other code

        public function getFullPath()
        {
            return sprintf('%s/%d', self::GetUploadPath(), $this->getId());
        }

        // ... other code
    }
?>
```

Next, we will implement the uploadFile() function. All this function does is store the temporary path of the uploaded file in anticipation of the save() method being called. When save() is called on a new record of DatabaseObject_BlogPostImage, the preInsert() and postInsert() callbacks will be executed. The copying of the file from its temporary location to its new location will occur on postInsert().

Listing 11-13 shows the code for uploadFile(), which writes the temporary path to an object property for later use. Note that it also does some basic error checking to ensure the temporary file exists and is readable.

Listing 11-13. *Setting the Location of the Uploaded File so It Can Be Copied Across (BlogPostImage.php)*

```php
<?php
    class DatabaseObject_BlogPostImage extends DatabaseObject
    {
        protected $_uploadedFile;

        // ... other code

        public function uploadFile($path)
        {
            if (!file_exists($path) || !is_file($path))
                throw new Exception('Unable to find uploaded file');

            if (!is_readable($path))
                throw new Exception('Unable to read uploaded file');

            $this->_uploadedFile = $path;
        }
```

```
        // ... other code
    }
?>
```

Next, we will implement the preInsert() callback, which is called before the database record is inserted into the database. This function first ensures that the upload location exists and is writable, which will help us solve any permissions errors if the upload area hasn't been created properly. Then the ranking value for the image is determined, based on the other images that have been uploaded for the blog post. The ranking system simply uses numbers from 1 to *N*, where *N* is the number of images for a single post.

Since the new image is considered to be the last image for the blog, we can use the SQL max() function to determine its ranking. The only problem with this is that if no images exist for the given blog post, a value of null is returned. To avoid this problem, we will use the coalesce() function, which returns the first non-null value from its arguments.

The code for preInsert() is shown in Listing 11-14.

Listing 11-14. *Ensuring the File Can Be Written, and Determining Its Ranking (BlogPostImage.php)*

```php
<?php
    class DatabaseObject_BlogPostImage extends DatabaseObject
    {
        // ... other code

        public function preInsert()
        {
            // first check that we can write the upload directory
            $path = self::GetUploadPath();
            if (!file_exists($path) || !is_dir($path))
                throw new Exception('Upload path ' . $path . ' not found');

            if (!is_writable($path))
                throw new Exception('Unable to write to upload path ' . $path);

            // now determine the ranking of the new image
            $query = sprintf(
                'select coalesce(max(ranking), 0) + 1 from %s where post_id = %d',
                $this->_table,
                $this->post_id
            );

            $this->ranking = $this->_db->fetchOne($query);
            return true;
        }

        // ... other code
?>
```

Finally, we will implement the `postInsert()` callback. This is the function responsible for copying the image file from its temporary upload location to the uploaded files area of our web application. We will do this in `postInsert()` because if any SQL errors occurred before this point, the whole transaction could be easily rolled back, preventing the file from being incorrectly moved into the web application.

To move the file, we will use the PHP `move_uploaded_file()` function. This function is used for security reasons, as it will automatically ensure that the file being moved was in fact uploaded via PHP. This function will return `true` if the file was successfully moved and `false` if not. Thus we can use the return value as the `postInsert()` return value. Remember that returning `false` from this callback will roll back the database transaction. In other words, if the file could not be copied for some reason, the database record would not be saved.

Listing 11-15 shows the `postInsert()` method, which completes the image-upload functionality for the web application.

Listing 11-15. *Moving the Uploaded File to the Application File Storage Area (BlogPostImage.php)*

```php
<?php
    class DatabaseObject_BlogPostImage extends DatabaseObject
    {
        // ... other code

        public function postInsert()
        {
            if (strlen($this->_uploadedFile) > 0)
                return move_uploaded_file($this->_uploadedFile,
                                          $this->getFullPath());

            return false;
        }

        // ... other code
    }
?>
```

Once you have added this code, you will be able to upload images to blog posts via the form we added to the post preview page. Currently, though, we haven't implemented code to display these uploaded images, so to verify that your code is working, you should check that there are records present in the database table by using the following query:

```
mysql> select * from blog_posts_images;
```

You should also check that the file you uploaded is in /var/www/phpweb20/data/uploaded-files.

Sending Images

Now that users can upload photos to their blog posts, we must display their images both on the blog post preview page and on the actual blog page. Before we do this, however, we must write the code to send the images. We could use the built-in file serving from the web server, but since the original images as well as generated thumbnails will be stored in the application data directory, we will serve these files using PHP code.

To begin, we will simply output uploaded images in full, just as they were uploaded. We will build on this functionality later by adding the ability to resize images.

■Note The image resizing we will implement will generate thumbnails on demand. In other words, the first time a thumbnail of a particular size is requested, it will be generated and saved for later reuse. The advantage of doing this over creating thumbnails when the image is uploaded is that we can easily choose what size thumbnails we want in the template rather than deciding in the PHP code at upload time.

To send blog post images, we will create a new action handler in the `UtilityController` class we created earlier in this book. Currently this controller is used only for outputting CAPTCHA images, but we will now make it also send blog post images.

Listing 11-16 shows the start of the `imageAction()` method we will add to `UtilityController.php`. This file can be found in `./include/Controllers`.

Listing 11-16. *Initial Setup of the Image-Output Function (UtilityController.php)*

```php
<?php
    class UtilityController extends CustomControllerAction
    {
        // ... other code

        public function imageAction()
        {
            $request  = $this->getRequest();
            $response = $this->getResponse();

            $id = (int) $request->getQuery('id');

            // disable autorendering since we're outputting an image
            $this->_helper->viewRenderer->setNoRender();
```

As in many other action handlers in this book, we begin by retrieving the request object. In this function, we also retrieve the response object because we are going to send some additional HTTP headers. Namely, we are going to send the `content-type` header (to specify the type of data) and `content-length` header (to specify the amount of data in bytes).

Next, we retrieve the requested image ID from the URL. This means that to request the image with an ID of 123, the URL `http://phpweb20/utility/image?id=123` would be used.

The next step is to disable the automatic view renderer, since we are outputting an image and not an HTML template.

At this point, we will try to load the `DatabaseObject_BlogPostImage` record specified by the `$id` variable, as shown in Listing 11-17. If the image cannot be found, we use the `$response` object to send a 404 header and return. If the image does load, we simply proceed in the function.

Listing 11-17. *Loading the DatabaseObject_BlogPostImage Record (UtilityController.php)*

```
$image = new DatabaseObject_BlogPostImage($this->db);
if (!$image->load($id)) {
    // image not found
    $response->setHttpResponseCode(404);
    return;
}
```

At this point in the function, we can assume that a blog post image has been successfully loaded. As such, we must now determine what type of image it is and send the appropriate content-type header. The getImageSize() function we looked at earlier in this chapter also includes an appropriate header in the mime index of the returned array.

In addition to sending this header, we will also send the content-length header. This tells the browser how much data to expect. We can use the PHP filesize() function to determine the value for this (specified in bytes).

■**Note** Why is the content-length header important? Perhaps you have downloaded a large file in your browser, and the browser was unable to give you an estimate of remaining time. This is because the content-length header was not sent. The browser simply receives data until no more is available—without the header, it is not able to determine how much data is still to come. This is usually more of an issue for larger files.

Listing 11-18 shows the remainder of the imageAction() function. This code begins by retrieving the full filesystem path using getFullPath(). It then determines which type of image the file is and sends headers for the type and the size of the image using the setHeader() function. Finally, the actual image data is sent.

Listing 11-18. *Sending the Image Headers and Then the Image Itself (UtilityController.php)*

```
            $fullpath = $image->getFullPath();
            $info = getImageSize($fullpath);

            $response->setHeader('content-type', $info['mime']);
            $response->setHeader('content-length', filesize($fullpath));
            echo file_get_contents($fullpath);
        }
    }
?>
```

This completes the minimum code required to output uploaded blog post images. In order to test it, you can upload an image using the form we created earlier in this chapter, and then manually enter the image ID into the following URL: http://phpweb20/utility/image?id=*ImageID*.

Resizing Images

Depending on the context, you will often want to display uploaded images at different resolutions in different areas of your site. For example, on the blog post index page in our application, you might want small thumbnails (perhaps around about 100 pixels by 75 pixels) while on the blog post detail page you might want to show somewhat larger images (such as about 200 pixels by 150 pixels). In addition, you may want to allow the user to click on an image to show the image at full size.

In this section, we will build a simple mechanism to generate resized versions (that is, thumbnails) of uploaded images. We will build this system such that the desired dimensions can be specified in the URL and an image the appropriate size will be returned.

In order to do this, we will use the GD functions that are included with PHP. A popular alternative to GD is ImageMagick, but it requires that ImageMagick also be installed on the server, while GD is typically included in most PHP installations.

■**Note** The techniques we use here can be achieved using ImageMagick's convert tool. You can use this tool either by calling convert directly within your script, or by using the imagick PECL package. After lying dormant for several years, this package has recently gained new life and provides a simple interface to ImageMagick. The biggest drawback to using this package is that it needs to be built into the PHP server in addition to ImageMagick being installed on the server. More information about convert can be found at http://www.imagemagick.org/script/convert.php.

Creating Thumbnails

The image thumbnailer we will now create is fairly straightforward when you look at the individual pieces. We will create a new method in the DatabaseObject_BlogPostImage class called createThumbnail(), which generates a thumbnail for the loaded record based on the width and height arguments specified. This method will return the full filesystem path to the created thumbnail, which allows us to easily link the thumbnailer into the existing code to load and display images. Additionally, it allows us to simply return the path of the original file if the requested thumbnail is bigger than the original image. This saves unnecessary duplication of the image on the filesystem.

The other thing createThumbnail() will do is cache the thumbnails. Since creating thumbnails can be processor-intensive (depending on the size of the input and output images), we want to make this process as efficient as possible. Fortunately, it is very straightforward to cache the created thumbnails, as we will soon see.

Before we write createThumbnail(), we will add in another method, which we will call GetThumbnailPath(). This method will return the filesystem path to where created thumbnails should be stored. We will use the ./data/tmp directory as the base directory for this, and use a subdirectory within it called thumbnails, as shown in Listing 11-19.

Listing 11-19. *Retrieving the Thumbnail Storage Path (BlogPostImage.php)*

```php
<?php
    class DatabaseObject_BlogPostImage extends DatabaseObject
    {
        // ... other code

        public static function GetThumbnailPath()
        {
            $config = Zend_Registry::get('config');

            return sprintf('%s/tmp/thumbnails', $config->paths->data);
        }
    }
?>
```

Next, we can look at createThumbnail(), in which we begin by retrieving the path of the original file and some basic information about this file, which we will use later in the function. Listing 11-20 shows beginning of createThumbnail().

Listing 11-20. *Determining the Image Attributes for Later Use (BlogPostImage.php)*

```php
<?php
    class DatabaseObject_BlogPostImage extends DatabaseObject
    {
        // ... other code

        public function createThumbnail($maxW, $maxH)
        {
            $fullpath = $this->getFullpath();

            $ts = (int) filemtime($fullpath);
            $info = getImageSize($fullpath);
```

Determining the Width and Height of the Thumbnail

The first (and probably the most complicated) step of creating a thumbnail image is to determine the dimensions of the thumbnail. The createThumbnail() function accepts the maximum width of a thumbnail as its first argument, and the maximum height as the second argument. Note that the proportions remain the same as the original regardless of the specified width and height; we simply use these values to determine the maximum size.

We will allow for either of these arguments (but not both) to be set to 0. This means the image will be constrained only by the specified value (so if a maximum width of 100 is specified with a maximum height of 0, the image can be any height as long as it is no wider than 100 pixels).

We use the width and height values returned from getImageSize() in combination with the specified maximum width and height ($maxW and $maxH) to determine the width and height of the thumbnail ($newW and $newH). This code is shown in Listing 11-21, and is explained in the comments.

Listing 11-21. *Calculating the Width and Height of the Thumbnail (BlogPostImage.php)*

```
$w = $info[0];          // original width
$h = $info[1];          // original height

$ratio = $w / $h;       // width:height ratio

$maxW = min($w, $maxW); // new width can't be more than $maxW
if ($maxW == 0)         // check if only max height has been specified
    $maxW = $w;

$maxH = min($h, $maxH); // new height can't be more than $maxH
if ($maxH == 0)         // check if only max width has been specified
    $maxH = $h;

$newW = $maxW;          // first use the max width to determine new
$newH = $newW / $ratio; // height by using original image w:h ratio

if ($newH > $maxH) {        // check if new height is too big, and if
    $newH = $maxH;          // so determine the new width based on the
    $newW = $newH * $ratio; // max height
}

if ($w == $newW && $h == $newH) {
    // no thumbnail required, just return the original path
    return $fullpath;
}
```

Determining the Input and Output Functions

In order to create thumbnails with GD, we must turn the original image into a GD image resource (a special type of PHP variable). There is a different function to do this for each of the image types we support (JPEG, GIF, and PNG).

Once the thumbnail has been created, we need to output the new GD image resource to the filesystem. We must determine which function to use for this, also based on the type of image. While we could simply use the same image type for all thumbnails, we will use the input image type as the output image type.

Just as we did when writing the image uploader (Listing 11-9), we can check the third index of the getImageSize() result to determine which functions to use. This is shown in Listing 11-22.

Listing 11-22. *Determining the GD Input and Output Image Functions (BlogPostImage.php)*

```
switch ($info[2]) {
    case IMAGETYPE_GIF:
        $infunc = 'ImageCreateFromGif';
        $outfunc = 'ImageGif';
        break;
```

```
        case IMAGETYPE_JPEG:
            $infunc = 'ImageCreateFromJpeg';
            $outfunc = 'ImageJpeg';
            break;

        case IMAGETYPE_PNG:
            $infunc = 'ImageCreateFromPng';
            $outfunc = 'ImagePng';
            break;

        default;
            throw new Exception('Invalid image type');
    }
```

Generating the Thumbnail Filename

Next, we will generate a filename for the newly created thumbnail. We generate this based on the height and width of the thumbnail, as well as on the image ID and the date the original file was created. By using the creation date, the thumbnail will be regenerated if the file is ever modified.

■**Note** We haven't actually implemented functionality to allow the user to edit an uploaded image, but if you did, this timestamp would ensure new thumbnails would be generated automatically for the new image.

In addition to creating the filename, we must also determine the full path of the thumbnail and ensure that we can write to that directory, as shown in Listing 11-23. If the destination directory doesn't exist, we will create it. Note that this will typically only occur the first time this function is called.

Listing 11-23. *Generating the Thumbnail Filename, and Creating the Target Directory (BlogPostImage.php)*

```
        // create a unique filename based on the specified options
        $filename = sprintf('%d.%dx%d.%d',
                            $this->getId(),
                            $newW,
                            $newH,
                            $ts);

        // autocreate the directory for storing thumbnails
        $path = self::GetThumbnailPath();
        if (!file_exists($path))
            mkdir($path, 0777);

        if (!is_writable($path))
            throw new Exception('Unable to write to thumbnail dir');
```

Creating the Thumbnail

Now that we know the dimensions of the thumbnail, the input and output functions, and the thumbnail destination path, we can create the actual thumbnail. The very first thing we will do, however, is check whether the thumbnail already exists. This simple check (in combination with the previous filename generation) is the caching functionality. If the thumbnail exists, we simply skip the generation part of this code.

If the thumbnail doesn't exist, we read in the image to GD using the input determined in Listing 11-22. So if the original image is a PNG file, ImageCreateFromPng() is used. If an error occurs reading the image, we throw an exception and return from the function. The first portion of the thumbnail-creation code is shown in Listing 11-24.

Listing 11-24. *Reading the Image into GD (BlogPostImage.php)*

```
// determine the full path for the new thumbnail
$thumbPath = sprintf('%s/%s', $path, $filename);

if (!file_exists($thumbPath)) {

    // read the image in to GD
    $im = @$infunc($fullpath);
    if (!$im)
        throw new Exception('Unable to read image file');
```

When resizing an image with GD, the original image resource remains unchanged while the resized version is written to a secondary GD image resource (which in this case we will call $thumb). We must first create this secondary GD image using ImageCreateTrueColor(), with the $newW and $newH variables specifying the size.

We then use GD's ImageCopyResampled() function to copy a portion of the source image ($im) to the $thumb. The target image resource is the first argument, and the source image resource is the second argument.

The remainder of the arguments indicate the X and Y coordinates of the target and source images respectively, followed by the width and height of both images. This function is fairly powerful, and it also allows you to easily crop or stretch images.

The code to create the target image and resample the original image onto the new image is shown in Listing 11-25.

Listing 11-25. *Resampling the Original Image onto the New Image Resource (BlogPostImage.php)*

```
// create the output image
$thumb = ImageCreateTrueColor($newW, $newH);

// now resample the original image to the new image
ImageCopyResampled($thumb, $im, 0, 0, 0, 0, $newW, $newH, $w, $h);
```

Finally, we write this new image to the filesystem using the output function we selected in Listing 11-22 (stored in $outfunc). So if the original image was a PNG image, we would use ImagePng() to write the image to disk.

■Note The second argument to the output functions (ImagePng(), ImageJpeg(), and ImageGif()) specifies where on the filesystem the image file should be written. If this isn't specified, the image data is output directly to the browser. You could choose to take advantage of this if you didn't want to write the generated images to the filesystem.

Finally, we ensure that the image was written to the system, and if so we return the path to the newly created thumbnail. Listing 11-26 shows the code that writes the image to the filesystem and returns from createThumbnail().

Listing 11-26. *Writing the Thumbnail and Returning from createThumbnail() (BlogPostImage.php)*

```
            $outfunc($thumb, $thumbPath);
        }

        if (!file_exists($thumbPath))
            throw new Exception('Unknown error occurred creating thumbnail');
        if (!is_readable($thumbPath))
            throw new Exception('Unable to read thumbnail');

        return $thumbPath;
    }

    // ... other code
}
?>
```

Linking the Thumbnailer to the Image Action Handler

Now that we have the capability to easily create image thumbnails, we must hook this into our web application. We will do this by making some simple modifications to the imageAction() function we created in Listing 11-16.

We are going to provide the ability to specify the desired width and height in the URL, so it will be extremely simple to generate thumbnails as required. This means you can decide on the dimensions of the thumbnail in the templates that output the image, rather than having to hard-code these dimensions in your PHP code.

Because users could potentially abuse a system that allows them to generate thumbnails of any size, we will add a mechanism to make it more difficult for this to occur. This mechanism works as follows:

1. When an image is requested, the URL must include a parameter called a hash in addition to the image ID, width, and height. This parameter will be generated based on the ID, width, and height.

2. The imageAction() method will check the supplied hash against what the hash should be for the combination of ID, width, and height.

3. If the two hash values are different, we will assume the image was requested incorrectly, and a 404 error is sent back.

4. If the hash value is correct, we generate the thumbnail and send it back.

If the user manually changes the width or height in the URL, the hash will not match the request, so the thumbnail won't be generated.

Generating an Image Hash

To implement this system, we first need the ability to generate an image hash based on the given parameters. We will use this method both in the generation of URLs in the template, as well as to generate a hash based on the ID, width, and height supplied in the request URL.

Listing 11-27 shows the GetImageHash() method, which generates a string based on the supplied arguments using md5(). This code should be added to the BlogPostImage.php file in ./include/DatabaseObject.

Listing 11-27. *Generating a Hash for the Given Image ID, Width, and Height (BlogPostImage.php)*

```php
<?php
    class DatabaseObject_BlogPostImage extends DatabaseObject
    {
        // ... other code

        public static function GetImageHash($id, $w, $h)
        {
            $id = (int) $id;
            $w  = (int) $w;
            $h  = (int) $h;

            return md5(sprintf('%s,%s,%s', $id, $w, $h));
        }

        // ... other code
    }
?>
```

Generating Image Filenames

Next, we will implement a new Smarty plug-in called imagefilename, which is used to generate image filenames using the desired image ID, width, and height. This plug-in will allow us to include image thumbnails in our templates very easily.

For example, to include a thumbnail that is 100 pixels by 75 pixels of an image with an ID of 12, the following code would be used in the template:

```
<img src="{imagefilename id=12 w=100 h=75}" alt="" />
```

Based on the arguments in this example, we would want to generate a URL as follows:

```
/utility/image?id=12&w=100&h=75&hash=[hash]
```

Similarly, if you wanted to generate the image path for the full-sized image, you would use the following:

```
<img src="{imagefilename id=12}" alt="" />
```

In order to generate this URL, we would use the {geturl} plug-in created earlier, in conjunction with the arguments and the GetImageHash() method.

Listing 11-28 shows the code for the function.imagefilename.php file, which we will store in ./include/Templater/plugins.

Listing 11-28. *The imagefilename Plug-In, Used to Generate a Thumbnail Image Path (function.imagefilename.php)*

```php
<?php
    function smarty_function_imagefilename($params, $smarty)
    {
        if (!isset($params['id']))
            $params['id'] = 0;

        if (!isset($params['w']))
            $params['w'] = 0;

        if (!isset($params['w']))
            $params['h'] = 0;

        require_once $smarty->_get_plugin_filepath('function', 'geturl');

        $hash = DatabaseObject_BlogPostImage::GetImageHash(
            $params['id'],
            $params['w'],
            $params['h']
        );

        $options = array(
            'controller' => 'utility',
            'action'     => 'image'
        );

        return sprintf(
            '%s?id=%d&w=%d&h=%d&hash=%s',
            smarty_function_geturl($options, $smarty),
            $params['id'],
            $params['w'],
            $params['h'],
            $hash
        );
    }
?>
```

This function begins by initializing the parameters (the image ID, as well as the desired width and height). Next, it loads the `geturl` plug-in so we can generate the `/utility/image` part of the URL (the controller and action values are specified in the `$options` array that we create in this function). Next, we generate the hash for the given ID, width, and height, and then finally combine all of the parameters together into a single string and return this value from the plug-in.

Updating imageAction() to Serve the Thumbnail

We can now update the `imageAction()` method to look for the `w`, `h`, and `hash` parameters so a thumbnail can be served if required. We simply need to generate a new hash based on the `id`, `w`, and `h` parameters, and then compare it to the `hash` value in the URL. Once we have determined that the supplied hash is valid and that the image could be loaded, we continue on by generating the thumbnail and sending it.

Instead of calling `getFullPath()`, we will call `createThumbnail()`, which returns the full path to the generated thumbnail. Since `createThumbnail()` throws various exceptions, we will call `getFullPath()` as a fallback. In other words, if the thumbnail creation fails for some reason, the original image is displayed instead. You may prefer instead to output an error.

The other code in `imageAction()` operated on the returned path from `getFullPath()`, so we don't need to change any of it—`createThumbnail()` also returns a full filesystem path.

Listing 11-29 shows the new version of `imageAction()`, which belongs in the `UtilityController.php` file in `./include/Controllers`.

Listing 11-29. *Modifying imageAction() to Output Thumbnails on Demand (UtilityController.php)*

```php
<?php
    class UtilityController extends CustomControllerAction
    {
        // ... other code

        public function imageAction()
        {
            $request  = $this->getRequest();
            $response = $this->getResponse();

            $id = (int) $request->getQuery('id');
            $w  = (int) $request->getQuery('w');
            $h  = (int) $request->getQuery('h');
            $hash = $request->getQuery('hash');

            $realHash = DatabaseObject_BlogPostImage::GetImageHash($id, $w, $h);

            // disable autorendering since we're outputting an image
            $this->_helper->viewRenderer->setNoRender();

            $image = new DatabaseObject_BlogPostImage($this->db);
            if ($hash != $realHash || !$image->load($id)) {
```

```php
            // image not found
            $response->setHttpResponseCode(404);
            return;
        }

        try {
            $fullpath = $image->createThumbnail($w, $h);
        }
        catch (Exception $ex) {
            $fullpath = $image->getFullPath();
        }

        $info = getImageSize($fullpath);

        $response->setHeader('content-type', $info['mime']);
        $response->setHeader('content-length', filesize($fullpath));
        echo file_get_contents($fullpath);
    }
  }
?>
```

Managing Blog Post Images

Now that we have the ability to view uploaded images (both at their original size and as thumbnails) we can display the images on the blog post preview page.

In this section, we will modify the blog manager to display uploaded images, thereby allowing the user to easily delete images from their blog posts. Additionally, we will implement Ajax code using Prototype and Scriptaculous that will allow the user to change the order in which the images in a single post are displayed.

Automatically Loading Blog Post Images

Before we can display the images on the blog post preview page, we must modify DatabaseObject_BlogPost to automatically load all associated images when the blog post record is loaded. To do this, we will change the postLoad() function to automatically load the images.

Currently this function only loads the profile data for the blog post, but we will add a call to load the images, as shown in Listing 11-30. Additionally, we must initialize the $images array.

Listing 11-30. *Automatically Loading a Blog Post's Images When the Post Is Loaded (BlogPost.php)*

```php
<?php
    class DatabaseObject_BlogPost extends DatabaseObject
    {
        public $images = array();

        // ... other code
```

```php
    protected function postLoad()
    {
        $this->profile->setPostId($this->getId());
        $this->profile->load();

        $options = array(
            'post_id' => $this->getId()
        );
        $this->images = DatabaseObject_BlogPostImage::GetImages($this->getDb(),
                                                                $options);


    }

    // ... other code
}
?>
```

The code in Listing 11-30 calls a method called GetImages() in DatabaseObject_ BlogPostImage, which we must now implement. This function, which we will add to BlogPostImage.php in ./include/DatabaseObject, is shown in Listing 11-31. Note that we use the ranking field as the sort field. This ensures the images are returned in the order specified by the user (we will implement the functionality to change this order shortly).

Listing 11-31. *Retrieving Multiple Blog Post Images (BlogPostImage.php)*

```php
<?php
    class DatabaseObject_BlogPostImage extends DatabaseObject
    {
        // ... other code

        public static function GetImages($db, $options = array())
        {
            // initialize the options
            $defaults = array('post_id' => array());

            foreach ($defaults as $k => $v) {
                $options[$k] = array_key_exists($k, $options) ? $options[$k] : $v;
            }

            $select = $db->select();
            $select->from(array('i' => 'blog_posts_images'), array('i.*'));

            // filter results on specified post ids (if any)
            if (count($options['post_id']) > 0)
                $select->where('i.post_id in (?)', $options['post_id']);

            $select->order('i.ranking');
```

```
        // fetch post data from database
        $data = $db->fetchAll($select);

        // turn data into array of DatabaseObject_BlogPostImage objects
        $images = parent::BuildMultiple($db, __CLASS__, $data);

        return $images;
    }
  }
?>
```

Displaying Images on the Post Preview

The next step in managing images for a blog post is to display them on the preview page. To do this, we must make some changes to the preview.tpl template in the ./templates/ blogmanager directory, as well as adding some new styles to ./htdocs/css/styles.css.

Earlier in this chapter we created a new element in this template called #preview-images. The code in Listing 11-32 shows the additions we must make to preview.tpl to display each of the images. We will output the images in an unordered list, which will help us later when we add the ability to reorder the images using Scriptaculous.

Listing 11-32. *Outputting Images on the Blog Post Preview Page (preview.tpl)*

```
<!-- // ... other code -->

<fieldset id="preview-images">
    <legend>Images</legend>

    {if $post->images|@count > 0}
        <ul id="post_images">
            {foreach from=$post->images item=image}
                <li id="image_{$image->getId()}">
                    <img src="{imagefilename id=$image->getId() w=200 h=65}"
                        alt="{$image->filename|escape}" />

                    <form method="post" action="{geturl action='images'}">
                        <div>
                            <input type="hidden"
                                    name="id" value="{$post->getId()}" />
                            <input type="hidden"
                                    name="image" value="{$image->getId()}" />
                            <input type="submit" value="Delete" name="delete" />
                        </div>
                    </form>
                </li>
            {/foreach}
        </ul>
    {/if}
```

```
<form method="post"
      action="{geturl action='images'}"
      enctype="multipart/form-data">

    <div>
        <input type="hidden" name="id" value="{$post->getId()}" />
        <input type="file" name="image" />
        <input type="submit" value="Upload Image" name="upload" />
    </div>
</form>
</fieldset>

<!-- // ... other code -->
```

As you can see in the code, we use the new `imagefilename` plug-in to generate the URL for an image thumbnail 200 pixels wide and 65 pixels high. We also include a form to delete each image in this template. We haven't yet implemented this functionality (you may recall that we left a placeholder for the delete command in the blog manager's `imagesAction()` method), but this will be added shortly.

Listing 11-33 shows the new styles we will add to `styles.css` in `./htdocs/css`. These styles format the unordered list so list items are shown horizontally. We use floats to position list items next to each other (rather than using `inline` display), since this gives greater control over the style within each item. Note that we must add `clear : both` to the div holding the upload form in order to keep the display of the page intact.

Listing 11-33. *Styling the Image-Management Area (styles.css)*

```css
#preview-images ul {
    list-style-type : none;
    margin          : 0;
    padding         : 0;
}

#preview-images li {
    float           : left;
    font-size       : 0.85em;
    text-align      : center;
    margin          : 3px;
    padding         : 2px;
    border          : 1px solid #ddd;
    background      : #fff;
}

#preview-images img {
    display : block;
}
```

```
#preview-images div {
    clear : both;
}
```

Once this code has been added, the image display area should look like the page in Figure 11-2.

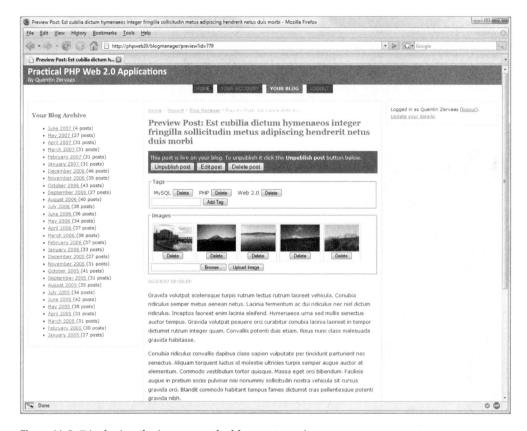

Figure 11-2. *Displaying the images on the blog post preview page*

Deleting Blog Post Images

The next step in the management of blog post images is to implement the delete functionality. We will first implement a non-Ajax version to delete images, and then modify it slightly to use Scriptaculous for a fancier solution.

Before we complete the delete section of the images action in the blog manager controller, we must make some small changes to the DatabaseObject_BlogPostImage class. Using DatabaseObject means we can simply call the delete() method on the image record to remove it from the database, but this will not delete the uploaded image from the filesystem. As we saw in Chapter 3, if we define the postDelete() method in a DatabaseObject subclass, it is automatically called after a record has been deleted. We will implement this method for DatabaseObject_BlogPostImage so the uploaded file is removed from the filesystem.

Additionally, since thumbnails are automatically created for each image, we will clean up the thumbnail storage area for the image being deleted. Note that this is quite easy, since we prefixed all generated thumbnails with their database ID.

Listing 11-34 shows the postDelete() function as it should be added to DatabaseObject_ BlogPostImage in ./include/DatabaseObject. First, we use unlink() to delete the main image from the filesystem. Next, we use the glob() function, which is a useful PHP function for retrieving an array of files based on the specified pattern. We loop over each of the files in the array and unlink() them.

Listing 11-34. *Deleting the Uploaded File and All Generated Thumbnails (BlogPostImage.php)*

```php
<?php
    class DatabaseObject_BlogPostImage extends DatabaseObject
    {
        // ... other code

        public function preDelete()
        {
            unlink($this->getFullPath());

            $pattern = sprintf('%s/%d.*',
                                self::GetThumbnailPath(),
                                $this->getId());

            foreach (glob($pattern) as $thumbnail) {
                unlink($thumbnail);
            }

            return true;
        }

        // ... other code
    }
?>
```

Now when you call the delete() method on a loaded blog post image, the filesystem files will also be deleted. Remember to return true from postDelete()—otherwise the SQL transaction will be rolled back.

The other method we must add to this class is one that gives us the ability to load an image for a specified blog post. This is similar to the loadForUser() function we implemented for blog posts. We do this so that only the logged-in user will be able to delete an image on their blog posts. Listing 11-35 shows the code for the loadForPost() function, which is also added to BlogPostImage.php.

Listing 11-35. *Restricting the Load of Images to a Particular Blog Post (BlogPostImage.php)*

```php
<?php
    class DatabaseObject_BlogPostImage extends DatabaseObject
```

```
    {
        // ... other code

        public function loadForPost($post_id, $image_id)
        {
            $post_id = (int) $post_id;
            $image_id = (int) $image_id;

            if ($post_id <= 0 || $image_id <= 0)
                return false;

            $query = sprintf(
                'select %s from %s where post_id = %d and image_id = %d',
                join(', ', $this->getSelectFields()),
                $this->_table,
                $post_id,
                $image_id
            );

            return $this->_load($query);
        }

        // ... other code
    }
?>
```

Now that these changes have been made to DatabaseObject_BlogPostImage, we can implement the non-Ajax version of deleting an image. To do this, we simply need to implement the delete part of imagesAction() in BlogmanagerController.php. Remember that we left a placeholder for this when we originally created this method in Listing 11-5. The code used to delete an image is shown in Listing 11-36.

Listing 11-36. *Deleting an Image from a Blog Post (BlogmanagerController.php)*

```php
<?php
    class BlogmanagerController extends CustomControllerAction
    {
        // ... other code

        public function imagesAction()
        {
            // ... other code

            else if ($request->getPost('delete')) {
                $image_id = (int) $request->getPost('image');
                $image = new DatabaseObject_BlogPostImage($this->db);
                if ($image->loadForPost($post->getId(), $image_id)) {
                    $image->delete();
```

```
                    $this->messenger->addMessage('Image deleted');
                }
            }

            // ... other code
        }
    }
?>
```

If you now click on the "Delete" button below an image, the image will be deleted from the database and filesystem, and a message will appear in the top-right flash messenger when the page reloads.

Using Scriptaculous and Ajax to Delete Images

Now that we have a non-Ajax solution for deleting images, we can enhance this system slightly to use Ajax. Essentially what we will do is send an Ajax request to delete the image when the "Delete" button is clicked, and use Scriptaculous to make the image disappear from the screen.

There are a number of different Scriptaculous effects that can be used to hide elements, such as Puff, SwitchOff, DropOut, Squish, Fold, and Shrink, but we are going to use the Fade effect. Note, however, that we are not applying this effect to the image being deleted; we will apply it to the list item (`<li>`) surrounding the image.

Modifying the PHP Deletion Code

In the imagesAction() function of BlogmanagerController.php, the code redirects the browser back to the blog post preview page after completing the action (uploading, reordering, or deleting). This is fine for non-Ajax solutions, but if this occurs when using XMLHttpRequest, the contents of the preview page will unnecessarily be returned in the background.

To prevent this, we will make a simple change to the redirection code at the end of this function. As we have done previously, we will use the isXmlHttpRequest() function provided by Zend_Controller_Front to determine how to proceed.

Because we want to check whether or not the image deletion was successful in the JavaScript code, we will also modify the code so it sends back JSON data about the deleted image. We will send this back using the sendJson() method we added in Chapter 6.

Listing 11-37 shows the changes to this method in BlogmanagerController.php. This code now only writes the deletion message to the messenger if the delete request did not use Ajax. If this distinction about writing the message isn't made, you could delete an image via Ajax and then refresh the page, causing the "image deleted" message to show again.

Listing 11-37. *Handling Ajax Requests in imageAction() (BlogmanagerController.php)*

```php
<?php
    class BlogmanagerController extends CustomControllerAction
    {
        // ... other code
```

```php
    public function imagesAction()
    {
        // ... other code

        $json = array();

        // ... other code
        if ($request->getPost('upload')) {
            // ... other code
        }
        else if ($request->getPost('reorder')) {
            // ... other code
        }
        else if ($request->getPost('delete')) {
            $image_id = (int) $request->getPost('image');
            $image = new DatabaseObject_BlogPostImage($this->db);
            if ($image->loadForPost($post->getId(), $image_id)) {
                $image->delete();
                if ($request->isXmlHttpRequest()) {
                    $json = array(
                        'deleted'  => true,
                        'image_id' => $image_id
                    );
                }
                else
                    $this->messenger->addMessage('Image deleted');
            }
        }

        if ($request->isXmlHttpRequest()) {
            $this->sendJson($json);
        }
        else {
            $url = $this->getUrl('preview') . '?id=' . $post->getid();
            $this->_redirect($url);
        }
    }
}
?>
```

Creating the BlogImageManager JavaScript Class

To create an Ajax solution for deleting blog post images, we will write a new JavaScript class called BlogImageManager. This class will find all of the delete forms in the image-management section of preview.tpl and bind the submit event listener to each of these forms. We will then implement a function to handle this event.

Listing 11-38 shows the constructor for this class, which we will store in a file called BlogImageManager.class.js in the ./htdocs/js directory.

Listing 11-38. *The Constructor for BlogImageManager (BlogImageManager.class.js)*

```
BlogImageManager = Class.create();

BlogImageManager.prototype = {

    initialize : function(container)
    {
        this.container = $(container);

        if (!this.container)
            return;

        this.container.getElementsBySelector('form').each(function(form) {
            form.observe('submit',
                            this.onDeleteClick.bindAsEventListener(this));
        }.bind(this));
    },
```

This class expects the unordered list element that holds the images as the only argument to the constructor. We store it as a property of the object, since we will be using it again later when implementing the reordering functionality.

In this class, we find all the forms within this unordered list by using the getElementsBySelector() function. This function behaves in the same way as the $$() function we looked at in Chapter 5, except that it only searches within the element the function is being called from.

We then loop over each form that is found and observe the submit event on it. We must bind the onDeleteClick() event handler to the BlogImageManager instance so it can be referred to within the correct context when the event is handled.

The next thing we need to do is implement the onDeleteClick() event handler, as shown in Listing 11-39.

Listing 11-39. *The Event Handler Called When a Delete Link Is Clicked (BlogImageManager.class.js)*

```
    onDeleteClick : function(e)
    {
        Event.stop(e);
        var form = Event.element(e);

        var options = {
            method     : form.method,
            parameters : form.serialize(),
            onSuccess  : this.onDeleteSuccess.bind(this),
            onFailure  : this.onDeleteFailure.bind(this)
        }

        message_write('Deleting image...');
        new Ajax.Request(form.action, options);
    },
```

The first thing we do in this method is stop the event so the browser doesn't submit the form normally—a background Ajax request will be submitting the form instead.

Next, we determine which form was submitted by calling `Event.element()`. This allows us to perform an Ajax request on the form action URL, thereby executing the PHP code that is used to delete a blog post image.

We then create a hash of options to pass to `Ajax.Request()`, which includes the form values and the callback handlers for the request. Before instantiating `Ajax.Request()`, we update the page status message to tell the user that an image is being deleted.

The next step is to implement the handlers for a successful and unsuccessful request, as shown in Listing 11-40.

Listing 11-40. *Handling the Response from the Ajax Image Deletion (BlogImageManager.class.js)*

```
onDeleteSuccess : function(transport)
{
    var json = transport.responseText.evalJSON(true);

    if (json.deleted) {
        var image_id = json.image_id;

        var input = this.container.down('input[value=' + image_id + ']');
        if (input) {
            var options = {
                duration   : 0.3,
                afterFinish : function(effect) {
                    message_clear();
                    effect.element.remove();
                }
            }

            new Effect.Fade(input.up('li'), options);
            return;
        }
    }

    this.onDeleteFailure(transport);
},

onDeleteFailure : function(transport)
{
    message_write('Error deleting image');
}
};
```

In Listing 11-37 we made the delete operation in `imagesAction()` return JSON data. To determine whether the image was deleted by the code in Listing 11-40, we check for the `deleted` element in the decoded JSON data.

Based on the image_id element also included in the JSON data, we try to find the corresponding form element on the page for that image. We do this by looking for a form input with the value of the image ID. Once we find this element, we apply the Scriptaculous fade effect to make the image disappear from the page. We don't apply this effect to the actual image that was deleted; rather, we remove the surrounding list item so the image, form, and surrounding code are completely removed from the page.

When the fade effect is called, the element being faded is only *hidden* when the effect is completed; it is not actually removed from the DOM. In order to remove it, we define the afterFinish callback on the effect, and use it to call the remove() method on the element. The callbacks for Scriptaculous effects receive the effect object as the first argument, and the element the effect is applied to can be accessed using the element property of the effect. We also use the afterFinish function to clear the status message.

After we've defined the options, we can create the actual effect. Since we want to remove the list item element corresponding to the image, we can simply call the Prototype up() function to find it.

Loading BlogImageManager in the Post Preview

Next, we will load the BlogImageManager JavaScript class in the preview.tpl template. In order to instantiate this class, we will add code to the blogPreview.js file we created in Chapter 7.

Listing 11-41 shows the changes we will make to preview.tpl in the ./templates/ blogmanager directory to load BlogImageManager.class.js.

Listing 11-41. *Loading the BlogImageManager Class (preview.tpl)*

```
{include file='header.tpl' section='blogmanager'}

<script type="text/javascript" src="/js/blogPreview.js"></script>
<script type="text/javascript" src="/js/BlogImageManager.class.js"></script>

<!-- // ... other code -->
```

Listing 11-42 shows the changes we will make to blogPreview.js in ./htdocs/js to instantiate BlogImageManager automatically.

Listing 11-42. *Instantiating BlogImageManager Automatically (blogPreview.js)*

```
Event.observe(window, 'load', function() {

    // ... other code

    var im = new BlogImageManager('post_images');
});
```

If you now try to delete an image from a blog post, the entire process should be completed in the background. Once the "Delete" button is clicked, the background request to delete the image will be initiated, and the image will disappear from the page upon successful completion.

Deleting Images when Posts Are Deleted

One thing we have not yet dealt with is what happens to images when a blog post is deleted. As the code currently stands, if a blog post is deleted, any associated images will not be deleted. Because of the foreign key constraint on the blog_posts_images table, the SQL to delete a blog post that has one or more images will fail. We must update the DatabaseObject_BlogPost class so images are deleted when a post is deleted.

Doing this is very straightforward, since the instance of DatabaseObject_BlogPost we are trying to delete already has all the images loaded (so we know exactly what needs to be deleted), and it already has a delete callback (we implemented the preDelete() function earlier). This means we can simply loop over each image and call the delete() method.

■**Note** DatabaseObject automatically controls transactions when saving or deleting a record. You can pass false to save() or delete() so transactions are not used. Because a transaction has already been started by the delete() call on the blog post, we must pass false to the delete() call for each image.

Listing 11-43 shows the two new lines we need to add to preDelete() in the BlogPost.php file in the ./include/DatabaseObject directory.

Listing 11-43. *Automatically Deleting Images When a Blog Post Is Deleted (BlogPost.php)*

```php
<?php
    class DatabaseObject_BlogPost extends DatabaseObject
    {
        // ... other code

        protected function preDelete()
        {
            // ... other code

            foreach ($this->images as $image)
                $image->delete(false);

            return true;
        }

        // ... other code
    }
?>
```

Now when you try to delete a blog post, all images associated with the post will also be deleted.

Reordering Blog Post Images

We will now implement a system that will allow users to change the order of the images associated with a blog post. While this may not seem overly important, we do this because we are controlling the layout of images when blog posts are displayed.

Additionally, in the next section we will modify the blog index to display an image beside each blog post that has one. If a blog post has more than one image, we will use the first image for the post.

Drag and Drop

In the past, programmers have used two common techniques to allow users to change the order of list items, both of which are slow and difficult to use.

The first method was to provide "up" and "down" links beside each item in the list, which moved the items up or down when clicked. Some of these implementations might have included a "move to top" and "move to bottom" button, but on the whole they are difficult to use.

The other method was to provide a text input box beside each item. Each box contained a number, which determined the order of the list. To change the order, you would update the numbers inside the boxes.

For our implementation, we will use a drag-and-drop system. Thanks to Scriptaculous's Sortable class, this is not difficult to achieve. We will implement this by extending the BlogImageManager JavaScript class we created earlier this chapter.

▪**Note** As an exercise, try extending this reordering system so it is accessible for non-JavaScript users. You could try implementing this by including a form on the page within <noscript> tags (meaning it won't be shown to users who have JavaScript enabled).

Saving the Order to Database

Before we add the required JavaScript to the blog post management page, we will write the PHP for saving the image order to the database. First, we need to add a new function to the DatabaseObject_BlogPost class. This function accepts an array of image IDs as its only argument. The order in which each image ID appears in the array is the order it will be saved in.

Listing 11-44 shows the setImageOrder() function that we will add to the BlogPost.php file in ./include/DatabaseObject. Before updating the database, it loops over the values passed to it and sanitizes the data by ensuring each of the values belongs to the $images property of the object. After cleaning the data, it checks that the number of image IDs found in the array matches the number of images in the post. Only then does it proceed to update the database.

Listing 11-44. *Saving the Updated Image Order in the Database (BlogPost.php)*

```php
<?php
    class DatabaseObject_BlogPost extends DatabaseObject
    {
        // ... other code

        public function setImageOrder($order)
        {
            // sanitize the image IDs
            if (!is_array($order))
                return;

            $newOrder = array();
            foreach ($order as $image_id) {
                if (array_key_exists($image_id, $this->images))
                    $newOrder[] = $image_id;
            }

            // ensure the correct number of IDs were passed in
            $newOrder = array_unique($newOrder);
            if (count($newOrder) != count($this->images)) {
                return;
            }

            // now update the database
            $rank = 1;
            foreach ($newOrder as $image_id) {
                $this->_db->update('blog_posts_images',
                                   array('ranking' => $rank),
                                   'image_id = ' . $image_id);

                $rank++;
            }
        }

        // ... other code
    }
?>
```

In order to use this function, we must update the imagesAction() function in BlogmanagerController.php (in ./include/Controllers). Listing 11-45 shows the code we will use to call the setImageOrder() method in Listing 11-44. After calling this method, the code will fall through to the isXmlHttpRequest() call, thereby returning the empty JSON data. The submitted variable that holds the image order is called post_images. Scriptaculous uses the ID of the draggable DOM element as the form value, as we will see shortly.

Listing 11-45. *Handling the Reorder Action in the Action Handler (BlogManagerController.php)*

```php
<?php
    class BlogmanagerController extends CustomControllerAction
    {
        // ... other code

        public function imagesAction()
        {
            // ... other code

            else if ($request->getPost('reorder')) {
                $order = $request->getPost('post_images');
                $post->setImageOrder($order);
            }

            // ... other code
        }
    }
?>
```

Adding Sortable to BlogImageManager

It is fairly straightforward to add Sortable to our unordered list; however, we must also add some Ajax functionality to the code. When a user finishes dragging an image, we need to initiate an Ajax request that sends the updated image order to the server so the setImageOrder() function (in Listing 11-44) can be called.

Sortable allows us to define a parameter called onUpdate, which specifies a callback function that is called after the image order has been changed. The callback function we create will initiate the Ajax request. Before we get to that, though, let's look at creating the Sortable list.

By default, Sortable operates an unordered list. It is possible to allow other types of elements to be dragged (although there may be some incompatibility with dragging table cells), but since we are using an unordered list we don't need to specify the type of list.

Another default that Sortable sets is for the list to be vertical. This means the dragging direction for items is up and down. Since our list is horizontal, we need to change this setting by specifying the constraint parameter. We could set this value to horizontal, but since the list of images for a single post may span multiple rows (such as on a low-resolution monitor) it would not be possible to drag images on the second row to the first (and vice versa). To deal with this, we simply set constraint to be false.

Since our list is horizontal, we must change the overlap value to be horizontal instead of its default of vertical. Sortable uses this value to determine how to calculate when an item has been dragged to a new location.

Listing 11-46 shows the code we must add to the constructor of the BlogImageManager JavaScript class in ./htdocs/js/BlogImageManager.class.js. Note that this code uses the onSortUpdate() function, which we have not yet defined.

Listing 11-46. *Creating the Sortable list (BlogImageManager.class.js)*

```
BlogImageManager = Class.create();

BlogImageManager.prototype = {

    initialize : function(container)
    {
        // ... other code

        var options = {
            overlap    : 'horizontal',
            constraint : false,
            onUpdate   : this.onSortUpdate.bind(this)
        };

        Sortable.create(this.container, options);
    },

    // ... other code
};
```

Now we must define the onSortUpdate() callback function. This is called when an item in the sortable list is dropped into a new location. In this function we initiate a new Ajax request that sends the order of the list to the imagesAction() function. Sortable will pass the container element of the sortable list to this callback.

When sending this request, we must send the updated order. We can retrieve this order using the Sortable utility function serialize(), which retrieves all values and builds them into a URL-friendly string that we can post. As mentioned previously, the unordered list we've made sortable has an ID of post_images. This means that if we have three images with IDs of 5, 6, and 7, calling Sortable.serialize() will generate a string such as this:

```
post_images[]=5&post_images[]=6&post_images[]=7
```

PHP will automatically turn this into an array. In other words, the equivalent PHP code to create this structure would be as follows:

```
<?php
    $post_images = array(5, 6, 7);
?>
```

This is exactly what we need in setImageOrder().

Listing 11-47 shows the code for onSortUpdate(), as described above. Another thing we do in this code is to update the status message on the page to notify the user that the order is being saved. In addition, we define the onSuccess() callback, which we will use to clear the status message once the new order has been saved.

Listing 11-47. *The Callback Function That Is Called after the List Order Has Changed (BlogImageManager.class.js)*

```
BlogImageManager = Class.create();

BlogImageManager.prototype = {

    // ... other code

    onSortUpdate : function(draggable)
    {
        var form = this.container.down('form');
        var post_id = $F(form.down('input[name=id]'));

        var options = {
            method      : form.method,
            parameters  : 'reorder=1'
                        + '&id=' + post_id
                        + '&' + Sortable.serialize(draggable),
            onSuccess   : function() { message_clear(); }
        };

        message_write('Updating image order...');
        new Ajax.Request(form.action, options);
    }
};
```

Note When you add this code to your existing class, remember to include a comma at the end of the previous function in the class (onDeleteFailure()). Unfortunately, this is one of the pitfalls of writing classes using Prototype: each method is really an element in its class's prototype hash, and therefore needs to be comma-separated.

Based on how the HTML is structured for the image-management area on the blog preview page, there is no simple way to define the URL for where image-reordering requests should be sent. Since all of our image operations use the same controller action, we will determine the URL by finding the form action of any form in the image-management area. We will also expect the form being used to have an element called post_id that holds the ID of the blog post.

If you now view the blog post preview page (with multiple images assigned to the post you are viewing), you will be able to click on an image and drag it to a new location within the list of images. Figure 11-3 shows how this might look.

Figure 11-3. *Changing the order of blog post images by dragging and dropping*

Displaying Images on User Blogs

The final thing we need to do to create a dynamic image gallery for users is to make use of the images they have uploaded and sorted. To do this, we must display the images both on the blog posts they belong to as well as in the blog index.

When displaying images on a post page, we will show all images (in their specified order) with the ability to view a full-size version of each. On the index page we will only show a small thumbnail of the first image.

Extending the GetPosts() Function

When we added the image-loading functionality to the DatabaseObject_BlogPost class in Listing 11-30, we didn't add the same functionality to the GetPosts() function within this class. If you recall, GetPosts() is used to retrieve multiple blog posts from the database at one time.

We must now make this change to GetPosts() so we display images on each user's blog index. We can use the GetImages() function in DatabaseObject_BlogPostImage to retrieve all images for the loaded blog posts, and then simply loop over the returned images and write them to the corresponding post.

The new code to be inserted at the end of GetPosts() in BlogPost.php is shown in Listing 11-48. Note that the $post_ids array is initialized earlier in the function.

Listing 11-48. *Modifying DatabaseObject_BlogPost to Load Post Images (BlogPost.php)*

```php
<?php
    class DatabaseObject_BlogPost extends DatabaseObject
    {
        // ... other code

        public static function GetPosts($db, $options = array())
        {
            // ... other code

            // load the images for each post
            $options = array('post_id' => $post_ids);
            $images = DatabaseObject_BlogPostImage::GetImages($db, $options);

            foreach ($images as $image) {
                $posts[$image->post_id]->images[$image->getId()] = $image;
            }

            return $posts;
        }

        // ... other code
    }
?>
```

Because of this change, all controller actions that call this method now automatically have access to each image, meaning we now only need to change the output templates.

Displaying Thumbnail Images on the Blog Index

The other thing we have done during the development of the code in this book is to output all blog post teasers using the blog-post-summary.tpl template. This means that in order to add a thumbnail to the output of the blog post index (be it the user's home page or the monthly archive) we just need to add an <img> tag to this template.

Listing 11-49 shows the additions we will make to blog-post-summary.tpl in ./templates/ user/lib. After checking that the post has one or more images, we will use the PHP current() function to retrieve the first image. Remember that we must precede this with @ in Smarty so current() is applied to the array as a whole and not to each individual element.

Listing 11-49. *Displaying the First Image for Each Post on the Blog Index (blog-post-summary.tpl)*

```
<div class="teaser">
    <!-- // ... other code -->

    <div class="teaser-date">
        <!-- // ... other code -->
    </div>

    {if $post->images|@count > 0}
        {assign var=image value=$post->images|@current}
        <div class="teaser-image">
            <a href="{$url|escape}">
                <img src="{imagefilename id=$image->getId() w=100}" alt="" />
            </a>
        </div>
    {/if}

    <!-- // ... other code -->
</div>
```

We must also add some style to this page so the output is clean. To do this, we will float the .teaser-image div to the left. The only problem with this is that the image may overlap the post footer (which displays the number of submitted comments). To fix this, we will also add clear : both to the .teaser-links class.

Listing 11-50 shows the changes to the styles.css file in ./htdocs/css.

Listing 11-50. *Styling the Blog Post Image (styles.css)*

```
/* ... other code */

    .teaser-links {
        /* ... other code */
    }

    .teaser-image {
        float       : left;
        margin      : 0 5px 5px 0;
    }

/* ... other code */
```

Once you have added these styles, your blog index page should look similar the one in Figure 11-4.

Figure 11-4. *The blog index page displaying the first image for posts that have images*

Displaying Images on the Blog Details Page

The final change we must make to our templates is to display each of the images for a blog post when viewing the blog post details page. This will behave similarly to the blog post preview page, except that we will also allow users to view a larger version of each image. To improve the output of the larger version of each image, we will use a simple little script called Lightbox.

First, we must alter the `view.tpl` template in the `./templates/user` directory. This is the template responsible for displaying blog post details. We will make each image appear vertically on the right side of the blog by floating the images to the right. This means we must include them in the HTML output before the blog content, as shown in Listing 11-51.

Listing 11-51. *Displaying Each of the Post's Images (view.tpl)*

```
<!-- // ... other code -->

<div class="post-date">
    <!-- // ... other code -->
</div>

{foreach from=$post->images item=image}
    <div class="post-image">
        <a href="{imagefilename id=$image->getId() w=600}">
            <img src="{imagefilename id=$image->getId() w=150}" />
        </a>
    </div>
{/foreach}

<div class="post-content">
    <!-- // ... other code -->
</div>

<!-- // ... other code -->
```

As you can see from this code, we display a thumbnail 150 pixels wide on the blog post details page and link to a version of the image that is 600 pixels wide. Obviously, you can change any of these dimensions as you please.

Now we must style the output of the .post-image class. As mentioned previously, we need to float the images to the right. If we float each of the images to the right, they will all group next to each other, so we must also apply the clear : right style. This simply means that no floated elements can appear on the right side of the element (similar to clear : both, except that a value of both means nothing can appear on the right or the left).

The full style for .post-image that we will add to styles.css is shown in Listing 11-52.

Listing 11-52. *Floating the Blog Post Images to the Right (styles.css)*

```
.post-image {
    float       : right;
    clear       : right;
    margin      : 0 0 5px 5px;
}
```

Once this style has been applied, the blog post output page should look similar to Figure 11-5.

Figure 11-5. *Displaying All Images Belonging to a Single Post*

Displaying Larger Images with Lightbox

Lightbox is a JavaScript utility written by Lokesh Dhakar used to display images fancily on a web page. Typical usage involves clicking on a thumbnail to make the main web page fade while a larger version of the image is displayed. If you have multiple images on the page, you can make Lightbox display next and previous buttons to move through them. Additionally, there is a close button to return to the normal page, as well as keyboard controls for each of these operations.

The best part of Lightbox is that it allows you to easily show enlarged versions of your images without navigating away from the page. Additionally, it allows you to easily keep your images accessible for non-JavaScript users, since the large version of the image is specified by wrapping the thumbnail image in a link. This means that if the browser doesn't support JavaScript, the browser will simply navigate to the larger image directly.

Installing Lightbox

Lightbox requires Prototype and Scriptaculous, which we already have installed. Download Lightbox (version 2) from `http://www.huddletogether.com/projects/lightbox2` and extract the downloaded files somewhere on your computer (not directly into your web application, since we don't need all of the files).

Next, you must copy the `lightbox.js` file from the `js` directory to the `./htdocs/js` directory of our application. Additionally, since this code assumes that `lightbox.js` will be in the root directory of your web server (which it isn't in our case), we must make two slight changes to this file. Open `lightbox.js` and scroll down to around line 65, and simply change the `"images/loading.gif"` value to include a slash at the beginning, and do the same for the next line:

```
var fileLoadingImage = "/images/loading.gif";
var fileBottomNavCloseImage = "/images/closelabel.gif";
```

Next, you must copy the `lightbox.css` file from the `css` directory to the `./htdocs/css` directory of our application. No changes are required in this file.

Finally, copy all of the images from the `images` directory to the `./htdocs/images` directory of our web application. You can skip the two JPG sample images that are in that directory, as they are not required.

■Note Ideally, we would keep the Lightbox images organized into their own directory (such as `./htdocs/images/lightbox`); however, you must then make the necessary path changes to `lightbox.js` and `lightbox.css`.

Loading Lightbox on the Blog Details Page

Next, we must make the Lightbox JavaScript and CSS files load when displaying the blog post details page. We only want these files to load on this page (unless you want to use Lightbox elsewhere), so we will add some simple logic to the `header.tpl` template in `./templates` to accomplish this.

Listing 11-53 shows the code we will add to this template to allow the Lightbox files to load.

Listing 11-53. *Adding a Conditional Statement for Lightbox to Load (header.tpl)*

```
<!-- // ... other code -->
    <head>
        <!-- // ... other code -->

        {if $lightbox}
            <script type="text/javascript" src="/js/lightbox.js"></script>
            <link rel="stylesheet" href="/css/lightbox.css" type="text/css" />
        {/if}
    </head>
<!-- // ... other code -->
```

Now we can modify view.tpl in ./templates/user to tell header.tpl to include the Lightbox files. To do this, we will add lightbox=true to the first line of this template, as shown in Listing 11-54.

Listing 11-54. *Loading Lightbox on the Blog Post Details Page (header.tpl)*

```
{include file='header.tpl' lightbox=true}
<!-- // ... other code -->
```

Linking the Blog Post Images to Lightbox

Finally, we must tell Lightbox which images we want to display. This is done by including rel="lightbox" in the anchor that surrounds the image. If you use this code, though, no previous or next buttons will be shown. You can instead group images together by specifying a common value in square brackets in this attribute, such as rel="lightbox[blog]". Listing 11-55 shows the changes we will make to view.tpl in ./templates/user to use Lightbox.

Listing 11-55. *Telling Lightbox Which Images to Use (view.tpl)*

```
<!-- // ... other code -->

{foreach from=$post->images item=image}
    <div class="post-image">
        <a href="{imagefilename id=$image->getId() w=600}" rel="lightbox[blog]">
            <img src="/utility/image?id={$image->getId()}&amp;w=150" />
        </a>
    </div>
{/foreach}

<!-- // ... other code -->
```

That is all that's required to use Lightbox. When the page loads, the lightbox.js script will automatically search the document for links with that rel attribute and create JavaScript events accordingly.

Now when you click on one of the images, the screen will change as shown in Figure 11-6.

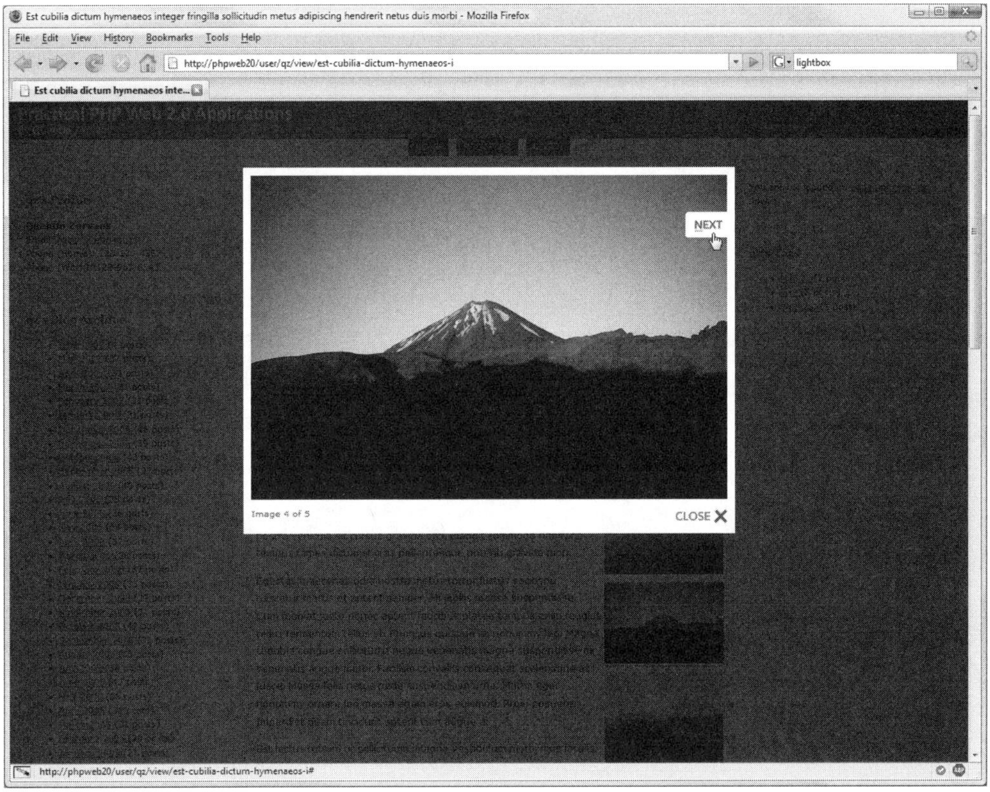

Figure 11-6. *Using Lightbox to display an enlarged blog post image*

Summary

In this chapter, we have given users the ability to upload photos and images to each of the blog post images. In order to do this, there were a number of different issues we had to look at, such as correct handling of file uploads in PHP.

We then built a system to generate thumbnails of images on the fly according to the width and height parameters specified in the URL. This allowed us to easily include images of different sizes depending on where they needed to be displayed in the application.

Next, we used the Scriptaculous `Sortable` class to add image-reordering capabilities, so the user could easily choose the order in which their images would be displayed simply by dragging and dropping the images.

Finally, we modified the display of the user's blog to display all images. We also used the Lightbox script to display larger versions of images seamlessly within the blog post page. In the next chapter, we will be implementing search functionality in our web application using the `Zend_Search_Lucene` component of the Zend Framework.

CHAPTER 12

■■■

Implementing Site Search

The next step in the development of our web application is to provide a search tool for users to find content on the web site. Essentially what we will be doing is allowing people to search based on content in blog posts, as well as on tags that have been assigned to those posts.

Implementing site search consists of two major steps:

- **Creating and managing full-text indexes.** Whenever a new post is created, we must add it to the index. Similarly, when a post is edited, the index must be updated accordingly, and if a post is deleted, then it must be removed from the index. We will be using the Zend_Search_Lucene component of the Zend Framework to manage these indexes.

- **Performing searches and displaying results.** We will include a search form on the web site. Users will be able to enter their desired search term, which we must then accept and use to query the search index. Once we find the matching documents, we will output those results to the user.

Another feature we will be implementing is an Ajax-based search suggestion tool. This means when somebody begins to type a search query, suggestions will be provided based on what other users have also searched for. This is loosely based on the Google Suggest tool.

Introduction to Zend_Search_Lucene

Zend_Search_Lucene is the text search tool that comes with the Zend Framework. It is a general-purpose tool (based on the Apache Lucene project) that allows the developer to index their documents as they please, as well as providing users with a powerful interface to query the created indexes.

Each entry in a search index is referred to as a *document*. A document consists of one or more fields, as decided by the developer. You can use five field types for each field in a document. I describe each of these in the "Zend_Search_Lucene Field Types" section.

When you add new content to your application, you create a new document in the search index. Likewise, you can delete documents from the index. One restriction with Zend_Search_Lucene is that you cannot update an existing document in the index. Rather, you must delete it and then add it again.

Comparison to MySQL Full-Text Indexing

Although Zend_Search_Lucene is not the only tool available for creating full-text indexes, it has various advantages over other solutions, the biggest being that it is a native PHP solution. This means that regardless of the platform we use or the database we use, we can use Zend_Search_Lucene to provide our web application with searching capabilities.

Since the database server we have been primarily developing for in this web application has been MySQL, we will briefly look at the native MySQL solution for full-text indexing.

When creating a new table in MySQL, you can specify a column as fulltext, meaning MySQL will automatically maintain a full-text index for that column. This allows you to perform SQL queries against this column.

For example, to create a database table that holds searchable news articles, you could create a table in MySQL using the following:

```
create table news_articles (
    article_id      serial          not null,
    title           varchar(255)    not null,
    body            text            not null,

    primary key (article_id),
    fulltext (title, body)
);
```

You would then be able to search in this table using the MySQL match() … against syntax. For example, to find all records matching the keyword MySQL, you would use the following SQL query:

```
select * from news_articles where match(title, body) against ('MySQL');
```

The match() … against syntax returns a score based on the relevance of each row that is matched. The results are automatically sorted by this score. You can retrieve this score by including match() … against in the column list:

```
select *, match(title, body) against ('MySQL') as score
    from news_articles
    where match(title, body) against ('MySQL');
```

Because maintenance of the index is automated, no extra work is required to maintain the index. This is a big advantage over the method we will be using, although there are some other drawbacks, such as the following:

- Full-text configuration is global to the server. By default, search terms must be at least four characters to be used. You can change this setting, but it will apply to all databases running on the server. The same applies to the list of the stop words. A *stop word* is a word that is ignored when performing a search. Words such as *the* or *to* are examples of stop words.

- If you want to run your application on a different database server, then this solution will not be available.

It is primarily because of this second restriction that we will instead use a native PHP solution. Additionally, there may be times when you write web applications that use no database at all, in which case you would have no choice but to use a solution such as Zend_Search_Lucene.

■Note If you are using PostgreSQL, then a good solution for a full-text indexing extension is Tsearch2. One drawback with this extension is that it must be compiled into the server. Although this is fine if you manage your own web servers, it can be difficult to get access to this extension in a shared hosting environment.

Zend_Search_Lucene Field Types

Five different field types are available for storing document data in a Zend_Search_Lucene document. Each serves a distinctly different purpose, and it is likely that you will typically use several of these field types for each stored document.

- Keyword: This field type is used to hold data that users can search on, as well as being included in the returned search data. It is typically used for data such as a date or URL, since the value stored in the index is exactly as you specify it.

- UnIndexed: If you want to store data with an indexed document but you don't want that data to be searchable, then you use this field type. This is useful for storing extra data with the document that you use when displaying the search results.

- Binary: This field type works similarly to the UnIndexed field type, except that it is for binary data. An example of binary data you may want to store with an indexed document is a thumbnail image or icon representing that data.

- Text: This is the field type you use for data you want users to be able to search on, as well as data that will be returned in the search results. This differs from the Keyword type in that the data is tokenized, meaning the data is split up into separate words (hence whitespace and other nonword characters are ignored), with each returned token indexed.

- UnStored: This field type allows you to add searchable data to the document just like the Text field; however, when a document is found from searching on data using this field type, unlike the Text type, that data isn't returned with the results.

You can structure the data to be indexed in many ways using these different field types. For instance, you may want to retrieve a database ID only in search results and then manually look up the corresponding data before presenting it to the user. In this scenario, you would use an UnStored field type to add the searchable content as well as UnIndexed to store the corresponding database ID. This is the method we will be using.

Field Naming

Every field you add to an indexed document must have a name. There are two reasons for this. First, when a search has been performed and you are displaying the search results to the user, you need a way to reference the stored data. Second, the advanced querying capabilities of Zend_Search_Lucene allow users to search on a specific field.

For example, if you were to create an index of all news articles in your web site, you might include a field called author (which would be of type Text since we want it to be searchable and to be returned in results) to hold the name of the person who wrote the article.

If you wanted to find all articles by me (Quentin Zervaas), you would use the search term author:"Quentin Zervaas".

■Note The entire author name must be quoted, since not doing so would mean in this case that the author field was searched for Quentin while the main index was searched for Zervaas. Although the intended results would be returned, other records may also be returned (such as articles by someone called Quentin that also happened to have the word Zervaas in any of the indexed fields).

This leads us now to the default search field that is used. In the previous example, we specified the author field must be searched; however, if no field is specified (that is, only the search term is specified), then all indexed fields are searched.

We will look at some more advanced queries later in this chapter once we have integrated the indexing capabilities.

Indexing Application Content

Now that we have briefly looked at how Zend_Search_Lucene is structured, it is time to create indexes for the content in our web application. We will be indexing the content from all published blog posts, including the content, title, tags, and timestamp.

We must also make a number of changes to the existing system to ensure indexes are correctly maintained. Specifically, this includes the following:

- When a new blog post is created (or existing post is sent live), it must be added to the search index.

- When an existing post is deleted (or sent from live to draft), it must be removed from the search index.

- When a blog post is modified, it must be removed from the search index and readded.

Additionally, since the index must be initially created at some point, we are going to write code to rebuild the entire index from scratch.

Because rebuilding an index from scratch is an expensive process (in terms of the time taken as well as the memory and CPU cycles used), it is not something you want to do frequently. Because of this, we must do our best to keep the index as up-to-date as possible. You may want to supplement this by rebuilding the index periodically (such as weekly) using a cron job.

To index all blog posts in the web application, we will first write code to generate an indexable document for each blog post. This is done using the Zend_Search_Lucene_Document class. Following this we will implement the functionality listed previously.

Indexing Multiple Types of Data

The search index we build in this application is specifically geared toward blog posts. In a larger web application, you may have other content you want to index also. In that instance you may want to have one index for each type of data (then when a search is performed, you search each index), or you have one index containing all searchable data.

Each of these methods has its own advantages and disadvantages. For example, if you use a single index for all types of data

- It is simpler to search across all indexes in one operation since all searchable data is in one place.

- You must keep track of the kind of data each document in the index is. For example, if you are indexing data about news articles as well as about uploaded files, you must differentiate between these somehow when you display search results to users.

On the other hand, if you use one index for each type of data

- It is more difficult to search because you have to search every index when a search is performed.

- It gives you more leverage to create different types of searches on your site. For example, if you want a form to allow users to search only in uploaded files, then you simply search the corresponding index. If you also have an index that holds information about news articles, you can skip searching this completely.

Ultimately it comes down to your own needs, depending on the type of application you are implementing and the search capabilities you need to provide.

Creating a New Zend_Search_Lucene_Document

As mentioned earlier this chapter, each entry in a Zend_Search_Lucene index is referred to as a document. To create a document that can be added to a search index, we use the Zend_Search_Lucene_Document class. After instantiating this class, we add all of the required fields and data accordingly. Once this has been done, the document can be added to the index.

In this section, we will write a new function for the DatabaseObject_BlogPost class that builds and returns such a document. We are not actually concerned with adding this document to the search index yet. We will deal with this later this chapter.

Listing 12-1 shows the beginning of the getIndexableDocument() method we add to the BlogPost.php file (in the ./include/DatabaseObject directory).

Listing 12-1. *Creating the Indexable Document (BlogPost.php)*

```php
<?php
    class DatabaseObject_BlogPost extends DatabaseObject
    {
        // ... other code

        public function getIndexableDocument()
        {
            $doc = new Zend_Search_Lucene_Document();
            $doc->addField(Zend_Search_Lucene_Field::Keyword('post_id',
                                                    $this->getId()));
```

After instantiating the Zend_Search_Lucene_Document class, we add a field to hold the ID of the blog post. Each document in the index will have its own internal ID; however, we are not able to set this ourselves, so we must still store the relevant blog post ID from our database.

In the previous section, we looked at the five different types of fields we can add to an indexable document. There is a static method in the Zend_Search_Lucene_Field class for each of these types. This creates an object compatible with the addField() method. The name of the field is the first argument, while its value is the second argument.

In the post_id field we use the Keyword type. These are the reasons we use this type:

- We want to retrieve the document from the index later using this ID (that is, we want to search on this ID).

- We want to retrieve the ID from any search results so the database data can be loaded accordingly.

- It is not textual data that needs to be tokenized (therefore ruling out the Text type).

Next we must add the data we want users to be able to search on to this document. Since we want to search on this data but we don't need to store it in the index (since we will retrieve the found blog posts from the database), we can use the UnStored field type.

Listing 12-2 shows the code we use to index the other fields for a blog post. Since the blog post content is actually made up of HTML tags, we must strip these tags since they are not relevant to the search results. Additionally, tags returned from getTags() are in an array, so we must turn these into a single string by using join().

Listing 12-2. *Adding the Indexable Fields to the Document (BlogPost.php)*

```php
        $fields = array(
            'title'     => $this->profile->title,
            'content'   => strip_tags($this->profile->content),
            'published' => $this->profile->ts_published,
            'tags'      => join(' ' , $this->getTags())
        );
```

```
            foreach ($fields as $name => $field) {
                $doc->addField(
                    Zend_Search_Lucene_Field::UnStored($name, $field)
                );
            }

            return $doc;
        }

        // ... other code
    }
?>
```

Retrieving the Index Location

Next we will add a utility function to DatabaseObject_BlogPost that returns the location on the file system of the search index data. We will be storing the search index in a directory called search-index within the application data directory (./include/data). Assuming your permissions are set up so this directory is writable by the web server, the files will be automatically created on the file system when we create the index.

Listing 12-3 shows the code for the getIndexFullpath() method that we add to BlogPost.php in ./include/DatabaseObject. We will use this function whenever we need to access the index, that is, when adding documents to the index, deleting documents from the index, and querying the index.

Listing 12-3. *Returning the Location of the Search Index (BlogPost.php)*

```php
<?php
    class DatabaseObject_BlogPost extends DatabaseObject
    {
        // ... other code

        public static function getIndexFullpath()
        {
            $config = Zend_Registry::get('config');

            return sprintf('%s/search-index',
                           $config->paths->data);
        }

        // ... other code
    }
?>
```

Building the Entire Index

Before we integrate the automatic maintenance of indexed documents, we will now write a function to build the entire index from scratch. This is useful the very first time we try to index a new document because the index will not yet exist.

Typically you won't need to build an index from scratch, but in addition to building the index when you first integrate this functionality, you may need to rebuild the indexes if the data goes missing or is corrupted. For example, if you needed to move the web application to a new server, you would copy the database, application files (such as PHP scripts and templates), and images uploaded (assuming you used the method described in Chapter 11). You wouldn't, however, move the data that is automatically generated by the application, such as compiled templates or search indexes. In this case you would rebuild the indexes on the new server.

To build the index from scratch, all we need to do is call the GetPosts() function to retrieve all live posts and then loop over each document and call the getIndexableDocument() method on the blog post object accordingly.

Listing 12-4 shows the setup code for the static buildIndex() function that we add to DatabaseObject_BlogPost. We use the create() method from the Zend_Search_Lucene class to create a new index, with the first and only argument being the file system path of the index. When we query the index later, we will be using the open() method instead of create(). We use the getIndexFullpath() from Listing 12-3 as the argument to create().

Listing 12-4. *Creating a New Search Index (BlogPost.php)*

```php
<?php
    class DatabaseObject_BlogPost extends DatabaseObject
    {
        // ... other code

        public static function RebuildIndex()
        {
            try {
                $index = Zend_Search_Lucene::create(self::getIndexFullpath());
```

Since we are building the entire index from scratch, we must now retrieve all existing blog posts in the database and add them to the index. Thankfully, everything we need to achieve this is already in place.

First, we call the GetPosts() function to retrieve all the blog posts. Since we don't want people to find unpublished blog posts in their searches, we retrieve only live posts. Next, it is simply a matter of looping over the returned posts and adding them to the index using the addDocument() method. This method takes an instance of Zend_Search_Lucene_Document as its only argument, which is exactly what the getIndexableDocument() function we created earlier in this chapter returns. This is shown in Listing 12-5.

Listing 12-5. *Retrieving All Blog Posts and Adding Them to the Index (BlogPost.php)*

```
$options = array('status' => self::STATUS_LIVE);
$posts = self::GetPosts(Zend_Registry::get('db'),
                        $options);

foreach ($posts as $post) {
    $index->addDocument($post->getIndexableDocument());
}
```

Finally, we must save the changes to the index. This is done by calling the `commit()` method on the index. Listing 12-6 shows the code we use to this, as well the code for handling any errors that might occur. Note that we use the logging capabilities we implemented earlier in the book to track any errors that might occur.

Listing 12-6. *Saving Changes to the Index and Handling Errors (BlogPost.php)*

```
            $index->commit();
        }
        catch (Exception $ex) {
            $logger = Zend_Registry::get('logger');
            $logger->warn('Error rebuilding search index: ' .
                          $ex->getMessage());
        }
    }

    // ... other code
}
?>
```

We will modify other parts of this class shortly to call this function, but in the meantime, if you want to test this function, you can add the following call to one of your existing controller actions:

```
DatabaseObject_BlogPost::RebuildIndex();
```

If this call works correctly, you will have a directory called /var/www/phpweb20/data/search-index in your application that is populated with the various files that Zend_Search_Lucene creates.

Indexing and Unindexing a Single Blog Post

We must make several changes to the `DatabaseObject_BlogPost` class to ensure blog posts are correctly stored in the index. All of these changes will be triggered in the events that are called when records are created, updated, or deleted.

Before we handle each of these events, we are going to implement two new methods to this class. The first we will use to add a single blog post to the search index (which we also use for updates to blog posts), while the second will be used to remove a blog post from the index.

Adding a Single Blog Post to the Index

We will now create a function called addToIndex() that is responsible for adding a single live blog post to the index. Since we will also be using this function when a blog post is updated, we need to add functionality so the index is updated correctly.

Zend_Search_Lucene does not allow a document in an index to be updated, so in order to reindex a document, the old version must be removed from the index before readding the new version. Therefore, we must query the index to find the old document and remove it accordingly, as you will soon see.

First, we must open the index so we can add the document to it, as shown in Listing 12-7. Note that we are using the open() method rather than the create() method. In fact, calling open() on a search index that does not yet exist throws an exception, so we simply handle this exception by calling the rebuildIndex() method we created earlier this chapter.

Listing 12-7. *Opening the Index for Modification (BlogPost.php)*

```php
<?php
    class DatabaseObject_BlogPost extends DatabaseObject
    {
        // ... other code

        protected function addToIndex()
        {
            try {
                $index = Zend_Search_Lucene::open(self::getIndexFullpath());
            }
            catch (Exception $ex) {
                self::RebuildIndex();
                return;
            }
```

Note This is the point in the code where the index is initially created (if it does not yet exist). Rebuilding the index at this point will include the current blog post; therefore, we can return from this method immediately, since the remainder of the method deals with adding this single blog post to the index.

Second, we must find any existing records for the current blog post in the search index (so we can delete that record before creating a new one). For a new blog post, none will be found, but if an existing live post is being updated, then there should be one match.

Although Zend_Search_Lucene features a built-in query parser, we prefer in this case to manually build a query using the Zend_Search_Lucene API. If you recall from the getIndexableDocument() method, we indexed the ID of the blog post in the post_id field. All we need to do now is to search for that ID. Once again, we wrap all this code in a try … catch statement because our later actions on the index may result in a thrown exception.

As we see in Listing 12-8, we call the find() method on the index to execute a search query. We then loop over the returned results and call delete() on each. We must pass the internal ID (not the blog post ID) of the indexed document to delete().

Listing 12-8. *Finding Any Existing Entries in the Index for the Current Blog Post (BlogPost.php)*

```
try {
    $query = new Zend_Search_Lucene_Search_Query_Term(
        new Zend_Search_Lucene_Index_Term($this->getId(), 'post_id')
    );

    $hits = $index->find($query);
    foreach ($hits as $hit)
        $index->delete($hit->id);
```

Many options are available for building a query as we have done here. I recommend you read http://framework.zend.com/manual/en/zend.search.lucene.searching.html for further details on this. The available classes allow you to build some powerful queries.

■**Note** When we handle user searches later this chapter, we don't really need to deal with building a query manually. Zend_Search_Lucene provides a powerful syntax to query an index in many different ways, as you will see. However, as mentioned, you should build the query programmatically if the complete scope of the query is known (as in this case).

Now that any possible existing entries for the current post have been deleted (in fact, pending deletion, commit() must be called for the action to be final), we reindex the current post. We want to index the post only if it is live, as you can see in Listing 12-9.

Listing 12-9. *Reindexing a Live Blog Post and Committing Changes to the Index (BlogPost.php)*

```
    if ($this->status == self::STATUS_LIVE)
        $index->addDocument($this->getIndexableDocument());

    $index->commit();
    }
    catch (Exception $ex) {
        $logger = Zend_Registry::get('logger');
        $logger->warn('Error updating document in search index: ' .
                    $ex->getMessage());
    }
}

    // ... other code
}
?>
```

As you may have noticed, by structuring the code the way we have, we automatically deal with the case where a user sends a live post back to draft. That is, this function will remove it from the index and not write it back (since the `status` property will no longer indicate the post is live).

Removing a Blog Post from the Index

Next we write a function to remove a blog post from the index. In fact, the function we have just written includes this as part of it; however, we are going to create a stand-alone function to achieve the same thing. This allows us to call it from the `preDelete()` function in `DatabaseObject_BlogPost`.

Although duplication in code should typically be avoided, we make an exception here because this will reduce the overhead in opening and closing the search index. The only real differences between this function and the last is that we don't have a call to `addDocument()`. Additionally, we don't bother rebuilding the index from scratch if it can't be opened.

Listing 12-10 shows the `deleteFromIndex()` function that we use to remove a blog post from the search index.

Listing 12-10. *Removing a Blog Post from the Search Index (BlogPost.php)*

```php
<?php
    class DatabaseObject_BlogPost extends DatabaseObject
    {
        // ... other code

        protected function deleteFromIndex()
        {
            try {
                $index = Zend_Search_Lucene::open(self::getIndexFullpath());

                $query = new Zend_Search_Lucene_Search_Query_Term(
                    new Zend_Search_Lucene_Index_Term($this->getId(), 'post_id')
                );

                $hits = $index->find($query);
                foreach ($hits as $hit)
                    $index->delete($hit->id);

                $index->commit();
            }
            catch (Exception $ex) {
                $logger = Zend_Registry::get('logger');
                $logger->warn('Error removing document from search index: ' .
                        $ex->getMessage());
            }
        }
    }
```

```
        // ... other code
    }
?>
```

Triggering Search Index Updates

Now that the key functions for managing search index data are in place, we must trigger these functions accordingly. Five different events must be handled:

- When a post is created

- When a post is updated

- When a post is deleted

- When a tag is added to a post

- When a tag is removed from a post

Note that at this point in the code, we don't care whether the post is live, since the addToIndex() function we just created will check this.

When a Post Is Created

To handle this case, we add a call to addToIndex() in the postInsert() function that already exists in the BlogPost.php file in ./include/DatabaseObject, as shown in Listing 12-11.

Listing 12-11. *Automatically Adding New Blog Posts to the Index (BlogPost.php)*

```php
<?php
    class DatabaseObject_BlogPost extends DatabaseObject
    {
        // ... other code

        protected function postInsert()
        {
            $this->profile->setPostId($this->getId());
            $this->profile->save(false);

            $this->addToIndex();

            return true;
        }

        // ... other code
    }
?>
```

When a Post Is Updated

To handle this case, we add a call to addToIndex() in the postUpdate() function that already exists, as shown in Listing 12-12.

Listing 12-12. *Updating the Search Index When a Blog Post Is Updated (BlogPost.php)*

```php
<?php
    class DatabaseObject_BlogPost extends DatabaseObject
    {
        // ... other code

        protected function postUpdate()
        {
            $this->profile->save(false);

            $this->addToIndex();

            return true;
        }

        // ... other code
    }
?>
```

When a Post Is Deleted

Once again to handle this case, we add to the appropriate DatabaseObject callback. In this case, we add a call to deleteFromIndex() to the preDelete() function, as shown in Listing 12-13.

Listing 12-13. *Removing a Blog Post from the Index Upon Deletion (BlogPost.php)*

```php
<?php
    class DatabaseObject_BlogPost extends DatabaseObject
    {
        // ... other code

        protected function preDelete()
        {
            // ... other code

            $this->deleteFromIndex();

            return true;
        }

        // ... other code
    }
?>
```

When a Post's Tags Are Changed

The final two events to be handled are when a tag is either added to a post or removed from a post. I have grouped them together here since they are similar cases. Basically, we just add a call to addToIndex() to both the addTags() and deleteTags() methods, as shown in Listing 12-14.

Listing 12-14. *Updating the Search Index When Tags Are Modified (BlogPost.php)*

```php
<?php
    class DatabaseObject_BlogPost extends DatabaseObject
    {
        // ... other code

        public function addTags($tags)
        {
            // ... other code

            $this->addToIndex();
        }

        public function deleteTags($tags)
        {
            // ... other code

            $this->addToIndex();
        }

        // ... other code
    }
?>
```

■**Note** I have not included a call to addToIndex() in the deleteAllTags() method, simply because this method is used only when deleting a blog post. If it were included, then there would be extra unnecessary overhead involved in deleting a blog post since the post would be reindexed before being removed.

Whenever you save or delete a blog post (or add/remove tags) now, the index will be updated accordingly. We haven't yet implemented the ability to search the index; however, you can test whether the index is being modified by viewing the ./data/search-index directory before and after saving a blog post to see whether the files have changed.

Creating the Search Tool

Now that the blog content is automatically being indexed whenever a user creates or edits a blog post, we can add an interface to the search index to the web site. In other words, we can add a search form.

In the following sections, we will extend the application templates to include a clearly visible search form, as well as writing a new controller action to handle search requests. This action will query the search index accordingly and display results to the user.

In addition to implementing this functionality, we will also look at the different types of searches made available using Zend_Search_Lucene.

Adding the Search Form

We'll first add a search form to the application template. We will add this form to the top of the left column of the site. You may prefer to add it to the main header of the site, but I've decided to include it here for the purposes of this chapter.

Listing 12-15 shows the form code we add to the footer.tpl template (from the ./include/ templates directory). This is fairly straightforward, since all the hard work is done in the script to which this form submits. Note that we have removed the placeholder code we had for the left column if no $leftcolumn template is specified.

Listing 12-15. *The Application Search Form That Will Now Appear Site-Wide (footer.tpl)*

```
<!-- // ... other code -->

<div id="left-container" class="column">
    <div class="box" id="search">
        <form method="get" action="{geturl controller='search'}">
            <div>
                <input type="text" name="q" value="{$q|escape}"
                        id="search-query" />
                <input type="submit" value="Search" />
            </div>
        </form>
    </div>

    {if isset($leftcolumn) && $leftcolumn|strlen > 0}
        {include file=$leftcolumn}
    {/if}
</div>

<!-- // ... other code -->
```

The value of the q (short for query) form input will be prepopulated by the $q variable. This will be made available only from the search page. This means by default the field will be empty, although when a search has been performed, it will be prepopulated with the search term.

Once you have added this HTML to your code, a typical page in your web application should look like Figure 12-1. Note the search form now at the top of the left column.

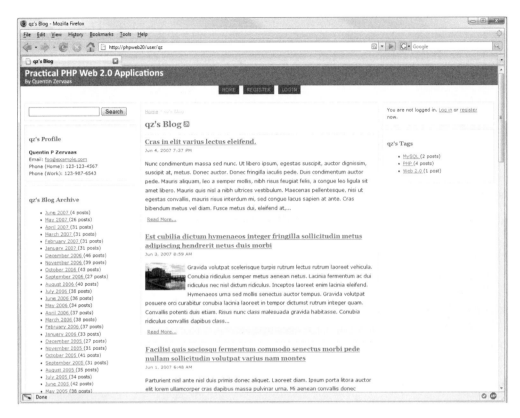

Figure 12-1. *The web application now with a search form*

Handling Search Requests

In the search form we added in Listing 12-15, the form action was to be submitted to the URL /search. We must now create a new action handler to deal with requests to this URL. To do so, we must create a new controller called SearchController, meaning requests to /search will automatically be routed to the indexAction() function of this controller.

First up we will create the new controller with minimal functionality. Listing 12-16 shows the code for the SearchController.php file, which we store in ./include/Controllers. So far all this does is retrieve the submitted query from the request and then write it back to the view controller. Additionally, the page title of Search is set.

Listing 12-16. *Creating the SearchController Class (SearchController.php)*

```php
<?php
    class SearchController extends CustomControllerAction
    {
        public function indexAction()
        {
```

```
            $request = $this->getRequest();

            $q = trim($request->getQuery('q'));

            $this->breadcrumbs->addStep('Search');
            $this->view->q = $q;
        }
    }
?>
```

We must also create the template for outputting search results. For now we will create an empty placeholder, as shown in Listing 12-17. This code should be stored in a file called index.tpl in the ./templates/search directory (you may have to create this directory).

Listing 12-17. *The Search Results Page (index.tpl)*

```
{include file='header.tpl'}

{include file='footer.tpl'}
```

You should now be able to enter a query in the search form we created and submit the form. When submitted, you will be taken to this search page. Obviously no results will be shown yet; however, the submitted query should reappear in the search box.

Querying the Search Index

Next we must extend the indexAction() function so it will actually search in the index. Although performing the actual lookup in the index is trivial, the whole process is slightly more complicated, because of the following reasons:

- We will be generating paged results. That is, we are going to show only five results from a search at a time. If there are more than five results, then a list of pages will be displayed so the user can view the other results.

- After finding the matches in the index, we must load the corresponding blog posts accordingly. If you recall, we did not actually store the blog post data in the index, so instead we must call the GetPosts() function of DatabaseObject_BlogPost to retrieve these posts.

The first thing we are going to do is build an array of search summary information. This is data we assign to the template to help output the paging and results information. Listing 12-18 shows the initialization of this array. The values in this array will be modified throughout this function.

■**Note** This array also contains the master value for the maximum number of results to return (the limit value). If you want to display a different number of search results on a single page, then you can simply change this value.

Listing 12-18. *Building Search Summary Data (SearchController.php)*

```php
<?php
    class SearchController extends CustomControllerAction
    {
        public function indexAction()
        {
            $request = $this->getRequest();

            $q = trim($request->getQuery('q'));

            $search = array(
                'performed' => false,
                'limit'     => 5,
                'total'     => 0,
                'start'     => 0,
                'finish'    => 0,
                'page'      => (int) $request->getQuery('p'),
                'pages'     => 1,
                'results'   => array()
            );
```

The parameters in this array are as follows:

- `performed`: This is a Boolean value that indicates whether a search was performed. If this script is called with an empty search term, then a search is not performed. This allows us to differentiate between a search with no term and a search with no results.

- `limit`: The maximum number of results to be returned per page in the search. This value is not modified later in the function.

- `total`: The total number of results found based on the specified query term. This value will be updated after the search is performed.

- `start`: This indicates the position in the results of the first result that is displayed. Note that this begins at 1 and not 0. So if the `limit` is set to 5, this value would be set to 1 on the first page, 6 on the second page, and so on.

- `finish`: This indicates the position in the results of the last result that is displayed. So if the `limit` is 5 and the user is viewing the second page, then this value would be set to 10.

- `page`: This parameter determines which page of results to show. This is set by the URL parameter p. Valid values are in the range 1…N, where N is the total number of pages.

- `pages`: The total number of pages of results found. This is calculated by dividing the number of results by the page limit. We use this value to ensure the page parameter is valid.

- `results`: An array to hold the search results. After finding matching blog posts, we will retrieve the posts and write them to this array.

Next we try to open the search index and perform the search. We wrap this code in `try` … `catch` so we can handle any errors that may occur trying to query the search index. Additionally, we use this exception handler to deal with empty queries.

If the specified query is empty, we throw an exception so the remainder of the code isn't executed. Note that this will result in the `performed` variable in the `$search` array to remain set to `false`, thereby allowing us to detect when a search hasn't been performed.

As you can see in Listing 12-19, we call the `find()` function on the index to perform the search. Since the `$q` variable is a string, the `Zend_Search_Lucene` query parser is invoked automatically. We will look at some examples of queries that can be performed shortly.

Listing 12-19. *Opening the Search Indexing and Performing the Search*

```
try {
    if (strlen($q) == 0)
        throw new Exception('No search term specified');

    $path  = DatabaseObject_BlogPost::getIndexFullpath();
    $index = Zend_Search_Lucene::open($path);
    $hits = $index->find($q);
```

Now that the search has been performed, we can update the values in the `$search` array as we need. Listing 12-20 shows the code we use to do this.

First, we update the performed value to `true` since the search has in fact now been performed. Second, since the results are returned in an array, we can call `count()` to determine the total number of matches.

Next, we use the total and the limit to determine the number of pages. Since this typically won't return a round number, we use `ceil()` to round the number to the nearest integer. We can now ensure the current page is a valid value. We use the `min()` and `max()` functions to ensure the number is no less than 1 and no more than the total number of pages. If no page was specified in the URL, this will result in the page being set to 1.

After we finish updating this array, we will need to extract the results for the current page from the `$hits` array. Since this array begins at zero, we need to determine which results to take from this array. To calculate this, we use the current page and multiply it by the number of results per page. However, if you use the first page as an example, this would mean the offset for the first page is `1 * 5 = 5`, rather than 0. As such, we must subtract 1 from the page number first.

Using the value in `$offset`, we can determine the `start` and `finish` values. The `start` value will always be the offset plus one (since the returned results are zero-indexed but the `start` and `finish` values begin at 1). The `finish` value can be calculated by using the start value plus the number of hits per page, subtracted by 1. Note that if the final page of results isn't a complete page, then this number will be wrong. As such, we also use the `total` value to determine the correct `finish` value.

Listing 12-20. *Updating the Search Summary Information (SearchController.php)*

```
$search['performed'] = true;
$search['total'] = count($hits);
$search['pages'] = ceil($search['total'] / $search['limit']);
$search['page']  = max(1, min($search['pages'], $search['page']));


$offset = ($search['page'] - 1) * $search['limit'];


$search['start']  = $offset + 1;
$search['finish'] = min($search['total'],
                        $search['start'] + $search['limit'] - 1);
```

Next we must extract the results for the current page from the returned hits, as shown in Listing 12-21. To do this, we use the array_slice() function in conjunction with the $offset and $search['limit'] values. We can then loop over the remaining results and extract the post_id field we set when indexing the blog posts.

We can then call the GetPosts() function to retrieve the matched blog posts. Be aware, though, that GetPosts() will not return the posts in the order they were returned from the search index. To correct this, we simply loop over the original $post_ids array we created and write each post to the results array accordingly.

Listing 12-21. *Extracting the Relevant Results and Retrieving Data from the Database (SearchController.php)*

```
$hits = array_slice($hits, $offset, $search['limit']);
$post_ids = array();
foreach ($hits as $hit)
    $post_ids[] = (int) $hit->post_id;

$options = array('status'  => DatabaseObject_BlogPost::STATUS_LIVE,
                 'post_id' => $post_ids);

$posts = DatabaseObject_BlogPost::GetPosts($this->db,
                                           $options);

foreach ($post_ids as $post_id) {
    if (array_key_exists($post_id, $posts))
        $search['results'][$post_id] = $posts[$post_id];
}

// determine which users' posts were retrieved
$user_ids = array();
foreach ($posts as $post)
    $user_ids[$post->user_id] = $post->user_id;
```

```
                    // load the user records
                    if (count($user_ids) > 0) {
                        $options = array(
                            'user_id' => $user_ids
                        );

                        $users = DatabaseObject_User::GetUsers($this->db, $options);
                    }
                    else
                        $users = array();
```

Finally, we can close the exception handler block (which doesn't need to actually do anything). We can then also set the page title according to the search that was performed. This means the search term will be included in the page and browser title. Additionally, we then write the search summary data to the view, as shown in Listing 12-22.

Listing 12-22. *Completing the Search Request and Assigning Results to the Template (SearchController.php)*

```
                }
                catch (Exception $ex) {
                    // no search performed or an error occurred
                }

                if ($search['performed'])
                    $this->breadcrumbs->addStep('Search Results for ' . $q);
                else
                    $this->breadcrumbs->addStep('Search');

                $this->view->q = $q;
                $this->view->search = $search;
                $this->view->users = $users;
            }
        }
?>
```

Displaying Search Results

Now that the search data is being generated for all user searches and assigned to the template, we must modify the search results template we created earlier this chapter.

We must include several elements in this template consistent with most search engines. These include the following:

- A message to perform a search if one was not performed (that is, if the page was accessed with an empty search term).

- A message if no results were found for the specified search term.

- A summary of the returned results if there are matches. This includes the total number of matches as well as which results are being shown.

- Each of the search results. We can reuse the `blog-post-summary.tpl` template we created earlier for displaying the summary of a single blog post.

- A list of all the pages found. In other words, if the result limit is 5 and there were 23 results in total, then there will be 5 pages. We need to provide links so the user can access subsequent pages.

Listing 12-23 shows the beginning of the `index.tpl` template in `./templates/search`. We first check that a search has been performed, and if so, we check whether any results were returned. If not, we display a message accordingly; otherwise, we proceed to display the summary information and loop over the results.

Listing 12-23. *Ensuring a Search Has Been Performed and Displaying the Results Accordingly (index.tpl)*

```
{include file='header.tpl'}

{if $search.performed}
    {if $search.total == 0}
        <p>
            No results were found for this search.
        </p>
    {else}
        <p>
            Displaying results {$search.start}-{$search.finish} of {$search.total}
        </p>

        {foreach from=$search.results item=post}
            {assign var='user_id' value=$post->user_id}
            {include file='user/lib/blog-post-summary.tpl'
                    post=$post
                    user=$users.$user_id
                    linkToBlog=true}
        {/foreach}
```

Next we output the paging information, as shown in Listing 12-24. We use the Smarty `{section}` construct to loop once for each page in the total results. Note that `{section}` begins at zero and loops accordingly to the `loop` parameter. Since we show users page numbers beginning at 1, we use the `index_next` variable rather than `index` so the page numbers don't begin at zero. The other thing we do is highlight the current page in the pager so the user can easily identify the active page.

Listing 12-24. *Linking to Each Results Page (index.tpl)*

```
<div class="pager">
    {section loop=$search.pages name=page}
        {assign var=p value=$smarty.section.page.index_next}
        {if $p == $search.page}
            <strong>{$p}</strong>
        {else}
            <a href="{geturl controller='search'}?q={$q|escape}&amp;p={$p}"
                >{$p}</a>
        {/if}
    {/section}
</div>
```

Note We have included only the pager beneath the search results. You may prefer to display it above and below the results. In this case, you may want to save the code in Listing 12-24 to a separate template and include it at the top and bottom accordingly.

We complete this template by closing the `if … else` statements and displaying a message prompting the user to search if they haven't yet done so, as shown in Listing 12-25.

Listing 12-25. *Completing the Search Results Template (index.tpl)*

```
    {/if}
{else}
    <p>
        Please use the search form in the left column to find content.
    </p>
{/if}

{include file='footer.tpl'}
```

As a final improvement to this page, we should style the `.pager` class so the pages are centered on the page. The CSS we add to `styles.css` in `./htdocs/css` is as follows in Listing 12-26.

Listing 12-26. *Styling the Page Listing (styles.css)*

```
.pager {
    text-align   : center;
    border-top   : 1px dashed #eee;
    padding-top  : 5px;
    font-size    : 85%;
}
```

If you now perform a search, you will be shown results similar to those in Figure 12-2.

Figure 12-2. *Results from performing a search in our web application*

Types of Searches

Now that our search engine is working, it would be useful to know how to actually query it. Earlier this chapter you saw some brief examples of the most basic searches you can perform with Zend_Search_Lucene. You can find further details of the query language used at http://framework.zend.com/manual/en/zend.search.lucene.query-language.html, but I will now cover some examples.

When we indexed blog posts, we added five fields to each indexed document (post_id, title, content, published, and tags). When a search is performed normally, all of these fields are searched for the given terms. Zend_Search_Lucene allows a user to search in one or more of these fields if they choose simply by prepending the field name to the search term. For instance, if a user wanted to search for blog posts based on their tags, they would include tags: in front of the term (since that is the name of the field we used when indexing the blog posts).

Specifically, if you wanted to find blog posts with the tag PHP, you would use this:

```
tags:PHP
```

Additionally, you can search for phrases by surrounding the query in quotes. So if you knew a post existed with a title of Holiday Photos, you could use the following search to the find the post:

```
title:"Holiday Photos"
```

The most important thing when you consider these different types of searches is that you let users know how to use the search tool. You should typically have some brief instructions on the search page to let them know how to do things such as searching based on tags.

Adding Autocompletion to the Search Tool

We have just finished creating an interface to the indexes we created earlier in the chapter, meaning users can now search for content from each of the users in our web application. The solution we created does not require the user to have any JavaScript capabilities, since all functionality is performed on the server side. We will now extend this search tool to use Ajax to help the user choose a search term.

This feature is based on the Google Suggest tool, which you can find at http://www. google.com/webhp?complete=1. Google Suggest allows users to search on Google just as they would normally, except when they begin to type a search term, an Ajax request is performed in the background to find the most relevant searches beginning with those characters they have already typed. The results are returned in real time, allowing the user either to finish typing what they've already started or to select one of the found terms (either with their arrow keys or with their mouse).

Providing Search Suggestions

To make suggestions to users as to what they should search for, we need some data to generate these suggestions. We'll use the tags that users have assigned to their blog posts as suggestions.

Thus, if they begin to type the term *MySQL*, when they have typed *my*, the following SQL query would be used to find suggestions for them:

```
SELECT DISTINCT tag
    FROM blog_posts_tags
    WHERE tag LIKE 'my%'
    ORDER BY lower(tag)
```

We want to provide suggestions based on tags only for live posts; thus, we must check that the tag found from `blog_posts_tags` belongs to a live post. To do this, we use an SQL join against the `blog_posts` table.

To get a list of suggestions for partial search string, we will add a new method called `GetTagSuggestions()` in the `BlogPost.php` file (in `./include/DatabaseObject`). Listing 12-27 shows this method. It takes the partial tag as its second argument (after the database connection), while the optional third argument specifies the number of the tags to return.

Listing 12-27. *Generating a List of Tags Based on a Partial Search Term (BlogPost.php)*

```php
<?php
    class DatabaseObject_BlogPost extends DatabaseObject
    {
        // ... other code

        public static function GetTagSuggestions($db, $partialTag, $limit = 0)
        {
            $partialTag = trim($partialTag);
            if (strlen($partialTag) == 0)
                return array();

            $select = $db->select();
            $select->distinct();
            $select->from(array('t' => 'blog_posts_tags'), 'lower(tag)')
                    ->joinInner(array('p' => 'blog_posts'),
                                't.post_id = p.post_id',
                                array())
                    ->where('lower(t.tag) like lower(?)', $partialTag . '%')
                    ->where('p.status = ?', self::STATUS_LIVE)
                    ->order('lower(t.tag)');

            if ($limit > 0)
                $select->limit($limit);

            return $db->fetchCol($select);
        }

        // ... other code
    }
?>
```

The returned data is an array with no more than $limit elements (unless the value of $limit is 0, in which case all found tags are returned).

Creating an Action Handler to Return Search Results

The next step is to create a new method in the SearchController class to return the search suggestions. The suggestions will be returned in JSON format based on a partial search string that will be supplied to the method. In the next section, we will write Ajax code to call this function as the user types in their search query.

Listing 12-28 shows the code for the suggestionAction() method, which belongs in the SearchController.php file in ./include/Controllers. It uses the GetTagSuggestions() method in Listing 12-27, as well as the sendJson() method we implemented in Chapter 6.

Listing 12-28. *Returning All Matching Search Terms in JSON Format (SearchController.php)*

```php
<?php
    class SearchController extends CustomControllerAction
    {
        public function suggestionAction()
        {
            $q = trim($this->getRequest()->getPost('q'));

            $suggestions = DatabaseObject_BlogPost::GetTagSuggestions($this->db,
                                                                      $q,
                                                                      10);

            $this->sendJson($suggestions);
        }
    }
?>
```

You can test that this functionality works by visiting `http://phpweb20/search/`
`suggestion?q=term`, where `term` is the partial tag for which you want to find suggestions.
To return valid results, you must have live posts in your database with tags that match the
term you supply.

Retrieving Search Suggestions

Our next step is to write a JavaScript class that will retrieve suggestions from the
`suggestionAction()` function we just wrote when the user types a search query. The way
this will work is to monitor the search query input box. When the user types a query, an
Ajax request will be performed to retrieve those results and then display them to the user.

One important thing to be aware of is that you don't want to retrieve the suggestions every
time the user enters a single character, since this will not only slow down the user's experience
but will also consume excessive server resources. Thus, the way it will work is to display search
suggestions only after the user has stopped typing. To achieve this, every time the user types a
key, we begin a timer. Once the timer expires, we initiate the Ajax request. If the user presses
another key before the timer expires, the existing timer is cancelled, and a new one is created.

Listing 12-29 shows the beginning of the `SearchSuggestor` class. We store this in a file
called `SearchSuggestor.class.js` in the `./htdocs/js` directory. First we set the URL that provides the search suggestions (which is the `suggestionAction()` function we created in the
previous section).

We then set the timer delay of 200 milliseconds (or 0.2 seconds). Additionally, we define a
placeholder to hold the timer returned from the `setTimeout()` function. Finally, we add a
placeholder to hold the current query.

■**Note** Although we specify the delay here in seconds, `setTimeout()` accepts the delay in milliseconds.
This means we must multiply the delay by 1,000. We do this only as a convention since Prototype and
Scriptaculous do the same thing.

Listing 12-29. *Beginning the SearchSuggestor Class (SearchSuggestor.class.js)*

```
SearchSuggestor = Class.create();

SearchSuggestor.prototype = {

    url   : '/search/suggestion',
    delay : 0.2,

    container : null,
    input : null,
    timer : null,
    query : null,
```

Next we write the `initialize()` function, which is the naming Prototype uses for class constructors, as shown in Listing 12-30. The argument for this function is the container of the search form (which we called #search).

We then find the form query input (using its name of q). We add the `keypress` event to this element, since we want to start the timer to initialize an Ajax request every time a key is pressed. Once again, we must use the Prototype `bindAsEventListener()` function so we can define the event handler within this class.

Because modern web browsers save the values you type into forms so they can display them next time, this will interfere with the autocompletion we are implementing. We therefore set the `autocomplete` attribute on the input element to disable this. You could also use `autocomplete="off"` in the HTML code, but this is nonstandard HTML and will cause the document to be invalid.

Listing 12-30. *The SearchSuggestor Constructor (SearchSuggestor.class.js)*

```
    initialize : function(container)
    {
        this.container = $(container);
        if (!this.container)
            return;

        this.input = this.container.down('input[name=q]');
        if (!this.input)
            return;

        this.input.setAttribute('autocomplete', 'off');
        this.input.observe('keypress',
                        this.onQueryChanged.bindAsEventListener(this));
    },
```

Now we define the `onQueryChanged()` function, which is called whenever a key is pressed in the search form. Listing 12-31 shows this function, which first cancels an existing timer if one is set and then creates a new timer. When the timer expires, the `loadSuggestions()` function will be called.

Listing 12-31. *Stopping and Starting Timers When a Key Is Pressed (SearchSuggestor.class.js)*

```
onQueryChanged : function(e)
{
    clearTimeout(this.timer);
    this.timer = setTimeout(this.loadSuggestions.bind(this), this.delay * 1000);
},
```

Now we must write the function to initiate the Ajax request and retrieve the search suggestions. First we retrieve the current query value from the form and trim it using `strip()` (remove the whitespace). Next we check the length of the query. If the query is empty or if it is the same as the previous query, we return from the function. If we didn't do this, then a new Ajax request would be performed even if the user simply pressed a key that didn't change the query (such as an arrow key). Once we determine the query can be submitted, we update the class `query` property to remember the query for the next time.

At this stage, we can perform the Ajax request to retrieve the search results. We use the `onSuggestionLoad()` function as the callback handler for the Ajax request. Although we define that function in Listing 12-32, we don't actually do anything with the results yet. We will build on this function and the rest of this class later in the chapter.

Listing 12-32. *Initiating the Ajax Request and Handling the Response (SearchSuggestor.class.js)*

```
loadSuggestions : function()
{
    var query = $F(this.input).strip();
    if (query.length == 0 || query == this.query)
        return;

    this.query = query;

    var options = {
        parameters : 'q=' + query,
        onSuccess  : this.onSuggestionLoad.bind(this)
    };

    new Ajax.Request(this.url, options);
},

onSuggestionLoad : function(transport)
{
    var json = transport.responseText.evalJSON(true);
}
};
```

■**Tip** The `$F()` function is a Prototype shortcut to retrieve the value from a form element. In the previous code, you could also use `this.input.getValue()` as another Prototype way of retrieving the value.

Loading the SearchSuggestor Class

Although we have not yet completed the SearchSuggestor class, we can add it to our site template. To do this, we must first load the SearchSuggestor.class.js file and then load the class in the onload callback we created in the scripts.js file earlier in the book.

Listing 12-33 shows the changes that are to be made to header.tpl in ./templates to load the SearchSuggestor.class.js file.

Listing 12-33. *Loading the SearchSuggestor Class in the Site Template (header.tpl)*

```
<!-- // ... other code -->

<script type="text/javascript" src="/js/SearchSuggestor.class.js"></script>
<script type="text/javascript" src="/js/scripts.js"></script>

<!-- // ... other code -->
```

At this stage, however, the SearchSuggestor class is not actually being used. We must modify the init() function in the scripts.js file to bind the class to the query text input. As mentioned previously, the argument to the SearchSuggestor function is the ID of the container holding the search form in footer.tpl. Listing 12-34 shows the code we add to the scripts.js file.

Listing 12-34. *Instantiating the SearchSuggestor Class on Page Load (scripts.js)*

```
function init(e)
{
    // ... other code

    new SearchSuggestor('search');
}
```

Displaying Search Suggestions

The next step is to display each of the found search results to the user. We will do this by creating an unordered list and displaying it directly beneath the search input. This will require changes both to the SearchSuggestor class and to the site CSS.

To display the search suggestions directly beneath the input without affecting the normal flow of the page, we must make the list's position absolute. For this to work, we must also make the parent container's position (#search) relative.

After making the necessary changes to the JavaScript, HTML like the following will be generated. Note that we don't actually include this in our templates at all, since we will be building the <ul> element using the appropriate DOM functions.

```
<div class="box" id="search">
    <form method="get" action="/search">
        <!-- // ... other code -->
    </form>
```

```
<ul>
    <li>Search suggestion 1</li>
    <li>Search suggestion 2</li>
    <li>Search suggestion 3</li>
</ul>
</div>
```

Listing 12-35 shows the styles we add to the styles.css file (in ./htdocs/css) to make the generated list display directly beneath the search text input.

Listing 12-35. *Styling the Search Suggestion Container (styles.css)*

```
#search { position : relative; }

#search-query {
    width   : 170px;
    border  : 1px solid #707070;
    padding : 2px;
}

#search ul {
    position        : absolute;
    list-style-type : none;
    width           : 174px;
    margin          : -2px 0 0 0;
    padding         : 0;
    background      : #f7f7f7;
    border          : 1px solid #707070;
    font-size       : 85%;
}

#search li {
    padding : 2px;
    margin  : 0;
}
```

Now we modify the SearchSuggestor class to display the search suggestions in the list. The first thing we do is modify the onSuggestionLoad() function, as shown in Listing 12-36. All the returned suggestions will be held in the array called json, so we pass this to the showSuggestions() function that we will create shortly.

Next we use the Scriptaculous Builder class to create the unordered list. We then loop over the list of terms and create a list item for each one. We then update the list item so the search term is used as the item content. Finally, we add the list to the search container.

Listing 12-36. *Displaying Suggestions After the Ajax Request Completes (SearchSuggestor.class.js)*

```
// ... other code

onSuggestionLoad : function(transport)
```

```
{
    var json = transport.responseText.evalJSON(true);
    this.showSuggestions(json);
},

showSuggestions : function(suggestions)
{
    this.clearSuggestions();

    if (suggestions.size() == 0)
        return;

    var ul = Builder.node('ul');

    for (var i = 0; i < suggestions.size(); i++) {
        var li = $(Builder.node('li'));
        li.update(suggestions[i]);
        ul.appendChild(li);
    }

    this.container.appendChild(ul);
},
```

Another thing we do in the showSuggestions() function is clear any existing terms before new ones are shown. We do this using clearSuggestions(), which is shown in Listing 12-37. This is called regardless of whether any search suggestions have been found; if there are no suggestions, there is nothing to show, and if there are suggestions, then we want to show only the new ones, not ones that were previously there.

Listing 12-37. *Removing Existing Search Suggestions from the Search Container (SearchSuggestor.class.js)*

```
clearSuggestions : function()
{
    this.container.getElementsBySelector('ul').each(function(e) {
        e.remove();
    });

    this.query = null;
}
};
```

One more minor change we must now make is to the loadSuggestions() function. Currently in this function if the search term is empty, then we don't bother performing this Ajax request. We must now make it so in addition to not performing the Ajax request, the current list of suggestions is hidden. The reason we add this is because if the user highlights the search input and presses Backspace, the term would be deleted but the suggestions would remain. The code in Listing 12-38 fixes this issue.

Listing 12-38. *Clearing Suggestions When the Search Term Is Cleared (SearchSuggestor.class.js)*

```
loadSuggestions : function()
{
    var query = $F(this.input).strip();

    if (query.length == 0)
        this.clearSuggestions();

    if (query.length == 0 || query == this.query)
        return;

    // ... other code
},
```

Adding Mouse Navigation to Results

Although the search suggestions are now being displayed when the user begins to enter a search term, it is not yet possible to do anything useful with these suggestions. The first thing we are going to do is allow users to click one of the suggestions. This will trigger the search form being submitted using the selected term.

To do so, we must first handle the mouseover, mouseout, and click events for each list item. The functionality we want to occur for each event is as follows:

- When the mouse is over a suggestion, highlight the suggestion. We do this by creating a new CSS style called .active and adding it using the Prototype addClassName() method.

- When the mouse moves away from a suggestion, remove the .active class using removeClassName().

- When a search term is clicked, replace the term currently in the search input with the clicked term and then submit the form.

First, we will add the new CSS style. We will simply make the active item display with a red background and white text. Listing 12-39 shows the new CSS selector we add to styles.css.

Listing 12-39. *Styling the Active Search Suggestion (styles.css)*

```
#search li.active {
    background : #f22;
    color      : #fff;
    cursor     : pointer;
}
```

Now we use the observe() method to handle the three events discussed earlier. Listing 12-40 shows the code we add to the showSuggestions() function to observe these events, as well as the suggestionClicked() function that we call from within the click event.

Listing 12-40. *Handling the Mouse Events with the Search Suggestions (SearchSuggestor.class.js)*

```
// ... other code

showSuggestions : function(suggestions)
{
    this.clearSuggestions();

    if (suggestions.size() == 0)
        return;

    var ul = Builder.node('ul');

    for (var i = 0; i < suggestions.size(); i++) {
        var li = $(Builder.node('li'));

        li.update(suggestions[i]);

        li.observe('mouseover',
                    function(e) {
                        Event.element(e).addClassName('active')
                    });

        li.observe('mouseout',
                    function(e) {
                        Event.element(e).removeClassName('active')
                    });

        li.observe('click',
                    this.suggestionClicked.bindAsEventListener(this));

        ul.appendChild(li);
    }

    this.container.appendChild(ul);
},

suggestionClicked : function(e)
{
    var elt = Event.element(e);
    var term = elt.innerHTML.strip();

    this.input.value = term;
    this.input.form.submit();

    this.clearSuggestions();
},

// ... other code
```

As you can see, in the `suggestionClicked()` event handler, the first thing we do is determine which suggestion was clicked using the `Event.element()` function. We can then determine what the search term is by retrieving the `innerHTML` property of the element (we also use `strip()` to clean up this code in case extra whitespace is added to it).

We then update the value of the form element and submit the form. Additionally, we clear the suggestions after one has been clicked, preventing the user from clicking a different suggestion while the form is being submitted.

Adding Keyboard Navigation to Results

The final thing we do to improve the search suggestions is to add keyboard controls to the suggestions. Essentially what we want to be able to do is let the user choose a suggestion using their up and down arrow keys. The keyboard handling rules we will add are as follows:

- If the user presses the down arrow and no term has been highlighted (that is, set to use the `.active` class), then select the first term.

- If the user presses the down arrow and a suggestion is highlighted, move to the next suggestion. If the user presses down when the last suggestion is highlighted, then select no suggestion so the user can hit Enter on what they have typed so far.

- If the user presses up and no term is selected, then select the last suggestion.

- If the user presses up and a suggestion is highlighted, move to the previous suggestion. Select no suggestion if up is pressed when the first suggestion is selected.

- Submit the search form with the highlighted term when Enter is pressed.

- Hide the suggestions if the Escape key is pressed.

As you can probably tell, the work involved with adding keyboard controls is slightly more involved than adding mouse controls.

The first thing we are going to do is to write some utility functions to help us select items and to determine which item is selected.

Listing 12-41 shows the `getNumberOfSuggestions()` function that we add to `SearchSuggestor.class.js`, which simply counts the number of list items present and returns that number. This is helpful in determining the item index of the next or previous item when using the arrow keys.

Listing 12-41. *Determining the Number of Suggestions Showing to the User (SearchSuggestor.class.js)*

```
SearchSuggestor = Class.create();

SearchSuggestor.prototype = {

    // ... other code
```

```
getNumberOfSuggestions : function()
{
    return this.container.getElementsBySelector('li').size();
},
```

■Note When you add this function and the other new functions in this section to
`SearchSuggestor.class.js`, make sure the comma is correctly placed after the close brace of each function in the class (except for the final one).

Next we write a function to select an item (that is, to apply the `.active` class) based
on its numerical index in the list of items. This list is zero-indexed. Listing 12-42 shows the
`selectSuggestion()` class, which works by looping over all list items and adding the `.active`
class if it matches the passed-in argument. Note that this function also deselects every other
list item. In effect we can use this function to ensure no items are selected at all by passing an
invalid index (such as `-1`).

Listing 12-42. *Selecting a Single Suggestion Based on Its Index (SearchSuggestor.class.js)*

```
selectSuggestion : function(idx)
{
    var items = this.container.getElementsBySelector('li');

    for (var i = 0; i < items.size(); i++) {
        if (i == idx)
            items[i].addClassName('active');
        else
            items[i].removeClassName('active');
    }
},
```

Next, we write a function to determine the index of the item that is currently selected,
shown in Listing 12-43. This is in some ways the opposite of the `selectSuggestion()` function.
It works almost identically, but rather than updating the class name, it checks instead for the
presence of the `.active` class. If no items are currently selected, then `-1` is returned.

Listing 12-43. *Determining the Index of the Selected Suggestion (SearchSuggestor.class.js)*

```
getSelectedSuggestionIndex : function()
{
    var items = this.container.getElementsBySelector('li');

    for (var i = 0; i < items.size(); i++) {
        if (items[i].hasClassName('active'))
            return i;
```

```
        }

        return -1;
    },
```

Now we write a function called getSelectedSuggestion(), which is shown in Listing 12-44. This function is identical to getSelectedSuggestionIndex() except that it returns the actual search term that is selected rather than its index in the list. We will use this function when the user hits Enter while a term is selected.

Listing 12-44. *Determining the Search Suggestion That Is Currently Selected (SearchSuggestor.class.js)*

```
getSelectedSuggestion : function()
{
    var items = this.container.getElementsBySelector('li');

    for (var i = 0; i < items.size(); i++) {
        if (items[i].hasClassName('active'))
            return items[i].innerHTML.strip();
    }

    return '';
}
};
```

The final thing we must do is modify the onQueryChanged() function, which is the event handler we defined that is called whenever a key is pressed in the search input. Currently, all the function does is clear any existing timers and set a new timer for fetching suggestions. We will now add handlers for specific keys to this function (in addition to the timer-handling code).

Listing 12-45 shows the code we use to handle the Enter key being pressed. When the user hits Enter, if a suggestion is highlighted, then we want to populate the search input with this term and submit the form. If no term is highlighted, then we submit the form with whatever the user has typed so far. When the search term populates the input, we clear the suggestions, just as we did in the mouse-handling code.

Also, note that we leave the call to clearTimeout() in front of the switch() statement. This is because we will be returning from the keys handled in the switch() statement, but we still want to cancel the timer. All normal key presses will travel beyond the switch() statement and trigger the new timer.

Listing 12-45. *Searching on the Selected Term When the User Hits Enter (SearchSuggestor.class.js)*

```
SearchSuggestor = Class.create();

SearchSuggestor.prototype = {

    // ... other code
```

```
onQueryChanged : function(e)
{
    clearTimeout(this.timer);

    switch (e.keyCode) {
        case Event.KEY_RETURN:
            var term = this.getSelectedSuggestion();
            if (term.length > 0) {
                this.input.value = term;
                this.clearSuggestions();
            }
            return;
```

Next we handle the Escape key being pressed. This case is fairly simple, because all we need to do is to hide the search suggestions, as shown in Listing 12-46.

Listing 12-46. *Hiding the Search Suggestions When the User Hits Escape*

```
        case Event.KEY_ESC:
            this.clearSuggestions();
            return;
```

We now handle the trickier case where the user presses the down arrow key. According to the rules we specified earlier in this section, we want to select the first term if no term is selected; otherwise, we want to select the next term. As another special case, if the last term is selected, then pressing the down arrow should result in no suggestion being selected.

Listing 12-47 shows the code we use to determine which suggestion should now be selected as a result of the down arrow being pressed. We make use of the utility functions we just created to help with this.

Listing 12-47. *Selecting the Next Item When the Down Arrow Is Pressed (SearchSuggestor.class.js)*

```
        case Event.KEY_DOWN:
            var total = this.getNumberOfSuggestions();
            var selected = this.getSelectedSuggestionIndex();

            if (selected == total - 1) // currenty last item so deselect
                selected = -1;
            else if (selected < 0)      // none selected, select the first
                selected = 0;
            else                        // select the next
                selected = (selected + 1) % total;

            this.selectSuggestion(selected);
            Event.stop(e);
            return;
```

To handle the case where the up arrow is pressed, we basically just do the opposite of the down arrow calculations. Listing 12-48 shows the code for this case. This code also includes the final call of the function to initiate the new timer. Note that this won't be called for presses of the Enter, Escape, up arrow, and down arrow keys, because we've returned from each of them in this function.

Listing 12-48. *Selecting the Previous Suggestion When the Up Arrow Is Pressed (SearchSuggestor.class.js)*

```
            case Event.KEY_UP:
                var total = this.getNumberOfSuggestions();
                var selected = this.getSelectedSuggestionIndex();

                if (selected == 0) // first item currently selected, so deselect
                    selected = -1;
                else if (selected < 0) // none selected, select the last item
                    selected = total - 1;
                else                    // select the previous
                    selected = (selected - 1) % total;

                this.selectSuggestion(selected);
                Event.stop(e);
                return;
        }

        this.timer = setTimeout(this.loadSuggestions.bind(this), this.delay * 1000);
    },

    // ... other code
};
```

If you now type a search term in the search box (assuming some existing searches have already taken place), you will be shown a list of suggestions for your search, as shown in Figure 12-3.

You might want to add some extra functionality to the tool in the future, such as displaying the number of results that would be returned if the user were to perform the given search. The difficulty in providing features such as this is that they are resource intensive. You need to perform the search of each term in real time (not recommended) to determine how many results the search would return, or you need to cache the result counts so the data can be accessed quickly.

In any case, you need to be aware of the implications of adding features like this to your server. Even the suggestion lookup tool as it is results in a new HTTP request and database query each time, so imagine if you had hundreds or thousands of people using the search tool at any one time.

Figure 12-3. *Search suggestions are now being displayed below the search input.*

Summary

In this chapter, we created a fully functioning search engine for our web application using Zend_Search_Lucene. We achieved this by creating a search index for all of the blog posts in the application. We altered the blog management code so the index is automatically maintained when posts are created, updated, or deleted.

Next we added a search form to the website to allow users to find blog posts. The powerful querying syntax of Lucene meant posts could be found based on several criteria, including the title, the body, or its tags.

Finally, we improved the search form to behave similarly to Google's Suggest interface. This provides users with some suggestions on what to search for, based on the tags registered users have applied to their blog posts.

In the next chapter, we will be looking closely at Google Maps. We will extend the blog functionality so users can add locations to their blog posts and display those maps accordingly.

CHAPTER 13

■ ■ ■

Integrating Google Maps

All of the code we have developed so far in this book has been self-contained with no reliance on any outside services. Frequently in your web development endeavors you will need to integrate features that you don't necessarily have the resources to provide. Or it simply may be that an outside service provides you with access to data you wouldn't otherwise be able to access.

In this chapter, we will be integrating Google Maps (`http://maps.google.com`) into our web application as an example of using third-party services. Specifically, we will allow users to assign one or more locations to each of their blog posts and then display a map marking the location when visitors view the respective blog post.

Many other services are available on the Internet that can be used on your web site (or even desktop applications), such as displaying product information and reviews using Amazon Web Services or processing credit card payments (using PayPal, Google Checkout, or one of the many other similar options available).

In addition to displaying maps with Google Maps, we will also make use of the geo microformat, extending what we learned about microformats in Chapter 10.

Google Maps Features

The Google Maps API is a well-documented and comprehensive JavaScript API that gives developers a wide range of options for displaying maps and controlling how their maps behave. Before we begin planning our usage of the maps, let's take a look at some of the key features available.

Geocoding

Gecoding is the process of converting a street address into geographical coordinates (latitude and longitude). For example, Google's address is 1600 Amphitheatre Pkwy, Mountain View, California. If you were to enter this address into the Google Maps geocoder, then the coordinates of latitude `37.423111` and longitude `-122.081783` would be returned. These coordinates can then be used to mark locations on the displayed map.

Google provides two ways to access its geocoder. The first method is to use their JavaScript interface to look up addresses. This allows you to look up and add new points on your map from within the client-side web browser.

469

The second method to access the geocoder is to query their geocoder web service on the server side. This makes it easy to look up addresses and save the results in your database for future use, and it doesn't therefore rely on the end-user having a JavaScript-enabled web browser.

For any given request, the geocoder may return zero, one, or several matches. Since an API key is required to access Google Maps (which we will create shortly) and each IP address has a limitation on the number of geocoder requests daily (15,000), an incorrect key or too many requests might be the cause for no matches being returned. Note that these errors are indicated in the status section of the response.

Note An API key is what Google uses to control access to their services. For you (as a web site owner or developer) to use Google Maps on your own web site, you must have an API key. When a user tries to load a map from your site, your API key is used in the request.

If multiple addresses are found (perhaps you entered an address such as 123 Main St. without specifying the town), it is up to you as the developer to determine which address is the one you were after. The response includes an accuracy rating with each matched address. The rating indicates to what level the response is accurate (such as country, region, city, street, intersection, or an exact match).

We will use the client-side geocoder in this chapter to look up addresses entered by users when they try to add locations to their blog posts.

Displaying Maps

When displaying a map with Google Maps, you must provide an HTML element on your page in which to hold the map. The map will automatically fill the entire width and height of the specified element.

Additionally, the objects in the following sections can be placed on maps as required.

Map Controls

When the map is initially displayed, there will be no controls displayed. Controls are buttons on the map that allow the user to manipulate the display. The available controls are as follows:

- **Zoom.** The user can zoom in or zoom out using the appropriate buttons or slider.

- **Panning.** The user can move the map north, south, east, or west using the panning buttons.

- **Map Type.** The user can choose the type of map displayed, which by default includes a street map, a satellite map, or a combination of the two (called a *hybrid* map).

- **Mini-map.** This a small map that sits in the corner of the main map that is zoomed out further than the main map, allowing users to change the location of the map more quickly for large distances.

- **Map scale.** This indicates how many meters, yards, kilometers, or miles the displayed distance represents.

Figure 13-1 shows an example map that includes each of these controls.

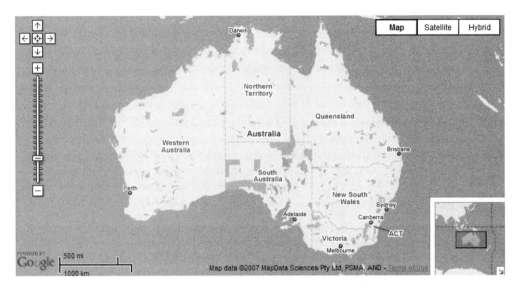

Figure 13-1. *A sample map showing various map controls*

The Google Maps API allows you to add any of these controls as required. Additionally, you can choose which corner of the map to anchor the control. By default, the zoom and panning buttons are in the top-left, the map type buttons are in the top-right, the mini-map is in the bottom-right, and the scale is in the bottom-left.

Although we will not be doing so in this chapter, the API also allows developers to create custom controls that can be overlaid on the map. For example, if you wanted to use graphical icons to switch between the map types instead of the text buttons, you could do so by creating a custom control.

Map Overlays

A map overlay is any object (aside from the map controls) that appears on top of the map that isn't actually part of the map yet moves with the map as it is panned. The use of overlays is essential to portray any useful custom information to your users. The different types of overlays available in Google Maps are as follows:

- **Markers.** A marker represents a single point on the map. It is possible to use any icon you desire to display the marker, although the simplest solution is to use the built-in icon (shown in Figure 13-2). A map can have any number of markers, although there may be scalability issues you need to take into account for a large number of markers.

■**Note** The Google Maps API provides a class (`google.maps.MarkerManager`) that can be used to manage a large number of points. Since loading a large number of points (hundreds or thousands) can result in a large amount of memory use in the client web browser, then how these points are loaded and displayed needs to be managed—there's no sense in loading points that are in Europe when the user is viewing North America. Since we will not be displaying a large number of markers at any one time in this book, we will not be using this class. However, if you wanted to extend the functionality we add this chapter to display every location of every blog post in our database, then you would consider using this class.

- **Information windows.** An information window is a callout box you can add to your map that points to a specified point on the map (which may or may not have a corresponding marker). Within the information window you can display any HTML content you please (such as text, links, or images). This is commonly used to display information after a marker has been clicked. The API also allows you to display tabbed information windows, allowing you to display multiple pages of information in a single information window.

- **Polylines.** By specifying a series of points, you can draw lines on the map using the polyline classes. Google uses this on its own maps to display driving directions between locations. You can use this feature in many ways, such as if you want to plot the path and distance of your morning jog (since the distance between two points can be calculated using their latitude and longitude).

Figure 13-2 shows an example of what a marker and information window looks like on a map.

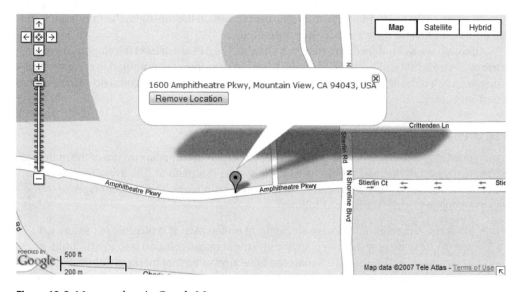

Figure 13-2. *Map overlays in Google Maps*

We will be using markers to display one or more points on users' blog posts as required. We will look at some advanced usage of markers as we will allow users to click and drag markers to a new location if they please.

Controlling Maps

In addition to using the controls that can be added to maps, it is also possible to control maps programmatically. For example, you must choose where to center the map initially; you can use code to switch between satellite and street map view, and you can open or close information windows as required using function calls.

The code we write in this chapter will use a combination of programmed map control as well as allowing users to control the map as they please. For example, when a marker is dragged to a new location, we will make its information window appear, but we will also allow the users to close and reopen the window as they please.

Planning Integration

Now that we have an idea of the functionality that Google Maps provides, it's time to plan how we use the available features. As mentioned previously, we are going to allow users to add one or more locations to each of their blog posts. In doing so, we must consider a number of issues:

- We will use the geocoder to find the coordinates of each location being added by the user. This means we must add a map to the blog manager section of the site and display a marker when they enter an address.

- Since the found location might not be the exact point the user wants to display, we will allow them to drag the marker to any location on the map that they please.

- We will save the coordinates and a description for each point in the database.

- For each post that has locations assigned to it, we must display the map on the post details page, as well as including an information window showing the description for every marker that is added.

Limitations of Google Maps

Although the terms and conditions of Google Maps state there is no limit to the number of page views for each map, there is a limitation for the number of geocoder requests. Each IP address has a limit of 15,000 geocoder requests per day. This means when the geocoder is used from a user's web browser, the request counts against their quota (not your server's). Note, however, that if you use the server-side geocoder, then each request counts against your server's IP address.

Theoretically, you could perform a geocoder request every time somebody viewed the page with the address that was added; however, you could potentially go over the limit, meaning the geocoder request would fail (we discuss the different error codes returned from the geocoder shortly).

It is unnecessary and slower to perform the geocoder request for every view, especially since the locations for a given blog post won't change. Because of this, it is important to cache the geocoder response for later use. Although we won't be caching the entire response, we will be caching the latitude and longitude for each point in the database.

Browser Compatibility

Google Maps is compatible with all modern graphical browsers. Obviously since it is completely reliant on JavaScript, users must have JavaScript enabled in their browser. In case a user has a browser that does support JavaScript but doesn't support Google Maps (perhaps it's an older browser or a browser with an incomplete JavaScript implementation), the `google.maps.BrowserIsCompatible()` function is available to check whether the browser has the capabilities Google Maps requires.

In addition to using `google.maps.BrowserIsCompatible()` to ensure Google Maps will work, we should also provide a non-JavaScript solution for users viewing blog posts that have location data. To handle this case, we will simply display a list of any saved locations that belong to a post (using microformats) rather than displaying a map.

Because we have implemented similar solutions in previous chapters, I have chosen not to include a non-JavaScript implementation in this chapter for the management of blog post locations. However, I have included notes later about how to approach the issue.

Documentation and Resources

Since I cannot cover every part of the API in this chapter, it is very much worth your while to use the documentation provided by Google if you want further information about using Google Maps.

For an introduction to how Google Maps works (including many examples), it is worth reading `http://www.google.com/apis/maps/documentation/index.html`.

For the complete API reference (that is, documentation of all classes, functions, and corresponding arguments), visit `http://www.google.com/apis/maps/documentation/reference.html`.

■**Note** We will be using the Google Ajax API loader (`http://code.google.com/apis/ajax/documentation`), meaning all classes belong in the `google.maps.*` namespace. This means dropping the G from the beginning of each class name as it appears in the documentation and adding `google.maps.` instead. For example, to create a new latitude/longitude point, we use the `google.maps.LatLng` class rather than the documented `GLatLng` class.

Creating a Google Maps API Key

To use Google Maps on your own web site, you must create an API key. A unique API key must be created for every domain on which you want to display maps (every subdomain must also have its own key).

To create a key, you must visit `http://www.google.com/apis/maps/signup.html` and enter your web site domain name. It is free to create a key (although you must agree to Google's terms and conditions, available at the sign-up URL).

> ■**Note** You will also need a Google account to create a key. If you have used any of Google's other services (such as Gmail), then you already have an account.

Once you've created the API key, add it to your application configuration file. We will add it to the settings.ini file using the key google.maps.key. Listing 13-1 shows the line we add to the end of settings.ini.

Listing 13-1. *Storing the API Key in the Application Settings File (settings.ini)*

```
google.maps.key = "your key here"
```

Adding Location Storage Capabilities

Before we actually begin integrating Google Maps in our application, we must do what we have done for other functionality we've added to the application: create a new database table and a DatabaseObject subclass to manage the database data.

Creating the Database Table

First let's create a new database table. We will call this table blog_posts_locations, and a single record will hold one location for one blog post. Each post can have any number of locations associated with it.

Listing 13-2 shows the schema for blog_posts_locations, which can be found in the schema-mysql.sql file.

Listing 13-2. *The MySQL Database Table for Storing Blog Post Locations (schema-mysql.sql)*

```
create table blog_posts_locations (
    location_id     serial             not null,
    post_id         bigint unsigned not null,
    longitude       numeric(10, 6)  not null,
    latitude        numeric(10, 6)  not null,
    description     text               not null,

    primary key (location_id),
    foreign key (post_id) references blog_posts (post_id)
) type = InnoDB;
```

As usual, the corresponding PostgreSQL schema can be found in the schema-pgsql.sql file.

Creating the DatabaseObject_BlogPostLocation Class

We must also create a new class that extends from DatabaseObject in order to manage the data in this table. Listing 13-3 shows the DatabaseObject_BlogPostLocation class, which we store in the BlogPostLocation.php file in ./include/DatabaseObject.

There are no new concepts in this code, because parts of classes covered earlier in this book have been combined to create this class. The key thing to notice is the inclusion of the GetLocations() method, which allows us to fetch all of the locations for a single blog post easily.

Listing 13-3. *Managing Location Data in the blog_posts_locations Table (BlogPostLocation.php)*

```php
<?php
    class DatabaseObject_BlogPostLocation extends DatabaseObject
    {
        public function __construct($db)
        {
            parent::__construct($db, 'blog_posts_locations', 'location_id');

            $this->add('post_id');
            $this->add('longitude');
            $this->add('latitude');
            $this->add('description');
        }

        public function loadForPost($post_id, $location_id)
        {
            $post_id     = (int) $post_id;
            $location_id = (int) $location_id;

            if ($post_id <= 0 || $location_id <= 0)
                return false;

            $query = sprintf(
                'select %s from %s where post_id = %d and location_id = %d',
                join(', ', $this->getSelectFields()),
                $this->_table,
                $post_id,
                $location_id
            );

            return $this->_load($query);
        }

        public static function GetLocations($db, $options = array())
        {
            // initialize the options
            $defaults = array('post_id' => array());

            foreach ($defaults as $k => $v)
                $options[$k] = array_key_exists($k, $options) ? $options[$k] : $v;

            $select = $db->select();
```

```php
        $select->from(array('l' => 'blog_posts_locations'), 'l.*');

        // filter results on specified post ids (if any)
        if (count($options['post_id']) > 0)
            $select->where('l.post_id in (?)', $options['post_id']);

        // fetch post data from database
        $data = $db->fetchAll($select);

        // turn data into array of DatabaseObject_BlogPostLocation objects
        $locations = parent::BuildMultiple($db, __CLASS__, $data);

        return $locations;
    }
}
?>
```

Modifying Blog Posts to Load Locations

The next change we make is to the DatabaseObject_BlogPost class. We are going to make this class automatically load all saved locations, just as it does with its profile and any assigned images. Doing so makes it easy for us to include the saved locations when outputting a blog post.

To do so, we call the GetLocations() function we added to DatabaseObject_BlogPostLocation in the postLoad() function of BlogPost.php, as shown in Listing 13-4. Note that we can reuse the $options array used for retrieving images.

Listing 13-4. *Automatically Loading Saved Locations When Loading a Blog Post (BlogPost.php)*

```php
<?php
    class DatabaseObject_BlogPost extends DatabaseObject
    {
        // ... other code

        public $locations = array();

        // ... other code

        protected function postLoad()
        {
            $this->profile->setPostId($this->getId());
            $this->profile->load();

            $options = array(
                'post_id' => $this->getId()
            );
            $this->images = DatabaseObject_BlogPostImage::GetImages($this->getDb(),
                                                                    $options);
```

```php
        $this->locations = DatabaseObject_BlogPostLocation::GetLocations(
            $this->getDb(),
            $options
        );
    }

    // ... other code

}
?>
```

Additionally, we must modify the GetPosts() function in this same class so locations are loaded automatically when blog posts are (meaning if you wanted to you could easily list locations on any of the blog post index pages). To do so, we make the changes shown in Listing 13-5.

Listing 13-5. *Loading Locations Automatically in GetPosts() (BlogPost.php)*

```php
<?php
    class DatabaseObject_BlogPost extends DatabaseObject
    {
        // ... other code

        public static function GetPosts($db, $options = array())
        {
            // ... other code

            // load the locations for each post
            $locations = DatabaseObject_BlogPostLocation::GetLocations($db,
                                                                       $options);

            foreach ($locations as $l)
                $posts[$l->post_id]->locations[$l->getId()] = $l;

            return $posts;
        }

        // ... other code

    }
?>
```

We now have the necessary structures in place to load locations when blog posts are loaded, thereby allowing us to easily display the locations (or add them to the map).

Creating Our First Map

The remainder of this chapter will be dedicated to extending the blog post manager to allow users to add locations to their blog posts and then display them on their public blog accordingly. We will add a new page to the blog post management area that displays a map while also allowing the user to enter an address. We will then search on this address using the geocoder and add the found location to the map. Once the location has been added, the user will be able to move or remove the location from the map, or they will be able to add more locations.

All of this functionality will be implemented using a combination of the Google Maps API as well as using Ajax to save location data in our application database. We will develop a new class to manage the map as well as to send location data between the browser and our server.

To begin with, we'll create the most basic map possible to fit within our application, and then we'll build on it as we continue through this chapter.

Creating a New Blog Manager Controller Action

The first thing to do is to create a new action in the BlogmanagerController.php file. This page will simply be a placeholder to display the Google map and the form to add new locations. Since all functionality will be implemented via Ajax, this action won't need to do anything other than loading the blog post that locations are being added to. We will create another action handler shortly to deal with loading, saving, and removing locations from a blog post via Ajax.

Listing 13-6 shows the code for locationsAction(), which we add to BlogmanagerController. php in ./include/Controllers.

Listing 13-6. *The New Controller Action for Managing Locations (BlogmanagerController.php)*

```php
<?php
    class BlogmanagerController extends CustomControllerAction
    {
        // ... other code

        public function locationsAction()
        {
            $request = $this->getRequest();

            $post_id = (int) $request->getQuery('id');

            $post = new DatabaseObject_BlogPost($this->db);
            if (!$post->loadForUser($this->identity->user_id, $post_id))
                $this->_redirect($this->getUrl());

            $this->breadcrumbs->addStep(
                'Preview Post: ' . $post->profile->title,
                $this->getUrl('preview') . '?id=' . $post->getId()
            );
            $this->breadcrumbs->addStep('Manage Locations');

            $this->view->post = $post;
        }
    }
?>
```

If you were to now view this controller action (assuming you passed in a valid blog post ID in the URL of `http://phpweb20/blogmanager/preview?id=PostId`), an error would be displayed since we haven't created the corresponding template.

Listing 13-7 shows a template we can use for now until we create the map display code. This file is written to `locations.tpl` in the `./templates/blogmanager` directory.

Listing 13-7. *A Starting Template for Managing Blog Post Locations (locations.tpl)*

```
{include file='header.tpl' section='blogmanager' maps=true}

<div id="location-manager"></div>

{include file='footer.tpl'
        leftcolumn='blogmanager/lib/left-column.tpl'}
```

We will use the `#location-manager` div to hold the map. Note that we include `maps=true` when including `header.tpl`. We will modify that template shortly so the Google Maps API is loaded when this variable is specified.

Linking to the locationsAction() Function

Before we complete the template for the newly created action handler, we are going to link to it from the blog post preview page. Similarly to how tags and images are displayed on this page, we are going to add a block above the blog content that lists all locations that belong to the post. To cut down on page load time, we are not going to display the map on this page. Rather, we will provide a link to `locationsAction()` (which in turn will display the map).

First we display a block in the `preview.tpl` file in `./templates/blogmanager` that lists each existing location along with a link, as shown in Listing 13-8. We add this between the image management area and the blog post details.

Listing 13-8. *Displaying Locations in the Blog Post Preview Page (preview.tpl)*

```
<!-- // ... other code -->

<fieldset id="preview-locations">
    <legend>Locations</legend>

    <ul>
        {foreach from=$post->locations item=location}
            <li>{$location->description|escape}</li>
        {foreachelse}
            <li>No locations have been assigned to this post.</li>
        {/foreach}
    </ul>

    <form method="get" action="{geturl action='locations'}">
        <div>
```

```
            <input type="hidden" name="id" value="{$post->getId()}" />
            <input type="submit" value="Manage Locations" />
        </div>
    </form>
</fieldset>

<!-- // ... other code -->
```

Additionally, we must add some new styles to the `styles.css` file (in `./htdocs/css`) in order to make this block look like the tag and image management blocks, as shown in Listing 13-9.

Listing 13-9. *Styling the Locations Summary on the Blog Post Preview Page (styles.css)*

```
/* ... other code */

#preview-locations {
    margin     : 5px 0;
    padding    : 5px;
}

#preview-locations input, #preview-locations li {
    font-size  : 0.95em;
}

/* ... other code */
```

Displaying Your First Google Map

Now that the basic infrastructure in the blog manager is ready, we can begin our actual Google Maps implementation. To begin, we will look at how to load the Google Maps API as well as how to initialize and display the map. We will do this by creating a new JavaScript class in which all calls to the API are contained.

Loading the Google Maps API

The first thing we are going to do is load the Google Maps JavaScript file. Like most of the other scripts we have loaded in our application, we will load this in the `<head>` section of our HTML document. To do so, we must load the file from `header.tpl`.

Just like we did with Lightbox in Chapter 11, we want to load the Google Maps API only when we actually display a map. As such, we will add a conditional include for loading the JavaScript file.

To load the API, you must load the script at `http://www.google.com/jsapi?key=KEY`, where *KEY* is the Google Maps API you created earlier in this chapter and wrote to the application settings file.

■**Note** As mentioned previously, we are using the Google Ajax API loader, so if you have used Google Maps in the past, this URL may be different from what you're used to using. Using this loader allows you to easily use different Google APIs in your code while needing to load only one JavaScript file.

Since we require the `google.maps.key` setting we added earlier in this chapter to load the API, we require access to this value in the template. To make this available, we are going to assign the application settings to the template by default. This is not something we have needed in the past; however, it may be something you use if you want to output other application settings directly.

To allow this, we must make a minor change to the `CustomControllerAction` class, which is used to set up the default template data. Listing 13-10 shows the change we make to this class, which can be found in the `./include/Controllers/CustomControllerAction.php` file.

Listing 13-10. *Assign the Application Settings to the Template (CustomControllerAction.php).*

```php
<?php
    class CustomControllerAction extends Zend_Controller_Action
    {
        // ... other code

        public function postDispatch()
        {
            // ... other code
            $this->view->config = Zend_Registry::get('config');
        }
    }
?>
```

Now we can use the settings to load the Google Maps API. Listing 13-11 shows the code we add to `header.tpl` to load the required JavaScript if the `$maps` variable is set to `true`.

Listing 13-11. *Loading the Google Maps API If the $maps Variable Is True (header.tpl)*

```
<!-- // ... other code -->
<head>
    <!-- // ... other code -->

    {if $maps}
        <script type="text/javascript"
src="http://www.google.com/jsapi?key={$config->google->maps->key|escape}"></script>
    {/if}
</head>
<body>
    <!-- // ... other code -->
```

Beginning the BlogLocationManager JavaScript Class

We will now begin to write a new JavaScript class called BlogLocationManager, which will be responsible for loading the map, initiating geocoder requests, and initiating Ajax requests to load, save, update, and delete markers.

Because many features will be going into this class—bringing together the Google Maps API with what you learned previously in this book—we will build the class step by step. Initially, we'll display a hybrid map (combination of satellite and street map) with some basic controls, centered on the Googleplex—home of the people who brought you Google Maps!

■**Note** You must specify a starting point when displaying a Google map, so we'll simply use the coordinates returned by a geocoder request of Google's own address, as described earlier in this chapter. Once we have our own locations to display, we'll center the map on those locations instead, but for now we'll use this location so you can see how to actually use the API.

The first thing we must do in this class is to actually load the Google Maps API. Even though I said we loaded it earlier, in fact all we did is load the generic Google API. This API is used to load a number of different APIs offered by Google. To do so, we use the google.load() method. The first argument is the name of the API we want to load (in this case it is maps), while the second argument is the version of the API.

■**Tip** Being able to specify the version number allows you to run any version of the Google Maps API you please. For example, if an upgrade was made by Google that broke an existing application of yours, you could temporarily force your application to use the older version until you make your application compatible with the newest version.

For our purposes, we simply specify 2 as the API version, which uses the latest version of the Google Maps 2 code. As such, we need to call google.load('maps', '2') to load the Google Maps API. We do this before declaring the class so the API is ready to be used when the class is instantiated.

Listing 13-12 shows the initialization of the class. Inside the constructor (initialize()), we observe the onload event on the page. The Google documentation recommends that you display the map only after the page has completed loading. We will look at the loadMap() function shortly. As we have done previously for classes we have written, we bind the call to loadMap() to this so we have the correct context when inside the function.

Note that we store this code in a file called BlogLocationManager.class.js in the ./htdocs/js directory.

Listing 13-12. *Initializing the BlogLocationManager Class (BlogLocationManager.class.js)*

```
google.load('maps', '2');

BlogLocationManager = Class.create();

BlogLocationManager.prototype = {

    container : null,    // DOM element in which map is shown
    map       : null,    // The instance of Google Maps

    initialize : function(container)
    {
        this.container = $(container);
        Event.observe(window, 'load', this.loadMap.bind(this));
    },
```

Next we implement the loadMap() method, which is responsible for creating the map, as well as adding all of the controls and markers. We must perform some basic tasks related to managing maps correctly in our browsers. The first thing to do is call the google.maps.BrowserIsCompatible() function to ensure the user's browser can display maps. If it can't, we simply return from the function, thereby not making any calls to the maps API.

The other thing we do—which is extremely important—is to observe the window unload event. This means when the browser closes or the user navigates to a new page, we call the unloadMap() function. This allows us to perform any map shutdown code required, which we will soon see is important when we cover unloadMap().

Listing 13-13 shows the code we use to check for compatibility and to unload the maps correctly.

Listing 13-13. *Ensuring Browser Compatibility and Destructing the Map Correctly (BlogLocationManager.class.js)*

```
    loadMap : function()
    {
        if (!google.maps.BrowserIsCompatible())
            return;

        Event.observe(window, 'unload', this.unloadMap.bind(this));
```

We are now free to create the map by instantiating the google.maps.Map2 class. This class takes the container in which the map will be displayed as its first argument (additionally you can specify further options to customize the map in the second argument; however, we will not be using this).

Once the map has been created, we make the map display by setting the center of the display using setCenter(). This function takes an instance of google.maps.LatLng as its first argument, the zoom level as its second argument (with 20 being the maximum zoom level), and the type of map as the third argument (optional). The API documentation states that this method must be called before adding any controls or overlays to the map.

To make a hybrid map appear, we use G_HYBRID_MAP as the map type. The default value for the map type is G_NORMAL_MAP, while a satellite map can be specified using G_SATELLITE_MAP. Note that you can also use the setMapType() method to change the map type.

Next we can add controls to the map using the addControl() method. By default, six different controls are available to be added, although it is possible to create custom controls. We will add MapTypeControl (allows you to switch between map, satellite, and hybrid), LargeMapControl (a control with buttons to pan and zoom), ScaleControl (displays the map scale), and OverviewMapControl (displays a mini-map in the corner at a lower zoom level). The other available controls are SmallMapControl (the same as LargeMapControl but without zoom slider) and SmallZoomControl (zoom buttons only).

Listing 13-14 shows the remainder of the loadMap() function, which creates the maps, adds controls, and finally centers on the Googleplex.

Listing 13-14. *Initializing the Map and Centering on the Googleplex (BlogLocationManager.class.js)*

```
this.map = new google.maps.Map2(this.container);
this.map.setCenter(new google.maps.LatLng(37.423111, -122.081783),
                   16,              // zoom level
                   G_HYBRID_MAP);   // map type
this.map.addControl(new google.maps.MapTypeControl());
this.map.addControl(new google.maps.ScaleControl());
this.map.addControl(new google.maps.LargeMapControl());
this.map.addControl(new google.maps.OverviewMapControl());
},
```

Finally, we must create the unloadMap() function, which is called when the window unload event is fired. To unload the map, we simply need to make a call to google.maps.Unload(), a Google API function that cleans up internal data structures to release memory. If this function is not called, then browser memory leaks may occur (depending on the browser).

Listing 13-15 shows the code for unloadMap() as well as closing this initial version of BlogLocationManager.

Listing 13-15. *Correctly Unloading Google Maps (BlogLocationManager.class.js)*

```
unloadMap : function()
{
    google.maps.Unload();
}
};
```

Loading BlogLocationManager

To use this class, we must now load and instantiate on the locationsAction() template. We do this by loading the class in the ./templates/header.tpl file, as well as instantiating the class in the ./htdocs/js/scripts.js file.

Listing 13-16 shows the changes we make to header.tpl. This code assumes that if we've chosen to load the maps (as we did by including maps=true when including header.tpl from

./templates/blogmanager/locations.tpl) and we're in the blogmanager section, then we load the BlogLocationManager class.

Listing 13-16. *Loading the BlogLocationManager JavaScript Class (header.tpl)*

```
<!-- // ... other code -->
{if $maps}
    <script type="text/javascript"
src="http://www.google.com/jsapi?key={$config->google->maps->key|escape}"></script>

    {if $section == 'blogmanager'}
        <script type="text/javascript"
                src="/js/BlogLocationManager.class.js"></script>
    {/if}
{/if}
<!-- // ... other code -->
```

Next we modify the locations.tpl template in ./templates/blogmanager so that BlogLocationManager is instantiated, as shown in Listing 13-17. Although this will create an instance of the class as soon as the line is read by the web browser, the map will be loaded only after the page has finished loading.

Listing 13-17. *Instantiating the BlogLocationManager Class (locations.tpl)*

```
{include file='header.tpl' section='blogmanager' maps=true}

<div id="location-manager"></div>

<script type="text/javascript">
    new BlogLocationManager('location-manager');
</script>

{include file='footer.tpl'
        leftcolumn='blogmanager/lib/left-column.tpl'}
```

As we just mentioned, we must specify a height for #location-manager. Google Maps will automatically fill its entire container, so we must specify a height so the map is loaded correctly (note that divs are block elements so automatically have a 100 percent width by default). Listing 13-18 shows the new selector we add to styles.css.

Listing 13-18. *Setting the Height of the Map Container (styles.css)*

```
#location-manager { height : 400px; }
```

If you now log in to the web application and try to manage locations for an existing blog post, you should see a map on your page, similar to that in Figure 13-3.

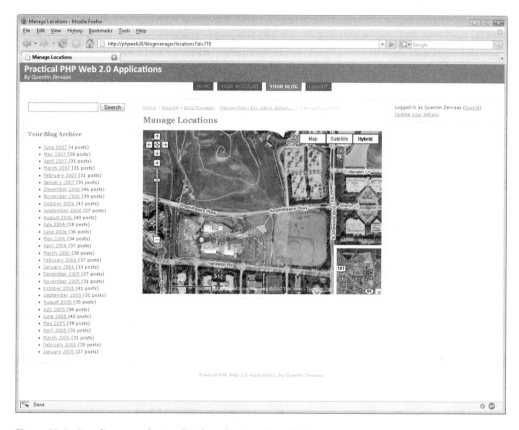

Figure 13-3. *Our first map being displayed using Google Maps*

Managing Locations on the Map

The next step is to extend the location management page and JavaScript class to allow users to enter the address they want to add to their map. We will then perform a geocoder request to find the coordinates for the entered address and add it to the map. Additionally, we will use Ajax in the background to save the location to the database for the active blog post.

Once an address is displayed on the map, the user will have the option of dragging it to a new location (which will result in the new coordinates being saved via Ajax) or deleting it altogether from the map.

Handling Location Management Ajax Requests

We'll first create a new action handler (once again in `BlogmanagerController`) to handle each of the different possible Ajax requests, each of which will return JSON data to the requesting script. The four different actions we are going to handle are as follows:

- **Get.** We use this action to return each of the locations saved in the database for the current blog post. Initially there will be no locations to return.

- **Add.** This is called to save a new location to the database. We will write a new form-processing class to aid with this. Once a new location has successfully been saved to the database, we will return its ID as well as the coordinates and description. When the location data is returned, we will add it to the Google map.

- **Delete.** This action is called to remove a location from the database. We must also tell the Google map to remove the location from its display in real time.

- **Move.** This action is used to update the coordinates of an existing location. It will be initiated after the user drags and drops a location to a new point on the map.

The New Location Form Processor

As mentioned earlier, to add new locations to the database, we must write a new form processor. This class is almost identical to other form-processing classes we have written throughout this book, so it is just shown in Listing 13-19. We store it in a file called BlogPostLocation.php in the ./include/FormProcessor directory.

Listing 13-19. *Processing New Locations and Saving Them Accordingly (BlogPostLocation.php)*

```php
<?php
    class FormProcessor_BlogPostLocation extends FormProcessor
    {
        protected $post;
        public $location;

        public function __construct(DatabaseObject_BlogPost $post)
        {
            parent::__construct();

            $this->post = $post;

            // set up the initial values for the new location
            $this->location = new DatabaseObject_BlogPostLocation($post->getDb());
            $this->location->post_id = $this->post->getId();
        }

        public function process(Zend_Controller_Request_Abstract $request)
        {
            $this->description = $this->sanitize($request->getPost('description'));
            $this->longitude   = $request->getPost('longitude');
            $this->latitude    = $request->getPost('latitude');

            // if no errors have occurred, save the location
            if (!$this->hasError()) {
                $this->location->description = $this->description;
                $this->location->longitude   = $this->longitude;
                $this->location->latitude    = $this->latitude;
                $this->location->save();
```

```
            }

            return !$this->hasError();
        }
    }
?>
```

Additionally, we must modify the `DatabaseObject_BlogPostLocation` class to ensure valid coordinates are being set. Just as we did when saving new users to the database, we create the `__set()` method in this class to preprocess these values.

Listing 13-20 shows the code we add to the `BlogPostLocation.php` file in the `./include/DatabaseObject` directory. All we are doing is formatting the latitude and longitude into a number with six decimal points (the Google API documentation states that this precision corresponds to a resolution of 4 inches/11 centimeters).

Listing 13-20. *Formatting the Latitude and Longitude (BlogPostLocation.php)*

```php
<?php
    class DatabaseObject_BlogPostLocation extends DatabaseObject
    {
        // ... other code

        public function __set($name, $value)
        {
            switch ($name) {
                case 'latitude':
                case 'longitude':
                    $value = sprintf('%01.6lf', $value);
                    break;
            }

            return parent::__set($name, $value);
        }

        // ... other code
    }
?>
```

Creating the locationsManage Controller Action

Now that the form processor is complete, we can write the action handler used to manage locations. As stated earlier, this must handle four different operations (get, add, delete, and move).

First, we must initialize the function, shown in Listing 13-21. Since all of the Ajax requests will specify the action and post_id parameters, we extract them from the request and then try to load the corresponding blog post. Additionally, since we will be returning JSON data for each action, we initialize the $ret array, which will hold the return data.

Listing 13-21. *Initializing the Action Handler and Loading the Blog Post (BlogmanagerController.php)*

```php
<?php
    class BlogmanagerController extends CustomControllerAction
    {
        // ... other code

        public function locationsManageAction()
        {
            $request = $this->getRequest();

            $action  = $request->getPost('action');
            $post_id = $request->getPost('post_id');

            $ret = array('post_id' => 0);

            $post = new DatabaseObject_BlogPost($this->db);

            if ($post->loadForUser($this->identity->user_id, $post_id)) {
                $ret['post_id'] = $post->getId();
```

Next we handle the first of the operations: get. When a blog post is loaded, its corresponding locations are loaded automatically (remember we added that functionality to the postLoad() function earlier this chapter).

To complete this action, we loop over these locations and add to the $ret array accordingly, as shown in Listing 13-22. The data required to add the locations to the map include the location ID, its coordinates, and its description.

Listing 13-22. *Handling the get Action (BlogmanagerController.php)*

```php
            switch ($action) {
                case 'get':
                    $ret['locations'] = array();
                    foreach ($post->locations as $location) {
                        $ret['locations'][] = array(
                            'location_id' => $location->getId(),
                            'latitude'    => $location->latitude,
                            'longitude'   => $location->longitude,
                            'description' => $location->description
                        );
                    }

                    break;
```

Now we handle the add operation, which uses the form processor we just created. When we extend the BlogLocationManager JavaScript class later in this chapter, we will actually render the new location on the map only once the form processor has completed correctly.

Additionally, the point will be rendered only based on the returned JSON data. As such, if there's an error adding the point to the database, we don't include it in the return data. Listing 13-23 shows the code we use to process the new location.

Listing 13-23. *Processing the Request to Add a New Location (BlogmanagerController.php)*

```
case 'add':
    $fp = new FormProcessor_BlogPostLocation($post);

    if ($fp->process($request)) {
        $ret['location_id'] = $fp->location->getId();
        $ret['latitude']    = $fp->location->latitude;
        $ret['longitude']   = $fp->location->longitude;
        $ret['description'] = $fp->location->description;
    }
    else
        $ret['location_id'] = 0;

    break;
```

Next, we handle the delete operation. This is simply a matter of loading the location to be deleted using the submitted location_id value and then calling the delete() method, as shown in Listing 13-24. Additionally, we set the location_id value in the return data so we can remove the point from the map once its deletion has been confirmed.

Listing 13-24. *Deleting Locations from the Database (BlogManagerController.php)*

```
case 'delete':
    $location_id = $request->getPost('location_id');
    $location = new DatabaseObject_BlogPostLocation($this->db);
    if ($location->loadForPost($post->getId(), $location_id)) {
        $ret['location_id'] = $location->getId();
        $location->delete();
    }

    break;
```

Finally, we process the move operation. This works by loading the location and then updating the longitude and latitude. We return the location data from this method so we can replot the point once the request has been confirmed. Typically this will result in no change, but if for some reason the new location isn't saved, then the point will be moved back to the location that is saved in the database.

Listing 13-25 shows the code we use to update a single point in the database and close the locationsmanageAction() function.

Listing 13-25. *Processing the Move Location Request (BlogmanagerController.php)*

```
case 'move':
    $location_id = $request->getPost('location_id');
```

```
                            $location = new DatabaseObject_BlogPostLocation($this->db);
                            if ($location->loadForPost($post->getId(), $location_id)) {
                                $location->longitude = $request->getPost('longitude');
                                $location->latitude  = $request->getPost('latitude');
                                $location->save();

                                $ret['location_id'] = $location->getId();
                                $ret['latitude']     = $location->latitude;
                                $ret['longitude']    = $location->longitude;
                                $ret['description'] = $location->description;
                            }
                            break;
                    }
                }

                $this->sendJson($ret);
            }
        }
?>
```

▪Note The previous code is used purely to process Ajax requests for managing locations. Since you should provide a non-JavaScript solution to all forms, try updating the previous function to handle normal form requests. Most of the functionality you require is already in place, but you'll need to use the Google geocoder web service (located at http://maps.google.com/maps/geo) to determine the coordinates of the submitted location (as you will see soon, the form element the address will be held in is called location). You can find more information about this web service at http://www.google.com/apis/maps/documentation/services.html#Geocoding_Direct. Additionally, once the previous function has finished processing, you will need to return to the locationsAction() controller action rather than sending JSON data. You can check whether you need to process the Ajax or the non-Ajax request by using $request->isXmlHttpRequest().

Creating the Address Lookup Form

Now that the PHP code to manage locations has been completed, it's time to develop the client-side part of the solution. First we must extend the locations.tpl template to display a form to allow users to add new locations. We set this form up just like a normal HTML form, which makes developing the non-Ajax version simpler (see the previous exercise). In the BlogLocationManager JavaScript class, we will extract the URL and post ID from the form.

Note that we also change the instantiation of BlogLocationManager to include the form as the first argument to the constructor in addition to the container in which the map is held. We will update the class accordingly shortly.

Listing 13-26 shows the new version of locations.tpl, stored in ./templates/blogmanager. The added or changed lines are highlighted accordingly.

Listing 13-26. *The Locations Management Template with Add Location Form (locations.tpl)*

```
{include file='header.tpl' section='blogmanager' maps=true}

<form method="post"
      action="{geturl action='locationsmanage'}"
      id="location-add">

    <div>
        <input type="hidden" name="post_id" value="{$post->getId()}" />

        Add a new location:
        <input type="text" name="location" />
        <input type="submit" value="Add Location" />
    </div>
</form>

<div id="location-manager"></div>

<script type="text/javascript">
    new BlogLocationManager('location-manager', 'location-add');
</script>

{include file='footer.tpl'
         leftcolumn='blogmanager/lib/left-column.tpl'}
```

Extending the BlogLocationManager JavaScript Class

It is now time to build on the BlogLocationManager class we developed earlier in this chapter. Because the changes we will be making are somewhat extensive, I will cover creation of the class from start to finish rather than simply adding to the existing code.

All code developed in the following sections belongs in the BlogLocationManager.class.js file in the ./htdocs/js directory.

Required Methods

Because the functionality we are implementing is somewhat complex, there are a large number of methods we need to create. Here is a list of each of the methods we will create in BlogLocationManager, including the arguments passed and a brief description of what the method does:

- initialize(container, form): This sets up the class and links the add location form to the map by observing the necessary events.

- loadMap(): This creates the actual map and displays it once the page has loaded. Additionally, it will initiate the request to fetch all existing locations for the current blog post.

- `zoomAndCenterMap()`: This automatically zooms the map in as far as possible to display all of the locations. This will be called when the map is initially loaded and also when a new location is added. If there are no locations to work with, the map will show the entire earth.

- `addMarkerToMap(location_id, lat, lng, desc)`: This adds a marker to the map based on the arguments. This includes creating an information window that displays a delete button. If a marker with the given `location_id` already exists, then the existing marker is removed, and the new one is added.

- `removeMarkerFromMap(location_id)`: This removes a marker from the map based on the first argument. If the marker doesn't exist, then nothing happens.

- `hasMarker(id)`: This checks whether a marker exists for the given location ID.

- `loadLocationsSuccess(transport)`: This handles the response from the Ajax request to retrieve locations (called when the map is first shown). This loops over each returned location and adds it to the map with `addMarkerToMap()`.

- `onFormSubmit(e)`: This is the event handler for when the form to add a new location is submitted. This will initiate a request to the geocoder.

- `createPoint(locations)`: This handles the response from the geocoder by submitting the first match back to the server using Ajax to save it to the database.

- `createPointSuccess(transport)`: This handles the response from the Ajax request to save the point. If the point was successfully saved, this will then call `addMarkerToMap()` to display the new point on the map.

- `dragComplete(marker)`: This is called after a marker has been dragged and dropped to a new location. We initiate the Ajax request to save the new coordinates (the move action) to the database.

- `onDragCompleteSuccess(transport)`: This handles the response from the Ajax request to save a dragged marker's new location. This method expects to receive the latitude and longitude of the point so it can be replotted. This means if for some reason the new coordinates were not saved, the point will revert to the location saved in the database.

- `onRemoveMarker(e)`: This is the event handler called when the remove location button is clicked on a marker's information window. This will initiate the Ajax request to delete the location from the database.

- `onRemoveMarkerSuccess(transport)`: This is called after the Ajax request to delete a location from the database successfully returns. This function will remove the marker from the map.

- `unloadMap()`: Just like in the previous version of this class, this is responsible for cleaning up the map. This involves calling the `google.maps.Unload()` API function.

Class Initialization

To begin this class, we set up a number of variables used to hold the object properties, as well as creating the initialize method. Listing 13-27 shows the code we use to create the class and set up holders for the processor URL, the post ID, the map container, the map object, and the geocoder object. Remember that we need to load the Google Maps API at the start.

This code belongs in the `BlogLocationManager.class.js` file in the `./htdocs/js` directory.

Listing 13-27. *Creating the Class Properties (BlogLocationManager.class.js)*

```
google.load('maps', '2');

BlogLocationManager = Class.create();

BlogLocationManager.prototype = {

    url       : null,

    post_id   : null,    // ID of the blog post being managed
    container : null,    // DOM element in which map is shown
    map       : null,    // The instance of Google Maps
    geocoder  : null,    // Used to look up addresses
```

Next we create a new hash to hold all the markers that are on the map. We could use an array for this; however, we are indexing the hash by the location ID, allowing us to easily access the marker for the corresponding database record. This makes it easier since we don't need to search for the item we're looking for—we can simply use the location ID as the key to retrieve the item. Also, note that we use the Prototype $H() method to extend the hash.

We also create a new instance of Prototype's `Template` class to hold the layout for marker information windows (see Chapter 5 for more information about the `Template` class). This template will display the location description with a button to remove the location from the database below it. When adding a new marker (with `addMarkerToMap()`), we will use this template and attach the `click` event to the created button.

Listing 13-28 shows the code used to create the markers hash and information window template.

Listing 13-28. *Creating an Information Window Template and a Hash to Hold All Markers (BlogLocationManager.class.js)*

```
    markers    : $H({}), // holds all markers added to map

    markerTemplate : new Template(
        '<div>'
      + '    #{desc}<br />'
      + '    <input type="button" value="Remove Location" />'
      + '</div>'
    ),
```

Now we create the `initialize()` method (the class constructor). In this method, we access the add location form to retrieve the URL of the locations manager action as well as the post ID (using the Prototype `$F()` function, a shortcut to retrieve the value of a form element).

We then create the geocoder object using the `google.maps.ClientGeocoder` class. We could instantiate this when a geocoder request is initiated; however, since it may be used multiple times, it's just as easy to create it once now.

Finally, we observe two events, as shown in Listing 13-29. First, the window `onload` event is used since the map should be created and displayed only after the page has loaded. Second, we observe the `onsubmit` event on the location add form.

Listing 13-29. *The Class Constructor, Setting Up Class Properties and Observing Events (BlogLocationManager.class.js)*

```
initialize : function(container, form)
{
    form          = $(form);
    this.url      = form.action;
    this.post_id  = $F(form.post_id);
    this.container = $(container);

    this.geocoder = new google.maps.ClientGeocoder();

    Event.observe(window, 'load', this.loadMap.bind(this));
    form.observe('submit', this.onFormSubmit.bindAsEventListener(this));
},
```

The loadMap() Function

Next we create the `loadMap()` function, which is somewhat similar to the earlier version of `loadMap()` we created, in that we check for browser compatibility and set up the window `onunload` event. We can now call the new `zoomAndCenterMap()`, which we will look at next, rather than hard-coding the map to center on the Googleplex.

After this we create the various map controls. The mini-map (`google.maps.OverviewMapControl` class) is first assigned to the `overviewMap` variable. This allows us to hide it immediately. This means the mini-map appears as a small arrow in the bottom-right corner, which can subsequently be opened by the user if required.

Next we change the way zooming works in the map. First we allow the user to zoom the map by double-clicking it (using the `enableDoubleClickZoom()` function), and then we enable smooth zooming (using `enableContinuousZoom()`) so when the map zooms, it gradually moves to the new zoom level.

Finally, we initiate the Ajax request to retrieve existing locations from the database. This uses the `get` operation that we created in `locationsManageAction()`. We will shortly look at the `loadLocationsSuccess()` callback the Ajax request uses. Listing 13-30 shows the full code for the `loadMap()` function.

Listing 13-30. *Creating the Map and Loading Existing Locations (BlogLocationManager.class.js)*

```
loadMap : function()
{
    if (!google.maps.BrowserIsCompatible())
        return;

    Event.observe(window, 'unload', this.unloadMap.bind(this));

    this.map = new google.maps.Map2(this.container);
    this.zoomAndCenterMap();

    this.map.addControl(new google.maps.MapTypeControl());
    this.map.addControl(new google.maps.ScaleControl());
    this.map.addControl(new google.maps.LargeMapControl());

    var overviewMap = new google.maps.OverviewMapControl();
    this.map.addControl(overviewMap);
    overviewMap.hide(true);

    this.map.enableDoubleClickZoom();
    this.map.enableContinuousZoom();

    var options = {
        parameters : 'action=get&post_id=' + this.post_id,
        onSuccess  : this.loadLocationsSuccess.bind(this)
    }

    new Ajax.Request(this.url, options);
},
```

The zoomAndCenterMap() Function

As explained earlier, to initialize the map, we need to set its center; however, since each blog post can have multiple points, we want to make all points visible. Rather than showing a map of the entire world, we want to zoom the map as far in as possible (while still showing all points), since that will make it easier to see each point.

To do this, we implement the zoomAndCenterMap() function, which determines the centermost point of the map based on the locations that have been added. Additionally, it determines the highest possible zoom level that can be used while still showing all of the added locations.

This function works by first calculating a rectangle that surrounds all points (also called a *bounding box*). The Google Maps API provides a class called google.maps.LatLngBounds, which does exactly this. When instantiated, the bounding box is essentially empty since we haven't added any coordinates to it. To do so, we call the extend() function on the bounding box, which automatically extends it based on the point passed to extend() (an instance of google.maps.LatLng).

Next we check whether the bounding box is empty (like it will be if no locations have been added to the blog post yet). In this instance, we simply hard-code coordinates and set a zoom level of 1. This effectively displays a map of the whole earth. The specific coordinates don't really matter at this zoom level, so we just use 0,0.

In the case where the bounding box is not empty (that is, where there is at least one point on the map), we call the getBoundsZoomLevel() function on the map object, passing the bounding box as its only argument. This function returns the highest possible zoom level that includes the entire box. Because we run the risk of points hiding behind map controls (since they are in the corners), we decrease the zoom level by 1 as a small buffer.

Finally, we call setCenter() on the map object to reposition it at the center of the bounding box (retrieved by calling getCenter()) and the zoom level we just calculated. Listing 13-31 shows the code for zoomAndCenterMap(). We make several calls to this function, because it is a handy reset function to give the user a complete overview of the current state of the map locations.

Listing 13-31. *Automatically Recentering the Map Based on Added Locations (BlogLocationManager.class.js)*

```
zoomAndCenterMap : function()
{
    var bounds = new google.maps.LatLngBounds();
    this.markers.each(function(pair) {
        bounds.extend(pair.value.getPoint());
    });

    if (bounds.isEmpty()) {
        this.map.setCenter(new google.maps.LatLng(0, 0),
                     1,
                     G_HYBRID_MAP);
    }
    else {
        var zoom = Math.max(1, this.map.getBoundsZoomLevel(bounds) - 1);
        this.map.setCenter(bounds.getCenter(), zoom);
    }
},
```

Adding Locations with addMarkerToMap()

Next we create addMarkerToMap(), which adds a new marker onto the map with a corresponding information window (which will not be shown initially). The function is reasonably complex, because we must observe the events necessary for dragging markers as well as for removing them from the map.

Listing 13-32 shows the beginning of this function, in which we first remove any existing point that already exists for id (the ID of the location database record). We will look at removeMarkerFromMap() shortly.

Next we create the new marker by using the google.maps.Marker class. The first argument is an instance of google.maps.LatLng (which we create using the lat and lng arguments), while the second is a list of specific options for that marker. In our case, we set the title to be description (this is used as the hover text for the marker), and we set the draggable property to true, allowing the marker to be dragged.

Additionally, we assign the ID of the location to the location_id property. Although this isn't a standard property for markers in Google Maps, we need this value later when handling a marker being dragged to a new location.

Listing 13-32. *Creating the New Draggable Marker (BlogLocationManager.class.js)*

```
addMarkerToMap : function(id, lat, lng, desc)
{
    this.removeMarkerFromMap(id);

    this.markers[id] = new google.maps.Marker(
        new google.maps.LatLng(lat, lng),
        { 'title' : desc, draggable : true }
    );
    this.markers[id].location_id = id;
```

Next we set up the dragging options. Because of the way the Google Maps API handles the drag events, we can't use the normal way of binding functions to this like we have in our other Prototype-based classes.

Inside the handler function, this refers to the marker being dragged. Since we want to call the dragComplete() method of our BlogLocationManager class, we need a different way to refer to the BlogLocationManager instance. To do this, we create a temporary variable called that, meaning that inside the dragend handler function, this refers to the marker that was dragged, while that refers to the BlogLocationManager instance.

▓**Note** If the Google Maps API passed the dragged marker as an argument to the event handler, then this workaround would not be required.

Once the marker has been created, we can add it to the map, as shown in Listing 13-33.

Listing 13-33. *Setting Up Marker Dragging and Then Adding It to the Map (BlogLocationManager.class.js)*

```
    var that = this;
    google.maps.Event.addListener(this.markers[id], 'dragend', function() {
        that.dragComplete(this);
    });
    google.maps.Event.addListener(this.markers[id], 'dragstart', function() {
        this.closeInfoWindow();
    });

    this.map.addOverlay(this.markers[id]);
```

Next we must create the information window, which will use the template created in Listing 13-27 for its content. To evaluate the template, we must pass the list of variables as the second argument to evaluate(). In the template we created earlier, we use only the desc variable; however, you might want to display any of the other variables in it also.

Once the HTML has been created, we need to attach the click event to the close button. To do this, the button must exist in the DOM and not just in an HTML string. We use the Scriptaculous Builder class to create the node in the DOM. We can then extract the button from the returned DOM so we can observe the click event on it.

Finally, we attach the created node to the marker using bindInfoWindow(). If we wanted to create the window and display it immediately, we would call showInfoWindow() instead. The other advantage of using bindInfoWindow() is that it automatically sets up the marker to open the information window when clicked (if we used showInfoWindow(), we would also need to then observe the onclick event to reopen it after it is closed).

Listing 13-34 shows the code we use to build the HTML node and attach the onclick event to the close button. We will look at the onRemoveMarker() function called when the button is clicked shortly.

Listing 13-34. *Building the DOM Node for the Information Window and Adding It to the Marker (BlogLocationManager.class.js)*

```
var html = this.markerTemplate.evaluate({
    'location_id' : id,
    'lat'         : lat,
    'lng'         : lng,
    'desc'        : desc
});

var node = Builder.build(html);
var button = node.getElementsBySelector('input')[0];

button.setAttribute('location_id', id);
button.observe('click', this.onRemoveMarker.bindAsEventListener(this));

this.markers[id].bindInfoWindow(node);

return this.markers[id];
},
```

Removing Markers Using removeMarkerFromMap()

Next we add the ability to remove markers from the map. This is not the same as deleting a location from a blog post (we do that using the delete button's click event handler, which in turn will call removeMarkerFromMap()).

Rather, this method is used to make the marker no longer appear on the map as well as unsetting the corresponding entry in the markers hash. It uses the hasMarker() method to see that the marker actually exists. We will implement hasMarker() next.

Listing 13-35 shows the code for `removeMarkerFromMap()`. After ensuring the marker exists, it calls the `removeOverlay()` API method on the `google.maps.Map2` object. After that, we use the Prototype `remove()` method to remove the element from the `markers` hash.

▌**Caution** In Prototype 1.6.0, the `remove()` method on the `Hash` object will be replaced by the `unset()` method.

Listing 13-35. *Removing a Marker from the Map (BlogLocationManager.class.js)*

```
removeMarkerFromMap : function(location_id)
{
    if (!this.hasMarker(location_id))
        return;

    this.map.removeOverlay(this.markers[location_id]);
    this.markers.remove(location_id);
},
```

Checking to See Whether a Marker Exists with hasMarker()

To determine whether a marker exists on the map, we implement the `hasMarker()` method. This works by searching the array keys for the provided location ID. The `indexOf()` JavaScript function returns `-1` if the argument isn't found; otherwise, it returns the array index of the element.

Listing 13-36 shows the code for `hasMarker()`. This method is used by the `removeMarkerFromMap()` and `onDragCompleteSuccess()`.

Listing 13-36. *Checking to See Whether a Marker Exists (BlogLocationManager.class.js)*

```
hasMarker : function(location_id)
{
    var location_ids = this.markers.keys();

    return location_ids.indexOf(location_id) >= 0;
},
```

Displaying Saved Locations with loadLocationsSuccess()

Next we handle the response from the earlier Ajax request to fetch existing blog post locations. You have seen several times earlier in this book how to handle returned JSON data. After decoding the data, we first ensure the response matches the current blog post and that the `locations` array is set.

Next we loop over each of the locations and call `addMarkerToMap()` accordingly. Once this has completed, we call `zoomAndCenterMap()` so the user can see all of the markers, as shown in Listing 13-37.

Listing 13-37. *Handling the Ajax Response for Existing Locations (BlogLocationManager.class.js)*

```
loadLocationsSuccess : function(transport)
{
    var json = transport.responseText.evalJSON(true);

    if (json.locations == null)
        return;

    json.locations.each(function(location) {
        this.addMarkerToMap(
            location.location_id,
            location.latitude,
            location.longitude,
            location.description
        );
    }.bind(this));

    this.zoomAndCenterMap();
},
```

Handling the Add Location Form Submission

Next we implement the onFormSubmit() function, which is called when the user submits the add location form. First we cancel the browser submitting the form by calling Event.stop() since we will be using the client-side geocoder to look up the entered location.

Then we retrieve the value of the added location. If the location isn't an empty string, we initiate a geocoder request by calling getLocations(). We use the createPoint() function as the callback when the request completes, as shown in Listing 13-38.

Listing 13-38. *Initiating a Geocoder Request When the Add Location Form Is Submitted (BlogLocationManager.class.js)*

```
onFormSubmit : function(e)
{
    Event.stop(e);

    var form = Event.element(e);
    var address = $F(form.location).strip();

    if (address.length == 0)
        return;

    this.geocoder.getLocations(address, this.createPoint.bind(this));
},
```

Handling the Geocoder Response with createPoint()

We now handle the response from the geocoder's `getLocations()` function. This returns JSON data containing details about the geocoder request, such as the request status and all the matching locations.

Note The data returned from this function is structured similarly to if you use the geocoder web service mentioned earlier this chapter. You can find an example of the data returned at `http://www.google.com/apis/maps/documentation/services.html#Geocoding_Direct`.

The first thing we do now is to check the status of the request. The data is held in a variable called `locations` (the name of the function's only argument), so the status value can be found in `locations.Status.code`. Listing 13-39 shows the different status codes. If at least one location is successfully found, the status value will equal `G_GEO_SUCCESS`.

Just to demonstrate how to handle these errors, I've included a `switch` statement that handles and describes each of the different errors that can occur. The error message is then written to the status box at the top of the column on the right.

Listing 13-39 shows the code we use to handle the different status codes that are returned. Note that if the request isn't successful, we simply return from the function after writing the status message, since the code following this is only for requests that have at least one returned location.

Listing 13-39. *Handling the Different Status Codes That Can Be Returned*

```
createPoint : function(locations)
{
    if (locations.Status.code != G_GEO_SUCCESS) {
        // something went wrong:
        var msg = '';
        switch (locations.Status.code) {
            case G_GEO_BAD_REQUEST:
                msg = 'Unable to parse request';
                break;
            case G_GEO_MISSING_QUERY:
                msg = 'Query not specified';
                break;
            case G_GEO_UNKNOWN_ADDRESS:
                msg = 'Unable to find address';
                break;
            case G_GEO_UNAVAILABLE_ADDRESS:
                msg = 'Forbidden address';
                break;
            case G_GEO_BAD_KEY:
                msg = 'Invalid API key';
                break;
```

```
                case G_GEO_TOO_MANY_QUERIES:
                    msg = 'Too many geocoder queries';
                    break;
                case G_GEO_SERVER_ERROR:
                default:
                    msg = 'Unknown server error occurred';
            }
            message_write(msg);
            return;
        }
```

Next we extract the first location from the list of returned locations, held in the `locations.`
`Placemark` array. To simplify matters, we just ignore any subsequent locations that are returned.
You may want to handle this differently (such as adding all of the locations and letting the user
then delete the ones they don't want).

Note Each returned place mark has an accuracy field associated with it. This lets you easily determine
the type of location that is returned. For example, an accuracy value of 8 means "address level accuracy,"
while 1 means "country level accuracy." You can find the different accuracy levels at `http://www.google.`
`com/apis/maps/documentation/reference.html#GGeoAddressAccuracy`.

We'll send the first location (placemark) found in the geocoder data back to the server
using Ajax. This is so we can save it to the database for the current blog post.

The response for each placemark includes a formatted address for the found placemark,
so even if the user doesn't include correct punctuation or capitalization of their location, the
geocoder will return a nicely formatted string (available in the `address` field).

The coordinates of the location can be retrieved from the `placemark.Point.coordinates`
array. The first element is the longitude, while the second is the latitude. A third element
(which we do not use) indicates the elevation.

Listing 13-40 shows the remainder of the `createPoint()` function, which extracts the place
mark and initiates the Ajax request.

Listing 13-40. *Submitting the New Location via Ajax (BlogLocationManager.class.js)*

```
        var placemark = locations.Placemark[0];

        var options = {
            parameters : 'action=add'
                    + '&post_id=' + this.post_id
                    + '&description=' + escape(placemark.address)
                    + '&latitude=' + placemark.Point.coordinates[1]
                    + '&longitude=' + placemark.Point.coordinates[0],
            onSuccess  : this.createPointSuccess.bind(this)
        }

        new Ajax.Request(this.url, options);
    },
```

Handling Successful Location Creation

Next we create the createPointSuccess() function, which is called after the response from the Ajax request in Listing 13-38 is returned. We first decode the JSON data from the response, and then we ensure the data corresponds to the current blog post.

We next create a new marker based on the returned data, which automatically displays the marker on the map. Since there is no function call available to open an information window after it has been bound to a marker, we simply trigger the click event on the marker, resulting in the information window opening.

Finally, we center and zoom the map so the new location is visible, as shown in Listing 13-41.

Listing 13-41. *Handling the Response from Creating a New Location (BlogLocationManager.class.js)*

```
createPointSuccess : function(transport)
{
    var json = transport.responseText.evalJSON(true);

    if (json.location_id == 0) {
        message_write('Error adding location to blog post');
        return;
    }

    marker = this.addMarkerToMap(
        json.location_id,
        json.latitude,
        json.longitude,
        json.description
    );

    google.maps.Event.trigger(marker, 'click');

    this.zoomAndCenterMap();
},
```

Saving New Coordinates for Dragged Locations

When creating new markers in addMarkerToMap(), we told the dragend event to call the drag-Complete() function. We receive the dragged marker as the only argument to this function. Using the location_id property we added to the marker when creating it, we can determine to which database record the marker corresponds. We then retrieve the new point coordinates and trigger the Ajax request to save them, as shown in Listing 13-42.

Listing 13-42. *Saving the New Coordinates for a Dragged Marker (BlogLocationManager.class.js)*

```
dragComplete : function(marker)
{
    var point = marker.getPoint();
    var options = {
```

```
            parameters : 'action=move'
                        + '&post_id=' + this.post_id
                        + '&location_id=' + marker.location_id
                        + '&latitude=' + point.lat()
                        + '&longitude=' + point.lng(),
            onSuccess  : this.onDragCompleteSuccess.bind(this)
        }

        new Ajax.Request(this.url, options);
    },
```

Handling the Response from Saving a Dragged Location

Next we handle the response from sending the Ajax request to save a dragged marker's
new location. When a marker's new location is saved in locationsManageAction() (in
BlogmanagerController), the location is returned via JSON.

We check the returned location_id value to ensure the marker exists on the map, and if
so, we readd it to the map using the given coordinates. If the new coordinates weren't saved,
then the old ones will be returned, therefore replotting the location in its previous location.
Finally, we trigger the click event on the marker so the information window opens.

Listing 13-43 shows the code for the onDragCompleteSuccess() function.

Listing 13-43. *Confirming the Coordinates of the Saved Location (BlogLocationManager.class.js)*

```
onDragCompleteSuccess : function(transport)
{
    var json = transport.responseText.evalJSON(true);

    if (json.location_id && this.hasMarker(json.location_id)) {
        var point = new google.maps.LatLng(json.latitude, json.longitude);

        var marker = this.addMarkerToMap(
            json.location_id,
            json.latitude,
            json.longitude,
            json.description
        );
        google.maps.Event.trigger(marker, 'click');
    }
},
```

Removing Markers from the Map

When the remove marker button is clicked in an information window, the onRemoveMarker()
function is called. The first thing we need to do is to determine which button was clicked.
We can then determine which database record the button corresponds to by retrieving the
location_id attribute.

Next we initiate the Ajax request to delete the record from the database. We use the onRemoveMarkerSuccess() function that we will look at shortly to handle the response from this Ajax request. The actual marker is removed only once it has been confirmed that the record has been deleted from the database.

Listing 13-44 shows the code for the onRemoveMarker() function, called when the remove button is clicked form a marker's information window.

Listing 13-44. *Removing a Marker from the Map and Database (BlogLocationManager.class.js)*

```
onRemoveMarker : function(e)
{
    var button = Event.element(e);
    var location_id = button.getAttribute('location_id');

    var options = {
        parameters : 'action=delete'
                    + '&post_id=' + this.post_id
                    + '&location_id=' + location_id,
        onSuccess  : this.onRemoveMarkerSuccess.bind(this)
    };

    new Ajax.Request(this.url, options);
},
```

Confirming the Deletion of the Marker

After the marker has been deleted, the onRemoveMarkerSuccess() method will be called to handle the response. It is only when this method is called that the marker is actually removed from the map. We do this using the removeMarkerFromMap() method, as shown in Listing 13-45.

Listing 13-45. *Handling the Response from the Location Deletion Ajax Request (BlogLocationManager.class.js)*

```
onRemoveMarkerSuccess : function(transport)
{
    var json = transport.responseText.evalJSON(true);

    if (json.location_id)
        this.removeMarkerFromMap(json.location_id);
},
```

Unloading the Map

As we saw earlier this chapter, we need to unload the map after the user browses away from the page (or if they close their browser). To achieve this, we simply called the google.maps.Unload() function, as shown in Listing 13-46, thereby completing the BlogLocationManager class.

Listing 13-46. *Unloading the Map with GUnload() (BlogLocationManager.class.js)*

```
unloadMap : function()
{
    google.maps.Unload();
}
};
```

Using BlogLocationManager

Once you have successfully updated your BlogLocationManager class with the code just covered, you will be able to easily add a new location simply by entering its address. For example, if you created a blog post about an upcoming event at Microsoft, you could enter Microsoft's address (1 Microsoft Way, Redmond), and your map would be updated accordingly, as shown in Figure 13-4. Note also the image shows the background HTTP request that occurs to save the location to the database.

Additionally, if the point wasn't sitting on the map exactly where you wanted it, you can click and drag it to a new location, which will automatically trigger a new Ajax request to save the updated coordinates when the marker is released.

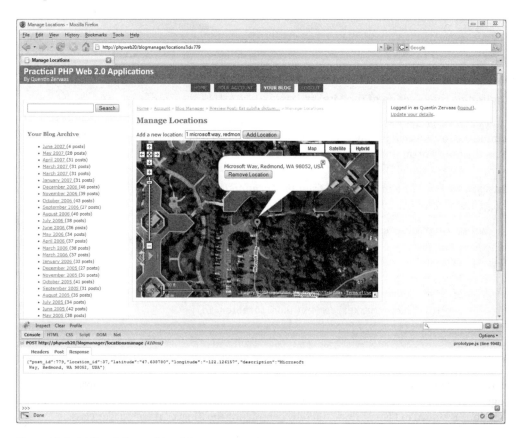

Figure 13-4. *Adding Microsoft's address to our map*

■Note You can try to extend the capabilities of the location editor by allowing users to change the description. The simplest way would be to create a new switch case in the `locationsManageAction()` function that retrieved the new description from the request and updated the corresponding location (remember to pass the post ID and location ID in the Ajax request). You would then modify the information window to allow editing of the description and initiate the Ajax request when the user confirms the new description. Scriptaculous provides a class called `Ajax.InPlaceEditor` that allows users to double-click an HTML element, which then replaces the element with a text input or textarea field. When the user clicks away from the field, an Ajax request is initiated to save the new value. For more details on this class, you can view http://wiki.script.aculo.us/scriptaculous/show/Ajax.InPlaceEditor.

Displaying the Map on Users' Public Blogs

The final thing we need to do in this chapter is to display added locations on the blog post details page. The functionality required to achieve this is only a subset of that required to manage locations, because we simply add each location to the map and then center the map on those locations.

In the following sections, we'll create a new JavaScript class (called `BlogLocations`) to help us display the locations, and then we'll update the blog post display page to use the new class. Note that this class will only ever be used if there is at least one location on a blog post. If a post has no locations, then we don't display the map at all.

We will use the geo microformat when outputting locations to the map. The `BlogLocations` JavaScript class will search the page for all locations using this microformat and then add each found location to the map.

Outputting Locations Using the Geo Microformat

The geo microformat is a subset of the hCard microformat that we looked at in Chapter 10, used to include longitude and latitude coordinates on a page. We'll use this microformat to output any locations added to a blog post when the live post is viewed.

There are several way to mark up this data using geo, each of which uses the class name geo for the root element. The first way allows the inclusion of the coordinates only:

```
<div class="geo">
    <span class="latitude">37.423111</span>,
    <span class="longitude">-122.081783</span>
</div>
```

Alternatively, you can specify the coordinates using the `<abbr>` HTML tag and using the title tag as the machine-readable coordinate and the value of the element a human-readable format, like this:

```
<div class="geo">
    <abbr class="latitude" title="37.423111">+37° 25' 23.20"</abbr>,
    <abbr class="longitude" title="-122.081783">-122° 4' 54.42"</abbr>
</div>
```

The only problem with using either of these methods is that it doesn't allow us to include the location name with the coordinates. To cater for this, the geo microformat also allows the following format:

```
<abbr title="37.423111;-122.081783" class="geo">
    1600 Amphitheatre Pkwy, Mountain View, California
</abbr>
```

In this example, the value of the `<abbr>` is a descriptive version of the location, while the latitude and longitude are specified as the `title` attribute.

■Tip For more information about the geo microformat, read either `http://microformats.org/wiki/geo` or `http://microformatique.com/?page_id=132`.

We can now modify the blog post output page so locations are displayed on the page using this format. Listing 13-47 shows the code we add to the `view.tpl` template in `./templates/user`.

Listing 13-47. *Outputting Each Location Using the Geo Microformat (view.tpl)*

```
{include file='header.tpl' lightbox=true}

<!-- // ... other code -->

{if $post->locations|@count > 0}
    <div id="post-locations">
        <h2>Locations</h2>

        <ul>
            {foreach from=$post->locations item=location}
                <li>
                    <abbr class="geo"
                        title="{$location->latitude};{$location->longitude}">

                        {$location->description|escape}
                    </abbr>
                </li>
            {/foreach}
        </ul>
    </div>
{/if}

<!-- // ... other code -->

{include file='footer.tpl'
        leftcolumn='user/lib/left-column.tpl'
        rightcolumn='user/lib/right-column.tpl'}
```

In this code each of the locations is already available in the $post->locations variable, since we modified DatabaseObject_BlogPost earlier this chapter to automatically load them. We loop over this array and output any found locations in an unordered list. If there are no locations, we don't output anything.

If you now view a blog post that has at least one location assigned to it, you will see these locations listed on the page beneath the blog post details. Additionally, the Firefox Operator plug-in will find this location, as shown in Figure 13-5.

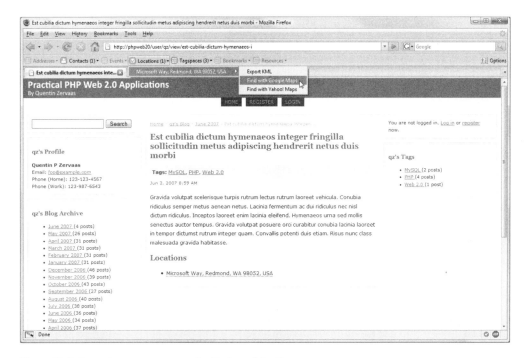

Figure 13-5. *Locations are automatically found by Operator.*

Creating the BlogLocations Class

We'll now write a JavaScript class to load the Google map on the blog post detail page. This class will search for locations we just added using the geo microformat and then add them to the map. We will call this class BlogLocations and store it in a file called BlogLocations.class.js in the ./htdocs/js directory.

Once again, we must initialize the class by loading the Google Maps API, setting up the map container, and observing the window onload event. Instead of passing the actual element in which the map will be shown to the constructor, we will pass the #post-locations element added in Listing 13-47. The map container will be a div inside #post-locations with a class name of .map. We will add this to the template shortly.

Listing 13-48 shows the code we use to initialize the BlogLocations class. Note that the template we use to display the information window is simplified because we don't need to display the remove location button. Once again, you may want to change this layout.

Listing 13-48. *Initializing the BlogLocations Class (BlogLocations.class.js)*

```
google.load('maps', '2');

BlogLocations = Class.create();

BlogLocations.prototype = {

    container   : null, // DOM element in that holds locations
    mapContainer : null, // DOM element that holds the map
    map         : null, // The instance of Google Maps

    markers    : $A([]), // holds all markers added to map
    markerTemplate : new Template('<div>#{desc}</div>'),

    initialize : function(container)
    {
        this.container = $(container);

        if (!this.container)
            return;

        this.mapContainer = this.container.down('.map');

        if (!this.mapContainer)
            return;

        Event.observe(window, 'load', this.loadMap.bind(this));
    },
```

Next we implement the `loadMap()` function, which is similar to the `BlogLocationsManager` class we implemented earlier this chapter in that we create the map and then set up various controls.

Listing 13-49 shows the code for `loadMap()`, which loops over all the elements that are found with the `.geo` class. Since the latitude and longitude are in the same string, we must split the string to extract them.

The reason we call `zoomAndCenterMap()` twice is because the map must be centered before adding any controls or overlays (according to the API documentation), and we want to center it on any found locations once they have been added.

Listing 13-49. *Displaying the Map and Adding the Locations (BlogLocations.class.js)*

```
    loadMap : function()
    {
        if (!google.maps.BrowserIsCompatible())
            return;

        Event.observe(window, 'unload', this.unloadMap.bind(this));
```

```
        this.map = new google.maps.Map2(this.container.down('.map'));
        this.zoomAndCenterMap();

        this.map.addControl(new google.maps.MapTypeControl());
        this.map.addControl(new google.maps.ScaleControl());
        this.map.addControl(new google.maps.LargeMapControl());

        this.map.enableDoubleClickZoom();
        this.map.enableContinuousZoom();

        this.container.getElementsBySelector('.geo').each(function(geo) {
            var coords = geo.title.split(';');
            this.addMarkerToMap(
                coords[0],
                coords[1],
                geo.innerHTML
            );
        }.bind(this));

        this.zoomAndCenterMap();
    },
```

Next we look at the `zoomAndCenterMap()` function, as shown in Listing 13-50. The algorithm for determining the viewport coordinates and zoom level is identical to `BlogLocationsManager`.

Listing 13-50. *Zooming and Centering the Map Based on the Added Locations (BlogLocations.class.js)*

```
    zoomAndCenterMap : function()
    {
        if (this.markers.size() == 0) {
            this.map.setCenter(new google.maps.LatLng(0, 0),
                               1,
                               G_HYBRID_MAP);

            return;
        }

        var bounds = new google.maps.LatLngBounds();
        this.markers.each(function(marker) {
            bounds.extend(marker.getPoint());
        });

        var zoom = Math.max(1, this.map.getBoundsZoomLevel(bounds) - 1);
        this.map.setCenter(bounds.getCenter(), zoom, G_HYBRID_MAP);
    },
```

Finally we look at the addMarkerToMap() function, as shown in Listing 13-51. This method creates the marker and corresponding information window for the arguments that are passed in, before being added to the map and being written to the markers array. The marker is stored in the markers array since the zoomAndCenterMap() needs to know all of the markers in order to work properly.

Listing 13-51. *Creating a New Marker and Adding It to the Map (BlogLocations.class.js)*

```
addMarkerToMap : function(lat, lng, desc)
{
    var marker = new google.maps.Marker(
        new google.maps.LatLng(lat, lng),
        { 'title' : desc }
    );

    var html = this.markerTemplate.evaluate({
        'lat'       : lat,
        'lng'       : lng,
        'desc'      : desc
    });

    marker.bindInfoWindowHtml(html);

    this.map.addOverlay(marker);
    this.markers.push(marker);
},

unloadMap : function()
{
    google.maps.Unload();
}
};
```

Updating the Blog Post Display Template

Now that the BlogLocations class is complete, we must update the blog post display template to use the class.

As mentioned, we are displaying the map on the page only if there is at least one location to display. Therefore, we must conditionally set the maps argument to true when including the header.tpl template. We can do this by calling $post->locations|@count, since nonzero values evaluate to true (in other words, if there are no locations, then the maps argument will be set to 0, which is effectively false).

Listing 13-52 shows the code we add to view.tpl in the ./templates/user directory to display the map.

Listing 13-52. *Displaying the Map on the Blog Post Details Page (view.tpl)*

```
{include file='header.tpl' lightbox=true maps=$post->locations|@count}

<!-- // ... other code -->

{if $post->locations|@count > 0}
    <div id="post-locations">
        <h2>Locations</h2>

        <ul>
            {foreach from=$post->locations item=location}
                <li>
                    <abbr class="geo"
                        title="{$location->latitude};{$location->longitude}">

                        {$location->description|escape}
                    </abbr>
                </li>
            {/foreach}
        </ul>

        <div class="map"></div>
    </div>

    <script type="text/javascript" src="/js/BlogLocations.class.js"></script>
    <script type="text/javascript">
        new BlogLocations('post-locations');
    </script>
{/if}

<!-- // ... other code -->

{include file='footer.tpl'
        leftcolumn='user/lib/left-column.tpl'
        rightcolumn='user/lib/right-column.tpl'}
```

We must also update the styles.css file (in ./htdocs/css) to set a height for the maps container. Additionally, since we don't want any images to overlap the map (since they are floated right), we add the clear : both style, as shown in Listing 13-53.

Listing 13-53. *Styling the Map Container (styles.css)*

```
#post-locations .map {
    height     : 400px;
    clear      : both;
}
```

Once you have updated this template and style sheet accordingly, your blog posts will be displayed with a map of any assigned locations, similar to that of Figure 13-6. This shows the location of Microsoft like we added in the previous section.

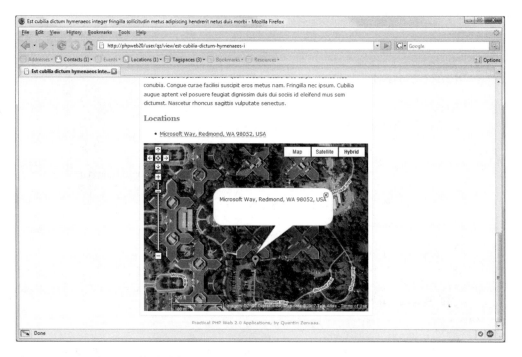

Figure 13-6. *Displaying all of a blog post's locations*

Summary

So there you have it—we have now added some fairly advanced mapping functionality to our application using Google Maps. What we did here really only scratched the surface of what can be done using the Google Maps API, but you can see how powerful it is.

Although Google probably doesn't recommend it, the Google geocoder on its own is a powerful tool that can be used in a wide range of applications (especially when you consider Google offers a non-JavaScript version of the geocoder that you can use on the server side).

To recap, the key concepts and features we covered in this chapter were as follows:

- Using a third-party service in conjunction with our own code to provide advanced functionality to users that we don't have the resources to provide ourselves. Be aware, though, that most third-party services are typically server-side based (as opposed to JavaScript).

- Creating structured classes with the help of Prototype to help manage a large number of Ajax operations. Since most Ajax requests will typically result in at least two functions (one to initiate the request and one to handle the response), the code can quickly grow and become unmanageable if not planned initially.

- Displaying and customizing maps using the Google Maps API. There are many different ways to customize maps, such as choosing which controls are displayed as well as for rendering markers and information windows. We didn't even touch on drawing poly-lines or polygons, but some powerful effects can be achieved by combining all of these features.

- Querying address and location data using the Google Maps geocoder. With a JavaScript interface as well as a web service (that returns XML or JSON data), it is easy to request location data regardless of whether the end-user has JavaScript enabled in their browser.

- Using the geo microformat to output locations in both a human- and machine-readable format and then reading this microformatted data using JavaScript.

This brings us now to the final chapter of the book. In Chapter 14 we will look at some of the issues involved in the deployment and maintenance of web applications, including tying up some of the loose ends that have been created thus far in the code we have developed.

CHAPTER 14

■ ■ ■

Deployment and Maintenance

So far in this book we have developed a somewhat complete web application. Although features can be added to an application, there is an old saying that the last 10 percent of the development of an application takes 90 percent of the time.

What this typically refers to are all the little details in making the application something that can be used reliably by many people. In this chapter, I will cover some of the details that this refers to, such as handling errors and notifying the user accordingly that something went wrong, deploying the application on a production server, using application logs, and backing up the application.

Application Logging

In Chapter 2 we set up logging capabilities for our web application, meaning we can record when various events occur. Although the only events we actually recorded were related to user logins and blog indexing, the idea was that we put a foundation in place that can easily be used anywhere in the application whenever required.

Having said that, a logging system isn't much use if there's no way to use the log. In the following sections, I will talk more about the logging system and show how it can be extended and used.

The reason for looking at the logging system first in this chapter is that the changes we will make later in this chapter for handling site errors rely partly on the features added here.

E-mailing Critical Errors to an Administrator

Zend_Log provides the ability to have multiple writers for a single logger. A *writer* is a class that is used to output log messages, be it to a file (as we have done so far), a database, or an e-mail.

The Zend Framework doesn't ship with a writer that can e-mail log messages, but we can easily write our own by extending the Zend_Log_Writer_Abstract class. We then register the new writer with the logger so critical errors can be sent to the e-mail address we will add to the application configuration.

Creating the Log Writer

The main log writers that come with the Zend Framework are the stream writer (for writing to files) and the database writer. Both of these writers record the message to their target locations as soon as the message is logged. If we were to do the same thing for our e-mail writer, then a new e-mail would be sent for every recorded message. Since a single request could result in several log messages, we must accumulate log messages and send them in one e-mail message at the completion of the request.

Thankfully, Zend_Log simplifies this by allowing us to define a method called shutdown(), which is automatically called (using PHP 5 class deconstructors) when the request completes. The shutdown() function we create will use Zend_Mail to send an e-mail to the nominated address.

We will call this class EmailLogger, which we store in ./include/EmailLogger.php. Listing 14-1 shows the constructor for this class. We create an array in which to hold the log messages until they are ready to be sent. Additionally, we use Zend_Validator to ensure a valid e-mail address has been included in the constructor arguments. By implementing the setEmail() function, we can easily change the target e-mail address during runtime if required.

The other key line of code to note here is the final statement where we instantiate Zend_Log_Formatter_Simple. With Zend_Log you can create a custom formatter, used to define how a log message appears in the writer's output. We will use the built-in Zend_Log_Formatter_Simple class (you saw an example of its output in Chapter 2), but you could also use the built-in XML formatter or create your own.

■**Note** If you want to use a different formatter, you would typically call the setFormatter() method on the writer once it has been instantiated rather than changing the code in the writer.

Listing 14-1. *Initializing the EmailLogger Class (EmailLogger.php)*

```php
<?php
    class EmailLogger extends Zend_Log_Writer_Abstract
    {
        protected $_email;
        protected $_events = array();

        public function __construct($email)
        {
            $this->_formatter = new Zend_Log_Formatter_Simple();
            $this->setEmail($email);
        }

        public function setEmail($email)
        {
            $validator = new Zend_Validate_EmailAddress();
            if (!$validator->isValid($email))
                throw new Exception('Invalid e-mail address specified');

            $this->_email = $email;
        }
```

Next we must create the _write() method, shown in Listing 14-2. This is an abstract method that is called internally when a new log message is recorded. In this method we simply need to write the message to the $_events array. As noted earlier, this array is used to hold the messages that are to be e-mailed until the e-mail is actually sent.

Before the message is written to the array, we must format the message using the formatter. If you prefer, you can write the raw message to the array here and format it when generating the e-mail body in shutdown().

Listing 14-2. *Formatting the Log Message and Then Accumulating It for Later Use (EmailLogger.php)*

```
protected function _write($event)
{
    $this->_events[] = $this->_formatter->format($event);
}
```

Finally, we implement the shutdown() method. As mentioned, this method is called automatically when the request ends. Our objective in this method is to generate an e-mail subject and body and then send the message using Zend_Mail. Obviously, if there are no log messages, then we don't want to send an e-mail at all, which is why the code checks whether $this->_events is empty before creating the e-mail.

Listing 14-3 shows the code for shutdown(). You may want to use different text for the subject and body than what I've listed here. I have simply included the number of messages in the subject and then joined the messages to make up the body.

■**Note** The default formatter puts a line feed after each message, so by joining on an empty string, each message will appear on a new line.

Listing 14-3. *Sending the Log Message E-mail in shutdown() (EmailLogger.php)*

```
public function shutdown()
{
    if (count($this->_events) == 0)
        return;

    $subject = sprintf('Web site log messages (%d)',
                        count($this->_events));

    $mail = new Zend_Mail();
    $mail->addTo($this->_email)
        ->setSubject($subject)
        ->setBodyText(join('', $this->_events))
        ->send();
    }
}
?>
```

Specifying the E-mail Recipient

Next we must define who receives the log e-mail. To do this we add a new setting to the configuration file (./settings.ini). Listing 14-4 shows this new value—remember to insert your own e-mail address accordingly.

Listing 14-4. *Specifying the Log Recipient (settings.ini)*

```
logging.file = /var/www/phpweb20/data/logs/debug.log
logging.email = admin@example.com
```

■**Note** You may have noticed there is a catch-22 developing. If the application cannot read the settings file (for example, if the file is missing or doesn't have read permissions), then the log file path and the recipient e-mail address cannot be determined for Zend_Log to record the error. We will resolve this in the "Site Error Handling" section by using the Apache server configuration.

Adding the EmailLogger Writer to Zend_Log

The next step is to instantiate the EmailLogger class and notify the logger about it. Before we can do this, there is one important step we have not covered yet. That is to filter messages by their priority. We want to send e-mails only for critical errors (while still writing all other messages to the filesystem log). This means we will filter out messages that don't have the priority levels Zend_Log::CRIT, Zend_Log::ALERT, and Zend_Log::EMERG.

To do this we use the Zend_Log_Filter_Priority class. This filter accepts the priority level as the first argument to the constructor. The default priority comparison operator is <=, meaning all messages matching that argument and lower will be matched. In our case, we will specify Zend_Log::CRIT as the priority level (this evaluates to a priority level of 2), which will therefore include Zend_Log::ALERT (priority level 1) and Zend_Log::EMERG (priority level 0).

Once the filter has been created, we add it to the writer using the addFilter() method. Listing 14-5 shows the code we add to the application bootstrap file, located in ./htdocs/index.php.

Note that in the EmailLogger class we implemented earlier, an exception is thrown if the provided e-mail address is invalid. Thus, we must catch this exception accordingly. In this code, we continue if an invalid e-mail address is used; however, in the code we add later this chapter, we will handle this using a global exception handler.

Listing 14-5. *Adding the E-mail Logger to the Application Bootstrap (index.php)*

```php
<?php
    // ... other code

    // create the application logger
    $logger = new Zend_Log(new Zend_Log_Writer_Stream($config->logging->file));

    try {
        $writer = new EmailLogger($config->logging->email);
```

```
        $writer->addFilter(new Zend_Log_Filter_Priority(Zend_Log::CRIT));
        $logger->addWriter($writer);
    }
    catch (Exception $ex) {
        // invalid e-mail address
    }

    Zend_Registry::set('logger', $logger);

    // ... other code
?>
```

To test that this works, you can simply add a fake message such as the following in your code. Just remember to remove it afterward; otherwise, you will receive many e-mails.

```
$logger->crit('Test message');
```

Now whenever a critical message is recorded in your application logger, you will automatically be e-mailed! If you have an e-mail address that sends you an SMS message whenever you receive an e-mail, you can be instantly notified when something critical occurs.

■**Caution** With a system such as this, you must be very careful how the e-mail reporting works, since you will be e-mailed for every single HTTP request on your site that generates an error. If you run a high-traffic site, it's likely you will bog down your own server and perhaps even be blacklisted from your mail server for sending so much e-mail. Because of this, you should strongly consider adding extra mechanisms so that duplicate messages aren't sent within a short timeframe. For example, you could hash the generated messages and write this hash to the filesystem (using either the application temporary directory or the system temporary directory). Then the next time you go to send an e-mail, look for the hash of the new messages; if it exists and its age is less than *n* minutes (such as 15 minutes), you can safely skip sending the e-mail.

Using Application Logs

It's difficult to say exactly how you should use your log files because everybody's mileage will differ. Certainly the e-mail capabilities improve the system in that you will be instantly notified if something goes wrong, but it's also good to audit application data.

As an example, we're tracking user login attempts. We are recording both successful and unsuccessful attempts. We recorded successful attempts with the "notice" priority, while we recorded unsuccessful attempts with "warning" priority.

If you wanted to find all unsuccessful login attempts, command-line tools such as grep will aid you with this:

```
# cd /var/www/phpweb20/data/logs
# grep -i "failed login" debug.log
2007-09-03T16:06:55+09:00 WARN (4): Failed login attempt from 192.168.0.75 user test
```

■**Note** The `-i` option for `grep` means the search is case-insensitive.

It can also be useful to watch the log files in real time when developing new functionality. This is especially so when you can't easily output debugging information directly to your browser (such as in an Ajax subrequest or when using a third-party service). You can use `tail -f` to achieve this, which means `tail` monitors the file for any changes and displays any new data in the file as it is written.

```
tail -f /var/www/phpweb20/data/logs/debug.log
```

■**Tip** You can press Ctrl+C to exit from `tail` when using the `-f` option. Also note that when you run this command, the last ten lines will be shown before monitoring for new content, just like when you run `tail` normally (assuming you don't specify the number of lines to be shown).

Another consideration you may need to make is managing the log files, since they can potentially grow quite large on a high-traffic site that records lots of debugging information. You may want to consider using a tool such as `logrotate`.

In any case, a solid foundation is now in place for your application logging and auditing needs. You can now easily add logging capabilities to any new classes you develop.

Site Error Handling

We are now going to change our code to handle any errors that may occur when users access the site. Several kinds of errors can occur in the day-to-day running of your web site:

- **Database errors.** This is any error relating to accessing the database server or its data. For example, the following are possible errors that may occur:

  - Connection errors, caused because the server or network may be down, the username or password are incorrect, or the database name is incorrect.

  - Query errors, caused when the SQL being used is invalid. If your application has been correctly developed and tested, then these should never occur.

  - Data errors, caused by violating a constraint in the database. This may occur if you enter a duplicate value in a unique field or if you delete data from a table that is referenced elsewhere via a foreign key. Once again, this should not occur if the application has been developed and tested correctly.

- **Application runtime errors.** This is a fairly broad title for basically any error (including uncaught exceptions) that occurs in code. Examples of application errors that may occur are as follows:

  - Filesystem and permission errors, such as if the application tries to read a file that doesn't exist or that it is not allowed to read. Similarly, if the application tries to write a file but isn't allowed to, then this will also cause an error. A file that your application reads that is in the incorrect format may also cause an error.

  - If your application accesses web services on remote servers, then how well your application runs is partly dependent on these servers. For example, if you process credit card payments using a third-party gateway, then that gateway must be operational for you to make sales on your site.

- **HTTP errors.** These are errors that occur based on the user's request. The most common HTTP error (and the one that we are going to cover in this section) is a 404 File Not Found error. Although many different errors can occur, other common errors are 401 Unauthorized (if a user tries to access a resource that they must be logged in for) and 403 Forbidden (if the user simply isn't allowed to access the resource).

■**Note** First, because of the Apache rewrite rules we set up for our application in Chapter 2, we won't be handling 404 errors in the "traditional way" that people do with Apache (using `ErrorDocument 404`). Rather, we will generate 404 errors when a user tries to access a controller or action that does not exist. Second, the 401 and 403 errors don't apply to our application, even though we have a permissions system. This is because we've implemented our own user login and permissions system, so the traditional HTTP codes don't apply.

Although we could have included the aforementioned error handling when setting up the application (specifically, for handling database and 404 errors), I have chosen to group it all together into this single section so you can see how the system reacts to errors as a whole.

Note that in some cases we have already handled various application errors that occur. An example of this is catching exceptions that have been thrown in various circumstances, such as in Chapter 12 when implementing blog post indexing capabilities.

In the error handling we are now going to implement, we will add handling capabilities to two areas of the application:

- Before the request is dispatched. This is to handle any errors that occur prior to dispatching the result with `Zend_Controller_Front`. In other words, it'll deal with any errors that occur with code inside the `index.php` bootstrap.

- While the request is being dispatched. This is to handle any errors that occur within the application, such as in a controller action or in one of the many classes we have written (errors that we haven't yet handled, that is). This also includes HTTP errors such as when the file isn't found (404).

Objectives of Error Handling

Before we implement any error handling, we must determine what we're actually trying to achieve by handling the error. An error handling system should do the following:

- **Notify the user that an error occurred.** Whether it is a system error or user error that has occurred, the user should still know that something went wrong and their request could not be completed correctly.

- **Record the error.** This may involve either writing the error to a log file or notifying the system administrator, or both. Typically a user error (such as a 404 error) is not something you'd need to notify the administrator about (although logging 404 errors can be useful in statistics analysis).

- **Roll back the current request.** If a server error occurs halfway through a client request, then any performed actions should be rolled back. Let's use the example of having a system that saves a user-submitted form to a local database and submits it to a third-party server. If the third-party server is down (resulting in an error), then the form shouldn't be saved locally and the user should be notified so. Note that our application isn't required to handle errors in this manner.

■**Note** This example is somewhat crude. In actual fact, if you had such a system, you would typically have an external process (such as a cron job/scheduled task) that was responsible for communicating with the third-party server rather than performing the action in real time while completing the user request. The local database record would then have a status column to indicate whether the form has been successfully submitted remotely. The example should demonstrate the point of rolling back the request.

Handling Predispatch Errors

First we are going to handle any errors that may arise prior to dispatching the user request. In our application, before we dispatch the request, we load the configuration file, initialize the application logger, and connect to the database. Additionally, we are going to catch any errors that were not caught elsewhere (that is, in the dispatch loop).

Essentially what we are going to do is to wrap all of the code in the application bootstrap (./htdocs/index.php) in a single try … catch statement, meaning if any error occurs (that hasn't otherwise been handled) in any part of handling the user request, we can deal with it in a single spot.

Notifying the User of Errors

When we detect that an error has occurred, we are going to redirect the user's browser to a static HTML page that has no reliance on the database or even on PHP for that matter. This page will simply tell them that something went wrong and their request could not be completed.

Listing 14-6 shows the code for the error.html file, which we store in the ./htdocs directory. When using this in a production site, you will probably prefer to customize this page further (by adding your logo and CSS styles).

Listing 14-6. *Notifying the User the Site Is Undergoing Maintenance (error.html)*

```
<!DOCTYPE html
    PUBLIC "-//W3C//DTD XHTML 1.0 Strict//EN"
    "http://www.w3.org/TR/xhtml1/DTD/xhtml1-strict.dtd">

<html xmlns="http://www.w3.org/1999/xhtml" lang="en" xml:lang="en">
    <head>
        <title>This site is undergoing maintenance</title>
        <meta http-equiv="Content-Type" content="text/html; charset=iso-8859-1" />
    </head>
    <body>
        <div>
            <h1>Site Under Maintenance</h1>

            <p>
                This site is currently under maintenance.
                Please check back shortly.
            </p>
        </div>
    </body>
</html>
```

Catching Errors

Now that we have an error template to display when something goes wrong, we are going to make some changes to the bootstrap file. Instead of having several try … catch constructs in this file, we are going to have only one. This will encompass nearly all of the code in index.php.

The only problem with this, however, is that we won't be able to write any of these errors to the log file, since the logger will be created inside the try block and therefore will not be available in the catch block. To deal with this problem, we are going to create the logger first, and instead of using the value from the configuration, we will use the Apache SERVER_ADMIN variable. If the web server has been configured correctly, then this should contain a valid e-mail address with which to contact the administrator.

We will use the SERVER_ADMIN value initially in the code and then use the logging.email value in the configuration file once settings.ini has been successfully loaded. If this value isn't set correctly in the Apache configuration, then this will be caught by the exception handler. Since Zend_Log requires at least one writer, I have used Zend_Log_Writer_Null to ensure there will always be a writer. If this is not done, then an error will occur in the exception handler, since we write the exception message to $logger.

■Note Zend_Log_Writer_Null is a special writer that just discards all messages without actually writing or sending them anywhere.

Listing 14-7 shows the beginning of the bootstrap file, stored in ./htdocs/index.php. This entire file will be shown in the coming listings.

Listing 14-7. *Using the Apache Configuration to Determine the Log E-mail Address (index.php)*

```php
<?php
    require_once('Zend/Loader.php');
    Zend_Loader::registerAutoload();

    // setup the application logger
    $logger = new Zend_Log(new Zend_Log_Writer_Null());

    try {
        $writer = new EmailLogger($_SERVER['SERVER_ADMIN']);
        $writer->addFilter(new Zend_Log_Filter_Priority(Zend_Log::CRIT));
        $logger->addWriter($writer);
```

Note that we use the $writer variable to hold the EmailLogger object so we can change the target e-mail address shortly.

Next is Listing 14-8, in which we load the application configuration. Next we modify the $logger object so it will write to the filesystem, as well as send critical log messages to the e-mail address in settings.ini rather than the SERVER_ADMIN value.

Listing 14-8. *Altering the Logger to Use the Configuration Values (index.php)*

```php
    // load the application configuration
    $config = new Zend_Config_Ini('../settings.ini', 'development');
    Zend_Registry::set('config', $config);


    // alter the application logger
    $logger->addWriter(new Zend_Log_Writer_Stream($config->logging->file));
    $writer->setEmail($config->logging->email);

    Zend_Registry::set('logger', $logger);
```

Next we have the database connection code. As mentioned when we first created the database connection code in Chapter 2, the actual connection is not made until the first query is performed. As such, the first thing we must do is force the database connection to be made so we can trap any potential connection errors upon start-up—not halfway through handling a user request.

To force the connection to be made immediately, we simply need to call the getConnection() method on the adapter object after it is instantiated, as follows:

```
$db = Zend_Db::factory($config->database->type, $params);
$db->getConnection();
```

If the connection fails, then an exception is thrown, just like one is if the call to factory() fails. We simply need to catch this exception and write a log message accordingly like we did earlier when loading the configuration.

Tip In actual fact, if the connection fails, then the exception thrown uses the Zend_Db_Adapter_Exception class. The call to factory() will throw an exception using Zend_Db_Exception. This allows us to easily trap the different exceptions accordingly within the same block of code. Since it doesn't matter to us which error occurs (that is, any error is enough for us to stop), we won't worry about differentiating between the exception types.

Listing 14-9 shows the database connection code as it stands in index.php.

Listing 14-9. *Forcing a Database Connection at Start-Up (index.php)*

```
// connect to the database
$params = array('host'     => $config->database->hostname,
                'username' => $config->database->username,
                'password' => $config->database->password,
                'dbname'   => $config->database->database);


$db = Zend_Db::factory($config->database->type, $params);
$db->getConnection();

Zend_Registry::set('db', $db);
```

Next we look at Listing 14-10, which is the code used to set up the authentication, create the front controller, set up the view renderer (to use Smarty), and create custom routes. Nothing is changed in this code, apart from that it is now all within the try … catch statement opened in Listing 14-8. I have included this code here simply so the entire index.php is shown.

Listing 14-10. *Setting Up the Front Controller and Its Routes (index.php)*

```
// setup application authentication
$auth = Zend_Auth::getInstance();
$auth->setStorage(new Zend_Auth_Storage_Session());

// handle the user request
$controller = Zend_Controller_Front::getInstance();
$controller->setControllerDirectory($config->paths->base .
```

```
                                        '/include/Controllers');
    $controller->registerPlugin(new CustomControllerAclManager($auth));

    // setup the view renderer
    $vr = new Zend_Controller_Action_Helper_ViewRenderer();
    $vr->setView(new Templater());
    $vr->setViewSuffix('tpl');
    Zend_Controller_Action_HelperBroker::addHelper($vr);

    // setup the route for user home pages
    $route = new Zend_Controller_Router_Route(
        'user/:username/:action/*',
        array('controller' => 'user',
              'action'     => 'index')
    );

    $controller->getRouter()->addRoute('user', $route);

    // setup the route for viewing blog posts
    $route = new Zend_Controller_Router_Route(
        'user/:username/view/:url/*',
        array('controller' => 'user',
              'action'     => 'view')
    );

    $controller->getRouter()->addRoute('post', $route);

    // setup the route for viewing monthly archives
    $route = new Zend_Controller_Router_Route(
        'user/:username/archive/:year/:month/*',
        array('controller' => 'user',
              'action'     => 'archive')
    );

    $controller->getRouter()->addRoute('archive', $route);

    // setup the route for user tag spaces
    $route = new Zend_Controller_Router_Route(
        'user/:username/tag/:tag/*',
        array('controller' => 'user',
              'action'     => 'tag')
    );

    $controller->getRouter()->addRoute('tagspace', $route);
```

Next we complete this file by dispatching the request, as well as catching any exceptions that may thrown. This is shown in Listing 14-11.

Listing 14-11. *Catching Exceptions and Redirecting*

```
        $controller->dispatch();
    }
    catch (Exception $ex) {
        $logger->emerg($ex->getMessage());

        header('Location: /error.html');
        exit;
    }
?>
```

Because the `$logger` object was created before the `try` … `catch` construct, we are able to write messages to it in the exception handler.

Application Runtime Errors

Next we must write code to handle application errors such as 404 errors or other unexpected errors. To do this we use the error handler plug-in. By default, `Zend_Controller_Front` loads the error handler plug-in, which will automatically look for a controller class called `ErrorController`.

When an unhandled exception is thrown during dispatch, `Zend_Controller_Front` will route the request to the `errorAction()` method of the `ErrorController` class. Because the error handler plug-in is registered automatically, we don't need to make any changes to the boot-strap to accommodate this class.

▪**Note** It is possible to use a different controller and action to handle the error, but by default the `error` action of the `error` controller is used.

To get information about the error that occurred, we retrieve the `error_handler` parameter from the request. Listing 14-12 shows the code we use to create the `ErrorController` class. This code should be written to a file called `ErrorController.php` in the `./include/Controllers` directory.

Listing 14-12. *Initializing the Error Handler Class (ErrorHandler.php)*

```
<?php
    class ErrorController extends CustomControllerAction
    {
        public function errorAction()
        {
            $request = $this->getRequest();
            $error = $request->getParam('error_handler');
```

Next we determine the type of error that occurred by checking the type property of the $error object. This variable can have one of the following values:

- EXCEPTION_NO_CONTROLLER is used if the requested URL did not match a controller (for instance, http://phpweb20/asdf).

- EXCEPTION_NO_ACTION is used if the requested URL did match a controller but didn't match an action within that controller (such as http://phpweb20/account/asdf).

- EXCEPTION_OTHER is used for all other errors that occur, regardless of what causes the error. Thus, if a database error occurs, this error type will be used.

We will treat either of the first two errors as a 404 error, since they effectively result from an invalid URL being requested. To further modularize this code, we will create a separate action in ErrorController for handling 404 errors, which we will call error404Action().

The code in Listing 14-13 shows how we detect the different types of errors and then forward on 404 errors accordingly. We will implement the error404Action() function shortly.

Listing 14-13. *Detecting the Type of Error That Has Occurred (ErrorController.php)*

```
switch ($error->type) {
    case Zend_Controller_Plugin_ErrorHandler::EXCEPTION_NO_CONTROLLER:
    case Zend_Controller_Plugin_ErrorHandler::EXCEPTION_NO_ACTION:
        $this->_forward('error404');
        return;

    case Zend_Controller_Plugin_ErrorHandler::EXCEPTION_OTHER:
    default:
        // fall through
}
```

■**Note** It'd be nicer to name this function 404Action() rather than error404Action(); however, it is a syntax error to begin an identifier (that is, a function or a variable name) with a digit.

Effectively what this means is that 404 errors now move out of this method because of forwarding the request (using the _forward() utility method). The remainder of the code in this function now is used to handle all other errors (that is, errors with the type EXCEPTION_OTHER).

Because the error might have occurred in the middle of a page being rendered, we must first clear the response that has already been generated by calling clearBody() on the response object. If you do not do this, the user may see half of their requested page followed by the error message.

Finally, we log the error message using the critical priority level. This means it will be e-mailed to the system administrator as we saw earlier in this chapter.

Listing 14-14 shows the code we use to clear the response body and then log the error. Note that after this function ends, the Zend_Controller_Front view renderer will automatically try to display the error.tpl template in the ./templates/error directory that we have not yet created. We will do so next after completing the code for the ErrorHandler class.

Listing 14-14. *Clearing the Response Body and Logging the Error (ErrorController.php)*

```
        $this->getResponse()->clearBody();

        Zend_Registry::get('logger')->crit($error->exception->getMessage());
    }
```

■Tip If you want to see this particular error handler in action, you can simply try throwing an exception from one of your existing controller actions. For example, try adding `throw new Exception('Testing the error handling');` to the `indexAction()` function of the `./include/Controllers/IndexController.php` file and then opening `http://phpweb20` in your browser. If you do this, make sure you remove this line of code after you have tested that it works correctly!

Next up we implement the `error404Action()` function that the previous function forwards to if the requested controller or action is not found. Our goal in this function is to first record the error, then set the appropriate HTTP error code (so the user's browser can interpret the response accordingly), and finally display a message to the user.

Since 404 errors can happen frequently and don't typically indicate a big problem, we don't consider them to be critical. As such, we use the `Zend_Log::INFO` priority level (by calling the `info()` method on the logger). This means the message will be written to the log file but not e-mailed to the administrator. You may want to keep an eye on these messages since they may indicate an incorrect link somewhere.

The final step in this function is to create a page title (using the `$breadcrumbs` object) and assign the requested URI to the template so we can output it to indicate to the user that the file wasn't found. Listing 14-15 shows the code to be added to the `ErrorController.php` file.

Listing 14-15. *Handling 404 Errors by Writing to the Log and Sending the Appropriate Response (ErrorHandler.php)*

```
    public function error404Action()
    {
        $request = $this->getRequest();
        $error   = $request->getParam('error_handler');
        $uri     = $request->getRequestUri();

        Zend_Registry::get('logger')->info('404 error occurred: ' . $uri);

        $this->getResponse()->setHttpResponseCode(404);

        $this->breadcrumbs->addStep('404 File Not Found');
        $this->view->requestedAddress = $uri;
    }
}
?>
```

Creating the Error Display Templates

Now that the PHP code for the error handler is complete, we must create a template for each of the controller actions. First we create the template used to display a message when an application error occurs. The location of this file is `./templates/error/error.tpl`. This is the first time we've used this `error` directory, so you'll probably have to create it first. As noted earlier, you can throw a fake exception from an existing controller action to test this error handler.

Listing 14-16 shows the contents of the `error.tpl` file. Note that in this template I haven't included the header and footer templates since in our case these templates can potentially cause more code to execute (such as by using one of the Smarty plug-ins we wrote). This may result in an infinite error loop, so we try to simplify the template as much as possible.

Listing 14-16. *Notifying the User That a System Error Has Occurred (error.tpl)*

```
<!DOCTYPE html
      PUBLIC "-//W3C//DTD XHTML 1.0 Strict//EN"
      "http://www.w3.org/TR/xhtml1/DTD/xhtml1-strict.dtd">

<html xmlns="http://www.w3.org/1999/xhtml" lang="en" xml:lang="en">
    <head>
        <title>A system error occurred</title>
        <meta http-equiv="Content-Type" content="text/html; charset=iso-8859-1" />
    </head>
    <body>
        <p>
            An error occurred completing your request, please try again shortly.
            The system administrator has been notified of the problem.
        </p>
    </body>
</html>
```

Next we write the template used when a 404 error occurs. Note that unlike handling application errors, 404 errors can occur frequently, and they don't typically represent an underlying problem in the application. As such, we can use the normal header and footer to display this error.

Listing 14-17 shows the `error404.tpl` template, which we write to the `./templates/error` directory. Note that we use the `$requestedAddress` variable we assigned in the controller action.

Listing 14-17. *Displaying an Error Message to the User Using the Normal Site Layout (error404.tpl)*

```
{include file='header.tpl'}

<p>
    The file you requested
    (<strong>{$requestedAddress|escape}</strong>)
    could not be found.
</p>

{include file='footer.tpl'}
```

■**Tip** Many web sites take advantage of 404 errors by attempting to do something useful with the requested URI, such as performing a search. For example, if you try to access the PHP web site at `http://php.net` but specify an invalid URL, the site will automatically perform a search based on the terms in the request. If it finds a single exact match, it redirects you directly to the page, while if multiple results are found, it notifies you that an error occurred and then provides links to each page found in the search. This is especially useful for a quick lookup on PHP functions. For example, if you go to `http://php.net/mysql_query`, the 404 handler on the site triggers a search for *mysql_query*, which results in the manual page for the `mysql_query()` function being displayed.

Web Site Administration

As mentioned in Chapter 1, an administration area is an important part of any web site. This special part of the site is what allows the people who run the site to control application data or modify how the site operates.

Because of the work potentially involved in developing this area and the fact it doesn't present any new concepts that we haven't already covered in this book, we won't actually develop the admin area here. Instead, I will list some ideas for functionality you may want to implement as well as provide a starting point for the admin area. Additionally, I have included various administrator functions in the downloadable application source code.

Administrator Section Features

The features that you may want to include in your application's administraton area are listed next. These features are based on the functionality we have implemented in this book, although obviously if you decide to add new features to the application, you may need to add extra functionality here to manage the data belonging to the new feature.

User Management

This area is arguably the most important section that can be implemented, because it allows you to easily see who is accessing the application. Typically in the user management area, you will use the following features:

- Searching for existing users or browsing the user list.

- Updating a user's details (such as their username or password). Additionally, you should have an option to choose the user's type. This allows you to nominate users as administrators who can then access the administrator area.

- Contacting users. This may be by way of sending a periodical newsletter to all users.

■**Note** Be sure to give users the choice of whether they receive bulk e-mails that are sent. You can do this by adding a new setting to their user account (refer to the "Controlling User Settings" section of Chapter 9 for an example of how to implement new user settings).

- Deleting users. Typically you won't want to delete users from your database but on occasion you may need to do so.

■Note Before implementing delete functionality, you need to decide exactly how you want to deal with the deleted data. For example, if a User A leaves a comment on User B's blog (assuming you have implemented a commenting system), then you typically won't want to delete that comment even if you want to delete User A. Database foreign key constraints will prevent you from deleting the user record before all linked comments are deleted. As such, you must either not delete the user record (perhaps disabling the account instead) or update the comment so it is not linked against the user account.

Blog Post Management

In addition to being able to manage user accounts, it may be of use to be able to manage user posts. Typically you won't need to create new blog posts, but you may need to edit or delete a post containing offensive content.

Specifically, you would need almost identical functionality to the blog management functionality for normal users, which may include the following:

- Editing or deleting blog posts and comments associated with posts

- Browsing uploaded images and deleting offensive images if required

- Notifying users if any of their content has been changed (including telling them the reason why)

Auditing Application Logs

Earlier in this chapter we looked at some ways to use the application logs. In addition to searching the logs on the command line, you may want to add a web interface to search and browse the application log.

Some of the capabilities of log viewing may include the following:

- View log entries between two dates (or for a predefined period, such as "this week" or "last month").

- Filter by the priority of the log entry (that is, whether it is a critical message, information, or otherwise). See Chapter 2 for a discussion of the priority levels.

- Search for specific entries (such as for invalid logins).

Note that we are writing log entries to a filesystem file. With Zend_Log it is possible to record log entries to a database instead. You may find it easier to filter entries in a database rather than in a file.

Implementing Administration

Now that I've covered some of the features you may want to use in the administration area, I'll list some implementation notes to help you get started.

Permissions

First you need to consider the permissions of the administration section. Obviously you want only privileged users to be able to access this area. Thankfully, we already catered for this in Chapter 3 by defining permissions for a user type of administrator. The permissions defined in that chapter stated that the administrator role would be able to access the resource called admin.

Creating an administrator is simply a matter of signing up for a new account on the site and then manually updating the database record of the created record using SQL.

■**Note** Typically it is only this initial administrator for whom you will need to perform manual SQL queries. If you do indeed implement a user management tool for the admin area as discussed earlier, then you will be able to create subsequent administrators, but you still need to create the initial administrator using SQL.

For instance, if I wanted to update the user with the username qz to be an administrator, I could use the following SQL query on the application database:

```
mysql> update users set user_type = 'administrator' where username = 'qz';
```

Creating the AdminController Class

The next step for implementing an administration area is to create a new controller. To obey the permissions defined in Chapter 3, this controller must be called AdminController.

■**Note** Recall that the line used in Chapter 3 was $this->acl->allow('administrator', 'admin'), meaning the administrator role can access the admin controller, while other users cannot.

The code in Listing 14-18 shows a starting point for this controller and belongs in a file called ./include/Controllers/AdminController.php. Note that you will still have to create all necessary actions and templates accordingly.

Listing 14-18. *A Skeleton for the Administration Area (AdminController.php)*

```php
<?php
    class AdminController extends CustomControllerAction
    {
        public function indexAction()
        {

        }
    }
?>
```

Now if you try to access `http://phpweb20/admin`, you will be denied access unless your user type is `administrator`.

Application Deployment

We'll now look at the process of deploying our web application to a live server. So far, we have presumed that all development has taken place on a dedicated development server and that the users of the application don't have access to this server.

A typical setup for how versions of web applications are managed involves three types of servers:

- **Development server.** This is where new code is created and tested. The application may be working sometimes, while it may be completely broken at others. It is typically accessed only by the developers and testers.

- **Staging server.** Once the new version of the web application is complete, it is deployed to the staging server. This server is configured identically to the production server (the same operating system and versions of Apache and PHP and other such software). This application will be fully functional, yet its data may be static and stale (it is typically not a backup or a mirror server). It is typically accessed by developers and testers (and perhaps the client who has commissioned you to develop the application in order to approve changes). Deploying on the staging server provides a good opportunity to determine any "gotchas" that may arise while deploying to the production server.

- **Production server.** Once everything appears to be functioning correctly on the staging server, the new application version can also be deployed to the production server. This is the server that the real world sees, which contains the live database and up-to-date data.

In reality, the average web developer's process will not include the staging server since the development server can often double as the staging server. In the following sections, we will assume we are dealing only with a development and a production server to simplify matters.

Different Configurations for Different Servers

Before deploying the web application files to a production server, we must cater to different servers requiring different configurations. The reason for this is that we should be able to deploy all files to the production server and have them all ready to go straightaway without then having to modify the production configuration file.

For example, in your development environment the database server will probably be the same physical machine as your web server (meaning your PHP will connect to a server on "localhost"). In a production environment, this may not be the case. Many web hosts will separate their database servers from their web servers. Because of this, you may require different database connection settings. To deal with this, we add a new section to the `settings.ini` file of our application.

When we created the settings file in Chapter 2, all configuration strings were within a section called `development`, which was denoted in square brackets as follows:

```
[development]
```

We can define more sections in this file in the same manner. So if we wanted to have different settings for production, we would include the following line:

```
[production]
```

You would then define the settings for production following this line. The only problem with this, though, is that some settings may be identical for both development and production. To help with this, `Zend_Config` allows inheritance in configuration files.

In other words, for the production settings we can use all development settings and then override each one as required. We do this by defining the new section as follows:

```
[production : development]
```

Returning to the earlier example of using a different hostname for the database server in production, we could use the following configuration file:

```
[development]

database.type       = pdo_mysql
database.hostname   = localhost
database.username   = phpweb20
database.password   = myPassword
database.database   = phpweb20

; other development settings here

[production : development]

database.hostname   = 192.168.0.123
```

In this code, all settings (such as database username and password) used for development will also be used in production except for the hostname, which has been overridden.

Listing 14-19 shows the code you should add to the `settings.ini` file. Even if you don't intend on changing any settings, you will need to add this line for the code following this to work.

Listing 14-19. *Defining the Production Settings Section (settings.ini)*

```
[development]

; other development settings here

[production : development]
```

Telling the Bootstrap Which Configuration to Use

Once the configuration section for the production server has been created, we must change the bootstrap file so it loads the correct section. So far we have hard-coded the bootstrap to use the `development` section. The question is, how does the code know which section to load? To do this we must add some detection mechanism into the bootstrap.

The way we are going to do this is by writing values to the web server environment in the Apache configuration. Using the Apache SetEnv direct, we are going to write a value that specifies the name of the configuration section to use, as well as the name of the settings file to use.

We then modify the index.php bootstrap to read and use these values. These values don't have to be specified: if they are not included in the configuration, we will use a default settings file of settings.ini and a default configuration section of production.

▌Note Typically you won't need to change the filename of the settings file, but having the ability to do so can be useful. For example, if you wanted to run two separate web sites from the same code base, you can use a separate settings file for each site and then specify in the web server configuration for each site which file to use.

As mentioned earlier, the SetEnv directive is used in Apache to set an environment variable. The first value for this directive is the name of the environment variable, while the second value is the value. The values we will use are as follows:

```
SetEnv APP_CONFIG_FILE "settings.ini"
SetEnv APP_CONFIG_SECTION "development"
```

▌Note We will use an APP_CONFIG_SECTION value of development (rather than production), because I'm treating this section as though we're developing the application. Once you deploy it (using the instructions later in this chapter), you would then either set this value to production or omit it completely (since we will use production as the default).

These values can then be accessed from any of your PHP scripts in the $_SERVER variable. For example, to retrieve the config filename, you can use $_SERVER['APP_CONFIG_FILE'].

Listing 14-20 shows the changes we make to the web server configuration we created in Chapter 2 (Listing 2-1). These changes go in the /var/www/phpweb20/httpd.conf file. You will need to restart your web server for these values to take effect.

Listing 14-20. *Setting the Settings Filename and Section in the Apache Configuration (httpd.conf)*

```
<VirtualHost 192.168.0.80>
    ServerName phpweb20
    DocumentRoot /var/www/phpweb20/htdocs

    <Directory /var/www/phpweb20/htdocs>
        AllowOverride All
        Options All
    </Directory>

    php_value include_path .:/var/www/phpweb20/include:/usr/local/lib/pear
```

```
php_value magic_quotes_gpc off
php_value register_globals off

SetEnv APP_CONFIG_FILE "settings.ini"
SetEnv APP_CONFIG_SECTION "development"
</VirtualHost>
```

The next step is to update the application bootstrap file to use these values. Listing 14-21 shows the changes we make to the ./htdocs/index.php file so the configuration filename and section are no longer hard-coded.

Listing 14-21. *Using the Apache Environment Variables to Determine the Configuration (index.php)*

```php
<?php
    require_once('Zend/Loader.php');
    Zend_Loader::registerAutoload();

    // setup the application logger
    $logger=new Zend_Log(new Zend_Log_Writer_Null());

    try {
        $writer = new EmailLogger($_SERVER['SERVER_ADMIN']);
        $writer->addFilter(new Zend_Log_Filter_Priority(Zend_Log::CRIT));
        $logger->addWriter($writer);

        // load the application configuration

        $configFile = '';
        if (isset($_SERVER['APP_CONFIG_FILE']))
            $configFile = basename($_SERVER['APP_CONFIG_FILE']);

        if (strlen($configFile) == 0)
            $configFile = 'settings.ini';

        $configSection = '';
        if (isset($_SERVER['APP_CONFIG_SECTION']))
            $configSection = basename($_SERVER['APP_CONFIG_SECTION']);

        if (strlen($configSection) == 0)
            $configSection = 'production';

        $config = new Zend_Config_Ini('../' . $configFile, $configSection);
        Zend_Registry::set('config', $config);

        // ... other code
```

These changes begin by trying to read the APP_CONFIG_FILE section from the server variables. If no value was found (or the value was empty), the default value of settings.ini is used.

We do then the same thing to determine which configuration section to use (using APP_CONFIG_SECTION instead). Finally, we use these values when instantiating Zend_Config_Ini.

Note This code forces the settings file to be in the application root directory (/var/www/phpweb20) by using basename(). If you wanted the ability to store the file elsewhere on your system, you could modify this code to allow full paths in the APP_CONFIG_FILE setting.

Deploying Application Files with Rsync

To help with deploying application files (both the initial deployment and also for subsequent updates), you can use the rsync program. Rsync is a tool used to synchronize files and directories between two locations. Although programs such as FTP and SFTP can be useful, they are cumbersome to use to deploy updates (since files may span many directories).

Rsync works by determining the differences between Copy A (in our case, the copy on the development server) and Copy B (the copy on the production server) and then applying those differences to Copy B. By transmitting only the differences between the copies, the amount of data to be transmitted is minimized.

The fact that rsync can be used over an SSH connection makes it a very good way to synchronize the two copies of code. Note, however, that rsync must be installed on both servers (as well as SSH if that is being used).

If you don't already have rsync on your servers, it can be downloaded from http://rsync.samba.org. It is required on each server on which you want to synchronize files.

Let's now look at an example of using rsync. Assuming both servers have rsync installed, you can pull the files from development to production (by running rsync on the production server), or you can push the files from development to production (by running rsync on the development server).

If you wanted to deploy the application onto a fictional production server at production.example.com, you would issue the following command:

```
# rsync -rlptzv -e ssh /var/www/phpweb20 myUsername@production.example.com:/var/www
```

The arguments used in this command are as follows:

- -r: Copy files recursively (that is, copy all directories and subdirectories).

- -l: Copy symbolic links.

- -p: Preserve file and directory permissions.

- -t: Preserve times on files.

- -z: Compress data during the transfer.

- -v: Verbose output during execution.

- -e: Specify which shell to use as the transport. In this case we use ssh.

The next argument indicates the master copy of the files being synchronized, while the final argument is the copy that is being updated. In this case we are copying from the development server, so we can use a local path. If we were running rsync from production, then we would use a URL in this argument and a local path on the production server as the final argument.

The first time you run this command, all of the application files will be copied, while subsequent times only changed files will be copied. You can see this easily by running the command twice initially—the second time nothing will be copied.

■**Note** You can also use the -n argument for a preview of which files will be transferred without actually performing the transfer.

Backup and Restore

The next aspect of application management we'll look at is the backup and restore of data on the production server. In the following sections we will look at how to back up the MySQL database used in our application, as well as how to restore it again if required. The PHP code we have developed doesn't need to be backed up from the production server since it is only a copy of the development code (assuming you back up your local development code or use version control already).

In many hosting environments the web host will take care of backup for you; however, it is still useful to know how to make a backup anyway. This also allows you to copy real data from production to development so you have some real data to work with when developing new features.

■**Caution** In Chapter 11 we stored uploaded images on the filesystem when we developed the dynamic image gallery. I covered the advantages and disadvantages of doing so at the time. This section deals only with the backup and restore of the application database; however, be aware that you should be backing up these uploaded images also.

Exporting a Database

To export the application database, we use the mysqldump program. This will export the entire database (depending on the options specified) to a file that we can then save wherever required (such as on a backup server or on CD/DVD).

We can specify many options when using mysqldump that control how the data is exported (such as for exporting only the schema and not the data, or vice versa), but for our purposes the default options will suffice.

The command in Linux to export a database is as follows:

```
# mysqldump dbname
```

This will output the database schema and data to the terminal (stdout). Therefore, if you want to write this to a file, you must redirect the output to a file. In other words, we can use this:

```
# mysqldump dbname > filename.sql
```

And better yet, we can compress this output (since the database may be large) by first piping the data through gzip:

```
# mysqldump dbname | gzip > filename.sql.gz
```

Because we connect to our database using the phpweb20 username as well as a password, we must specify the -u and -p parameters so we can use the required credentials. Additionally, we can substitute the database name (phpweb20) into the earlier example:

```
# mysqldump -u phpweb20 -p phpweb20 | gzip > phpweb20.sql.gz
```

Once you have executed this command, you will have a compressed backup of the database in your current directory.

■**Tip** The PostgreSQL equivalent of mysqldump is the pg_dump tool. The arguments that must be supplied to this program differ slightly from mysqldump; however, the programs basically work the same.

Importing a Database

Now that you have a backup of the database, it is useful to know how to re-create the database from scratch. First you must create the database, as well as the permissions (as per the instructions in Chapter 2), if it doesn't already exist:

```
mysql> create database phpweb20;
```

Next you import the file from the command line. You can do this by decompressing the file and then piping the results to the mysql program. Note that we need to pass the --stdout argument to gunzip for this to work:

```
# gunzip --stdout phpweb20.sql.gz | mysql –u phpweb20 -p phpweb20
```

If the database dump is already decompressed, you can use the following command:

```
# mysql –u phpweb20 –p phpweb20 < phpweb20.sql
```

As you can see, exporting and importing database data are somewhat trivial. It can get slightly more complicated if you need to also manage a large set of permissions or if you have some other unique setup.

Some people prefer to split their database dumps by exporting the schema to one file and the actual data to another file. This allows you to restore the data in two separate steps, which is especially useful if you're just importing the data to a database that already has the necessary tables in place (such as if you were copying the data from production to the development database).

Summary

In this chapter, we looked at a number of topics relating to creating and managing web applications. These topics are quite important since they must all be considered when creating an application that will run smoothly with minimal maintenance.

Specifically, the topics we covered in this chapter were the following:

- Creating a useful logging system that can notify an administrator when a problem arises

- Handling errors that may occur during runtime by logging the error and notifying the end user that a problem occurred

- Handling 404 errors by telling the user the page they requested could not be found

- Creating an administration section that allows privileged users to control application data as required

- Creating multiple configurations for a web application to cater for each environment the application may be used (development, staging, and production)

- Deploying an application to a production server (including how to deploy updates)

- Backing up and restoring a MySQL database

With the conclusion of this chapter, you should have a solid understanding of what it takes to develop a web application from start to finish. The topics covered in this chapter should help you manage the code developed in earlier chapters in a real-world environment.

Although you may not require all of the functionality we have implemented in our Web 2.0 application, I hope it has put forward ideas and concepts that will help you to further develop this application or create your own from scratch.

Remember that these ideas are not set in stone—they are simply the way I prefer to do things. If you disagree with something I've done in this book, you should challenge it by trying your own way and deciding for yourself what works the best. Better yet, I hope you will challenge me directly so I may learn something new also.

Index

■E

forums.apress.com

FOR PROFESSIONALS BY PROFESSIONALS™

JOIN THE APRESS FORUMS AND BE PART OF OUR COMMUNITY. You'll find discussions that cover topics of interest to IT professionals, programmers, and enthusiasts just like you. If you post a query to one of our forums, you can expect that some of the best minds in the business—especially Apress authors, who all write with *The Expert's Voice*™—will chime in to help you. Why not aim to become one of our most valuable participants (MVPs) and win cool stuff? Here's a sampling of what you'll find:

DATABASES
Data drives everything.

Share information, exchange ideas, and discuss any database programming or administration issues.

INTERNET TECHNOLOGIES AND NETWORKING
Try living without plumbing (and eventually IPv6).

Talk about networking topics including protocols, design, administration, wireless, wired, storage, backup, certifications, trends, and new technologies.

JAVA
We've come a long way from the old Oak tree.

Hang out and discuss Java in whatever flavor you choose: J2SE, J2EE, J2ME, Jakarta, and so on.

MAC OS X
All about the Zen of OS X.

OS X is both the present and the future for Mac apps. Make suggestions, offer up ideas, or boast about your new hardware.

OPEN SOURCE
Source code is good; understanding (open) source is better.

Discuss open source technologies and related topics such as PHP, MySQL, Linux, Perl, Apache, Python, and more.

PROGRAMMING/BUSINESS
Unfortunately, it is.

Talk about the Apress line of books that cover software methodology, best practices, and how programmers interact with the "suits."

WEB DEVELOPMENT/DESIGN
Ugly doesn't cut it anymore, and CGI is absurd.

Help is in sight for your site. Find design solutions for your projects and get ideas for building an interactive Web site.

SECURITY
Lots of bad guys out there—the good guys need help.

Discuss computer and network security issues here. Just don't let anyone else know the answers!

TECHNOLOGY IN ACTION
Cool things. Fun things.

It's after hours. It's time to play. Whether you're into LEGO® MINDSTORMS™ or turning an old PC into a DVR, this is where technology turns into fun.

WINDOWS
No defenestration here.

Ask questions about all aspects of Windows programming, get help on Microsoft technologies covered in Apress books, or provide feedback on any Apress Windows book.

HOW TO PARTICIPATE:
Go to the Apress Forums site at **http://forums.apress.com/**.
Click the New User link.

You Need the Companion eBook